Dresden

Dresden

The Fire and the Darkness

SINCLAIR McKAY

VIKING
an imprint of
PENGUIN BOOKS

VIKING

UK | USA | Canada | Ireland | Australia
India | New Zealand | South Africa

Viking is part of the Penguin Random House group of companies
whose addresses can be found at global.penguinrandomhouse.com

First published 2020
001

Maps illustrated by Ian Moores

Set in 12/14.75 pt Bembo Book MT Std
Typeset by Jouve (UK), Milton Keynes
Printed and bound in Great Britain by Clays Ltd, Elcograf S.p.A.

A CIP catalogue record for this book is available from the British Library

ISBN: 978–0–241–38968–3

Contents

List of Illustrations

Inset 1

Inset 2

Inset 3

Picture Credits

The majority of the photographs come from private collections. Others are from: 2–8, 12–14, 16, 21, 30, 32–5, 46, 47, 52, 54, Getty; 9, 15, 19, 27, 31, 41, 58, Alamy; 11, 18, 36, 40, Mary Evans; 23, 56, Bridgeman; 42, 43, Terje Hartberg; 53, Deutsche Fotothek. Every reasonable effort has been made to trace copyright but the publisher welcomes any information that clarifies the copyright ownership of any unattributed material displayed and will endeavour to include corrections in reprints.

Maps

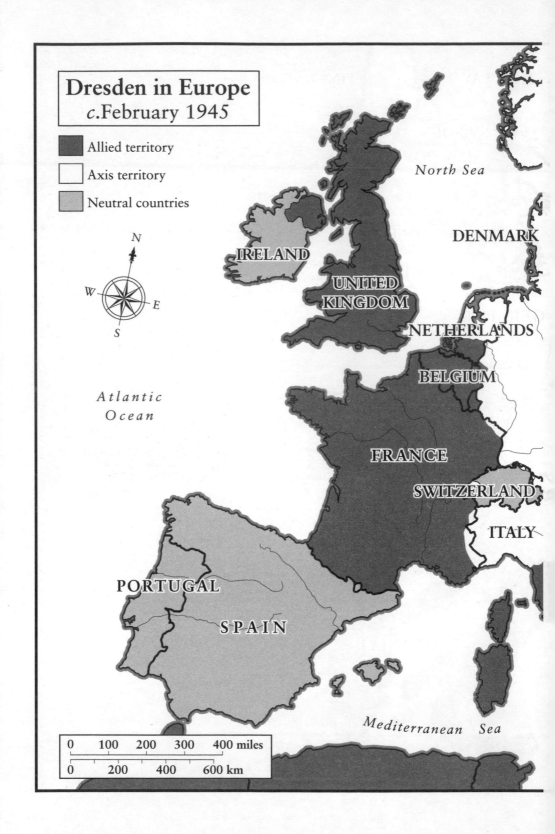

Dresden in Europe
*c.*February 1945

Allied territory

Axis territory

Neutral countries

N
W *E*
S

IRELAND

UNITED
KINGDOM

North Sea

DENMARK

NETHERLANDS

BELGIUM

*Atlantic
Ocean*

FRANCE

SWITZERLAND

ITALY

PORTUGAL

SPAIN

Mediterranean Sea

0   100   200   300   400 miles

0   200   400   600 km

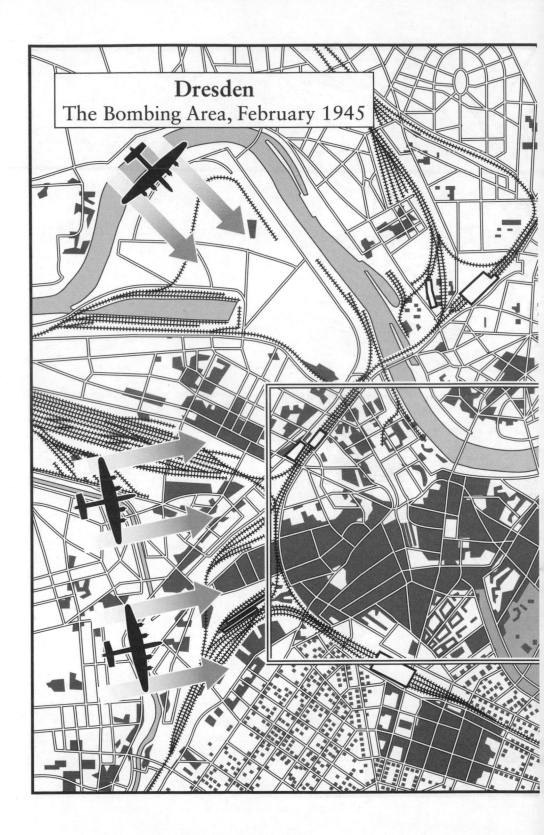

Dresden
The Bombing Area, February 1945

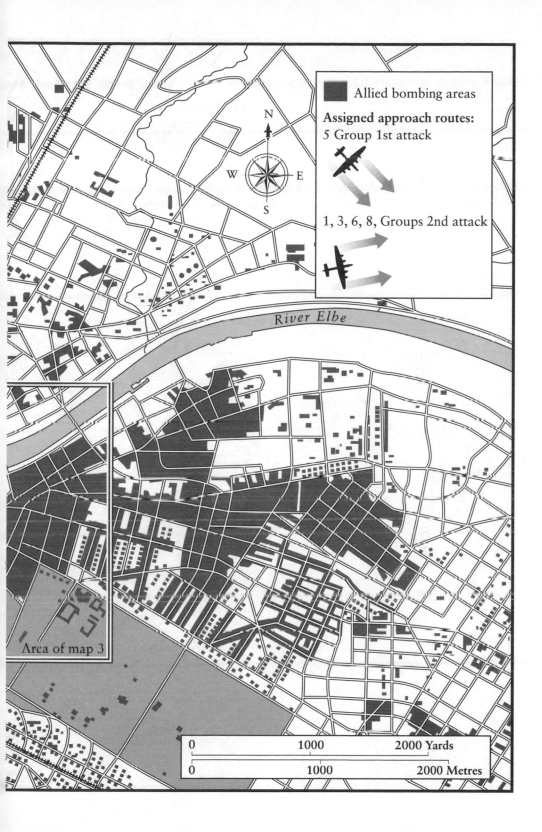

Dresden City Centre
*c.*1945

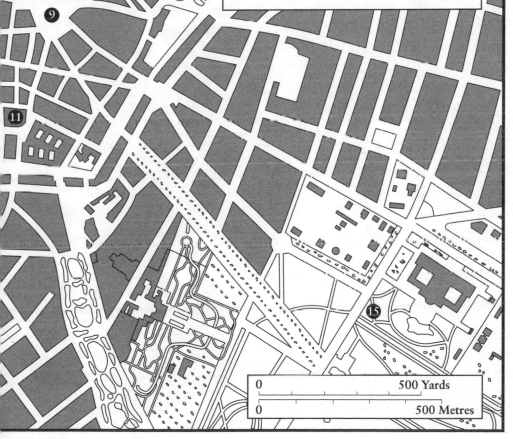

1. The Zwinger Palace and gardens
2. The Semper Opera House
3. The Japanese Palace
4. Augustus Bridge
5. Catholic cathedral
6. Dresden Castle and Green Vault
7. Brühl's Terrace
8. Frauenkirche
9. Neumarkt (New Market)
10. Altmarkt (Old Market)
11. Kreuzkirche
    (Church of the Holy Cross)
12. Central Theatre
13. Prager Strasse
14. Dresden central railway station
15. Grosser Garten (Grand Garden park)

River Elbe

0   500 Yards

0   500 Metres

Preface: The City in Time

By the castle wall, and in the shadow of the Catholic cathedral, winter twilight can occasionally bring an arresting effect. If you glance around, it is possible, just for a fleeting moment, that you will find yourself alone. And here in this triangle of cobbled paving and sculptured stone – the Schlossplatz, overlooked by the grand archway leading through to the castle courtyard, the church spire high and sharp against the amethyst sky – time can smoothly slip its moorings.

If you are knowledgeable about the history of art, you might imagine yourself in the early nineteenth century, a figure frozen in a painting by the Romantic artist Caspar David Friedrich, who lived in Dresden and depicted its steeples and domes, suffused in a lemon sunlight. You might allow yourself to roam yet further back: inhabiting a richly detailed Bellotto landscape. He too was drawn to the architectural elegance – the wide market squares and beautifully proportioned houses and civic buildings – of the city in the eighteenth century. Stand there long enough and there will be the music that those artists heard too: the bells of the cathedral. They strike, with some urgency, and clamour, and with a deeper, resonant note that sounds like anger.

And it is in this near-discordancy that the more recent, terrible past is also summoned, unbidden; many who stand or walk here now, cannot help imagining, even for a moment, the bass drone of the aeroplanes overhead; the sky bright with green and red marker flares; and then roaring flames in the gutted cathedral rising ever higher.

Such visions are not confined to this one spot. Just a few yards from this square is the elegant terrace that overlooks the River Elbe and its curiously wide banks. Now, as then, this stone walkway stretches along to the Academy of Arts with its glittering glass dome. Just as with the Catholic cathedral, any stroll along here somehow takes place in two different time streams; you are there, in the present, gazing along the curving valley of the Elbe; and at the same time, you are seeing, against the clear cold night sky, the hundreds of bombers swooping in from the west. You envisage the terrified crowd of people around you, trying to escape the furnace flare heat, making as if by instinct for the river. This is the macabre truth of Dresden: every vision of beauty carries a split-second awareness of the most terrible violence. All visitors to this city will have felt that momentary dislocation. Unease would be the wrong word; the sensation is not ghostly. But there is a sharp cruelty about the juxtaposition of the fairy-tale architecture and the knowledge of what lies beneath it. And of course illusion is built upon illusion: for much of the fairy-tale architecture we see today was previously obliterated in the cataclysm.

It should not be possible to see the city that expressionist artist Conrad Felixmüller sketched so wittily in the 1920s; to gaze upon the stone and glass that Margot Hille – seventeen-year-old apprentice brewery worker in the west of the city – would have seen on her way home from work throughout the war in the mid 1940s; or to see the comfortable bourgeois world that Dr Albert Fromme and the Isakowitzes and Georg and Marielein Erler moved through at the beginning of the century – the smart restaurants, the opera house, the exquisite galleries. It should not be possible to see any of these things because in just one night, on 13 February 1945, just weeks before that war ended, 796 bomber planes flew over that square, and that city, and in the words of one young witness, 'opened the gates of hell'. In the course of that single, infernal night, an estimated 25,000 people were killed.

Dresden has been rebuilt, slowly, and not without difficulties and conflicts. The minutely detailed restorations have been married with sensitive modern landscaping, so that the new buildings on the market squares are not immediately obvious. But the curious thing is that despite the miraculous reconstruction, we can still somehow see the ruins.

In the case of the eighteenth-century baroque church the Frauenkirche, which overlooks the New Market square, this is deliberate: you are meant to see how the pale stone of the restoration rising high into the sky contrasts with the blackened original masonry, the shattered stumps of which were almost all of what was left after the pilots of Bomber Command – and then, the following day, the US Eighth Air Force – flew over.

The city stands now as a sort of totem to the obscenity of total war: like Hiroshima and Nagasaki, Dresden is a name associated with annihilation. The fact that the city lay deep in the heart of Nazi Germany, and indeed had been an enthusiastic early adopter of the foulest National Socialist politics, added knots of extraordinary moral difficulty.

Across the decades, the stark morality (and immorality) of both the city and the act of destroying it with fire have been debated and analysed, with varying degrees of anger, remorse, pain and trauma. Such arguments are still very much part of the landscape. In Dresden, the past is in the present, and all have to tread carefully through these layers of time and memory.

An additional knot of difficulty lies in the city's more recent past: after the war, Dresden was subsumed into the German Democratic Republic, under the control of the Soviet Union. The Soviets took command of history, in the most literal sense; and the Soviets built new structures in the centre of the city that were supposed to reach out to the future. In the wave of continent-wide celebration that greeted German reunification in 1990, there were – and still are – a few who very sincerely regretted the collapse of the East German government.

One of Dresden's more celebrated citizens – Victor Klemperer, an academic who was one of the very few Jewish inhabitants left after most others had been deported to death camps – remarked after the war that the city was 'a jewel box'; and that was one of the chief reasons the firestorm commanded so much attention. It is certainly the case that other German cities and towns proportionally suffered more; Pforzheim, in the west, was attacked a few weeks after Dresden and the percentage of the population who were killed in the space of just a few minutes was higher than even the extraordinary number of fatalities in Dresden.

And there had been other firestorms too: in 1943, the wooden-based houses and apartments of Hamburg had tons of incendiaries showered from above; the fires had started, windows shattering, roofs buckling. And pilots above in the orange skies had watched with wonder as flames joined with flames across narrow streets, and joined into an ever larger cauldron of fire that began to bend the elements: air was sucked away, hurricane-force winds of searing heat blew upwards to the sky, and those people who had not simply been burned or baked to death found themselves instead suffocated, their lungs sharp with fire with every increasingly futile breath.

There was Cologne; Frankfurt; Bremen; Mannheim; Lubeck; other cities too. In a great many of them, quite apart from the impossible-to-imagine death tolls, there were the architectural losses: the palaces, opera houses and churches that had formed some notional symbol of European civilization.

Unlike many other cities in the west of the country, though, Dresden – close to the Polish and Czech borders, and about a hundred miles from Prague – already had a strong place in the international imagination. It had long been famous for its exquisite art collections, for its colourful Saxon history, and also for the inviting nature of the landscape that surrounded its beautiful baroque churches, cathedrals and pretty lanes. Then – as now – the city seemed to exist a step apart, deep in the valley of the River Elbe, ringed by gentle hills rising in the distance to picturesque forested mountains. In the early nineteenth century, philosopher Johann Gottfried Herder described Dresden as the 'German Florence', drawing admiring parallels between the two cities; and this in turn led to the more widely used 'Florence on the Elbe'.

But the city was also famous because it was not quaint. Dresden had never been simply a jewel box; it had also acquired pleasurable notoriety for the crackling vigour of its artistic life: the wildly innovative painters, the composers, the writers. Here were some of the earliest modernists; visionary architects with new ideas for perfect communities were drawn to the city too. Added to this, music seemed part of the chemical composition of these streets. It still does today: in the old city in the evenings, you will hear classical buskers and the echoes of cathedral choirs. Those echoes were heard many decades before.

So the story of Dresden – of its destruction and resurrection – presents an almost Shakespearean array of terrible ethical questions.

By acknowledging the suffering of all those many thousands of people that night – children, women, refugees, the elderly – and in the years afterwards, do we diminish the hideous crimes that had been committed all around them since the rise of the Nazi Party? By digging deeper into individual stories, are we at risk of fetishizing one notably beautiful place when villages, towns and cities across Europe were even more barbarically served?

Then there is the matter of how we view the hundreds of pilots that flew over, and dropped their fiery bombs on their target: these young men, exhausted, empty, freezing and profoundly afraid at the bitter end of a long conflict in which they had seen so many of their friends blasted out of the sky, were simply doing what they were told by their commanders. The crews of those planes – British, American, Canadian, Australian, among others – piloted, plotted courses, aimed guns at enemy fighters, lay on their stomachs over the bomb bays, talked to each other over intercoms, and clutched their superstitious mascots – be they cloth caps, special socks, or even a girlfriend's brassiere – close. A bra had more talismanic power than a crucifix. These men looked down through the darkness upon fires thousands of feet below, and threw yet more incendiaries into them, knowing that, at any moment, they too could be engulfed in flame and burned alive. How were these young men ever to defend themselves against the later accusations that they – and RAF Air Chief Marshal Arthur Harris, whom they nicknamed 'Butcher' – had participated in a war crime?

Even though this is in part a story about military power, we cannot necessarily think about it purely in terms of military history. Rather, we should try to further fathom the cataclysm by seeing it as much as possible through the eyes of those who were there, on the ground and in the air; those who were in command, and those who had no agency. For this is a tragedy that rippled out far beyond the war. With all the thousands of lives that were extinguished on that one night, there was also the crushing of culture and memory. And the horror of that night is still an electrically live political issue: the greatest care has to be taken not to give accidental support or succour to those who seek to exploit the distant dead today. Remembrance itself is a battlefield; there are those on the far right, in east Germany, and elsewhere, who continually seek to exploit the idea that native civilians in Nazi Germany were victims of atrocities too. Their arguments are compounded with outlandish conspiracy theories surrounding the reason for the bombing. Against them are those citizens who understand that these people cannot be allowed to hijack the events of that night for their own ends. That the past must be protected.

And perhaps one way to do that is simply to listen to the voices of those who were there. To explore the lives of those who were born in Dresden long before the darkness stole over it; and their children, born into that darkness; those who suffered the illimitable terror of that night; and those who had to find a way of rebuilding ordinary life in the dislocated years that followed.

There has been a very moving collaboration between the authorities in the modern city and volunteers working for an organization in Britain which has been focusing on helping Dresden in its reconstruction. The Dresden Trust has worked especially closely upon the painstaking rebuilding of the Frauenkirche.

The city and the Trust have made much of the symbiotic relationship between Dresden and Coventry, in the English midlands – the latter having been attacked and reduced to molten lead and red-hot stone and brick by the Luftwaffe in November 1940. The twinning of the cities is about the understanding that no such thing must ever be allowed to happen again.

But it is also important to see that the story of Dresden is about life, as well as death; it is about the infinite adaptability of the human spirit in the most extraordinary circumstances.

And now that these events pass from living memory, and we can see them with a clearer gaze less occluded by claims, counterclaims and propaganda, there is also an opportunity here for another sort of restoration: a remembrance of the Dresdeners and the texture of their everyday lives.

In recent years, the city's archives have been engaged in a remarkable effort to elicit as many testimonies and eyewitness accounts as they can. In an inspiring project of communal history, voices have been captured, memories resurrecting many who were lost. These were – are – the stories of a diverse range of citizens, of all ages, committed to paper at different times. There are accounts from those who were children at the time, as well as the diaries and letters and fragments left behind by older people who lived through the cataclysm and recorded the horror. From the quiet authority of Dresden's chief medical figure to the air-raid wardens; from the city's remorselessly persecuted Jews to the gentile Dresdeners who in shame tried to help; from the recollections of teenagers and schoolchildren to the extraordinary experiences of some of the older residents, the archives carry a kaleidoscopic portrait not just of one night but of an extraordinary historical moment in the life of an extraordinary city. There are a multitude of voices waiting to be heard, many for the first time.

And it is now time to see underneath those ruins and restorations to recreate the flavour of what was once – before the obscenity of Nazism – an unusually innovative and creative city. To walk long-vanished streets, and see them as the Dresdeners saw them. The story is not just one of astounding destruction; but also about how fragmented lives were somehow regenerated afterwards.

PART ONE
The Approaching Fury

1. The Days Before

In the early days of February 1945, the sharp air in Dresden carried a flavour of smoke. Although wartime coal supplies were never certain, the city's stoves and boilers were working against the morning frosts. The snow had gone but breath still lingered in the cold. The cobbles around the Frauenkirche were moist and treacherous, a potential hazard to those walking with hands thrust deep into overcoat pockets. The elderly gentlemen in hats making their way to work in the banks and the insurance companies near the Old Market each morning, maintaining a simulacrum of middle-class normality, watched their step.

Others moved more lightly through the narrow streets. Gerhard Ackermann, a young teenager dodging past the cream-and-brown liveried electric trams and the wooden greengrocery barrows, had managed to spend the best hours of the previous weekend at the cinema. Many German civilians at this point were throwing themselves into the alternative worlds conjured by films, watching them with a kind of hunger. The production Ackermann saw was *In flagranti*. Made a few months previously, and one of the last films to be produced under the Nazi regime, this was a screwball comedy, filled with farcical twists, involving a secretary becoming a private detective.[1]

Throughout that winter there had been films playing in all Dresden's eighteen cinemas. Among the grandest of these was the Universum Kino, a thousand-seater establishment with an upmarket clientele. Film was predominantly the enthusiasm of working-class Dresdeners, but the middle classes could be coaxed into theatres such as the Universum by highbrow costume dramas and adaptations of classic novels.[2] *In flagranti* was the last film to be shown in Dresden before the Nazis commanded that all cinemas in Germany shut down.[3] Young Ackermann's ticket would become a souvenir.

In any case, for many older Dresdeners, escapism was too great an effort. There was an instinctive and vertiginous understanding that the order of things, that the world they knew, was going to give way at any moment. These citizens could see for themselves that the rhythm of the city was fevered: the constant flow of trucks along the wide main roads and across the bridges, carrying young German soldiers and ordnance through the city and thence eastwards; the exhausted horses drawing behind them carts bearing equally tired refugee families from the countryside, making their painful way in the opposite direction.

There was real urgency amid all this movement. The Red Army under Marshal Georgy Zhukov had crossed the River Oder in Poland; the Soviets' bewildering and breath-catching momentum sustained from mid January, when they had broken through the German lines like an axe cleaving a rotten door. To the west, the Americans and British were exerting fresh pressure following the Battle of the Bulge, pushing their way through wet, freezing forests and small towns.

Many German civilians were starting to look at the prospect of US occupation with a quiet degree of ambivalence, but the idea of Soviet conquest inspired real, vocal fear. Stories of the sociopathic relish with which the Red Army in the east had descended upon countless women, as well as civilian males, had been relayed ahead of their arrival. None of the German farmers and agricultural workers and their families in those regions fleeing this ineluctable advance would have been aware that, at that moment, the future of both themselves and their nation was being decided at a resort on the Black Sea some 1,300 miles south-east of Dresden; that in a once-ornate palace in Yalta, Joseph Stalin, Winston Churchill and Franklin D. Roosevelt, the last jaundiced and visibly ill,[4] had been discussing details of how a defeated Germany was to be governed and kept subdued; of how the country would be split into four occupied zones – American, British, French, Soviet – and ruled under meticulously democratic principles. At the conference, Stalin's senior commanders requested that the transport nexus of Dresden, which would lie within the projected Soviet sphere of influence, be targeted by Anglo-American forces in order to hamper German movements to the east.[5]

By this stage of the war it was becoming clear that squadrons of heavy bombers were already outmoded; that the future of warfare was in the hands of physicists. The Americans were, in secret, close to producing the atomic weapon that the Nazis had unsuccessfully striven towards. Equally secretly, Stalin had been kept apprised of the work being carried out in the laboratories at Los Alamos in New Mexico by scientist and communist-sympathizer Klaus Fuchs.

German civilians must have found it hard to imagine any greater destruction than that which was already being wrought. On 6 February 1945 there were hugely destructive US Eighth Air Force raids on the towns of Chemnitz and Magdeburg. In the case of Magdeburg, 140 miles north-west of Dresden on the Elbe, the historic quarters of the city were already dust and rubble; a raid the previous month, broadly aimed at the oil refinery, had seen grand civic architecture as well as innumerable houses and apartments consumed in flame.[6]

Despite the daily radio bulletins telling of fierce German resistance to Allied predations and newspaper articles reassuring readers that Anglo-American aggression would be forestalled, every Dresdener knew that the city was attracting ever-greater enemy attention, the reconnaissance planes 'silvery against the sky', as then eleven-year-old Dieter Patz recalled.[7] Mothers tried to shield their children as far as possible from the war. Frieda Reichelt, who had a ten-year-old daughter called Gisela, was expecting another child that March. 'I was looking forward to the arrival of a new sibling,' recalled Gisela. 'Dresden seemed far from the war and we were careless of bombing raids. My mother enabled me as far as possible to have a nice childhood.'[8]

Despite the studied insouciance of many citizens, Dresden had already suffered raids from the Americans, one in the autumn of 1944 and another on 16 January 1945. The attackers had materialized from the daylight sky and killed several hundred people on each occasion. The primary target had been the vast marshalling yards not far from the Friedrichstadt hospital. To add to the tension, Dresden's early warning sirens had been howling neurotically – and unnecessarily – at the darkness almost every night, making proper sleep impossible for many. Even if the city had for some years seemed removed from the war, its inhabitants were constantly reminded of the conflict, even as they dreamed.

Nightly news reports that superior German forces were holding the Red Army back were undermined by whispered rumours that Berlin might fall at any moment. Unknown to Dresdeners, the authorities in Berlin had recently designated their city a 'defensive area'[9] – meaning that in the event of a mass Soviet incursion, German soldiers would be expected to turn the streets and squares into a battleground. Dresden, with a population of some 650,000 – about the same as Manchester in England, or, indeed, Washington DC – was to be part of an Elbe Line, under the command of General Adolf Strauss, stretching up the course of the river from Prague and thence through Germany to Hamburg – a front that, in theory, would be held definitively and bloodily by the Germans.

There were many in Dresden, on those quiet evenings in the blackout, who imagined that they could hear the noise of death echoing from the distant hills. There were hideous stories of multiple rapes and mutilations, and they were true. The Red Army was a little over sixty miles away. Hertha Dietrich, a single woman who lodged in the house of a retired stable manager, was anxious that she would not be able to bear the city falling to such people and declared that she 'would take the old man to her acquaintances' in another town further west.[10]

And how many in the city had heard the rumours that just a few days beforehand, the advancing Soviets had happened across a Nazi concentration camp? Certainly, academic Victor Klemperer and his wife had picked up the terrible intelligence of Auschwitz, the Soviet soldiers exploring the abandoned camp and finding thousands of living skeletons, prisoners who had been left behind to die. This nightmare discovery had been made on 27 January. The whispered speculation about it had reached Dresden, and it merely confirmed to Klemperer that his fears had been justified. When, over the last few years, his friends and neighbours had been told by the Gestapo to pack a bag for one short journey, he had known that they were being sent by train to their deaths.[11]

The few Jews who were left in Dresden had had their properties expropriated and were crammed into specially assigned houses, rundown and split into tiny apartments. They were cold and sparse;

the gas supply sputtered so that water could hardly be heated and at any time of day and night the residents might find themselves subject to violent, spitting house inspections by the authorities. Klemperer had seen countless Jews being handed 'deportation' papers; and he had seen how a pre-war Jewish population of thousands had been reduced to little more than a few dozen. Many in Dresden had the same suspicions, but everyone knew it was unwise to discuss such things openly. Both the local Gestapo and the police had the authority to execute anyone who was suspected of treachery, and damaging morale counted as treason.

Daily life was a challenge of seeing and yet not seeing, hearing and yet not hearing, but the dissolution of ordinary bourgeois standards was now taking startling forms. Rural refugees, who congregated down by the vast central railway station, could be seen squatting in adjacent alleys relieving themselves, because the queues for the station's lavatories were simply too long; this was not the kind of thing fastidious Dresdeners were used to witnessing.

Sixty-four-year-old Dr Albert Fromme saw increasing numbers of refugees from Silesia arriving at his clinic, ill, bewildered, halted part-way through their treks westward. Dr Fromme was the pre-eminent surgeon at the Dresden Friedrichstadt hospital, the leafy grounds of which lay between the Elbe and the marshalling yards. (Despite the conflict, the institution was still open to all.) Among the difficulties he faced were anxiety over stocks of medicines and pain-killers and the fact that fuel supplies for the hospital buildings were becoming sporadic.

Dr Fromme was one of Dresden's more influential citizens. Just a year beforehand he had been appointed president of the German Society of Surgery and in Dresden he had founded a much admired academy for physicians. However, this did not make him a member of the establishment because he had never been a member of the Nazi Party. The Fromme home was filled with sober oil paintings and a huge variety of books. According to his children, their father was a reserved figure – when he came home for his lunch every day he expected quiet and decorum in the house – but that is hardly remarkable, given his experience as a medic in the First World War, when he had not only seen obscenities in the trenches, but also fought desperately to save those who had suffered so horribly. How could he have been anything other than grave?

Now, his work in Dresden was all consuming. Every day as he walked the corridors of the hospital, the air sharp and fresh with disinfectant, he and his younger colleagues were facing logistical difficulties that in peacetime might have seemed insurmountable. But, like everyone else in Dresden, Dr Fromme had somehow adapted to his old world being tilted upon its axis.

Just a short walk from the crowded hospital was another venerable Dresden institution, the mighty Seidel und Naumann factory, through the gates of which its mass of workers entered and left daily. For long a household name – indeed, Dr Fromme swore by one of its carefully crafted products, his private typewriter – by February 1945 its production was angled almost entirely towards war work.

Two great chimneys dominated the skyline above the Seidel und Naumann complex: industrial echoes of the cathedral spires of the old city just half a mile to the east. There were other echoes too, of elegance. The factory buildings had an austere dignity, looking a little from the outside like large residential apartment blocks. These formed an enormous square, in the middle of which lay open space, allowing light into every section. Before the war – indeed, since the start of the century – the firm had been producing intricately detailed and beautifully designed household items. Its typewriters, sold under the labels 'Ideal' and 'Erika', were exported all over Europe. Its sewing machines similarly were found in parlours across the continent. Its bicycles were enduringly popular. The firm had proved equally innovative and elegant when it came to industrial relations. Seidel und Naumann provided its workers with not only a large canteen serving nutritious meals but also a company health scheme and recreational outings.

Before the outbreak of the war, the Dresden site employed some 2,700 people, but the composition of the workforce making their way daily through the factory gates on Hamburger Strasse was now very different. In the absence of fighting-age men, the great majority of those who worked here were female, many of them forced labour: Jewish women and even women from the USSR. The degradation of the workforce had developed stage by inexorable stage during the war, and by 1945 these slave labourers – haggard, haunted, inadequately clothed – had somehow become accepted by Dresdeners as part of the normal world. The nature of the work in the factories had changed dramatically too. And the purpose of the finished products – from detonating fuses for shrapnel shells to ignitors for depth charges and anti-aircraft guns – was kept strictly secret even from those who were working long hours to produce the parts for them. Both supply of and demand for domestic goods were understandably hollowed out.

There were still some working-age men employed in Dresden rather than serving in the military. The father of eleven-year-old Dieter Patz worked relatively close by in a metalworking unit that specialized in intricate instruments. The boy was certain that his father 'worked in a scissors factory'.[12] The truth, of course, was quite different: the plant had been turned over to the rather more intricate business of military parts years earlier, and for these skilled workmen there were now extra duties, including compulsory attendance of meetings of the Volkssturm at the end of each day.

The Volkssturm, in its broadest sense, was the last redoubt of the German military and comprised all the men who for whatever reason had not been conscripted. Each city and each district had its own platoon of often middle-aged or elderly men, but it was not attached in any formal way to the army. It had been resurrected only in 1944, and the men who were required to attend its meetings knew that there was little likelihood of their ever being provided with proper weapons or equipment. In other cities, some members had been handed responsibility for filling in the potholes and craters that had been left by bombing raids. There was a cult-like aspect to it too: the meetings were filled with Nazi exhortations to do with death, blood and honour, threaded through with quasi-mystical invocations of the ancient homeland. Patz simply recalled that when his father at last arrived home each day, 'it was way past the normal supper time, and he seemed utterly exhausted'.[13]

In terms of forced labour, it was the workforce at the Zeiss Ikon camera plant in the south-east of the city, near the Great Garden park, that had among the largest numbers. By 1942 the works were hugely important for the manufacture of precision instruments and optical technology for the military. Dresden's Jews – including the academic Victor Klemperer – were among those compelled to work there.[14] By February 1945, with so many shipped out to death camps in the east, the numbers at the factory had to be supplanted by extra forced labour: women brought in from Poland and from the fringes of the USSR. Here were sparse barracks for such workers to rest in; three-tiered bunks, inadequate heating, a perpetual shortage of food and weariness that eroded the soul. Yet moving among them were local women workers, fully paid, who either walked to work or caught the tram from the suburbs.

Such groups ought not to have been able to commingle without either intense resentment or horrified pity, yet they did. There were those everyday Dresden workers, Klemperer recalled, who certainly seemed to bear the Jews on the factory floor no sort of animosity, nor feel the need to keep separate from them, either out of hostility or silent sympathy. Instead, the atmosphere on the production line was frequently jocular.

As the working day began early for the free citizens of Dresden, so too were their children making their way to their schools, finding out whether they were open that day, assiduous about studies even in the increasing chaos around them. There had been extensive disruptions to timetables and schools had frequently closed, often to conserve fuel; children instead were left to play winter games in the city's parks and in the wooded suburbs. Some classrooms had been converted into makeshift field hospitals for wounded men brought back from the eastern front.

Any German child under thirteen in 1945 had grown up knowing nothing other than Nazi rule; this, to them, was the natural order of the world. Those few whose parents secretly questioned the order of things behind closed doors must have felt conflicted when asked to learn and repeat the propaganda so willingly absorbed by their classmates. Among the smarter establishments in the city – certainly in terms of academic pride and attainment – was the Vitzthum-Gymnasium, the school attended by Dr Fromme's elder son Friedrich. Throughout the course of the year, the establishment had suffered two major setbacks: first, the requisition of one of its main buildings for military use, necessitating a move to share premises with another school; then, in 1944, those premises were shattered by American bombs during a speculative daylight raid.

Among its pupils were many who would later become lawyers, engineers, doctors or journalists, but increasing numbers of the city's fifteen-year-old boys were being drafted, via the Hitler Youth, into military positions in anti-aircraft batteries, pointing guns at the night sky not just above Dresden but in other cities too.

All boys were required to participate in the Hitler Youth, even the quieter, bookish ones not suitable for defensive duties. Winfried Bielss, fifteen years old in 1945, had his own after-school responsibilities. They seemed not to impinge greatly upon his larger concern, which was stamp collecting. Winfried and his mother lived in an apartment in a genteel suburb on the north bank of the Elbe. His soldier father was, at that time, in Bohemia: one of the more vicious crucibles of Nazism. There, in Czechoslovakia, the local Jewish population had been almost completely exterminated, and other minorities such as the Romany were persecuted too. Now, Bielss's father was facing not merely Stalin's advancing forces but also local resistance groups who were fighting back with real vigour while, little more than a hundred miles away, his son was returning home for his supper.

Even in those sparse times there was red cabbage and fried potatoes – and as his mother exclaimed, there could be scant cause for unhappiness if one 'could still enjoy fried potatoes'.[15] Indeed, in peacetime, staple Saxon comfort recipes had always revolved around potato soup (with cucumber and sour cream) and potato dumplings (with buttermilk). The only real absence now was rich cakes, a traditional Dresdener yearning.

By those early days of February 1945, Bielss's Hitler Youth duties were centred on the grand central railway station; and they involved guiding the many disembarking refugees to their new temporary billets in the farms and villages that surrounded Dresden. The architecture of the station surely impressed upon all arrivals a sense of the city that Dresden had until recently been, with its elegantly curved long glass roofs and slickly designed platforms and concourse. Here was a structure that spoke of some cosmopolitanism; pan-European detailing in the whorls of the ironwork, in the light pouring in through those glass roofs, which gave a romantic haze to the rich smoke from the steam engines.[16] There had also until recently been refugees arriving from some bombed-out cities in the west as well. Added to this, there were German soldiers arriving on leave or to convalesce.

Those disembarking at the station were frequently pointed north, to the New Town – Neustadt – that lay on the other side of the river. The Neustadt had streets with a distinctly Parisian flavour: long, tall terraces, shops and restaurants on ground floors, a maze of hidden leafy courtyards behind. Meanwhile, matching this sophisticated feel in the old town – the Altstadt – near the railway station was the elegant and sumptuous Prager Strasse, a shopping street that, even in the vice-grip of the total-war economy, still exerted a strong pull on the imaginations and desires of many local people.

In a curious way, the windows of Prager Strasse's shops in earlier years had not only afforded glimpses of flashing beauty – richly coloured silks of indigo and emerald, chic haute couture, voluminous luxurious furs, the hard dazzle of jewellery – but also suggested a form of social stability: exquisite assets that unlike the cruelly inflationary German currency of the 1920s would keep their value, thus also buying their owners security and safety. There was no such security for many store owners, though; since the passing of the 1935 Nuremberg Laws forcing anti-Semitism deep into the constitutional heart of German life, business people had learned bitterly that such assets could be snatched – expropriated by the state. None the less, even by this later stage of the war this was still where the smarter ladies of Dresden society came to shop, dine and take coffee, albeit ersatz with an aftertaste of oats.

More down-to-earth Dresdeners favoured traditional stores such as Böhme, which by 1945 had become a thriving marketplace for gossip and war theories. There were modern department stores too:

Renner, on the Altmarkt (old market), even in the depleted war years, stocked everything from children's clothes to household goods. And a few streets up was an innovative shop that had once been called Alsberg. In contrast to the charmingly antiquated neighbouring streets, this was a temple of futuristic modernism, built with a carefully calibrated geometry of horizontals and subtle curves. Alsberg had been the first to introduce smooth escalators so that more genteel shoppers might not overexert themselves. Like so many other businesses both in this city and across Germany, it had been seized from its Jewish owners by the Nazi authorities as part of their Aryanization process; they changed the name to 'Möbius'.[17] The business would not have been much use to the owners as the decade wore on in any case: the Nazi boycott on Jewish shops was too thorough.

The ostentation of other, grander shops might have been regarded with a certain sardonic amusement by young working-class Dresden women such as seventeen-year-old Anita Auerbach; she was a waitress at The White Bow, a cheap and busy restaurant a few streets from the centre. In earlier years this had been an establishment filled with teetotal left-wing political radicals, an informal theatre of speeches and fiery meetings and long, shouting debates. One such prominent Dresden communist from those days, a young mother called Elsa Frölich, had been imprisoned by the Nazi authorities and subsequently released. She was now working as an accountant in a nearby cigarette factory that had been converted to manufacture ammunition. Frölich was one of the few in Dresden in February 1945 who yearned to see Stalin's forces in the streets.[18] The White Bow, however, was now teeming with German soldiers (and indeed the occasional furtive deserter, seeking to avoid scrutiny), its windows fogged from the steam of the hot vegetable broth that was served.

In the south-west of the city another young woman of seventeen, Margot Hille, had just a few months previously completed an apprenticeship that in peacetime might not have been available to her: she now had a full-time position in the Felsenkeller brewery, one of many breweries that thrived around the city. Established in the mid nineteenth century, the firm had excavated special tunnels for the purposes of brewing storage.[19] War had also brought a new sort of production line to the firm – darkly secret and deep within the factory – that of highly technical components for military machinery. But there was still beer too. Felsenkeller specialized in a strong lager advertised with the image of a smiling golden-haired boy in checked trousers holding aloft a foaming stein.

If there seemed something slightly unreal about local manufacturing and drink businesses continuing as though the world was on a stable footing, the sense was magnified back in the Altstadt, where the banks and insurance companies continued their daily business. Like the department stores, the Dresden banks had been subject to Nazi theft. One of the city's more prominent financial houses, owned by the Jewish Arnhold family, had been swallowed up by Aryanization in 1935; their bank was subsumed into the Dresdner Bank, which, although it had moved its head office to Berlin, still had substantial premises in Dresden.

Dresdner Bank's business was now wholly war-related, and its tendrils reached into every part of Nazi-dominated eastern Europe. It is fair to speculate that in those dark months, some senior figures within the bank would have known and understood for certain what had been happening in those concentration camps so deep in the eastern forests. Part of their business had been about financing such efforts, and finding ways of profiting from them. In the streets where Dresdner Bank's senior management operated, the bright red and black of the Nazi flag fluttered in the winter winds, the swastika stark against grey masonry.

Yet nearby were tokens of a city somehow not wholly steeped in war. There was (and is) the Pfunds Molkerei – an absurdly picturesque dairy shop, ornately decorated with nineteenth-century Villeroy & Boch hand-painted ceramic tiles, that represented an older Dresdener spirit, playful and blithe, a small temple to the virtues of sweetness.[20] A tourist attraction in peacetime, here were pastries and buttermilk – a draw not merely for children but also for parents who had never quite forgotten their intense childhood pleasures. Further along the river, vineyards covered the slopes of Schloss Eckberg, a splendidly grandiose nineteenth-century structure built in the style and spirit of an English castle by a local wealthy merchant.[21] Here and in many other nearby vineyards there was said to be an extraordinary terroir. Certainly it produced a subtle Riesling that was both light and as sharp as autumn apples. The Eckberg vineyard commanded a view of the river, and of the early twentieth-century bridge that was known locally as the Blue Wonder. It was also the bridge that many locals mentioned when they were discussing the advance of the Red Army. In these conversations, people wondered if this construction – considered a revolutionary piece of suspension engineering and a real source of local pride – would have to be sacrificed to slow the Soviets down.

The underlying fears of brutality and unstoppable violence were woven through with other profound anxieties. To each and every Dresdener, the city had a unique and perhaps sacred beauty: the cathedrals and churches and palaces that had lined the curve of the Elbe for centuries should have represented a form of eternity. Instead there was the fear that the barbarians would smash the beauty into dust. That religious sense of aesthetics had somehow found a way of coexisting with blood-red swastikas.

Yet the real shadow over the city was not being cast by the Soviets; instead, the broadly unsuspected threat lay in the secret plans and intentions of the Allies in the west.

2. In the Forests of the Gauleiter

The arguments, blazing and bitter, had long ago moved beyond ethics; possibly even beyond strict rationality. The exquisite calculations of military actions were being replaced with something more haphazard, and quite regardless of human mortality. This was the exhaustion of global war; especially apparent in those who were still haunted by the century's earlier conflict. But the idea that civilians could be legitimately targeted was not new. Three years previously, in 1942, Joseph Stalin had told Winston Churchill that British bombers should be targeting German houses as well as German industry. At the time, there were still those – especially among the American senior command – who believed that the fine distinction between military and civilian objectives was still possible, and indeed was morally necessary. But Churchill had not needed any such admonitions from Stalin: among senior British commanders and politicians, total war had already become an accepted fact. Before Stalin had made his views known, men such as the prime minister's singular scientific adviser Lord Cherwell were insisting that bombing raids against Germany should aim to 'de-house' the populations of the great cities; by doing so, they would begin to paralyse the industry and infrastructure of the entire country.[1] The term 'de-housing' had a calculatedly bland, technocratic flavour.

The most enthusiastic proponent of this idea was Air Chief Marshal Sir Arthur Harris of Bomber Command, whose name was to become inextricably intertwined with the fate of Dresden. A man whose only streak of sentimentality seemed to extend to beautiful rural landscapes and the farmers who tended them, Harris never had a flicker of doubt about the need to destroy German cities. He was wholly and blankly indifferent to the ultimate fates of the civilians who lived in them. Yet he could morally justify all of this with ease. In a talk he gave in 1942 he insisted that he was not interested in retribution for the havoc wreaked upon Britain by German bomb-ers.[2] This was, as he saw it, simply about bringing a swift end to the war; and he clung to this belief with religious fervour.

RAF Bomber Command was based among the green Chiltern hills thirty miles north-west of London. Twice-married Harris, whose fair hair was turning silver, operated out of a simple office adorned with a slender grandfather clock, a large desk with a single black telephone and an angled lamp, one wall featuring a painting of an evening landscape, another with a vast map of Europe, and a view from the window of thin poplar trees – a sharp contrast to the bright futurist modernism of the base's control room. He was very sociable; on evenings when he could be pulled away from his desk, he and his wife Therese threw dinner parties in their nearby home for a variety of figures, including senior US air commanders and diplomats, who always wrote afterwards to thank them for their sparkling hospital-ity.[3] Since Harris had taken over the command in 1942 at the age of fifty, he had succeeded in two urgent objectives: persuading the prime minister that the continued bombardment of German cities was just as vital as every other theatre of war (at a time when critics were arguing otherwise); and hugely increasing the numbers of aero-planes and crew members, with attendant leaps in technological and engineering progress. His intensely combative nature, directed as much at those above him as below, was renowned; his terms of abuse – always articulate, sometimes darkly witty – were intended to draw blood. Any who expressed moral qualms or doubts about the work of Bomber Command was a Fifth Columnist.[4]

But perhaps one of the reasons for this ever-burning ferocity was the astounding number of airmen who had lost their lives under his and his predecessor's command: to date some 50,000 crew members had been killed on raids, their bodies burning as they fell through dark skies. 'There is no parallel in warfare to such courage and determina-tion in the face of danger over so prolonged a period, of danger which at times was so great that scarcely one man in three could expect to survive his tour of thirty operations,' wrote Harris.[5] In addition to this, as Harris was later to point out, there were huge numbers of deaths in training; even among the skilled mechanics on east coast airbases, exposed around the clock to hard English winters, and working under such horrible pressure that they succumbed to diseases usually only found among the elderly.

Harris had been with the Royal Flying Corps in the First World War and his own moral compass had to an extent been set by the fields of blood below; he had remained in the RAF in those inter-war years, proving himself a brilliant and incisive organizer, as the service was wrestling to keep its independence from the army and navy, and his view of Germans, whether military or civilian, was unyieldingly hostile. Yet he denied that he wanted to see 'terror bombing'; he claimed he had 'never gone in for it'.[6] The reasoning was perhaps a little icier than that dismissive expression: he was interested in 'the destruction of German cities, the killing of German workers, the disruption of civilized community life', but as a means of shortening conflict and forestalling further carnage. He simply did not regard death by bombing as the worst way to lose life. When his superiors, such as Chief of the Air Staff Sir Charles Portal, insisted upon the bombers being used instead for highly specific industrial targets, Harris's already brittle patience would crack. He later stated that people who talked a lot about 'individual small targets' had clearly never given any thought to the 'European climate'; and that people who said 'that sort of thing' had clearly 'never been outside' or 'looked out of a window'.[7] This was a view that might have either amused or simply startled the commander of the United States Army Air Force in Europe, Carl 'Tooey' Spaatz. Major General Spaatz's 'oil plan' – sending hundreds of US planes from English airfields to fly in daylight across the continent, aiming at specific plants and refineries to disable German fuel supplies – was, especially in the autumn of 1944, accounted by others to have been a terrific success.

In early February 1945 Harris's bombers – working in conjunction with the US Eighth Air Force – had been attacking what Harris dismissively termed 'panacea targets':[8] largely synthetic-oil plants (which, when disabled, were far from fitting Harris's description – the damage caused genuine difficulties to supply lines). On 3 February there was an attack on Dortmund, intended to demolish the benzol works there. Similar plants at Osterfeld and Gelsenkirchen were attacked without success, but there were other effective strategic missions flown in those days too. On 7 February, for example, the Allied armies were about to move through the dense woods of the Reichswald on the Dutch border when bomber planes attacked the German troops stationed in the towns of Goch and Kleve, smashing roads, severing railways and so opening paths for the Allied troops to capture and move through. Harris was convinced that the conflict was edging closer to the point that decisive raids – well-rehearsed patterns involving a thousand bombers, sweeping irresistibly in a never-ending line over cities – would make the German High Command buckle. This long-established principle of area bombing, carried out in many hundreds of raids from Essen to Hanover, Cologne to Hamburg, Mannheim to Magdeburg, was to choke cities with helpless refugees. This was the point at which ordinary daily civilization could simply disintegrate.

To some senior figures in RAF Bomber Command, cities such as Dresden were now simply coloured zones upon detailed maps, populaces presided over by fanatical authoritarians. By this stage of the war, there were few who cared to make the exact distinction between civilians and soldiers, between German culture and Nazi cultism. Few had the time to envisage the lives of ordinary people.

There was a widespread fondness in Dresden for trees; a rich variety were encouraged and grown all over the city. Rudi Warnatsch, a boy living with his mother in a residential block, recalled vividly that 'the larger part of the courtyard was taken up with a cultivated garden. A magnificent chestnut tree and a linden tree were to be found there.'[9] In one of the smarter suburbs to the east of the city, Marielein Erler adored 'the great oaks and lindens' that stood in the park near her house.[10] Georg Frank's parents had planted a peach tree in their garden. Professor Victor Klemperer and his wife Eva had been intensely attached for both sentimental and culinary reasons to the cherry tree that stood in their back garden.[11] Its fruits came to symbolize the sweetness of the life that had been stolen from them.

In broader terms, the leafy streets and squares and courtyards reflected the unusual care that had been taken with the city's infrastructure. This was a city in which even the lower-cost housing for the working classes was of good quality for its time. Part of the reason was that there was in Dresden a decades-long tradition of obsession with hygiene, the richer industrialists frightened of the diseases that could threaten their workforces. Thus, people in the denser suburbs near the Altstadt lived in neat, ordered flats: four- or five-storey apartment blocks with well-scrubbed stairwells. A little to the south of the city, the middle classes favoured more opulent apartments, some of which featured 'winter garden' heated conservatory extensions.[12]

Trees also haunted the hinterland of Martin Mutschmann, the Gauleiter who held dominion over all Dresden lives. He felt most at home deep in the woods of the Saxon countryside, hunting. He was fascinated by traditional, ancient woodcrafts and by folk and fairy tales. If Dresden itself was a conscious expression of the value of art and harmony, then the man who ruled over it from the early 1930s right until the end of the war somehow represented a darker, more primitive unconscious current, something ungovernable that seemed more a part of those forests that lay close to the town. Mutschmann was Germany's longest-serving Gauleiter, who, together with his openly sadistic and greatly feared deputies, precisely represented the sort of enemy that Air Chief Marshal Harris believed could be vanquished only by the trauma of complete civic obliteration: implacable, fanatical, remorseless.

Gauleiter Mutschmann had a slight (and not flattering) facial resemblance to the actor Peter Lorre; his asymmetric eyes were prominent, his gaze glittering and unreadable. He had thin hair and a heavy gut. In February 1945 he was sixty-six years old. He had been Gauleiter of Saxony since 1925, and upon Hitler's ascent to power in 1933 was made its prime minister too. Mutschmann was among the very first to have joined the National Socialists in 1922. His implacably aggressive political views had been formed a long time before that. Mutschmann was close to the Führer and shared Hitler's intense fervour. And through him, Dresden had been clothed in all the raiment of fascism from the start – not merely the vast swastikas draped over all public buildings, but also the pervasive presence in the streets of the SS, the Hitler Youth, of the Nazi newspaper *Der Freiheitskampf*, the necessity for ordinary people in public arenas to give the stiff-armed salute and exclaim 'Heil Hitler'. Now, even in those first uncertain weeks of 1945 that saw traces of snow on the distant hills, Mutschmann had complete control not merely of the streets but of each and every private household: the old gentlemen, the mothers and their children, the young working women, the men in protected or reserved occupations.

Every coffee these Dresdeners drank in a restaurant, every film they went to see, any rationed purchase they made in a grocery shop, every telephone call, each and any interaction with the soldiers passing through the city on their way to distant fronts, all movements and utterances were potentially being monitored. Yet the people of Dresden had somehow found a way of adjusting to the relentless violence of his regime, to the grim tokens of oppression such as the signs on lamp posts in residential Johannstadt and other suburbs proclaiming them 'Jew zones'; to the way that the Gestapo and the police between them terrorized the remaining Jews while rooting out any form of political dissent elsewhere. Both in the workplace and at home, conversation was carefully guarded. It was not uncommon for ordinary men and women to be arrested late at night and interrogated into the early hours. No one was more than one forbidden word away from imprisonment. Or, indeed, very much worse.

On 8 February 1945, following a meeting of the Nazi People's Court, a judicial execution was carried out in the grey-flagstoned yard of the Dresden courthouse, just a little south of the central railway station. The victim: Dr Margarete Blank, forty-three, who had a rural medical practice and who now faced not the noose but the guillotine.[13] Her crime: while she was treating the children of an officer, she had expressed doubts about Germany securing any kind of final victory. Dr Blank was subsequently reported to the Gestapo, arrested, accused (falsely) of being a member of a resistance group and finally sentenced to death by decapitation. There was nothing secret about the use of the guillotine: under the Nazis a wide range of suspected Bolsheviks and resistance figures had perished beneath its heavy blade. Everyone in the city knew the possible penalty for ill-calculated remarks, passed on anonymously by colleagues and neighbours.

For Martin Mutschmann, it was clearly the duty of the people of Dresden to stand and fight whatever forces threatened the city. Any form of dissent or reluctance was treachery. This burly figure, locally nicknamed 'King Mu', had been raised not far from Dresden in a town called Plauen; he had left his Lutheran school at fourteen, in the final decade of the nineteenth century, had himself apprenticed and had gained proficiency in two perhaps unexpected disciplines: lacemaking and embroidery.

This was the industry for which Plauen had acquired international renown. The lace designs – both for clothing and for household use – were intricate but also expressive. There were great swirls of leaves and vines, hypnotic geometry, epic webs stretching across vast tablecloths. Even in an increasingly mechanical age, this was an occupation requiring habitual delicacy as well as concentration, and Mutschmann went on to become a master embroiderer. Yet outside of the workshop, his aggression very soon became apparent as he established his own lace business in the city. Colleagues recalled his frequently voiced hatred of Jews, especially those who had arrived from eastern Europe. Then a slump in the lace trade across the continent just before the First World War hit hard; this was not just a matter of cold economics but also changing tastes. The frilly fuss of lace was being displaced by the crisper, cleaner designs of early modernism.

Mutschmann, however, was certain he knew what was harming his world: the pernicious activities of the Jews. He was keen to scapegoat his Jewish competitors in Plauen for sabotaging the market. Indeed, he succeeded in rousing local feeling against Jewish businesses, and the town, which appeared so ordered and stable, came close to seeing a pogrom.

The squalor and the exhausting horror of the Great War made their mark: Mutschmann was invalided out of the conflict in 1916 – he later claimed this was the result of a kidney infection – and he returned to his business.[14] At its height, it had employed about 500 people, but there was no climbing out of this vertiginous slump. The jagged anarchy that came to Germany at the bitter end of the war – the violent battles between communists and right-wingers – further cemented Mutschmann's prejudices.

As Mutschmann saw it, this was a world that was being dragged down by an international Jewish conspiracy, and Germany's grovelling humiliation and abasement – its streets overrun with socialist firebrands – was the confirmation of their malign success. So Mutschmann joined the National Socialist German Workers' Party (NSDAP) in 1922 and quickly established a very strong bond with Hitler. At Christmas 1928 Mutschmann sent Hitler a book of fairy tales illustrated by Hermann Vogel, inscribed with Mutschmann's greetings from the Vogtland forest.[15]

Mutschmann's wife Minna (née Popp), whom he had married in 1909, played her own part in this new political life. She joined the women's section of the party. As her husband ascended the political ladder, so she played a role in organizing events, sometimes fundraising, attended by female fellow Nazis. Mutschmann's mother also joined.

By 1925, he was the Nazi Party's Gauleiter (chief party administrator) in Saxony, and it seemed to some that he was fixated on Saxon identity to the exclusion of any wider political ambitions. Hitler's triumphant assumption of power over Germany in 1933 in turn gave each regional Gauleiter a huge amount of new authority. The political violence came quickly to Dresden: a community hall meeting of around 2,000 'communists' ended in a staged brawl, leaving nine shot dead. The arrests of left-wing figures followed swiftly.[16] In addition, at this time Mutschmann was made Saxony's Reichsstatthalter (state governor). As he enjoyed vastly enhanced powers over the state, so the former lacemaker became increasingly absorbed with what he understood to be traditional Saxon culture and folk art.

In the Tharandt forest, he had a grand hunting lodge built, a curious structure topped with a truncated pyramid. Associates and allies were invited to stay for hunts. Mutschmann was obsessed by the pursuit – not just the sport but also, specifically, its part in the folk tapestry of the region. He had a statue of a stag installed near the entrance to the lodge. There was also a sculpture of a wild boar that stood near the house. He was attracted to the primitive atavism of such imagery. It has been suggested that interest in such things was part of a general Saxon move in the early part of the twentieth century to assert its own identity as Germany became ever more centralized and uniform. But the Nazi interest in folklore and legends spoke to something deeper and parareligious.

In terms of crafts, Saxony also had a rich history of puppetry: the large, unblinking, staring eyes of marionettes were used in productions aimed at adults as well as children. Mutschmann was photographed at an exhibition gazing with fascination at a display of them. The craft that went into the manufacture of the marionettes – the wires for the arms, the legs, the heads – was exquisite. Yet it was always acknowledged that there was something measurelessly unsettling about the unchanging expressions of these effigies; something that would make you a little reluctant to stay alone in a quiet room with them. The nineteenth-century writer E. T. A. Hoffmann, who lived for a time in Dresden, captured that sense in a fragment called 'The Automata', featuring a fairground marionette that answers questions mechanically and yet seems eerily able to see into the minds of the questioners.[17]

Throughout the 1930s and 1940s, in response to the satirical use of marionettes by unruly modernist artists such as the Dresdener Otto Griebel, the Nazis had established the Reichsinstitut für Puppenspiel (puppetry); among the puppets that featured in approved and pre-censored plays staged by the Hitler Youth were grotesquely caricatured Jewish figures, with hooked noses and large, terrible eyes. Those audiences watching the movements of the 'Aryan' marionettes will surely have had moments of self-reflection about the symbolism of the manipulators and the manipulated.

Mutschmann's interest in local Saxon sculpture and painting coloured his attitude to art in general. This was the man who, in the mid 1930s, banned jazz from Dresden (and later, in 1943, from the whole of Saxony), claiming it was 'degenerate music'.[18] As well as the underlying racism, there was also this sense that here was a musical form that was in its purest sense ungovernable, evoking responses that were anarchic and uncontained. This also extended to Mutschmann's attitude towards public expressions of humour. Perhaps because of an innate class sensitivity, he moved throughout the 1930s and the war years to eliminate in public discourse all jokes and humour at Saxony's expense. The area's dialect was often mocked (it still is by some in the west of Germany), as was its people's perceived rustic backwardness. One might imagine that the more sophisticated Dresdeners were both amused and bemused by the rural folk of the state, who even by the

1940s still inhabited a world in which the horse and cart was the main form of transport and manual farm labour the primary employment.

Not all Nazis were as unwilling to take a joke as Mutschmann. Indeed, there were some who felt in the earliest days of Hitler's rule that the odd satirical jab would be a useful outlet for sentiments that otherwise might build into more serious resistance. Right from the start of the Nazi era there had appeared a new subculture of 'whispered jokes', and the SS newspaper *Das Schwarze Korps* even went so far as to state that good-natured humour about authority, expressed openly, was healthy and to be encouraged. It cited a joke about Goebbels doing the rounds that the propaganda minister himself had got to hear, exclaiming, 'Oh, that old one again!'[19]

Later, such tolerance on the part of the SS wholly vanished, but Mutschmann had always been doctrinaire, governing Dresden with medieval brutality from 1933 onwards. Even on the sophisticated Prager Strasse, anyone failing to give the Nazi salute in greeting to an official could face instant arrest and imprisonment. In schools, Mutschmann insisted that all children were drilled in the values of the new regime, and any teacher felt to be even faintly resistant to such indoctrination was simply to be banned.

By 1935, under the Gauleiter's guidance, Dresden was taking an enthusiastic lead in the Nazi policy of sterilizing those with special needs and disabilities. In that year alone 8,219 sterilizations were performed in the city, more even than in Berlin, where there had been 6,550.[20] This was not a secret; it was reported prominently in the British press. Those who voiced ethical concerns were silenced, including 'a number of evangelical pastors' who were placed under 'protective arrest' – a measure that was 'unavoidable' in the interests of maintaining public order. These were pastors who had also spoken out about the ever-more pressing need for religious observance. The Gauleiter disagreed; the Nazi Natural Festival celebrating 1 May, for instance, 'took legal precedence over all church festivals'.[21] As with religion, so with culture.

The city's ornamental past was infused, as far as Mutschmann could make it, with the totalitarian vision. In 1934, when Hitler and Goebbels made a sweeping visit to the city to mark the first Reich

Theatre Week and were greeted by vast crowds of eager onlookers, Mutschmann accompanied them on a stroll through the baroque splendours of the Zwingergarten. The festival's first Nazi-sponsored performance took place in the Semper Opera House: a lavish production of Richard Wagner's opera *Tristan und Isolde*.

There were moments of social triumph for the Gauleiter too. In 1937 the Duke of Windsor, having abdicated as King Edward VIII, came to Dresden together with his new American wife prior to meeting Hitler. This was a tremendous moment for the Nazi Party, not merely for propaganda purposes but also to give its senior officials a sense of cultural acceptance. Gauleiter Mutschmann staged a grand banquet in the city to honour the duke's visit, after which Edward made an effusive speech to Mutschmann and the other Nazis present: 'As a student, I visited Germany for the first time to become acquainted with your language, your art and your literature. After twenty years, I return again as a student but this time to become acquainted with the essential problem – concerning the whole world – of the well-being of the working-class population.'[22] Gauleiter Mutschmann sought to impress the duke with an intricate scale model of the Zwinger Palace. Here was both enterprise and art, a contrast to the artlessness of the royal visitors.

Some eight years later, after six years of war, Dresden was a more huddled, threadbare city, the grand opera and galleries and museums reluctantly closed. It was a city that had still somehow not been wholly ground down by Mutschmann's blunt brutality. Yet the landmarks of fear were there for everyone to see. The florid Gothic bulk of the old courthouse on Mathildenstrasse, just a few streets away from the old town, housed a particularly brutal prison that all the citizens would have been aware of. The Mathilde, so named after the street, was used to confine and torture Jews, political dissidents, captured prisoners and Czech resistance figures. The conditions were medieval: straw on stone floor, wall shackles, whips. A few streets away, the once elegant Continental Hotel, across the road from the central railway station, was the headquarters of the local Gestapo. The incursion into commercial and civic space was deliberate: no corner of life was to remain free from the presence of the regime.

Little children still had footballs bearing swastikas; even some brands of toothpaste carried the symbol.

A notable absence in the city's wartime infrastructure was, with a single exception, the purpose-built air-raid shelter. Mutschmann had considered them an unnecessary expense. Instead, across the Altstadt countless musty cellars had been garnished with bare lightbulbs, sparse wooden sticks of furnishings. The exception was, of course, the concrete bunker built for Herr Mutschmann in the grounds of the city residence that he had expropriated from its Jewish owner.

Also active in the days before the bombardment was a figure who, for Dresden's Jews especially, had embodied the most hideous malevolence. Untersturmführer Henry Schmidt of the Dresden Gestapo – running a special department dedicated to persecuting Jews – had, like Mutschmann, lost none of his faith in the Nazi regime, nor in its power to prevail over the Western Allies and the Soviets. Schmidt, like Mutschmann, had come to the Nazis with zeal relatively early; and he had learned his craft in the secret police with an enthusiasm that had taken him all over the country.[23] By 1942 he had specifically requested a transfer to Dresden, not too far from where he had been brought up. He had exulted in his new responsibilities. In 1945 Schmidt was still young: a thirty-two-year-old man who had the power to condemn anyone he chose to death. The war crimes he committed in Dresden in the space of those three years alone were to make him a fugitive for many decades afterwards.

The apartment he lived in with his wife had been stolen from a Jewish couple who had been transported to Theresienstadt concentration camp and thence to their deaths. It was to him and his colleagues Hans Clemens and Arno Weser that any possible outbreaks of dissent among citizens were reported. Clemens – a blond, sturdy figure – had been noted and commended by his superiors for a particular ruthlessness and brutality that bordered on psychopathy; his interrogations in cells with bare white tiles were less about answers to questions and more about the simple exercise of inflicting terror and extraordinary cruelty.

Even in his ordinary dealings with Dresden citizens Clemens could not control the impulse to use physical violence and intimidation, whether he was carrying out an 'inspection' of a suspect's apartment or checking credentials in the street.[24] It cannot be known, as he walked through the old city, whether there was any part of his soul that had the slightest resonance with its gentle beauty.

That beauty was certainly very much appreciated by one of Dresden's more prominent civic leaders, although it did nothing to temper his bitter prejudices. Dr Rudolf Kluge was, for a time, the Burgomeister (or mayor) of the city. He had been born in Dresden in 1889, and although he had studied elsewhere, gaining a degree in law in Berlin, he always returned. Possibly the lurching economic plunges of the 1920s Weimar government hit him and his young family hard, for otherwise it is not entirely clear what made Dr Kluge join the NSDAP in 1928. But he came – with some ease – to occupy the darkest of moral positions: a key lawyer conjuring legal justifications not just for the Nazi Party but also for the entire new regime that was clamping itself around Germany's body politic.[25]

The other figure of real authority in the city by that first week of February was Hans Nieland, another early NSDAP loyalist and SS member, who had joined the party in 1926. He had studied for a doctorate in law; his thesis was entitled 'Power as a Governmental Concept of Law'.[26] As the Third Reich grew, Nieland was appointed to various dry technocratic positions involving civic structures. That did not mean that he was any less fervid about the virulent ideology. In 1940, at the comparatively young age of thirty-nine, he was appointed Burgomeister in place of Kluge, who stayed on as his deputy and later reassumed the position. It was, then, Nieland who should have been structuring the means for the city to defend itself, and Nieland who knew in February 1945 just how naked Dresden was.

In the 1930s Rudolf Kluge had been bathetically convinced that Dresden's tourist industry would be boosted by Hitler's conquests, bringing ever more fascinated visitors to this new centre of Germany.[27] In 1945, he could still gaze out of his window with love at the unbroken domes and spires of the city; yet this aesthete was stonily indifferent to the extraordinary suffering he had helped to inflict.

3. The Dethroning of Reason

In early February 1945 there were 198 Jewish people left in Dresden; before the Nazis came to power, there had been over 6,000. Even before the outbreak of war Dresden's Jews had had to endure the calculated wrecking and destruction of an architectural treasure, an act of sacrilege that was to be replicated throughout the continent. The grand synagogue that stood by the river at the eastern end of Brühl's Terrace, designed by gentile Gottfried Semper in the early nineteenth century, had been an ornament not merely to the Jewish population but to Dresden itself – the perfect architectural symbol for a community that was an organic part of the city's life, and with its own unmistakable identity. In the nineteenth century the synagogue had even attracted the dedicated anti-Semite Richard Wagner, who walked around it with avid curiosity.[1] Then, on 9 November 1938, came the terror orchestrated by the Gauleiter and his deputies that saw it burned to the ground: Kristallnacht. By February 1945 the site was long empty, as though a tooth had been extracted, leaving behind only some stubborn fragments of wall.

The synagogue's genesis lay in the nineteenth-century city's cosmopolitanism. Semper, who had already received the commission to build Dresden's grand opera house in the late 1830s, had been asked, for a modest additional sum, to build a synagogue on the edge of the Altstadt that would somehow blend in with the nearby baroque splendour of the Frauenkirche and other grand structures. But blending does not mean replicating, and the result was a brilliant addition to Dresden's already eclectic skyline. The exterior exhibited Byzantine influences: an octagonal tower, punctuated with windows, rose from the main rectangular body of the structure and at its western end stood two more slender towers topped with domes. Those domes spoke to the much larger effort of the Frauenkirche that rose over the streets close by, but they also strongly suggested an Eastern influence, an impression that was intensified inside the synagogue by distinctive and elegant curves and arches reminiscent of Moorish Spain or North Africa.[2] In addition, Semper had designed the synagogue so that pan-directional shafts of light would illuminate every corner.

The reason the synagogue had been designed by a gentile and not a Jew was, as historian Helen Rosenau suggested, because at that point in the mid nineteenth century, Jews were still finding it very difficult to enter certain trade guilds. Also, commissions of this nature were quite frequently offered to high-placed social contacts.[3] That aside, Semper's synagogue was a monument to all the possibilities of assimilation and, indeed, cross-cultural respect. This was not a building carefully hidden in a medieval ghetto: it took a proud and prominent position along the city's most fashionable promenading area. Until 1938 it was an integral element in that curving and sophisticated riverscape.

On the evening of 9 November 1938 the synagogue – as well as a huge number of shops and businesses that stretched right the way down Prager Strasse – became targets. Earlier in the day a low-ranking Nazi diplomatic official died, having been gunned down in Paris by a Polish Jew horrified by the treatment of his family back in Germany. Hitler's response was both incandescent and obscenely calculated: the word was spread through the SS in every German city. That night they would strike back. And in Dresden, young men stood in the square in front of the Rathaus (town hall), just round the corner from the synagogue, cajoling and whipping up the passions of passers-by who now were becoming a crowd. Nothing was left to the vagaries of spontaneity: a little earlier, SS men had stormed into the synagogue and sprayed all around with petrol, preparing it for conflagration; this done, they moved outside once more, awaiting the quiet signal.

In that square, in the darkness of that autumn evening, the men stood before metal braziers standing on cobbles, small flames leaping noiselessly, unruly shadows cast. As if by some twitch of morphic resonance, the violence began. Armed with staves and clubs, the men and their supporters set off towards the railway station, past the rich illuminations of the shop windows. They knew in advance which shops were Jewish owned. The different notes of shattering glass were a counterpoint to the guttural, ugly language of the shouting. The terror that was inspired in the shopkeepers and shop workers who were beaten up, arrested and dragged to cold imprisonment can only be imagined. And while this went on, another cohort of young men went back to the synagogue and set the fires roaring high.

Other citizens were not inert. Dresden's fire brigade received the call and were there commendably soon as the flames within the synagogue took a more adamant hold, the grey smoke rising higher into the murky autumn sky. Yet the firemen were not allowed to pass the ranks of SS men; they could only watch as, with a roar from within the building, its windows burst into the street. Eventually, they were allowed to intervene, but only to save the immediately adjoining structures. These were evacuated, though the cruelty some Jewish inhabitants faced outside in that cold air was just as frightening. They were surrounded by jeering, taunting young men and forced to watch as the walls of the synagogue began to collapse.[4] Other citizens looked on with horror, men and women who dared not move or decry the SS actions. Even by 1938, shows of defiance could result in imprisonment and beating.

Present at the fire was Dresden's Burgermeister, Dr Rudolf Kluge, who used the occasion to make a pronouncement. 'The symbol of the hereditary racial enemy,' he declared, 'has finally been extinguished.'[5] He was saying this of a building that had always been part of the landscape of his life; had he always gazed upon it, and the worshippers within, with such hatred? That night, over a hundred Jews around the city were murdered as their shops and businesses were shattered, ransacked and ruined; hundreds more were arrested and taken to the cells, to be subjected to stony-faced violence.

With the synagogue near collapse some hours later, its fabric cracking and creaking, the firemen were permitted to douse flames that might yet spread. Among them was a young man called Alfred Neugebauer, who had originally trained as a lithographer and who had a powerful interest in history and archaeology. The twin domes of the Semper Synagogue had been topped with polished metal Stars of David, each measuring some two feet across. One of these was retrieved and taken back to the fire station, where Neugebauer, experiencing a sudden rush of urgency, knew it had to be preserved and saved. He concealed it beneath a blanket and then took it home on his bicycle at the end of his shift. This was a dangerous act; the discovery of the symbol in any house search would have had Neuge-bauer marked out as a dissident. He hid it well, though, and as war came and he moved into various areas of civic defence, the six-pointed star stayed where it was and survived the conflict.[6]

As for the rest of the synagogue, Dr Kluge's office declared that the glowingly hot remains be dynamited and removed, the entire site razed under the pretext of public safety. The malice of the burning was compounded by the demand that the Jewish community pay for the work. There is a point when official callousness – enacting orders from higher above – transforms into malevolence. In the case of Dr Kluge, it was the way in which he ordered that a film unit should be present at the site of the ruined synagogue to capture the moments when the dynamite shattered the last of its foundations.[7] Anyone with the slightest moral qualm about this persecution might have taken care that it would not be preserved in such a way that the entire world might one day come to see. And so Dr Kluge's anti-Semitism was proved not merely authentic, but also completely sociopathic.

Yet in a wider sense, the story of what happened to the synagogue also perhaps helps to illuminate one of the enduringly terrible questions about Dresden – the mystery of how such violent hatred against Jews could possibly have festered in a city that had stood above all for art, and the intellect, and the commingling of cultures.

The opening of the Semper Synagogue in 1840 was confirmation that Jews were central to Dresden society. By the 1920s, when Dresden was a city of new electric trams, large banks, wealthy villas and adventurous shops and restaurants, the expanded Jewish population was very much at ease, its people moving among all the professions as well as the arts. More than this, the city had proved a safe haven for Jews from other, more aggressive parts of the country. Experienced dentist Erich Isakowitz came to Dresden with his young family in the early 1920s, having moved from a town in eastern Prussia where anti-Semitism had been on the rise.[8] Dresden by contrast offered a range of new friendships (and indeed a whole new range of clients for Isakowitz's dental surgery, the technology of which was thankfully becoming a little more sophisticated by the 1920s, at least in terms of pain relief and dentures that did not shatter). Aside from anything else, here in this city was to be found an abundance of intelligence: the teachers, professors and students at the very good university, the artists and writers who had been congregating here since the turn of the century, the bankers and the insurance brokers and the stockbrokers who dived deep into the city's cultural riches.

Whether at the cinema, the theatre, or any of the hundreds of cafes that served Dresdeners, there was little outward sense that the Jews were regarded as separate, or 'other'; Jewish children – such as Erich Isakowitz's daughter – attended the same schools as gentiles.[9] The Isakowitz family lived in a pleasant apartment block a little to the south of the grand railway station. Their home had central heating, telephone, quarters for a maid and a leafy conservatory, warm in winter winds.[10] Isakowitz had many patients for his dental practice, among whom was Eva Klemperer, the wife of university lecturer Victor. The stories of Klemperer and Erich Isakowitz point to a recurring philosophical and religious fault line in Germany: both men had served bravely in the First World War and both had risked their lives for their country. There was never any suggestion that this should be otherwise. So how was it that there could still be any questions in Dresden social circles about assimilation? (Indeed, in the case of Klemperer, who had actually converted to Protestantism for a time as a young man – and then again later, undergoing baptism as he embarked upon his academic career – the question gains extra resonance.)

The term assimilation, as used by gentiles, always suggested that Germans who held the Jewish faith were alien. Yet they had been born, brought up and educated in Germany and served in its armed forces. In Klemperer's accounts of gatherings in the 1930s, as it became ever clearer that Hitler was not some fleeting, temporary aberration but a fearsome phenomenon, there were agonized conversations among Dresden's gentiles and Jews alike about assimilation and non-acceptance, and about the desire (or, more realistically, fear-filled urgency) to emigrate to Palestine.[11]

All of this was something that Victor Klemperer tried to deny. He knew himself to be German; the Nazis were the ones who were 'un-German', to use his term. Indeed, right from his birth in Poland in 1881, and subsequent upbringing in Berlin, Klemperer's life had been flavoured by his enthusiastic and affectionate sense of his own German-ness. He had in his study a sabre that he had used in the First World War; Klemperer had afterwards been awarded the Cross of Merit for his volunteered services in the conflict. More specifically, Klemperer identified very strongly as a Prussian; the world and the politics that he most admired were made incarnate in Bismarck.

But he had always been alert to the world around him; immediately after the First World War, Klemperer very much disliked all colours of the new, aggressive radical politics, far left as well as far right. It was frantic, unstable, gravitating down towards violence. And with it came for the first time a prominent and noticeable new strain of anti-Semitism in this wild public discourse. The razor-slash atmosphere of street politics, combined with all the vicious economic blows and financial insecurity, was already fomenting loathing of moneyed Jewry before the Nazis made it their cold-eyed focus.

It was after the First World War that Klemperer had chosen to settle in Dresden with his non-Jewish wife Eva, who was an accomplished musicologist. There was already a more genteel form of anti-Semitism that had been embedded in the fabric of German society for some time. The reason Klemperer had converted to Christianity as a young man had nothing to do with his beliefs – he was not religious in any way – but was that certain professions and academic roles in German institutions were, during the reign of Kaiser Wilhelm, quietly, informally barred to those of the Jewish faith. In addition to this, Klemperer's strong sense of his Germanic identity was allied to a feeling that Protestantism was its most natural cultural expression.

Klemperer found secure tenure at the Technical University in Dresden. His field was philology and the Romance languages, as well as German studies. Amid the chaos of the 1920s – the hyperinflation, the national humiliation both of reparations and of the French occupation of the Ruhr and the resultant foaming, highly aggressive extremists on all political fronts – Klemperer and his wife none the less found their own sort of stability.

Hitler's ascendancy to the chancellorship in 1933 might just have been foretold, but the speed at which virulent, spitting Jew-hatred became embedded in day-to-day German culture could not. What began was a breathtakingly fast process of 'othering', enacted in cities right across the country but somehow with even more awful velocity in Dresden. April 1933 brought the start of the boycott movement, the government-sponsored campaign to persuade non-Jews to turn away from all Jewish businesses. As well as the terrible economic price, there were a thousand painful emotional wounds as well, Dresden fashion retailers and jewellers watching as previously loyal and friendly customers simply disappeared.

The venom coursed further through the civic veins: academics were forced to swear professions of loyalty to Hitler in public. This oath-taking began in schools but very shortly the order went out in the universities. Signed documents were not enough; these declarations of absolute obedience to the new government had to be heard and witnessed. Non-Jewish academics may have consoled themselves with the idea that all political regimes are transient, and that Hitler's party might be more transient than most. That illusory consolation would itself have been fleeting. Soon came the Nuremberg Laws, barring Jews both from a wide range of professions and from academic tenure.

No matter that he had been baptized a Christian in 1912, this was the case for Victor Klemperer. His removal from the university did not happen immediately; unlike his Jewish colleagues, he was granted some extra time because he was a war veteran. But when it became plain that his job was no longer open to him, there were further malicious blows. Not only was he not allowed to teach; he was also denied access to the university library. Now he could no longer even study for his own satisfaction or pleasure. Books that he yearned to read were now beyond his reach.[12] He had his academic pension to live on; but as the 1930s ground on, these funds began to diminish dramatically, until they vanished altogether. This was merely the start of the extraordinary ordeal that he and Eva were to be condemned to suffer.

★

By the mid 1930s many of Dresden's Jewish citizens started thinking more seriously about emigration. This was hardly a move to be made lightly, to abandon one's home in the hope of becoming at best 'a guest' (as the author Stefan Zweig put it)[13] in a foreign land. How could safety and security be guaranteed abroad?

The Aryanization of the German banks in 1935 – effectively straightforward theft by the government – compounded the growing sense of dread; even by then there were whispers and rumours about the new camps that had been established outside small German towns, suggestions that to be sent to such places meant that one would never return. The first inmates of these camps were largely political prisoners, communists and radical left-wingers violently opposed to Nazi ideology. Many were beaten with whips and truncheons. Some were found dead by concerned visiting lawyers such as Josef Hartinger, their bodies covered with wounds.[14] And many of them were Jewish.

In this rising miasma of anxiety, a number of Dresden Jews began making inquiries. As some were looking towards Palestine, which seemed a not wholly congenial prospect, others turned to Canada, to South Africa, to Argentina. In the case of the Isakowitz family, the preference was England. But by this stage it was not permitted for Jews simply to leave Germany; they had to pay a considerable ransom to the Nazi Party in order to do so. The more belongings and valuables any family had packed ready to be sent, the higher the proportion of that perceived wealth the Nazis were set on expropriating. Fortunately, and only after making considerable sacrifices, the Isakowitz family managed to leave, travelling to London and finding a semblance of security in Hampstead Garden Suburb.[15]

For the Jews who remained in Dresden, the sense of humiliation and threat continued to escalate with terrible effect. Professor Klemperer, already deprived of the work that he loved, suffered further hurt when the thuggish officers of the Gestapo snatched his typewriter from him. The Klemperers were no longer allowed to employ their cleaning lady; the new laws stated that Jews were forbidden to have Aryans working for them.

Added to this were surprising and distressing outbreaks of anti-Semitism from the most ordinary people. Klemperer recalled one day in the late 1930s when he visited the pharmacy to have a prescription made up. The young lady behind the counter simply pretended that he was not there. Another customer came into the shop; the girl beckoned him forward to the counter. The customer gestured towards Klemperer and told her that this gentleman was first in line. The assistant would not be contradicted; she would serve the other customer first.[16]

The expulsion of the Jews from their professions was excruciating, and not just because livings were lost. It was also the ruthless way in which entire proud identities were snatched away. As Stefan Zweig observed elsewhere, the deepest desire of European Jews in the first part of the twentieth century was not to acquire wealth – wealth was merely a means of getting a secure foothold in gentile society – but instead to become intellectuals. No one deep down wanted to be a merchant, but a great many dreamed of studying for a doctorate.[17] The old anti-Semitic stereotype of the acquisitive Jew piling up gold was hated by the Jewish community; conversely, intellectual endeavour in any sphere meant that Jews were not merely assimilated into society, but became an absolutely integral ingredient in its cultural life, stretching from writing to the performing arts to science.

This had as profound an impact in Dresden as it did in Vienna; the Jewish community had loved being so central to a city that thrived and flourished on a wide range of rich traditions. And the Nazis knew precisely what they were doing when they forbade the Jews from continuing in any intellectual pursuit – a calculated form of internal cultural exile aimed at the most sensitive of nerves. From there, the further stages of dehumanization were easily set in train.

In 1938 Jewish citizens of Polish heritage became the focus of Dresden's Nazis: as in other cities, they were to be removed from their homes and forcibly deported to Poland – a land where they had no home. And so it was that many Dresden Jews found themselves torn from the city they loved before being kept by the bewildered Polish authorities in holding camps: a frightening twilight existence in which statehood, citizenship and human rights were denied.

In the year that Germany went to war with Britain, Dresden's remaining Jews were evicted from their homes. In the vast majority of cases, these were quite simply stolen by the authorities. The

Klemperers, who lived in a modest, pleasant villa in the suburb of Dölzschen, felt this new oppression with dagger-like keenness. A little before this, they had had their phone line removed; Jews were now forbidden to communicate telephonically. Added to this had been a new by-law of exquisitely calibrated malice: Jews were no longer allowed to keep household pets. The Klemperers loved their cat; now they were obliged to have it destroyed.[18]

Those who had been torn from their family homes were moved to apartment buildings known as Judenhäuser; these buildings were horribly inferior to their previous accommodation: cramped, dimly lit and with unreliable gas supplies. Nazi officers could and did enter freely at all hours. On one occasion Klemperer was slapped around the face, and his wife was spat at.

The Klemperers' car was impounded. As the war deepened, travel restrictions extended to public transport: Jews were no longer allowed to ride on Dresden's trams. In addition to this came the order that all Jews must wear prominently a yellow star. On the streets of Dresden these had the most terrible lustre, not only making the dread and vulnerability all the heavier but also forcing friendly neighbours and ex-colleagues to gaze at a sign of humiliation they did not want to see. There were other degradations to come.

There seemed to be an almost childlike spite in the Dresden decree of 1942 that Jews were now forbidden to buy either flowers or ice cream. The latter by-law seemed aimed squarely at the few Jewish children who remained, an act of cruelty so calculated as to suggest something hotter, more lava-like, than sociopathy. It came on top of the edicts that Jews were no longer permitted on Brühl's Terrace, the promenade overlooking the Elbe, and there were certain paths in the Great Garden park that were also now declared to be off-limits.[19] The last time Jews had been banned from the riverside terrace was 200 years previously.

Professor Klemperer was trying to fathom this regime and all of its malevolence and to square it with his own love of Germany, which resonated with the deep conservatism of Bismarck and Kaiser Wilhelm. The Nazis and Hitler, by contrast, he saw as revolutionaries; they were, he thought, an incarnation of Romanticism, a movement that was all about the unstoppable tides of passion and feeling. Nazism was its darkest flowering, exulting in 'the de-throning of reason', 'the animalisation of mankind' and the 'glorification of the power idea, the predator, the blond beast'.[20]

But even as the war intensified, Klemperer was also interested to note that among Dresden's citizens, adherence to Nazism was by no means universal. Certainly he was followed and taunted and spat at by some boys in the Hitler Youth, but balancing that were innumerable small but vital acts of kindness from strangers: people commenting how distressed they were by the yellow stars; shopkeepers sneaking across small extra rations (the Jews were barely above starvation levels of subsistence). Then there were the much greater acts of kindness, the non-Jewish family friends who stayed loyal. There was Annemarie Köhler, who vitally provided a hiding place in her own home for Klemperer's written diaries: had they been found, the consequences would have been lethal.

Then there was the attorney Helmut Richter, who – astoundingly, in the circumstances – managed to save Klemperer's beloved house in Dölzschen. Richter used his legal prowess to raise a new mortgage on Klemperer's home. This meant that, even though the professor was forbidden to live in it, the deeds were still at least in his name. The house was leased to a Nazi; naturally, no rent was paid to Klemperer, but the fact that the property was still the professor's was truly remarkable. Yet even the most covert of actions had consequences. Attorney Richter had joined the Nazi Party years before, but by the start of the war in 1939 he had turned away from it in disgust. By 1943 Richter's antipathy, which manifested itself further than in simply rescuing his friend's house, could no longer be ignored by the Dresden authorities. He was arrested and sent to Buchenwald concentration camp and his death.[21]

Klemperer could see that, even though their persecution had echoes of medieval pogroms, the Nazis 'arrived not in the garb of the past, but in that of the most extreme modernity'.[22] This modernity needed labour, and he was among those forced into working for Zeiss Ikon until exempted on grounds of age. A special camp for some of the other workers was built a little north of the city, at Hellerberge. There is a spool of film, a recording, quite beyond shame, of the people arriving there. The men and women were stripped; and then, naked,

they were 'decontaminated' and 'deloused'. These details stayed out of
the camera's frame, but there is a surviving shot of a vast furnace being
fed, the inference from which apparently was that these barracks
would be very well heated. One cannot help but wonder if this shot
was included deliberately: a knowing note of premonition.[23]

From here, after months of labour, Jewish citizens found themselves suddenly facing transportation, a journey to the east in conditions
of pure horror. Each and every Jewish citizen was on a municipal
list. From this list were selected the names of those to be sent to Riga,
to Theresienstadt. As with the persecution of the Jews throughout
Nazi Europe, the implacable bureaucracy of death went beyond
any kind of reason. In the space of just one generation, the city was
participating, and not unwillingly, in a programme of methodical
genocide. Yet in the early days of 1945, Victor Klemperer was still
recording flashes of generosity from gentiles. It is a remarkable thing:
like a flower crushed beneath a rock that still instinctively feels for
the sunlight.

The moral stain had expanded outwards. Usually in times of war,
art is conscripted to the struggle, yet in the case of Dresden it had by
1945 been suffocated. As with the psychotic persecution of the Jews,
there seemed something quite extraordinary about a city whose soul
had been defined by rich culture and creativity now forcibly sup-
pressing and distorting that genius.

4. Art and Degeneracy

Hamlet was first performed in Dresden just ten years after William Shakespeare died. In 1626, a troupe of 'English comedians' staged what is now thought to be a shortened version of the tragedy.[1] There have even been suggestions that this production for Saxony's royal court involved the use of elaborate marionettes, the effigies miming the play within the play.

That detail would have greatly appealed to the twentieth-century Dresden modernist Otto Griebel. Among Griebel's brilliantly varied interests in the 1920s and 1930s was Dresden's continued tradition of marionette plays; he was gripped by the possibilities of mocking allegory that they offered. This in turn earned him the hostile attention of the authorities. By February 1945, as a forty-nine-year-old father of five who had been torn away from Dresden by the hurricane of war that had flung him to a corner of eastern Europe in reluctant military service as a draughtsman, Otto Griebel was now free and back with his family and what remained of his work in the darkened city. Although no special shelters had been built for the city's living population, some time back proper shelters had been provided for Dresden's many art treasures, among them Old Masters, including Rembrandts.

The elegant pensioner Georg Erler had his own private art collection in his smart home on Striesener Strasse, to the east of the city. He, like so many others, had long believed that Dresden would be spared. 'The will to destroy the enemy seemed to stop before our beautiful city of art,' he wrote.[2] Yet he did fear another force: the Red Army. In the early weeks of 1945, Herr Erler and his wife Marielein had debated how best to safeguard their aesthetic treasures, which included large oil paintings of distinguished family members, ornamental Meissen china and a rather beautiful antique six-armed chandelier 'made entirely of opalescent yellowish toned Bohemian glass'.[3] Mirroring the city's authorities, which had carefully packed the contents of the galleries and the castle and transported them to closely monitored networks of caves in the hills, the Erlers arranged to take their own art out of Dresden, making several trips across country to deposit it with relatives in the smaller town of Lüneburg.

Art can sometimes be symptomatic, as well as reflective or interpretive; whether tranquil or feverish, it can capture the temperature of a time. So much 1920s German art was raw and stark and brutal but, curiously, neither the talented Otto Griebel nor his radically innovative artistic contemporaries in Dresden seem to have detected the latent malevolence in Germany through the traumatized postwar period from 1918 onwards. Griebel's story – the way he was thrown so violently back and forth during those years – partly mirrors the story of art in Dresden down the centuries.

Theatre and art remained at the heart of the city even through the severely distorting times of hysterical censorship. The Nazis were not the first power in the city to try to bend the visions of art to their will. And nor were they the last. Yet over time, that freedom stubbornly reasserted itself. The city – chiefly during the eighteenth-century reign of Augustus the Strong – had accumulated the most astonishing range of artistic treasures: lustrous nativity portraits, extraordinary porcelain, the rich flashing reds and blues of rubies and sapphires embedded in sword hilts.[4] The range of the paintings – some executed in the city itself, others bought up from Amsterdam to Venice – spoke to sensibilities that were authentically and grandly pan-European. Here were portraits and annunciation scenes by Titian; madly populated landscapes from Jan Brueghel the Elder.[5]

And there were great artists who saw that Dresden itself was an ornament to be captured in its delicate beauty, and so, even by the harrowed days of 1945, Dresdeners still somehow understood themselves, through these works, to belong to an aesthetic world that stretched far beyond the rocky plains and the haunted forests of Saxony. Through the ages these artists had contrived to make the soul of Dresden genuinely cosmopolitan.

The Venetian Bernardo Bellotto, who had painted both Venice

and London and bathed them in a blue/gold sun, came to live in the city in the mid eighteenth century. Here, his landscapes were imbued with a silvery light: crisper, clearer and serving to draw closer attention to exquisite architectural detail. In a sense, he was transmitting the glory of others, for his eye captured in almost hyper-realist detail the stonework of the Catholic cathedral, the soft curving contours of the Frauenkirche dome. This was painting not just as a means of evoking aesthetic delight: it was a deliberate act of remembrance, a means of preserving that which could at any time be destroyed; war had come to Dresden before.[6] Centuries before that deathly grey February, painters had sensed the city's vulnerability.

Bellotto's most famous study of the city was to be linked strongly to the days and weeks around February 1945. 'Dresden from the Right Bank of the Elbe', the artist's position on the north-west bank of the river looking south-east towards that skyline, was executed in 1748 but could have been painted at any point since. The light is apple-bright, and this perfectly proportioned and detailed study of that curving river bend and all the proud churches and houses and academies along it was after the war to serve as an invaluable reference point.

Similarly, Johan Christian Dahl's 'View of Dresden at Full Moon', painted around 1838, is a poignant vision of a city that would have been equally familiar to both Bellotto and Victor Klemperer, depicted in a new and evocative way: in the rich blue of the night.[7] The light here is soft silver, with the dome of the Frauenkirche and the sharp spire of the Catholic cathedral in deep silhouette. Dahl, a Norwegian, had moved to the city in the early years of the nineteenth century and had formed a close friendship with the man who is now acknowledged as the city's pre-eminent artist: Caspar David Friedrich. It is in Friedrich's work that we see perhaps a little of Dresden's more numinous qualities, something a shade detached from the everyday, looking into distances and seeing worlds that are strange yet familiar. Friedrich had been born in Pomerania, but after precocious artistic success, he set up home in the kingdom of Saxony. Here was a Dresden artist steeped in Romanticism, most famous now for the lone wanderer on top of a mountain crag staring out over 'the sea of fog' and other lonely peaks. Here too were landscapes without people: vast ravines, blasted trees – and through the ruby mists of sunset, faraway spires rising into rich red skies; all the terror and the seduction of the sublime.

There were even more unsettling Friedrich images: the snow-patched ruins of an abbey; the iron gates before a cemetery. Dresden hills and meadows were depicted in eerie twilit tones.[8] These were paintings that appeared to have been summoned from dreams, and to later generations they also seemed freighted with all the troubling symbolism of the unconscious mind and, specifically, the German soul. The works of Friedrich were much admired by the Nazis, and it was not until the 1970s that this taint was dispelled. The attraction might have been partly this: in those faraway mists there rose towers and spires suggestive of a faith that seemed not wholly Christian – at least, not in its Catholic iteration. When you are up on the hills of Dresden on a foggy autumnal day, that arresting effect of impossibly sharp distant spires emerging from the clouds is there.

The sophistication of Dresden as a citadel of artistic thought and inno-vation, a zenith of European civilization, acquired more and more depth. And unlike other ornate cultural centres, it had a continuing attraction for young radical artists. The most famous of the groupings formed at the beginning of the twentieth century was Die Brücke (The Bridge). This was not the first German art movement to turn against established academies, or to attempt to form an idealized com-munity, but Die Brücke was seriously avant-garde.

Here was a group that rejected what it saw as bourgeois realism in favour of compositions that evoked deep inner feelings and turbu-lence; the work that emerged was later termed German expressionism, and for several decades it became an extraordinarily influential and wide-ranging genre. There were canvases that pulsed with glowing, clashing colour, heads and bodies depicted against sharp, strange angles; there were also chilling woodcuts depicting gas masks and death's heads, all executed with a tangible anger. This movement was to become the apotheosis of everything the Nazis loathed about modernism.

Die Brücke – which contained the seeds of a wider social and sexual revolution – had been founded in 1905 by two young architecture students enrolled at the Dresden Technical University: Fritz Bleyl and Ernst Ludwig Kirchner. There was an early passion for folk art, the wood sculptures to be found in the forested lands around. This interest in a less urban, more communal existence also manifested itself in terms of ostentatious sexual abandon in those forests with the artists' life models.

They were joined early on by Emil Nolde, his paintings luminously powerful.[9] The spirit of the movement was disseminated across Germany, and across Europe too. In Dresden, innovation fed further inventiveness; expressionism became fused with furious social satire and the determination to portray proletarian realities. In those years before the outbreak of the First World War, the city was nurturing the artistic talents of students Conrad Felixmüller, Otto Dix and Otto Griebel.

Of these, it was Dix's work that became immediately, viscerally, emblematic. In 1914, aged twenty-two, he had hurled himself like so many other young men into the First World War, carried along with the initial waves of exultation that marked the declaration of hostilities: the certainty that victory would be swift and honourable. And, of course, Dix, like his comrades, very quickly understood the squalid, mud-sucking, barbed-wire-torn truth. The young artist served bravely and was awarded the Iron Cross, but something new had entered his soul.

He returned to Dresden in 1919, and the art that he produced in the 1920s evoked physical shock. There was no more vague abstraction; instead, pitiless clarity. *Der Krieg* was a series of etchings depicting trench life and death. There was no heroism here; and no pity either. This world instead was simply one of unimaginable pain, visible in bulging eyes and filth, with all varieties of mud and death.[10] 'Stormtroopers Advancing Under Gas' remains one of the most totemic images of the cycle: the masks skull-like in this weird landscape of hell. Dix suffered continual nightmares involving crawling through bombed-out houses and rubble; his dreaming self spent every night in a phantasmal Dresden which had been destroyed.[11]

The artist – whose work came to be understood as part of a fresh movement called Neue Sachlichkeit (New Objectivity), depicting the dark social realities of Weimar life – was appointed a professor at the Dresden Academy of Art in 1927. One of his young peers – who had taught Dix about some of the technicalities of printing from woodblocks – was Conrad Felixmüller. Like Dix, Felixmüller had returned from the war an implacable radical.

This young man's speciality was woodcuts: strong, urgent, blending an urban industrial realism with the stabbing geometry of expressionism. Felixmüller had served in a medical capacity during the Great War, and on his return to Dresden he threw himself into the roiling cauldron of revolutionary politics. The months after the war had seen authority temporarily upended in what became known as the 'German Revolution': councils and industries occupied by workers and soldiers. The Bolshevik seizure of Russia the previous year seemed as though it might be repeated here, but with each and every advance by socialists and communists, there were the opposing forces of the right, who found their most eloquently violent articulation in the Freikorps: roaming armed squads composed in part of former soldiers. In the aftershocks of war, the brutality was transposed to city streets.

Germany in defeat resembled the expressionist horror of the famous 1920 film *Das Cabinet des Dr Caligari*, in which a young man – a somnambulist – with no will of his own is impelled to murder. His wide staring eyes have a flicker of haunted pathos, but as he moves through a disturbing landscape of sharp, dagger-like forms, it is also clear that he is irredeemably lethal. Some of Conrad Felixmüller's woodcuts carried a similar charge of expressionist menace: small rooms, lit by moonlight, where shadows are sharpened to threatening points.[12]

Also rising to prominence at that febrile time was Otto Griebel, an artist who had gone a step further than Felixmüller by joining the city's Workers' and Soldiers' Council. Griebel was a keen promoter of the Dadaist movement, which had both mischief and deadly seriousness. This was art that extended to every sphere – painting to poetry performances – and it embraced the nonsensical and made satirical fetishes of everyday manufactured objects and advertising. It was intended as an assault on all notions of stability: how could there be such fixed meanings in a world that at any moment could be torn apart with pure horror? Griebel's 1923 painting 'The Naked Whore' – depicting a topless blonde with a curious rictus smile in the act of lowering her drawers – was the most direct challenge imaginable to any of Dresden's more delicate sensibilities.[13]

And there were still such sensibilities; more traditionalist, figurative artists there and in other cities who resented the relationship between the expressionists and the art establishment. In Dresden, the most influential figure in this establishment was the director of the Old Masters Picture Gallery, Hans Posse. He was also to become one of the city's most horribly conflicted figures. Initially, from his lofty position, Posse championed this new shocking generation of artists. In 1926 he ensured that Dresden staged an International Art Fair: the works of local painters would hang alongside confrontational works from elsewhere.

Posse could not sense the subterranean pressures that were building, and when in 1933 he found himself facing an entirely new and hostile regime, his lack of a sure-footed response indicated to senior Nazi Party operatives that Posse did not share their views. Art was not some marginal activity; it lay at the very centre of the way the Nazis sought to transform German life. The term they used was *Gleichschaltung*, roughly meaning 'coordination'. It meant that all artistic endeavour had to conform strictly to Nazi ideals. Partly, this was down to the anger of Hitler, himself rejected twice for a place at Vienna's Academy of Fine Arts. Hitler was exactly the sort of painter that Posse disdained. His art was stolidly representational – studies of grand civic buildings, farmhouses, courtyards, and the like – and in the eyes of a modernist looked preposterously twee and kitsch.

Conversely, Hitler's hatred of modernism was something that he made very plain in his speeches. The German people did not want to have to consult pretentious guidebooks to decode what was happening in these nightmarish, distorted modernist paintings, or in the 'sick brains' of those who had produced them.[14] Even on the edge of war, Hitler regarded himself as an artist first and a politician second, as he told the British ambassador.

And so Dresden was selected for the first wave of Nazi art-shaming. Artists such as Dix, Felixmüller and Griebel had their work seized by the authorities and displayed in the Dresden Rathaus in the autumn of 1933, the intention being that townsfolk would come and articulate their loathing for these immoral paintings.[15] Without being named as such, this was the first exhibition of 'degenerate art'; a foretaste of the more comprehensive exhibition to come in Munich in 1937, comprising a mix of Jewish painters, perceived anti-militarists and indeed any abstractionist.

For Otto Dix, this reverse was profoundly menacing on several levels: he was removed from his job and banned from exhibiting past works. A couple of years later, forced to change his artistic style completely in order to find buyers for his new work, Dix fell back on landscape painting: mountains, plains and, in a nod to a Dresden artist that he loathed, snowy landscapes of remote villages and lonely graveyards that deliberately echoed the work of Caspar David Friedrich.[16] Dix had been reduced to the same kind of kitsch as Hitler.

Nor was life much easier for his sponsor, the gallery director Hans Posse; he too was removed from his post. But Posse was unaware that he and Hitler had a mutual friend, the art dealer Karl Haberstock, who identified and obtained looted works for the Führer, and who was likely to have mentioned the director to him. As a result, Hitler put Posse in charge of the entire Nazi art acquisition programme. Suddenly and unexpectedly this high-minded Dresden art expert was pulled deep into a swamp of criminal squalor. As the Nazi hierarchy grabbed and stole as much art as they could for themselves, Posse was there giving an illusion of respectability, buying fine German art that reflected all the values of the Third Reich.

There were still numinous realms that, despite their best efforts, the Nazis could never quite control. For, as well as painting, Dresden was also a city suffused with music, an art perhaps too sacred for the regime to defile. Its purest expression, in soul-piercing harmonies, was to be found in the Lutheran Church of the Holy Cross – the Kreuzkirche – in the Altstadt. The candle flames dancing in the darkness of the nave were a form of defiance in themselves; in previous years, such Catholic touches were not used, but it was important that the Nazis understood there was no room for their own additions. Other churches had seen iron crosses installed, fusing Christianity with Nazi militarism.

The Kreuzkirche had been famous for many decades – centuries, even – for its boys' choir that had been formed in the thirteenth century. Now, in the murkiest and most desperate hours of the war, that crystalline song was still known across the continent and indeed across the Atlantic. Even at that stage, over five years into the conflict, choristers were still being enrolled at the Kreuzschule, a grand Gothic building that lay close to the church, and it was still only those with the very finest voices and instinct for musicality who were admitted. The school was a boarding establishment with long dormitories, and a valuable refuge from the saturation of Nazi imagery and ideology that had otherwise filled the veins and arteries of the city.

But the war had pressed most terribly on the cantor, the man who conducted and directed the choir. Like so many other people in Dresden, he had been forced to make the most hideous compromise in order to remain in his position. Rudolf Mauersberger – glaringly bald, with a distinctive, amiable face – had been appointed to this hugely prestigious institution some fourteen years back, in 1931; the choir was already greatly celebrated, but he was poised to take this musical phenomenon out into a wider world.[17]

In one sense, Hitler and the Nazis offered no threat: what could be more perfectly emblematic of German culture than this institution? And yet from 1933 onwards there were tensions, and it was possibly because he had seen so many others in the city removed from their posts that Rudolf Mauersberger joined the Nazi Party. This was the time when university professors were being forced into 'confessing' their loyalty to the Führer in special ceremonies, when schoolteachers were being ordered to abandon complex curriculums in favour of a return to simplistic basics of mathematics and grammar, when even minor public servants were obliged to greet Nazi officials with a stiff-armed salute and a 'Heil Hitler!'

It was clear that Mauersberger loved his role as the choir's cantor. Certainly, his work with the choir and his efforts to bring the boys before international audiences transcended the grim reality of Dresden's gross Gauleiter and his new regime. In the mid 1930s, having taken the choir on a European tour, Mauersberger succeeded in arranging a trip to America, where the Kreuzchor performed before many appreciative audiences.[18] If anything, this would have given the new Hitlerian regime a note of real legitimacy: the pure musical genius of the choir and the sensitive settings of religious classics would have reassured many Americans that the Nazis appreciated civilization after all.

The tension between the Nazis and the Church – and especially the Kreuzchor – lay in an ideological conflict between spiritual and secular worship. Nazism claimed complete ownership of mind and body, while the Church had a rather older and more legitimate claim to the soul.

Catholics had the Pope to turn to; Hitler and his lieutenants, no matter their own personal dismissal of religious faith, understood the strength of the bonds to Rome, and knew that they could not strike too hard against the distant authority of the Vatican over German believers. (It was different in subjugated Poland, where Catholic priests, refusing to bow to secular demands, were imprisoned and brutalized.)

For Protestantism, however, the case was not quite the same; in the absence of a central unifying episcopal authority, the Nazis had more room to influence and coerce. And in the case of the Lutheran Kreuzchor, there was the simple brute fact that membership of the Hitler Youth was compulsory for the young choristers. Uniforms were mandatory, and the Hitler Youth had their own particular musical genre, including marches such as 'Vorwarts! Vorwarts!' and an adaptation of an old hymn with the words 'The rotten bones are trembling'.

There are some suggestions that Mauersberger was able to keep these and other Nazi favourites, including the party's official anthem, the 'Horst Wessel Song', out of the Kreuzkirche. The paraphernalia of the Hitler Youth – the armbands, belts and daggers – were rather more difficult to discard. An unattributed story had it that around 1943 Mauersberger and his choristers were engaged to perform elsewhere in Germany. They would be taking the train to their destination. The authorities demanded that the boys of the choir travel in their full Hitler Youth regalia. But Mauersberger had planned ahead. He did not board the train at the central station but at the next stop along, Dresden Neustadt, bringing the boys' school clothes – black jackets, white shirts with wide collars – with him so they could immediately change. He did not wish them to travel as Nazis, but as Kreuzchor singers.

Little more than a quarter of a mile away from the Kreuzkirche stood the city's other great shrine to sacred music. The Frauenkirche, which was not only an aesthetic marvel, but an engineering one too with its large distinctive dome looming some 220 feet (67 metres) above the streets of the Altstadt, had been built in the 1730s under architect George Bähr, inspired by the Italian baroque style. With the installation of its organ, the church saw Johann Sebastian Bach come to perform in 1736. Like the Kreuzkirche, the Frauenkirche had acoustics that were almost ethereal: the melodies and harmonies and counterpoints rising up past galleries and into the unusual pink-and-blue painted warmth of the dome interior.[19] Like its near neighbour, this was a Protestant church and the boys of the Kreuzschule would also perform there on special occasions, most recently a concert of Christmas carols and music with the city deep in the darkness of blackout in the winter of 1944.

Even in February 1945 this was a building that would still be recognized by Bach and by the great organ maker Silbermann: the gleam of dulled gold, the tortured altarpiece of Christ in the Garden of Gethsemane, and high above the brighter figures of saints among the rosy clouds of Heaven.

Sacred music was one thing: but the city was also famous internationally for opera – to many agnostics a form of religion in itself. And in this sphere, the Nazis, from Hitler downwards, had taken a very much more active interest. By February 1945 the Semper Opera House was no longer staging productions. The theatrical extravagance would not have been possible, still less appropriate, at that frayed point. The last show had been staged a few weeks previously at the end of 1944 – the comic opera *Fra Diavolo*, involving bandits, revolutionaries and an innkeeper's daughter, and which starred Dresden Opera's celebrated bass Kurt Böhme.[20] But the history of the institution was still very alive to the citizens of Dresden. Indeed, that history reflected all the most turbulent periods of Dresden politics;

not least when the opera was presided over by the young Richard Wagner in the 1840s.

It is curious now to contemplate the Dresden life of Hitler's favourite composer, for while Wagner made musical history staging premieres of his work here – *Rienzi*, *The Flying Dutchman* and *Tannhäuser* – he was also briefly pulled into a swirl of radical left-wing and anarchist politics. The twin streams of great art and intense politics always characterized the city.

As a boy, Wagner had briefly attended the Kreuzschule; a few years later, in 1842, as a young composer with a fast-building reputation, he was back in Dresden as Royal Saxon Court conductor. While there were those sceptical of his musical innovations, a great many others were swept up in a form of rapture. His operas, pulsating out across the country, also reinforced the idea of Dresden as a flashing cultural jewel, and were a strong lure to high society and the more refined classes. Ironically, this came at a moment in Wagner's political development (though his virulent anti-Semitism seems to have been a constant) when he was agitating for greater freedom for the individual, and indeed for the city of Dresden to have some semblance of representative democracy.

In the 1840s Saxony was still a kingdom under Frederick Augustus II. As well as writing articles for a local radical journal, Wagner became friends with the Russian anarchist Mikhail Bakunin, who had arrived in the city in the late 1840s. Here were fresh, fiery ideas about collectivism and class conflict; Wagner was intoxicated. In 1849, in the aftershocks of continent-wide revolutionary outbreaks, there was a brief uprising in Dresden that saw young people manning barricades in the streets. Wagner was swept up in the action and was then banished from the city.[21] Just over fifty years after that, the juvenile Adolf Hitler was attending a performance of *Lohengrin* in a hall in the Austrian city of Linz. By his own admission, the music overwhelmed him.[22] Wagner had entered his soul.

By the 1930s Hitler was also enraptured by the work of a living composer who had moved to Dresden: Richard Strauss. Hitler had been a particular enthusiast for Strauss's turn-of-the-century opera *Salome*; though he also fervently admired the later works *Elektra* and

Der Rosenkavalier. Most particularly the Nazis adored Strauss's lieder; these songs were, in contrast to the scale and scope of opera, intimate, composed for one instrument and one voice and often touching on elements of folk song, invoking maidens at spinning wheels or warriors returning to their farms after war.[23] Hitler played them extensively at Berchtesgaden.

But the elderly Strauss, despite the rich tonality of his music, was a modernist, and he was emphatically anti-nationalist. He had worked extensively with the Jewish poet Hugo von Hofmannsthal, and in the 1930s he set out upon a new collaboration with an Austrian writer, also Jewish, who had been charming readers across the continent. In 1934 Stefan Zweig and Strauss worked together on a new opera entitled *The Silent Woman.*[24] It was to receive its premiere at the Dresden Semper Opera House.

Both Strauss and Zweig knew that such a partnership was, even in the earliest days of the Hitler regime, forbidden. They also both knew that the names of Jews were no longer allowed on theatrical billboards. And yet Richard Strauss persisted in defiance. One reason – his strong loyalty to Zweig aside – was that he was to an extent already compromised and wished to establish some distance between himself and the Nazi hierarchy.

In 1933 Strauss had been appointed president of the Reich Chamber of Music – the department that would ensure that all music throughout the country would reflect the new regime and its ideals. He stated in letters to friends that this was not of his choosing; the position had been conferred upon him by Joseph Goebbels and there was the silent understanding that refusing it was out of the question. Here for the Nazis was a huge prize: a composer of worldwide fame and a vast following who, simply by being seen with Hitler, would help to confer both cultural respectability and indeed legitimacy upon the Nazis.

Strauss had private reasons for making such a terrible pact: his daughter-in-law was Jewish. He had to do everything that he could to protect her, and her extended family. This would become a constant struggle throughout the 1930s and 1940s, and any who were repelled by Strauss's apparent cordial cooperation with the Nazis were perhaps unaware of the razor-edged nature of his life, his loved ones under the nominal protection of a Gauleiter but subject to the constant menacing attentions of the Gestapo.

His artistic collaborator Zweig understood though; even as the consequences of Strauss's Dresden defiance were made clear. *The Silent Woman*'s run was ended by the Nazis after its second performance. Strauss was then removed as president of the Reich Chamber of Music after some letters he had written to Zweig about the stupidity and squalor of the Nazi regime had been intercepted by the Gestapo.

And though this did not mean that Strauss was completely excommunicated from Hitler's regime – they still employed the respectable weight of his name on the musical score for the 1936 Berlin Olympics – the composer had lost his freedom to be so outspoken ever again. Zweig, meanwhile, saw how this darkness was going to spread across the continent. He and his wife emigrated to England not long after, and made a home in the city of Bath. They subsequently sailed for Brazil.[25] The high culture of Europe had meant everything to Zweig; it had been his life. To see it so violated by the Nazis may have persuaded him that such a world could never be restored. He and his wife succumbed to despair: in 1942 they were both found dead from overdoses of barbiturates.

The Dresden opera house had seen other cruelties inflicted by the Nazis, including the swift dismissal of its chief conductor Fritz Busch. He himself was not Jewish but the reason for his sacking was his support for Jewish musicians and his refusal to pay any kind of respect to the Nazi regime. At the premiere of his production of *Rigoletto*, sponsored thugs in the audience started screaming a repeated slogan: 'Out with Busch!'[26] The performance was halted, and Busch understood that it would be impossible to remain in the land of his birth. He moved to England and took over as musical director of the Glyndebourne Festival Opera.

One popular mass art form that endured in Dresden despite constant hostile attention from the regime was the Sarrasani circus. This was a rather grander and more elegant affair than simply a large tent and attendant caravans; instead it was sited in a purpose-built circular

4,000-seat auditorium, designed by prominent architect Max Littmann, in a style not dissimilar to the opera house, in the Neustadt just north of the river. This had been its home since 1912; at around that time, the circus's original impresario Hans Stosch – who had renamed himself Sarrasani – had started dressing in the style of a Maharajah to project the global spirit of his circus.[27] His Italianate pseudonym had been inspired by a Balzac character, Sarrasine, who defied the wishes of his father, as Stosch had defied his.

There was a time when Stosch's circus featured not merely spectacular animal acts and energetic clowns, but also incredibly skilled acrobats and jugglers drawn from China and Japan who made their homes in Dresden. But, like all other fields of art and entertainment, it had in the 1930s been bent to the will of the Nazis. First they had accused it of being a 'Judenzirkus' and its roster of international acts was hugely diminished.[28] The intimidation continued, and seeking favour from the authorities, the circus had in the late 1930s staged special shows based on the Spanish Civil War and on uprisings in India against the English; in other words, it was forced into ideological conformity. By February 1945 the circus was being run by the late Stosch's daughter-in-law Trude. Unlike the cinemas, it was allowed to stay open; Sarrasani – with its horses, elephants, dancing girls and now strictly Aryan acrobats – was popular with the soldiers moving through the city.

In England, meanwhile, the winter winds that scoured from the east sliced across the North Sea and through the small towns of Lincolnshire, where local cinema-goers escaped the chill in plush theatres and immersed themselves in other worlds. In the early weeks of 1945, British audiences were thrilling to the Hollywood noir intensity of *Double Indemnity*. Entertainment of this sort was beyond value to twenty-eight-year-old Flight Lieutenant Leslie Hay.[29] His nickname 'Will', after the popular film comedian, was testament to this love. Unlike many of his RAF colleagues he was not a drinker, and so instead sought the silvery darkness to shut out all thoughts of his bombing missions. Hay had himself experienced the horror of being bombed; he was in London during the German Blitz of 1940 and on a few nights had been caught outside in the wet streets, forced to flatten himself against the cold pavement, keeping as low as possible as glass and brick exploded around him. Hay signed up for the RAF not out of any desire for revenge, as he was later at pains to point out, but simply because he understood how powerful a means of warfare this could be. He was married, and had been for several years; his young wife lived and worked in London while her husband's squadron was based in Fulbeck, a tiny village amid the fecund farmland on the black Lincolnshire fens. At the end of each leave, when she kissed him goodbye at King's Cross station, they gave each other meaningful looks; the constant, inescapable possibility of death was always there. Yet it was not so simple as that. As a pilot, Hay had a sensual love of flying; even as lightning-bright lines of flak were streaking past, he was intoxicated with the feel of his Avro Lancaster aeroplane, the sensation of swooping through the night.

There were some curious consolations on otherwise terrifying long-distance bombing raids. On one night, Hay's route towards the German target took him and his crew over the vast moonlit glittering spectacle of Mont Blanc. On another occasion, quite apart from all the other dangers of enemy fire, he was mesmerized by the materialization of ghostly yellow halo-like rings around the plane's propellers: this was St Elmo's Fire, an electrical phenomenon.

He was not impervious to the effect that his dropped bombs were having upon target cities like Dusseldorf and Munich, nor to the unfathomable strain that it put upon him and his fellow airmen, even as they flew through defensive fire that seemed to him like a vast infernal firework display. But like so many of his generation who knew in later years how extraordinary their own survival had been, Hay sought to frame his memories with human optimism.

In January 1945, after a hazardously long mission into Czechoslovakia to bomb a synthetic-oil factory, both Hay and his wife had every expectation that he had almost reached the end of his tour of duty. He learned upon his return that his tour had been extended from thirty operations to thirty-six. Hay's wife was horrified; he was merely stricken. Hay at that point was implacable about his duty; the cities that the Allies were targeting had no doubt been chosen with good reason and even the prettiest towns must surely have harboured wide ranges of clandestine munitions factories and laboratories for the development of secret weapons. Such raids were, to him, bleakly necessary. In a matter of days, Hay – among thousands of other airmen – was to be briefed about a mission to Dresden. It was a beautiful city, he knew, but had those famous decorative porcelain factories been turned to the development of terrible new missiles and rockets? In reality, the city's war work was more to do with precision instrumentation; but Hay's association of Dresden with intense scientific innovation was entirely correct.

5. The Glass Man and the Physicists

There was another sort of music in Dresden: the low hum of electrical generators and scientific equipment. Just half a mile south of the central railway station there were laboratories where men were conducting a wide variety of experiments with cathode rays and thermionic valves. Some had been there for decades, working towards creating extraordinary advances in everything from communications to electric transmission. They might have thought that they stood outside the bloody revolution, yet they too were forced to participate. The strain of staying focused on pure ideas and research while knowing that there were innovations to be made that would contribute towards the terrible ongoing conflict must have been great.

The ugly central buildings of the university with their red roofs and bulbous towers might have lacked the aesthetic appeal of Oxford or Heidelberg, but there was a pragmatism and adventurousness here which had made the institution an attractive prospect for engineers, mathematicians and physicists alike. It had certainly drawn the handsome young Heinrich Barkhausen, a prodigy in the field of electric technology in the earlier years of the century. Born in Bremen in 1881 (at around the time when his countryman Friedrich Siemens was travelling Europe giving lectures about the forthcoming wonders of mass electric lighting), Barkhausen showed an immense interest in all branches of the natural sciences.[1] He studied at institutions around the country, but at the startlingly young age of twenty-nine he was offered a professorship at Dresden's Technical University.

Barkhausen's continuing work, both before and after the Great War, led to some very significant breakthroughs that would later prove to have tremendous military application. Among these was a way of boosting higher frequency signals, which changed UHF radio use, but his was also an esoteric field of magnetism and resonance; the complex relationship between different natural force fields and sound, and the ways that both might be manipulated. Professor Barkhausen commanded the realm of *Schwachstromtechnik*: electrical communication engineering.[2] He had given his name to a discovery involving electromagnetics and acoustics: the Barkhausen Effect.

Such a man, it must be assumed, would have had little room spare in his mental landscape for any form of political ideology; his life was filled with dials, diodes, tuners, vacuum tubes, glass cylinders containing delicate instrumentation. But Professor Barkhausen and his colleagues were none the less drawn deeper into the maelstrom as soon as the Nazis came to power. As with all academics, they were forced to swear the oath of allegiance to Hitler, and when greeting superiors and colleagues or starting lectures they were required to give the Nazi salute. It was from this very same institute that Victor Klemperer had been dismissed, along with all his Jewish colleagues. Professor Barkhausen and all those who worked with him could see all too well what was happening on their campus.

By the 1930s, the technical electronic advances that Barkhausen had made were attracting intense interest from the military. He was working not just with UHF signals but also with microwaves, and these had the potential to unlock new possibilities for instantaneous communications across vast distances from theatres of war everywhere. In such an atmosphere, and at such a time, how could even the most abstracted of academics resist the pressure of totalitarianism? In 1938 Professor Barkhausen was sent to Japan for a period of joint research; with war just a year away, it is reasonable to presume that he and his counterparts in Japan would be engaged in technological work that would be harnessed militarily by their respective states.

Barkhausen watched from the Far East as the Axis powers challenged the world. The war progressed, and the professor found himself transferred once more, this time to work in Romania. But by 1944 Professor Barkhausen was back in his old Dresden home, and back in his familiar laboratory. He had walked the tightrope with success; the Nazis had not turned against him. And even in a near-empty university there were ever-more pressing lines of electronic research to pursue, including the quest to perfect voice synthesis (enabling a form of electrical encryption and interception proofing when messages were transmitted). Barkhausen had also found an extremely promising young protégé for his physics department, an insouciant youth from the Latvian capital Riga called Mischka Danos.[3]

Twenty-one-year-old Danos had seen in German-controlled Latvia the true depths of Nazi depravity. One winter's day he had taken himself off into the hills near Riga for some skiing. Some impulse made him avoid the more commonly used trails, and he moved through an empty landscape of snow and trees. But as he came to a hill, he was startled by a long procession of people, men, women and children, in dark clothing, climbing the incline. There was some form of spectacle unfolding at the top. Rapt with curiosity, the young man quietly ascended the hill. A silent line of people was standing around an enormous crater dug out of the earth. The crater was filled with corpses, freshly murdered. The people of Riga and the suburbs around had come to see the mass graves of the local Jews. Danos turned and left quickly. According to his widow Sheila Fitzpatrick, something within him was shut very tight that day. A keen piano player, he was never able to feel the emotional depths in Beethoven again, or at least could not allow that firmly closed door to be re-opened.[4] So how then had Danos come to the decision to leave Latvia and instead go to study in the very heart of Germany in 1944?

One very good reason was to avoid conscription into the German military on the eastern front, for young Latvians were being drawn into the Wehrmacht in increasing numbers. But even in 1944 there was also a student-exchange programme between Latvia and Germany, part of an effort by the Nazi authorities to spread German intellectual influence throughout the Baltic states. Danos and his family were of Hungarian descent, and perhaps the young man would have had second thoughts if he had been fully aware of his background, for, although unaware of it at the time and raised as a German-speaking Catholic, the Danoses were Jewish. When he had stood looking down into that mass grave he had had no inkling that he shared the heritage of those within, but even without this event, the irony of a brilliant young Jewish intellectual clamouring to travel so far into the heart of the Reich having borne witness to mass slaughter seems almost too extraordinary to contemplate.

The young man's reasoning was sharp. Danos, as Fitzpatrick explained, had always regarded the Nazi cult as a temporary aberration; by 1944, he and his mother were certain that it would be defeated, and soon.[5] Moreover, it could not be allowed to occlude his love and respect for the deeper wellsprings of German culture. In another ironic twist, Dresden, offering relative anonymity, would have been very much safer for Danos than Riga; other families of Jewish heritage in Riga had been denounced to the authorities. There was every possibility of that happening to Mischka Danos; but not if he was far away, living in east Germany.

Danos and Barkhausen found an immediate rapport, and the student was quickly promoted to be the professor's assistant. When the desperate searchlight of call-up caught the young man in its beam, Professor Barkhausen wrote to the authorities explaining that his assistant was engaged in vital war work at the university. And so it was that Danos – with his precocious expertise in electronics, radio technology and mathematical theory – became a fixture in those laboratories.

The university was surrounded by a number of grand houses, and some of these offered rooms for students; Danos lived in one that was both large and draughty. He soon made friends, but by February 1945 he was contemplating another move. His mother, a fashion designer, had left Riga for Prague, and Danos made frequent use of the Dresden-to-Prague express train to see her. But both could see how unstoppable the Soviet approach from the east was, and the prospect of life under Stalin seemed even grimmer than under the Nazis. Prospects in Dresden were little better. They foresaw Dresden being hit by artillery and soldiers wreaking bloody havoc in the streets. Their quiet plan was to pack up and travel far north, to Flensburg, on the border with Denmark. In those early days of February, Danos had secretly made up his mind to leave sometime closer to the end of the month and he was planning a discreet party for a few university friends which would be held in his room on the night of the 13th.

Professor Barkhausen well knew that he formed part of a grand Dresden tradition: the city's spirit of inquiry and lively – and profitable – invention. Men of science across the years have not always been noted for sharp commercial acumen, and many inventors failed to collect the ease-giving riches that might have been theirs, but the inventors of Dresden had always been different: they understood market forces, as well as more natural phenomena, very well indeed. It is an irony of Nazi rule in the city that this gleeful talent for profit-spotting from the most ingenious inventions was temporarily squashed. Historically, the city's lightning flashes of invention had always been closely allied with political power and influence. This history was also, of course, known to the Western powers, and was a factor when their strategists were selecting their bombing targets; Dresden had long been a byword for technical innovation as well as art.

This wild inventiveness, often the result of serendipity, had started in the early eighteenth century, with the scramble to reproduce the Chinese wonder of porcelain. For centuries, exquisite pieces from the Far East had been transported along the Silk Road and lusted after in the courts of European aristocrats, but no one in seventeenth-century Europe could either fathom or replicate a product that dated back hundreds of years, nor recreate the extraordinary translucency of the material or the delicacy of its decor. Porcelain was hugely valuable, hence its nickname 'white gold'.[6]

In the early 1700s Augustus II, Elector of Saxony, was set upon acquisition of gold; his appetite for luxury and for what might be termed status objects was insatiable. This in turn led to an accidental chain of events that brought him a means of creating porcelain. Augustus had secured the services of – or, to put it another way, kidnapped and held under house arrest – a young man who had built a rackety career around the courts of Germany by claiming to be an alchemist. Even in a new age of Newtonian mathematical revelation, powerful men persisted in their belief that gold could be conjured from base matter.

The young man was Johann Friedrich Böttger.[7] Augustus furnished him with a Dresden laboratory that also served as a prison, but Böttger persisted in escaping. Each time he was caught, the security was tightened. The patience of Augustus wore thin, and Böttger knew he would have to produce some kind of alchemical miracle. As he experimented with different soils, clays and minerals, he was obliged to create crucibles that were hard enough to resist the searing temperatures of molten gold; and ironically, in creating these red stoneware containers, he took a step to producing a much more tangible form of wealth.

Augustus had enlisted a local man of science, Ehrenfried Walther von Tschirnhaus, to help Böttger, and it was the older man who understood what might be achieved; far from the fantasy of conjured gold. Using local kaolin hewn from the hills, the men found that they could produce authentic white porcelain.

And swiftly thereafter followed the techniques of glazing, of painting, of the application of gold. The forms these new creations took established a fresh aesthetic while paying tribute to the Chinese source: tea and coffee sets decorated with Oriental scenes. There were also the leitmotifs that were to remain central for over 200 years: depictions of animals, flowers, pastoral vignettes. Figurines were crafted alongside the dinner services, vases and bowls.

The secret could not remain in one laboratory for long: soon porcelain was being produced across Europe. But the Dresden industry, moved a little downriver to Meissen, laid claim to particular quality. Each of its pieces carried the image of two crossed swords as a form of hallmark.[8] And what was once exclusive to the aristocrats and the rich across the years became attainable for the middle classes. The Meissen aesthetic was instantly identifiable; the pure pale blues, sober dark reds, the pinks and the greens gleaming on tiny cups; boisterous figurines of elaborately dressed courting couples; harlequins pulling faces; noblemen on fine steeds. Here were watchcases with floral motifs, bright yellow flowers flashing against the light.

In those early days, Augustus (still waiting for supplies of magically manufactured gold) took to the new art with enthusiasm, and those who succeeded him commissioned extraordinarily delicate and detailed tea sets, the tiny cups and pots swirling with colour and mazy patterns. A certain element of coy sentimentality lay at the heart of Meissen's rococo figurines: here were shepherds and shepherdesses and tiny white lambs, beautifully sculpted, evoking a pastoral innocence. This was why the Nazis were open about their love for porcelain: amid all their looting of art, the pieces senior party officials most coveted were antique Meissen.[9] In Dresden, the von Klemperer family (not immediately related to Victor Klemperer) had a collection of some 800 pieces. In the earliest days of the Nazi regime, before the systematic thefts, senior party leaders had even offered to buy them.

The pastoral leitmotifs mesmerized Hitler; Meissen spoke to his adoration of rustic idylls. And as it was, the Nazi Party inspired a vast boost in production of all forms of porcelain. Figurines became the most popular Christmas presents; this was partly because Hitler and his deputies so frequently gave porcelain as a gift. Himmler was heard to murmur that finely decorated china was 'one of the few things' that gave him any real pleasure.[10]

In all of its florid decoration and candy colourings, Meissen might to some eyes have seemed kitsch. Broadly, though, these were objects of desire in homes far beyond the German borders. By the 1930s huge numbers of British households owned Dresden porcelain. Their collections were of course highly unlikely to include any of the specially commissioned Nazi figurines made not at Meissen but by the Munich-Allach porcelain company. There was one depicting a boy in Hitler Youth uniform, banging a drum, and staring up at the sky as though entranced by a vision: this item was mass produced, selling thousands upon thousands. Another hugely popular figurine, often handed out by Nazi Party officials, was of an SS storm trooper.

Hitler's yearning for porcelain did not abate in the war years; even as late as 1944, pieces were being made specially for him. The Meissen manufacturing works had long been turned over to the production of teleprinters for the military, so a porcelain workshop was set up within Dachau concentration camp, further south.[11] Prisoners with appropriate skills, living with the daily possibility of imminent death, were marshalled into the most bitter slave work: producing intricate works of beauty and life within the razor-wire fenced compound of grotesque slaughter.

By February 1945 the Nazis had removed much of the most valuable antique Meissen porcelain from Dresden. Packed carefully into padded boxes, these sumptuous dinner services, and lifelike figurines with coats of plum red and flesh of pale peach, were hidden in nearby mountain caves. (After the war, the Soviets would show an equally passionate if not furiously greedy desire for not only the finished porcelain but also the means of its production. Art intertwined with international exports, even for the communists.)

Dresden inventors through the centuries were canny about keeping a firm hold of the patent rights to their inspirations, divine or otherwise, and the period from the late nineteenth century to the inception of the Nazi Party saw a quite startling outbreak of innovation of all varieties.

This was the city that produced the first mouthwash, in 1895; the result of a heretofore unsuccessful former department store assistant called Karl August Lingner going into partnership with his old friend Richard Seifert, a chemist.[12] Lingner had a fixation with health; and the idea for the mouthwash was not simply as a cure for dreadful-smelling breath. People at that time were swilling their mouths with anything from vinegar to brandy, but scientists had been examining the processes of tooth decay and Lingner and Seifert's new idea of making the liquid antiseptic, destroying lurking germs, was sensational. The product was called Odol; it became a household item not only in Germany but across the continent and in Britain too. It very swiftly made Lingner very rich. He was soon able to purchase a preposterously grand Dresden property, the Villa Stockhausen, a nineteenth-century chateau, complete with terrace, colonnades, two towers and vineyards on the slopes rushing down to the Elbe. It still stands in the east of the city, on a hill that overlooks the Altstadt.

Lingner had obsessions that went beyond money. He was a public hygiene reformist; indeed the promotion of healthy living came to subsume his working life.[13] Lingner applied such principles at his four-storey Dresden factory, where the working-class employees had access to showers and baths, their own modest homes lacking such facilities. They were also supplied with free milky coffee in their break periods, this to discourage the regrettable working-class enthusiasm for consuming alcohol while on duty. As with other Dresden employers, Lingner offered Christmas bonuses and the use of a company savings bank. Unlike them, he also encouraged workers to use a gymnasium in their lunch hours and after work.

The factory began making new lines and ranges: Pixavon shampoo, Kavon soap, Irex tooth powder. But Odol mouthwash became the essential bathroom item for Germany's middle classes: the liquid, flavoured with peppermint and oils, became the nation's most familiar taste and smell. The accumulating fortune from it enabled Lingner to look at the city of Dresden and turn its population into subjects for his hygiene anxieties. He proposed a disinfection facility clinic; those deemed to be carrying germs would be transported there in trucks while their belongings would be fumigated in a separate vehicle. Although this idea did not find general favour, Lingner did manage to institute a Centre for Dental Hygiene and also oversaw the opening of a children's clinic in the poorer streets of Johannstadt.

Like so many at the time, in various European countries, Lingner's notions of social hygiene slotted into broader ideas adjacent to eugenics and social Darwinism. He believed that races that did not seek to dominate would instead be doomed to submission.[14] There was a concomitant anxiety that urban life could cause degeneration: physical and spiritual.

Lingner became one of Dresden's most prominent grandees: his philanthropy ranged to staging spectacular night-time parades for King Friedrich August III, using hundreds of electric lights and teams of technicians. He also put together the Hygiene Exhibition of 1911, the city's very first international exhibition and one that naturally echoed his chief obsession. It was extremely popular: about five and a half million people bought tickets in order to listen to lectures on the merits of different meats and vegetables, the horrors of alcohol abuse and the pernicious harms of tobacco. The exhibition was promoted with posters featuring a staring, stylized eye – the Hygiene Eye.[15] The idea behind the image was that of a public watchfulness; the city's all-seeing eye staring hard at dirt of all varieties. Among the attractions were microscopes set up with slides of bacteria – for many visitors, the first glimpse of microbial life. There was glassware and mazes of tubes filled with ruby-red liquid intended to demonstrate how blood circulated around the body.

And then there was The Glass Man. He became an aesthetic as well as educational sensation. Here was a male figure, his skin fashioned from glass, and visible beneath it a pale skull, blue veins, ribs and all of his internal organs. The Glass Man stood with his arms stretched high, as though in supplication or worship. The vivid colours of his viscera mesmerized the crowds. His purpose was to illustrate the mechanics of the digestive tract, and the ways different foods were absorbed. He stood above the audience on a podium, somewhere between a cadaver and a robot. The Glass Man was also a vision of a future in which men and women would themselves be transparent to medical science: pulsing hearts, coursing blood, the rhythms of peristalsis, and all with the aim of creating new, healthier generations of Germans.

Lingner's views and concerns, shared by so many millions, were in part a reaction to the squalor that city life elsewhere had brought to the poor: not just the rackety sanitation, but also fears about promiscuity and sexual disease. Grimly, it was not coincidental that the clinical atmosphere of the time lent respectability to eugenics: just as scientists had begun to grasp inheritability, so too were conjured the dreams of engineering stronger children. Lingner did not inspire the Nazis, but his exhibition, later turned into a permanent Dresden Hygiene Museum, none the less was irresistibly attractive to them. He himself died in 1916; by the mid 1930s his legacy had been thoroughly appropriated.

The Hygiene Museum, attracting tens of thousands of visitors each year by the 1930s, was taken over by Dresden's Nazi authorities, who gave it an emphatic new slant: racial hygiene. The public were to be educated about the importance of keeping bloodlines pure; and about the races that posed the greatest danger of infection. Hitler had been hypnotized from the early 1920s by the scientific possibilities of eugenics: sterilization became a Nazi keyword.

Another branch of scientific ingenuity, though, had made the city a more attractive bombing target. From the earliest years of the century, Dresden had established itself as a thriving centre for optical technology: everything from telescopes and microscopes to the smartest cameras. Here was an industry relying on skill and precision but also a certain aesthetic flair. The cameras that were produced here had sleek designs that made them ardently sought after all over Europe.

But there was also a certain beauty to the industrial-scale optical instruments too. In 1926, still struggling in the economic aftershocks created by the hyperinflation of previous years, four large camera and optical firms decided, in desperation, on a merger: and that merger was to be world-beatingly successful. Zeiss Ikon was the company that rose out of those inflationary ashes. The cameras, with a smart logo, were for the time very innovative: the Ikoflex twin lens model, Contax rangefinders and the Ikonta folding cameras.[16]

The presiding genius of the company through the 1920s, until the advent of the Nazis, was Professor Emanuel Goldberg. Born in Moscow in 1881, and barred from various Russian academic institutions because of his faith – this was a fear-filled time of pogroms – Goldberg eventually emigrated to Germany confident that his intellectual appetite for the new science of photography and cinematography would be able to flourish. After huge academic success in Leipzig, Professor Goldberg came to Dresden in 1926 and was appointed the first managing director of Zeiss Ikon.[17] By this stage, he had already developed what was in essence the first home-movie camera – the Kinamo, which for its time was a miracle of compactness. It was also a shrewd device in marketing terms: a middle-class must-have that German skiing and mountain-climbing enthusiasts took on their holidays. Here in some ways was an industry that, in its delicacy and precision, was a harmonious counterpoint to the painstaking exactitude of the city's architecture, art and music.

Professor Goldberg also had an enthusiasm for micro-photography – the genesis of the microdot. He also postulated an early data-retrieval system, using photoelectrics. By 1931, such was his reputation that the International Congress of Photography was held in the city; he was awarded the Peligot Medal of the French Society for Photography and Cinematography.

When, in 1933, the Enabling Act brought the end of democracy, and when Dresden was very suddenly caught in the Nazi vice, Professor Goldberg might reasonably have imagined that his creative expertise would lift him above the malice of Gauleiter Martin Mutschmann. It did not. According to one account, the tactics the Nazis used to get rid of him were terribly simple: one day, they marched Professor Goldberg out of the Zeiss Ikon works, put him in a car and drove out of the city into the forest, where he was tied to a tree. After threatening him and his family, they freed one of his hands and made him sign a letter of resignation. Almost immediately, Professor Goldberg relocated his whole family to Paris.

Subsequently, Zeiss Ikon answered the urgent needs of a vastly expanding German military, not just the air force but precision optical engineering for the navy and for the army too. The factories were gradually cloaked with ever increasing secrecy, their optical products now clandestine means of aiding swift and brutal conquest. It says something for the suffocating darkness of the times that when, at the start of 1942, the city authorities announced there were to be further Jewish deportations (straight to the death camps in the east), the wartime management of Zeiss Ikon protested and asked that their Jewish slave workers be spared. This was hardly an act of mercy, more a cold-eyed calculation of the loss of skilled hands.[18] The next day the Gestapo, determined not to be cheated of their prey, insisted that, none the less, 250 Jews would be deported at once.

Yet by the beginning of 1945 there were Jewish women working at Zeiss Ikon who had been co-opted from concentration camps: 700 of them from Flossenbürg, another 300 from Auschwitz and Ravensbrück. They were treated with the same icy cruelty as their predecessors had been, and their co-workers would have seen very clearly exactly how hungry they were, and how miserable their rations. A number of prisoners lived on site in dormitories on the top floor of the factory, and aside from all the general discomforts of wooden bunks, reeking, scratching blankets and freezing air, there were those who considered this a stroke of real luck compared to the other possibilities. How had this darkness become so normalized in a city once famed as the most civilized place in Germany?

6. 'A Sort of Little London'

The small children of Dresden in 1945 had never heard an English or American voice; if they had, their parents would have been committing a clandestine criminal act. There were radio broadcasts – jaunty, friendly propaganda from the Allies – that were wholly forbidden. The Americans never seemed a heavy threat in the sense that the Soviets did: they appeared coercive rather than menacing. The pervasive popular culture of golden-hearted cinema cowboys had reached deep into Germany before the Nazis could wholly extinguish it.

But many of those Dresden children were also perfectly aware that the first serious bombing attacks upon the city, in the autumn of 1944 and at the very start of 1945, had been carried out by the Americans. This they gleaned from their parents. And these raids had been during the hours of daylight. The curious thing was that even after this strong foretaste of the hideous damage that could be wrought by the bombers, Dresdeners had remained complacent to the point of blitheness. The first American attack – carried out by thirty B-24 bombers aiming some seventy tons of explosive at the railway marshalling yards to the west of the Altstadt – was remembered with some clarity by Dieter Haufe, who had just recently turned eleven in October 1944. Because, inevitably, there were many bombs that did not hit their targets.

That 7 October, a Saturday, was 'a gorgeous warm Indian-summer day',[1] recalled Haufe. 'My mother and I were tending our recently planted peach tree' in the communal garden of their apartment block. Suddenly, to their shock, the city's air-raid sirens started wailing: a 'pre-alarm' signal. Throughout the war, Dresdeners had become quite accustomed to very frequent – and almost always false – alarms. Generally, though, these had come after dark. There was something unexpected about that unearthly low moan on such a rich autumnal afternoon. Mother and son first had to sprint up to their

1. 'Dresden from the Right Bank of the Elbe Below the Augustus Bridge', painted by Bernardo Bellotto c.1750. This prospect drew artists and musicians as well as sophisticated European and American travellers.

2. The stable courtyard of Dresden's castle in the heart of the Altstadt, c.1930s. This part of the castle, built in the sixteenth century and with space for jousting, was restored after the destruction of the war.

3. The Semper Opera House, one of Dresden's cultural glories, remained open until January 1945. Its productions were internationally renowned, although at the start of the Nazi era its support for Jewish artists brought violent repercussions.

4. A rich panorama overlooking the Altstadt in the 1930s. With the baroque geometry of the Zwingergarten in the foreground, the steeple of the Catholic cathedral close by, the treasures of Dresden's castle to the right and the dome of the Frauenkirche a few streets away, here was a landscape of architectural heritage.

5. The Altmarkt was the centre of the city's commerce, filled with sophisticated shops and restaurants. Author Erich Kästner recalled how, at the turn of the century, the square glowed with the colour of flower stalls.

6. Designed by Ernst Giese and Paul Weidner in 1892, Dresden's central railway station was a key link to the rest of Europe, lying on the main line from Berlin to Prague. Its elegant architecture was the first sight of the city for thousands of rural refugees from Silesia and Pomerania.

7. The Lutheran Church of Our Lady – the Frauenkirche – was a baroque masterpiece built in the eighteenth century by George Bähr; it had exquisite acoustics and was an aesthetic as well as religious draw for Dresdeners.

DRESDEN VIA HARWICH

INFORMATION FROM CONTINENTAL TRAFFIC MANAGER, L·N·E·R LIVERPOOL STREET STATION, LONDON, E.C.2, OR HULL: 71 REGENT STREET, W.I. Wm MÜLLER & Co (London) Ltd. 66 HAYMARKET, S.W.I. PRINCIPAL LNER STATIONS, OFFICES & TOURIST AGENCIES

8. As overseas travel became available to more and more people in the early 1930s, Dresden was advertised in British newspapers as a tourist destination. Under the Nazi regime, visitors were escorted by Party officials.

9. In early eighteenth-century Dresden, a young alchemist stumbled upon a secret that hitherto had been the preserve of the Chinese: porcelain. Dresden (and nearby Meissen) became synonymous with a sentimental style.

10. Dresden's Hygiene Exhibition in 1911 proved so popular that a Hygiene Museum remains in the city today. The poster was not intended to imply totalitarian surveillance, but the developing scientific wonders of the time.

11. Hitler in front of the Zwinger Palace, 1934. The purpose of the Führer's visit was to inaugurate German Theatre Week. When he attended a performance of Wagner's opera *Tristan und Isolde*, eager crowds lined the streets to welcome him.

12. Richard Strauss, pictured in the 1930s with a member of the Dresden Opera Company. The composer adored Dresden and many of his operas received their premieres there, although his relationship with the Nazis was razor-edged.

13. Hitler had a pathological loathing of modernist art, which he termed the product of 'sick brains'. In 1933 Dresden became the first German city to stage exhibitions designed to shame the artists whose work was on display.

14. Having recently abdicated the British Crown, the Duke of Windsor visited Dresden in 1937, where he gave a speech praising the regime's ideas for the working class before meeting Hitler. He is pictured with a scale model of the Zwinger Palace.

15. As with the Hitler Youth for German boys, membership of the League of German Girls was mandatory. In spite of the poisonous ideology, Dresden girls had a powerful sense of civic responsibility.

16. Dresden's most powerful politician, Martin Mutschmann, was close to Hitler. A former lace-maker, the Gauleiter was mesmerized by tales of the dark forests and with folk art, an exhibition of which he is seen attending.

17. Dr Albert Fromme was Dresden's most senior medical practitioner. He and his hospital colleagues kept working even in the midst of the inferno.

18. The acclaimed artist Otto Dix was one of Dresden's most influential figures; after the First World War, he was haunted by recurring nightmares of being trapped in burning ruins.

19. Professor Victor Klemperer, one of the very few Jews in Dresden to have survived the Nazi period. His diaries – which Jews were forbidden to keep – are an extraordinary record.

20. Otto Griebel's Dresden art and his marionettes both had an anarchic undertone hated by the Nazis.

fourth-floor apartment to grab their 'alarm packs – blankets, pillows, gas masks'. Dieter was also anxious to get 'my faithful companion Waldi' – the family's dachshund.

They ran down the stairs and into the cellar of the apartment block, which, like similar residential buildings across the city, had been prepared as a shelter. And there mother, son and dog sat with several of their neighbours under a bare lightbulb. Minutes later, the attack began. 'The noise grew stronger, rose into swelling drones,' remembered Haufe. 'There were several detonations. And then the electric light flickered.'

The prospect of being cast into complete darkness, with the seismic roars from above, was terrifying. 'Then, very close: a deafening bang – an insanely strong rush of air.' The boy remembered the procedure as 'automatic': speedily donning his child's gas mask, 'strapping it tight'. The light went out and there was nothing but blackness. In this murk and panic, there was now only one thought in the boy's mind: 'I will never see my mother again.' And under the onslaught, 'my body vibrated' and even 'my fingers tingled'. Then, silence. 'I pressed Waldi close to me.' Some moments later, 'A flaming candle appeared in front of my face.' It was held by a neighbour, 'Frau Schmidt from the second floor.'

The bombers seemed to have gone. But in the confusion, time took great gulping jumps. The boy found himself outside, with his dog but not his mother. The pavement, oddly, 'felt like cotton', a result of the thick layer of dust that now covered it. The apartment block opposite looked as though it had been demolished. The air was dense and throat-catching. But it was at that point that the boy heard his name being called; his mother was there, quite safe, just a few steps away.

Even a target as large as a railway marshalling yard was impossible to hit with complete certainty from a height of tens of thousands of feet, though the daylight made the American bombers more precise than they would otherwise have been. Some explosives either missed or deviated from their intended target. How could it be otherwise? As well as apartment blocks, and a chunk of the Seidel und Naumann factory, a large school was hit; if this attack had not come at the weekend, hundreds of children would have been killed. As it was, the city's death toll on that day was about 270. According to Haufe, Gauleiter Mutschmann ordered that news of mass fatalities be suppressed; bodies were buried not all at once, but at intervals, and mourning families were told that they would simply have to wait. Mutschmann might have been seeking to avoid any possible damage to morale. Yet as it was, the citizens – who could see perfectly well the destruction for themselves – seemed close to dismissive about the attack.

Another American raid, this time with the aim of disrupting all connections with the eastern front, came on 16 January 1945. Again, the roaring damage – as well as the apparent impunity of bombers operating in bright daylight, evading the attentions of Luftwaffe fighters scrambled from the airfield north of the city – seemed not to create much of an impression upon the wider city, though by that stage, when every day was filled with fear, perhaps there was little left that could surprise or shock. Fifteen-year-old Winfried Bielss, whose fascination for trains and public transport equalled his love for stamps, noted the damage that was caused to the city's 'Tram Line 5, which ended at St Paul's Cemetery'. The line, Bielss noted, 'was interrupted for several days'.[2]

Neither he nor any adult Dresdener could have had any notion in February 1945 that it was the railway lines rather than the factories that were the primary preoccupation of the US Air Force's commander Carl Spaatz, or that, while the British were to continue area bombing, the future plans agreed for American bombers focused on the heavily used connections that ran from Berlin through to Dresden and onwards from that busy junction on lines pointing outwards via the valley of the Elbe and the central European uplands.[3] In addition, the US Assistant Secretary of State for Air, Robert Lovett, concerned at growing numbers of American war casualties and at German resistance, and also at the possibility that the Nazis were developing new secret weapons, had recommended that air attacks be spread wider across the country. In terms of lending support to the Red Army, the targeting of Dresden had for some time been seen as legitimate.

Yet there were elderly Dresden citizens who would have remembered a time not so long back – perhaps now with some bewilderment – when Americans were not the enemy but in fact an integral part of the fabric of Dresden life. The same was true of the English. And certainly, at the start of the twentieth century, the English language had been perfectly common, spoken by English and American expatriates in the streets of Dresden and displayed in the English-language newspapers they bought from its newsstands. Even into the 1930s the city had attracted a variety of international visitors, distinguished and otherwise, and there had been boarding schools where many of the girls were native English speakers.

It was for this reason, as noted by Victor Klemperer, that local gossip in the early days of 1945, even after the January bombing raid by the Allies, was filled with speculation that Dresden had never been targeted in earnest because there was still too much residual affection for the city among the English and Americans. Indeed, Dresden had its own specialized urban rumour: that Winston Churchill wanted the city spared because his American grandmother had loved it so (other variations made the relation his aunt). Curiously, even though no reliable records exist, it is eminently possible that both Churchill's grandmother and his mother had been swirled briefly into Dresden's social maelstrom.

The grandmother, Clara Jerome (née Clarissa Hall), was an American heiress who, midway through the nineteenth century, savoured her first taste of Europe when her diplomat husband was posted to Trieste, and found herself intoxicated with the possibilities. Paris seemed very much more alive to her than Manhattan. Certainly, this was a great deal to do with the grandeur of her new social connections, but here too was a world filled with art and conversation and ideas. So it is perfectly natural to imagine that, at some stage, this ardent Europhile paid a visit to Dresden, which was, after all, home to a very lively American community throughout the nineteenth century and where might be encountered writers and academics who had found the city irresistible, and extended brief stays into lengthy sojourns.

The anglophone taste for the city had begun earlier, in the mid eighteenth century, when the future British prime minister Lord North visited Dresden with his friend the Earl of Dartmouth, who wrote: 'We spent a fortnight in a sort of little London, in a continual

hurry of amusements . . . We have danced a great deal, and have been
at 3 balls a night. I did not expect to see English country dances so
well danced, out of England . . . We are extremely happy here in the
fine weather we have enjoyed.'[4]

It was not long before notable Americans were discovering this
continental ornament. One such was the short-story writer and essay-
ist Washington Irving, author of 'Rip Van Winkle' and 'The Legend
of Sleepy Hollow'. He had travelled extensively throughout Europe
but had never been able to find anywhere to settle. Leaving Vienna in
the early 1820s, he happened across Dresden and was immediately
delighted. Here, he declared, was 'a place of taste, intellect and literary feeling'.[5] Irving was hoping to gather material for fiction inspired
by deep-rooted German folk tales, but sophisticated Dresden society
kept him far from the villages and the forests. There was great demand
from all corners of society – from artistic to diplomatic – to have
Irving grace their evenings. The months that he lived in Dresden were
testament to the city's openness towards Americans and other English
speakers, and this was to remain the case throughout the nineteenth
and early twentieth centuries. There was an English church, American
restaurants, a local English newspaper; for a small city, Dresden was
very accommodating: it was estimated to receive over 100,000 visitors
a year; a large number to be found threading their way through the
streets near the Albertinum art museum and the Frauenkirche.

Kathleen (later Dame Kathleen) Courtney was sent to Dresden at
the turn of the century after she left her boarding school in England.
She was enrolled at a finishing school where she was to learn German.[6] The city charmed her immediately, and she described how one
morning, simply looking out of her window at the school, she witnessed a comical cultural battle on the square below, the notes of an
American organ coming from the American church being ruthlessly
drowned out by a local Dresden street band.

Those finishing schools sent young ladies out to the opera in the
evening, and it was noted that the foyer resounded with the noise of
the English tongue. By 1909, one American socialite eagerly told the
English-language *Daily Record* that 'Dresden had impressed her as
quite the finest city for foreign residents she knew in Europe, being

infinitely superior to Paris or Berlin as far as climate, pretty surroundings, opportunities for artistic and musical education, and homelike conditions were concerned.'[7]

Naturally, the First World War brought all of this to an end, but only temporarily. By the 1920s and 1930s there was once again a strong influx of English visitors; there was a suggestion, indeed, that certain strata of British society were more sympathetic to the Germans than to the French following the slaughter on the battlefields, for the French were behaving so mercilessly over the matter of reparations.

The craze, meanwhile, for young English ladies to come to Germany to hone both etiquette and cultural experience did not let up throughout the 1930s. The advent of the Nazis, for many of the upper-class families of these young women, represented simply a new kind of order, a bulwark against the threat of filthy Bolshevism. So for a while Dresden continued to host numbers of debutantes, who would be invited to dances with dashing young German military officers, losing themselves in the extraordinary formality of uniforms and deep bows.

Meanwhile, the Nazis had also been assiduous at marketing the country to less socially exalted visitors. With the steady growth of the white-collar middle and lower-middle classes in Britain in the 1930s came a greater appetite for foreign travel, and the Nazi Ministry of Propaganda was adept at drawing curious souls. Even as early in the regime's life as 1934, when the streets of the cities convulsed with shocking political violence, there were advertisements in British newspapers reading: 'Germany is News!', followed by the strapline 'See Germany for yourself as it is today'.[8] There were 'Cook's Tours', run by the travel firm Thomas Cook and advertised to readers in the *Daily Mail* and *Daily Telegraph*. 'English-speaking guides' were promised; they were Nazis. In Dresden, as elsewhere, they did not feel that they had anything to hide. They wanted British travellers to see the imposed order in the streets and squares and to undertake guided tours of a surrounding countryside that they themselves viewed as quasi-mystical. In addition to this, Dresden's musical and artistic life was familiar even to readers of the more popular newspapers: the Dresden Opera Company's 1936 visit to London suffused the gossip columns with admiring Mayfair titbits.

★

By February 1945, the only British and Americans to be found in Dresden were underfed prisoners of war. Among them was a young American, twenty-two years old, called Kurt Vonnegut. He had been in Dresden since 10 January 1945, having been taken prisoner a week before Christmas as the Wehrmacht startlingly struck back against the Allies on the borders of Luxembourg and Belgium.[9] In the intervening weeks he had been granted a view of the sort of hell that men can seemingly plunge into with ease: disintegration of human feeling and sympathy and imperviousness to squalid death. Yet his life beforehand had not been without trauma. While he was undergoing military training in the US, close to his hometown Indianapolis, he returned on leave to see his mother to find that she had committed suicide by taking a combination of sleeping pills and alcohol.

There had been financial problems too. Vonnegut's family, originally from Germany, had interests in brewing and architecture, and prospered in the early years of the twentieth century until Prohibition in the 1920s destroyed the beer business, and the crash that rippled out from Wall Street in 1929 halted countless building projects in their tracks.

Young Vonnegut, who had studied at Cornell, was a pacifist. His original specialized subject was biochemistry. But both he and Jane Cox, the childhood sweetheart he had vowed to wed, were fascinated by journalism and writing. Vonnegut had always told his fiancée that they would be married in 1945. In 1944 he was shipped out from the US and across the Atlantic. Within weeks he and his company would be stepping into the darkness of Europe. He was a private, attached to military intelligence, and he was there in the freezing wet forests at the end of 1944 when the Battle of the Bulge saw the Wehrmacht infused with a demonic new energy. Private Vonnegut's company was cut off; he and 150 others were rounded up by German soldiers on 19 December. Thence began not just an ordeal, but also a terrible tutorial in the hinterland of human nature.

Vonnegut and his comrades were forcibly marched some sixty miles, the cold biting into their bones, boots grating the soles of their feet. They reached a town called Limburg, and it was here that the men were loaded into boxcars,[10] the sealed, windowless wooden crates that served as railway carriages. There was no room to manoeuvre, the floor crusted with frozen dung, and to add an element of existential absurdity the train remained stationary. Possibly because tracks ahead had been bombed by the Allies, these airless, cold goods wagons filled with half-conscious human freight were left standing in sidings for days on end.

Consequently, they themselves were now vulnerable to Allied bombs, and one crisp night there came an American raid during which the train was hit. Hundreds were killed or injured. Vonnegut and the other survivors were put into another rancid carriage and taken to a prisoner-of-war camp in Mühlberg, just a short distance outside of Berlin. According to Vonnegut, commissioned officers were not to be compelled to work; anyone of humbler rank, however, could be selected to help satisfy the ever more rapacious Nazi demand for labour.

The train journey to Dresden at that time – taking into account timetable changes caused by Allied attacks and to accommodate the extra services transporting Jews – would have taken between three and four hours. There must have been some way upon arrival that Vonnegut, herded from his barbaric conveyance, was able to glance around at the bridge over the Elbe, and the very pretty roofscape punctuated with spires and towers. For, as he later told Jane, he thought this was the first 'proper' city that he had ever seen.[11]

One of their shared literary heroes was Fyodor Dostoyevsky, author of *Crime and Punishment*; Vonnegut did not seem aware that this idol had himself lived in Dresden for several years, from the late 1860s to the early 1870s. What would the Russian have made of the city in 1945, his eye searching out all the agonies of moral compromise, the piercing awareness of sin and cowardice? Certainly, Kurt Vonnegut was fascinated by the gradations of morality he observed there. He swiftly satisfied himself that there was a sharp distinction between the sadists who made up the German guard parties and the inhabitants, past and present, of a city clearly as cultured as this one.

Vonnegut was put to work on a production line bottling malt syrup. Such sweet luxury was by February 1945 beyond most citizens of the Reich, but supplies were deemed important for pregnant mothers. The accommodation assigned to him and others in his group was in the abattoir complex: barracks set up in the slaughter-house. And he was to recall that in those nights of late January and early February 1945, the city's sirens appeared to react to the tiniest provocation, usually, it seemed, when it was quite another city receiv-ing a bombing raid. Vonnegut himself could not envisage Dresden as a target; it never apparently occurred to him that his own side might want to unleash a roaring fire on the beauty of the old city.

And so, after each day's shift, and after the uncomfortable, rib-jabbing, rifle-butt-thumping march back to the abattoir, after the grim evening rations of soup threaded with strings of horsemeat gristle and hard-to-swallow bread, he was not apprehensive about any threat from above. Indeed, he and his fellow soldiers must instead have been wondering quite how long it would be before either the Americans or the Soviets materialized on Dresden's bridges.

Similarly blithe was the twenty-six-year-old British rifleman and paratrooper Victor Gregg. He too had been taken prisoner in the later stages of 1944 after Arnhem. Like the American, London-born Gregg was put to work, but in his account the labour was initially comparatively congenial.[12] He was attached to a road-sweeping gang in the city, which gave him a chance to take in the extraordinary archi-tecture. The gangmaster – a native Dresdener – was apparently a man of high good humour. Gregg and a few other POWs were treated to stew, black bread and even beer.

Gregg was receiving such good rations that his strength levels were consistently high, and this in turn meant that he could contemplate escape. According to his own account, he tried to slip away from his barracks and his work parties twice, both times unsuccessfully. As a result he was detailed to rather more secure work duties. By the begin-ning of February 1945 Gregg and his fellow prisoners had been sent to work in a soap factory some way out of the city centre; the ingredients were in such pitifully short supply that Gregg and his party had to make it using pumice rather than the regular fats.

In all this time Gregg certainly sensed that Germany was nearing the end of its war, and he, like others, recalled Dresdeners telling him that the city would never be considered a target by the Allies, because it was both too precious historically and insufficiently important to the war effort. One day Gregg and his workmate Harry 'confused' a quantity of cement for pumice. The result was soon a grinding, roaring protesting machine, sparks and flames, and the outbreak of a fire that might well have burned the factory down.

The Gestapo were adamant that the duo had acted deliberately (which, of course, they had, despite Gregg's protestations). In Nazi Germany, sabotage could only carry one sentence. At a makeshift tribunal conducted with nightmarish speed, the pair were sentenced to death. Gregg and his friend were told they would face a firing squad on the morning of 14 February 1945. Harry put on a brave front, telling Gregg that he was sure something would turn up.

In an earlier, more elegant age, one particular RAF airman – later to become a successful novelist – would have revelled in Dresden's cosmopolitan atmosphere. But within a few days he would instead be in a briefing room being told why the city was a target for his bombs. Flight Sergeant Miles Tripp, twenty-one, was based near the small Suffolk town of Bury St Edmunds. For him and his six fellow bomber crew members, this town represented a solid reality from which they were becoming increasingly detached. With its pale-bricked market square, half-timbered shopping streets, its abbey and cinemas and pubs, this was the quiet world to which they returned after flying through darkness – and through occasional fugue states of terror – to bomb German cities.

Tripp was a bomb aimer: the man who lay on his belly on the floor of the Lancaster, watching the green and white and red flares thousands of feet below and using them as the prompt to unleash his load of explosives and incendiaries. At the start of one mission, convinced the pilot was about to mess up the take-off and crash the plane, Tripp suddenly found himself curled up with his knees to his chin and with no recollection of how he had scrambled into that position.[13]

He and the rest of the crew, who were days away from being told that they were to fly their longest, deepest mission into Germany yet, understood very well all the different degrees of mortal fear, and indeed the destabilizing elation that survival could bring. By the early days of February 1945 they were acutely, silently aware of the mortality rate for bomber crews, and of how it was more likely than not that their lives would soon end in blinding fireballs.

Like many who flew with Bomber Command, Tripp became unselfconsciously eccentric: his hair was for the time extraordinarily long; with his blue uniform, he wore a bright scarlet scarf.

In the first week of February 1945 he and his fellow crew members had been sent to bomb the Gremberg railway marshalling yards in Cologne. The mission over what he could see was the already ruined city scared him; despite the ferocity of the 1943 bombing attack that had left the historic town looking like a blasted cemetery, the defences still had bite; the skies around Tripp's bomber glowed with tracer fire from the ground seeking out his plane's fuselage, and there were the illusory 'scarecrows': rumoured rockets that visually imitated the explosion of an aircraft when hit, but which were in fact a tragic optical trick caused by other planes exploding. He watched another plane being hit and 'dropping like a stone'. The mission was judged a success, but the repeated intense levels of fear after having made over twenty-five such flights were corroding his psyche. The mission to come would be yet more haunting.

Upon his return from that Cologne bombing mission, Tripp made his way off base and to the Angel Hotel in the centre of Bury St Edmunds. Already there was his girlfriend Audrey, who was with the Women's Auxiliary Air Force. They regularly spent the night together in the Angel. In an age when only married couples were permitted to share rooms, the hotel staff, Tripp related, looked at them both with a special affection and understanding. Sometimes Tripp had a stock of 'wakey wakey' pills – officially supplied Benzedrine, intended to ward off tiredness on missions – as he felt it was a waste to 'go to bed with an attractive woman' only to fall asleep.

Those hours in the quiet dark of the hotel bedroom helped him to stay connected to life, and to sanity. In all the wartime tenderness of their affair, he and Audrey shared both intimacy and laughter. There was a defiance there, a spirit that extended beyond conflict and one that could prompt a restoration of faith, even to those who had lost it. Such consolations were grabbed by Tripp and so many other airmen with a kind of desperate hunger.

7. The Science of Doomsday

Sir Arthur Harris's memoirs, published in 1947, betrayed a boyish fascination with the power of vast infernos, referring to such terrible phenomena as 'fire tornadoes' and 'fire typhoon[s]'. He quoted a secret German document written in the aftermath of the July 1943 RAF bombing of Hamburg, describing it as a raid that 'went "beyond all human imagination"'.[1] Harris added that 'it must have been even more cataclysmic than the bursting of the two atomic bombs over Japanese cities'. He also quoted the German report of the firestorm that roared through the city, 'against which every human resistance was quite useless'.

This for him seemed less a matter for moral doubt and anxiety than about coolly analysing a mesmerizing man-made apocalypse. He was also at pains to point out that the creation of fire typhoons had been the aim of German bombers over Britain; they had succeeded in Coventry and failed in London, although that had seemed to be their goal; the Blitz, after all, was code-named Operation Loge after the fire-demon in *Das Rheingold*.

Harris also explained that there had been misconceptions on all sides at the start of the war about the style of bombing raids that would have the most impact, and that the British were hampered by erroneous thinking. 'High explosive bombs were invariably too small, and of the wrong kind,' Harris wrote. 'The standard 250lb general purpose bomb, as it was called, was a ridiculous missile.' And the sorts of bombs that were not 'ridiculous' were 'hardly considered'. These included blast bombs, which he claimed had the dual advantage of bringing down buildings while causing few casualties, as long as the population below was securely in shelters.

Then there had been the German tactic of spreading a bombing raid on a British city throughout the hours of the night. This was unlikely to create a conflagration, because in the gaps between the bombardments the hard-worked fire services could usually tame the flames, but the idea was to induce exhaustion among the emergency services and general civilian population alike. The difficulty for any side prosecuting this approach, mused Harris, was that defences began to be firmed up as the conflict wore on, and for the British bombers in those early stages of the war, ever more effective German anti-aircraft searchlights and guns meant a quite horrifying number of bombers were shot out of the sky, their industrial targets relatively unharmed. The principle of concentration became more important; the idea that a swift, massive raid with incendiary bombs might instead start hundreds of individual fires that could not all be put out. The ideal was to create an all-consuming fire.

Air Chief Marshal Harris had long contemplated the possibilities of such a tactic. In the aftermath of the First World War in 1919, when he was a squadron leader in Iraq, the British believed that the territory could be controlled by intimidation from the air rather than having troops on the ground.[2] Young Squadron Leader Harris, high in those Arabian skies, looking down on simple dwellings, mused on the effect of bombs: an entire village could be reduced to ashes within forty-five minutes. And short of shooting rifles into the air, there would be next to nothing that the people below could do about it.

The fact was that fire as a tool of warfare was something that appealed as much to unknowably old instincts as well as intelligence. By reducing everything to ash, fire cleansed and made new room for the victor. The Assyrians in the ninth century BC had developed combustible weapons; sulphuric fires in copper globes. There was the coming of so-called 'Greek fire' under the Byzantine Emperor Constantine Pogonatus – possibly a blend of naphtha, sulphur and quicklime, again producing intense flame – that could be launched at enemy ships. Here was a weapon forged by secret science. Only the Byzantines knew the exact formula, and only they knew the technique by which it could be mixed on ships in cauldrons, and then distilled into tubes or siphons prior to being discharged at the enemy, an operation that apparently created both an ear-splitting thunderclap and copious smoke. This Greek fire was a forerunner of phosphorous bombs, the burning substance that would consume both wood and flesh. It had been used in the Siege of Constantinople in 717–18, and in the centuries to come new admixtures would be launched from trebuchets.

The coming of gunpowder and the regimenting of increasingly professional, highly trained armies across Europe did nothing to quench the instinct to burn. Sometimes as a deprivation strategy it was vividly successful; in 1812, as Napoleon marched his forces deeper into Russia, those Russians pulling back before him set the land aflame, ensuring that with every mile the Grande Armée travelled the spectacle of desolation and hunger greeting his men would increase. It was said that significant parts of Moscow also went up in towering flames against the bleak winter skies; and greeted with this spectacle of death, Napoleon was forced to turn back. But those fires along the way had ruined supplies of both food and arms; and suddenly the prospect of retreat was now sharply flavoured with the possibility of mass slaughter.

Just a year later Napoleon was in Dresden, facing an alliance on the plains and in the forests of Bohemia of Russians, Prussians and other forces drawn from across central Europe. Dresden had seen fire and bombardment before, and simply because the city was beautiful, it did not mean that it or its people were fragile. Broadly, Dresdeners supported Napoleon, but as the Russian and Bohemian armies carefully advanced to the city's perimeter, there was no guarantee that he could hold the town. 'What artist has ever troubled himself with the political events of the day anyway?' wrote E. T. A. Hoffmann in 1813 as his windows shook from the distant explosions of battle. 'But a dark and unhappy age has seized men with its iron fist, and the pain squeezes from them sounds that were previously alien to them.'[3]

And while it was true that many European cities and towns had, throughout the centuries, found themselves caught in the middle of complex conflicts, which brought with them artillery and cannon fire, the firepower remained on the ground. The advent of air power at the beginning of the twentieth century immediately changed all that as Italian and British pilots, high above African plains, insouciantly dropped bombs on rebellious colonial subjects.

The ethical debates concerning the use of bombing had been

conducted since the early 1920s, as air forces across the world began to organize more effectively. There was a fine distinction drawn between 'terror bombing' – the indiscriminate dropping of explosives on residential areas and civilians – and 'morale bombing', in which factories and industrial plants were targeted, with civilians becoming collateral damage.[4] Italian general Giulio Douhet published *The Command of the Air* in 1921; his thesis was among the first in print to suggest that a sufficiently mighty attack from the air would extinguish the fighting courage of the civilian population to the extent that their rulers would have no choice but to capitulate.[5] However, a great many others were instantly repelled by this proposed new incarnation of total war. In Britain, there were draft rules discussed in Whitehall committees that 'embraced the premise that indiscriminate area bombardment was unlawful'.[6] Yet the idea that a sufficiently shocking bombardment would instantaneously shatter the enemy's will to fight on remained too tempting and also in a curious way seemed utilitarian: there might perhaps be sacrifice of the lives of non-combatants but surely better that than to repeat the charnel-house slaughter of millions in conflicts that ground on for years? In 1925 the military historian and former soldier Basil Liddell Hart referred to this as subduing the enemy 'through the spirit'.[7]

There were others, though, who took a more clear-sighted and icier view of the nature of this future war. In 1927 Lord Tiverton declared that 'the girl filling a shell at a factory is just as much a part of the machinery of war as the soldier who fires it. She is much more vulnerable and will certainly be attacked. It is impossible to say,' he continued, 'that such an attack would be unjustified.' Therefore, he concluded, 'an attack will be made upon the civilian population'.[8] This complemented the more famous Stanley Baldwin statement 'the bomber will always get through', and spoke of the same fears. In any new war with Germany, this would certainly be the aim of the enemy: the aerial bombardment not only of factories but of homes too, for if the workers were to witness their families and their houses destroyed, then they would be in no kind of state to return to the production lines needed for fast precision work on war materiel. The RAF and the War Office were also thinking back to the Great War, and the Great German Fire Plan for the Luftwaffe to drop as many incendiaries upon London as they could.

Even in the pre-nuclear era in the years before the Second World War, the popular imagination had been haunted by apocalyptic visions of destruction raining from the sky: authors as diverse as H. G. Wells and 'Sapper', the creator of the rabidly gung-ho Bulldog Drummond spy adventures, had depicted airships pouring poison down upon major cities. Wells's novel *The War in the Air*, published in 1908, envisaged fiendish German flying craft called Drachenflieger (dragon-flies), under the command of a Kaiser-like ruler attacking the east coast of America with chemical weapons.

The sickly premonitions of mass culture were matched with nervy speculation from senior government and establishment figures. As First World War Royal Flying Corps bomber and author Frank Morison observed in 1937, serious bombing onslaughts used as routine instruments of war would result in 'a gap in the continuity of human culture' that would be 'beyond all mending'.[9] There were those who sought to dampen increasingly bellicose rhetoric. In 1938, Neville Chamberlain announced that 'the deliberate bombing of civilians was contrary to international law'.[10] That law had already been thoroughly broken by Hitler and Mussolini from 1936 onwards as they began their infamous intercession in the Spanish Civil War. The hope that they might somehow be persuaded not to do it again seemed vain.

Yet even the Nazis seemed keen that the notorious 1937 bombing raid on the northern Basque town of Guernica fitted within a quasi-legalistic international framework. The Luftwaffe's avowed intent, the Nazis contended, was to damage rebel armaments and manufacturing plants, not to massacre the civilians of a town that had had little involvement in the conflict. Hundreds of civilians were killed, and three-quarters of the town's buildings were destroyed or made uninhabitable. Global political reaction was one of revulsion, yet the attack was studied closely too.

And it is striking that, no matter how sophisticated the developing technology throughout the ensuing war – from target finders to the strips of metal-foiled paper known as 'Window' dropped from aircraft to blind enemy radar, to more comprehensive 'electronic blankets' to do the same – the principles somehow remained ancient. This was not simply about attacks from the air, but about a very much more atavistic impulse. With Guernica had come a philosophy that put the attackers up among the ancient gods, like Zeus firing thunderbolts from the heavens and those below unable to defend themselves. The only truly rational response was fatalism. When exploring the international legality of such raids, the Germans, like others, were most interested in attacks that would destroy morale; if the citizens could see the unearthly power of these choreographed raids, then, it was reasoned, capitulation would follow swiftly.

Yet rationality seemed elusive on the part of both the aggressors and the victims. The Luftwaffe worked on perfecting the waves of destruction, and on the bombs that would shatter most effectively: in September 1939, following their incursion into Poland, the Germans launched repeated air raids on Warsaw. On the morning of 25 September, the largest and most carefully coordinated of these unleashed hundreds of tons of high explosives and incendiaries, starting vast fires on either side of the Vistula, filling the air with the smoke and embers from beautiful civic buildings and churches and blotting out the sun. In the fiery twilight of those crackling streets, it was expected that any armed resistance would give way immediately. It did not. Even though the city was captured two days later through the efforts of the army on the ground, it was clear that the bombing, while shocking the capital's citizens, had not cowed them.

When a weapon is available, the impulse is always to use it. The Nazi bombing of Rotterdam in 1940 – intended as an adjunct to the shock of ground invasion – pursued the leitmotif of unquenchable flame after the Nazi push into the Netherlands had been met with a level of resistance that caused some surprise. The plan was that troops and tanks would enter Rotterdam with flamethrowers following a precision bombing raid.[11] In fact, the raid was the exact opposite of precise.

Rotterdam's centre had a large number of medieval wooden-framed buildings, close-built streets and alleys patterned with the echoes of European history. The Luftwaffe swooped down from the skies, flying low to unload their explosives and incendiaries with apparent indiscrimination. Building after building yielded to the spread of the fire. Here was Nazism in its fresh flowering of nihilism, a willingness not just to destroy hundreds upon hundreds of non-active civilians but also to erase the beauty around them. This was the flourishing of a power that said: we can now wipe out civilizations. And in this rare case, it worked: when the Luftwaffe next threatened to return to reduce the medieval wonders of Utrecht to seething ash, the government of the Netherlands felt compelled to surrender. Their desire was not merely to protect Dutch citizens but to preserve the country's history and culture, irreplaceable landmarks of memory and belonging.

The Luftwaffe had also achieved an unintended side effect, an unexpected quirk of physics that reinforced the idea that, with enough research, they could visit a man-made apocalypse on any city of their choosing. The conflagrations spawned in the Rotterdam raid were too fierce and too many to be fought by the fire services on the ground, and as they spread, feeding their own intensity, so the nature of the air that nourished them changed as well. A column of intense, radiant heat was rising above the city, and in the remaining stumps of streets below, this was producing superheated vacuums in which breathing was impossible and that were causing untethered objects to rise from the ground. This was the sort of fire tornado that Harris and Chief of the Air Staff Charles Portal were to become so mesmerized by.

The phenomenon had been seen before. In 1871 parts of Wisconsin had been suffering prairie fires in prolonged dry spells, the orange sun hanging sickly in the smoke-laden sky. A gang of railway construction workers clearing brush from deep in the woods accidentally started another fire that, owing to some unique atmospheric conditions, including an insistent westerly wind, swiftly acquired an extraordinary intensity. Cold air was sucked into an ever-growing column of blinding heat, and the flames swept through illimitable acres of dry woodland.

The process was reported to have been amazingly, terrifyingly fast; other railway workers in the path of the sheet of flame roaring towards them were said simply to have combusted on the spot. According to one witness, the phenomenon actually 'sounded like freight trains'. The fire spread out further, and the flames approached the town of Peshtigo. It was faced with a 'wall of flame a mile high and five miles wide', now

burning at some 2,000 degrees centigrade – hot enough to turn sand
into glass. Wooden houses and churches were engulfed. Many years
later, this would be described as 'nature's nuclear explosion'.[12]

The Peshtigo Paradigm became the subject of American scientific
research; what was this phenomenon known as a 'fire whirl', so superheated that anyone standing in it might find themselves drawn
helplessly into the air, higher and higher, revolving in a tornado
while being burned alive? An estimated 1,200 people died in the
inferno; the numbers could not be precise owing to the often uniden-
tifiable nature of the remains. The fire, which had greedily consumed
1.2 million acres, eventually exhausted itself and countless survivors
were left with hideous burn injuries and what would now be termed
post-traumatic stress disorder.

There was another terrifying outbreak in 1881, in logging country
in Michigan; one witness later said: 'The onrushing flames would
leap high into the air then descend to the ground like a bouncing ball,
burn everything before them, then rise for another leap.'[13] This was a
'hurricane carrying a sheet of flame', and once more it had found
richly wooded country to spread across. There was a mushroom of
superheated air and flame that rose far into the sky. Onlookers
described it as 'the end of the world'.[14] And in its aftermath, there was
again a terrible scientific fascination about the effect that it had had
on animals and humans. Livestock had simply been cooked; sheep
and cows were charred. Humans too had been baked alive; many
were found without clothes, shrivelled. Of the survivors, many suffered hideous legacies, their feet and hands burned off. Others had
had their eyes burned out or their faces disfigured.

These rural catastrophes were followed in 1923 by fire typhoons visited upon two Japanese cities, sparked by the Great Kanto Earthquake.
People at Yokohama docks were suddenly startled and terrified by a
noise like unearthly thunder.[15] Then those on the piers were sent flying
as the ground beneath them shifted. Next came the tsunami, a monstrous wall of black water rolling across warehouses and homes, humans
reduced to tiny drowning specks in the maelstrom. And afterwards
came the fires, both to Yokohama and to Tokyo, seventeen miles to the
north, which had also been hit by the tremor. The earthquake sparked

flames, and in residential districts composed wholly of wooden houses, fires started leaping across streets, devouring all with speed. The nightmare intensity of the flames prompted religious responses. One onlooker said: 'If this were not hell, where would hell be?'[16] Elsewhere, a Jesuit priest was hypnotized by the horror of the spectacle: 'Each new gust of wind gave new impulse to the fury of the conflagration,' he said.[17]

But here was also a new and more terrible element: population density. Although the American firestorms had killed many, the destruction was spread over a huge and sparsely populated area. In crowded Tokyo, the pulsing heat and the approach of flames higher than any skyscraper caused mass urban panic. There were those who sought to flee but found themselves trapped in the suffocating crush of a crowd that was pushing against itself in all directions. The instinct to escape resulted in human gridlock.

Closer to the Sumida river, and with the air around them becoming steadily hotter, the panicking crowds made for the water. Yet for many, there was no sanctuary in the swirling currents, only exhaustion, and huge numbers drowned. The crowds still rushing from the surrounding streets soon started to overload the bridges crossing the river; some buckled and collapsed, taking with them many more lives.

This was a modern city, yet it and its inhabitants were helpless before a conflagration of such extraordinary force. Roads melted into viscous treacle; railway lines warped. All gas and electricity supplies were completely disabled. Telephone wires and poles along with electric cables simply disintegrated and vanished in the flames. There was nothing any fire-fighting team could do; 130 separate fires were conjoining with a rapidity that made them elemental.

In other parts of the city, with the air now filled with floating glowing embers and the deep roar of the rising flames, many sought escape by making for the city's open spaces, filling its squares and parks. What happened in one park was, again, biblical in its appalling scale. The sheets of flame were coalescing and they now produced what was termed locally as the 'dragon twist' – the fire tornado, or firestorm. Once more that terrifying inversion of gravity ensued, trees and bodies plucked from the ground into the maw of the superheated inferno. They would simply have melted.

The fire created hurricane-force winds, the effect of which was akin to a blast furnace. Clothes were shredded, torn off by the air itself; internal organs roasted. In some cases, depending on where the victim had been in relation to the fire, corpses might look little more than sunburnt. Conversely, in the worst instances, parts of them had been liquefied.

A western trader called Otis Poole observed: 'Over everything had settled a thick white dust, and through the yellow fog of dust, still in the air, a copper-coloured sun shone upon this silent havoc in sickly reality.'[18] The death toll was prodigious, in the region of 156,000 lives, though once again it was difficult to be exact when so often all that remained were fragments of jewellery and headless naked husks.

Since the advent of flight, military strategists had brooded on the age-old daydream of weapons so terrible that they would have the power to stop wars in an instant and make victory certain. Winston Churchill was contemplating after the First World War the idea of a weapon that could be created in a laboratory, and that would somehow contain hitherto unimagined destructive forces. He envisaged something 'the size of an orange'[19] which would be inconceivably more powerful, and generate a much greater blast, than any contemporaneous technology.

In the years after the slaughter in the trenches – the first conflict to be captured in detail on celluloid, thus bringing to the wider civilian population images of a black-and-white world of squalor and death – there was an understandable fear of the same kind of conflict recurring. The dream was of decisive air power that, simply by threatening innumerable lives, would paradoxically serve to save many, many others. It could in one sense be cleaner.

Yet this is not how Britain began its air war with the Germans. As Hew Strachan observed: 'The RAF did not enter the war with a well-developed plan to conduct a strategic bombing offensive, designed to kill as many German civilians as possible.'[20] Even if it had wanted to, the means were not there: flight distances were limited, navigational technology was still rudimentary. Its aircraft were not able to penetrate deep into Germany. In addition, there was a genuine anxiety that the targets should indeed be of the 'precision' variety – the great industrial works that were powering the Nazi war machine. Partly this was to do with the international rulings and guidelines that had been debated throughout the previous decade (as well as an important plea on the eve of conflict from the then neutral US and its President Franklin D. Roosevelt that civilian areas outside combat theatres should never be bombed) and also to do with a strategic sense that strikes against important infrastructure would keep the fighting contained; for there was the world after the war to consider as well.

The dissolution of a mutual code of aerial warfare was gradual. The Nazi attack on Rotterdam was a clear signal of intent. After the fall of France to the Germans in June 1940, when British forces were forced to retreat, the only way of taking the fight to the enemy was in the air. There was a British raid in August 1940 against Berlin, essentially at the limit of the RAF's range at that time, the targets including Berlin airport near the centre. Ninety-five bombers flew in the raid, and though they caused some casualties and disruption, both were comparatively light. None the less, the audacity inspired rage in Hitler. With the German expectation that the RAF's losses during that summer's Battle of Britain would soon render it effectively inoperable, Hitler authorized attacks on London. This, though, was not intended at the start as terror bombing; the targets – docklands, factories, power stations – were intentionally industrial rather than residential.

All the same, from the night of 7 September 1940 right the way through until the following May, for residents near the docklands of the East End and south London, life was turned inside out: bombs that sounded like the footsteps of giant ogres, sheets of flame hundreds of feet high bringing choking clouds of toxic smoke laced with burning sugar and cinnamon, the result of warehouse blazes. Families sat in almost absurdly inadequate shelters, and then emerged, giddy from lack of sleep, to see nothing where their homes had once been. For others, the sight of sliced-open houses, exposing fireplaces and bathrooms, was near hallucinatory. The author Virginia Woolf walked out of her house in Bloomsbury during an air raid, her arms held up to the sky as if drawing the bombers towards her.

Although it had become clear to the Germans by the autumn of 1940

that they had not vanquished the RAF, and that Hitler was not prepared to risk the invasion of England, the Luftwaffe continued with its
attacks on British cities. The bombers over London – even if they had
been aiming for factories – flew deeper into residential suburban districts. The effect of the unremitting nightly assault on the people below
seemed a curious mix of acceptance and mordant humour. The Nazis
were hoping for revolution; the closest they got was an organized
group of East End residents marching to the West End and demanding
entrance to the cellars of the luxurious Savoy Hotel.

Nor would the science of firestorms obtain here: among the precision
targets marked out for the Luftwaffe were the lanes of the City, London's financial and economic heart. Although close-built, the district
had already seen a previous fiery catastrophe some centuries earlier in
1666; there was very little in the way of timber construction to be
found there now. And while the narrow residential streets lying close
to St Paul's Cathedral between Aldersgate and Moorgate were so effectively bombed that they became nothing but dust and stumps of stone,
the fires sparked by the magnesium incendiaries would not take hold.

None the less, by 1941 Chief of the Air Staff Sir Charles Portal acknowledged that the approach of the RAF towards German targets was
to change. The idea of precision bombing mutated into area bombing.[21]
Real precision was still not possible, and it was absurd to pretend that it
was; with Germany effectively blacked out, and bombers facing not
merely the hazards of flak and enemy fighter aircraft but also the blankness of cloud cover, the idea that it was possible to aim, from thousands
of feet up, at the centre of a ball-bearing factory that lay somewhere in
a great pool of darkness was untenable. The targets were now large city
centres. Generally, the industry lay on the peripheries of these urban
areas. But the intention now was to create wider social havoc. The US
president was informed of the intensified strategy; there were no objections from America, and none from Stalin's Soviet Union either.

Thus, in March 1942, 234 Wellington and Stirling bombers took
off from bases in Norfolk, including RAF Marham, with the aim of
bringing fire to a medieval city on the Baltic Sea. Lübeck, once the
cornerstone of the Hanseatic League, linking a range of ports in
northern Europe, with a picturesque warren of historic lanes and

marketplaces, had some submarine construction works outside the centre; but as the new Air Chief Marshal Arthur Harris was to later admit, it was hardly the most crucial or urgent of targets.[22] Lübeck was, however, a laboratory in which a new theory would be tested.

There were three waves of bombers under a bright frosty moon, swooping over the silver river and canals. The first wave carried the 'Blockbuster' bombs, whose purpose was to smash down upon roofs and open them up, ready to receive the following incendiaries. Countless fires burst into life. Timber crackled, while the rich brown local brickwork baked and glowed. On that crisp dry night, the flames in the old city conjoined, gorging even on the great churches. The bells were melted. The death toll was not (by later standards) hugely high: some 300 mortalities. But in the space of several hours, about 15,000 people were made homeless. It had, from the point of view of Bomber Command, been a fantastic success; now they could bring roaring infernos to city after city.

Lübeck's most celebrated cultural figure was the author Thomas Mann, whose autobiographical novel *Buddenbrooks* – a sensational international success – was set largely in the city. He and his family had left Hitler's Germany many years beforehand. At the time of the raid, Mann was in America, making radio broadcasts for the BBC propaganda unit intended to be heard by his countrymen. (The Nazis forbade any citizen to listen to unauthorized broadcasts on pain of death, yet many still did.)

'Did Germany believe that it would never have to pay for the misdeeds which its lead in barbarism enabled it to commit?' Mann declared. 'It has hardly begun to pay – over the Channel and in Russia . . . Hitler is boasting that his Reich is ready for ten, even twenty years of war,' he continued. 'I assume that you Germans have your own ideas about that – for example, that after a fraction of this time, no stone will stand on top of another in Germany.'[23]

As fire takes hold, so too does the anger of war; by means of direct revenge, the Nazis launched the Baedeker Raids against Britain, so named because the targets were beautiful cities that had received three stars in the famous German guidebook. Like Lübeck, these targets had very little if anything by way of industrial or strategic significance: the aim was to cause anguish by obliterating old treasures. Exeter, Bath, York and Canterbury were among the historic targets; death tolls were in the hundreds and architectural gems – centuries-old guildhalls, quaint eighteenth-century shopping streets, the monastery houses adjoining Canterbury Cathedral – were irreplaceably obliterated.

This was bombing as deliberate sacrilege. It was not just the idea of sacred sites such as Canterbury facing wanton demolition; even secular architectural glories carried with them a uniqueness that spoke to the national soul. Along with science came psychology: the pain and the national humiliation of having such exquisite streets permanently mutilated would be intense.

And yet, here again, the Germans were aware that such raids would hardly form any kind of knockout blow; there was no possibility they would force Churchill and the Air Ministry to change their own tactics. Perhaps the bombed populations of Essen and Cologne, Magdeburg and Bremen might have derived some moments of satisfaction after learning that the ancient Roman structures in Bath had been endangered and destabilized by the Luftwaffe; yet that satisfaction would not have lasted long after once more gazing at the ruins created by the RAF.

But this was an instance of the shadow line of rationality being crossed; the Baedeker Raids had no purpose other than that of raw emotion. This in turn brought a further moral dimension to the philosophy of total war: the notion of blood-thumping vengeance enacted upon civilians. The technology to enable the slaking of such unthinking fury was by this stage improving daily. From the British point of view, the Gee navigation system – involving frequent timed radio pulses and on-board oscilloscopes – was bringing a much wider variety of potential targets, detectable by technology if not by the naked eye, into view, and making longer-range missions more practicable.

Some, however, were becoming ever more anxious about the moral issues raised by unleashing such power. This was a war increasingly fought by physicists as well as soldiers; scientists in laboratories were working as tirelessly as all those in the services to devise routes to victory. Some among those working for Bomber Command were tormented by dilemmas posed by their very own breakthroughs.

8. The Correct Atmospheric Conditions

There was a teenage boy boarding at Winchester, the venerable English public school, in the 1930s, who had been marked out as a little eccentric, chiefly because of his habit of smuggling complex mathematical texts under his cricket jumper when he was forced to play. The amused teachers would send the boy out onto the grass to field in positions where it was unlikely the ball would ever roll, and where he could comfortably stand and study the most extraordinarily abstruse theorems as the game was played all around him.

Here was a prodigy who delighted in the 'absolute elsewhere',[1] a popular slang phrase of the time denoting abstracted souls but deriving from the work of physicists who were beginning to explore new quantum realms. This teenager, a few years later, would find himself being drafted into one of the most sensitive of the war's nerve centres: and his wild mathematical skill would come to be coupled with a maturing moral sense; a deepening understanding of the desires and vulnerabilities of war. Dresden was destined to become a large part of that boy's moral and philosophical growth.

There is a map produced by Bomber Command in 1942, showing the city of Dresden and its public landmarks.[2] A note at the top warns that the hospitals on it were not to be hit. It is striking that the map-makers felt the need even to say such a thing: who would ever consider a hospital a target? But there is an unconscious cruelty there too, against weary bomber crews who had already seen more death than most: for even though they could make strenuous efforts to obey the injunction, the truth was that the available technology did not make it possible for them to achieve such delicate accuracy.

The teenage mathematician was to see all of this and more: Freeman Dyson won a place at Cambridge University just after the war broke out. He knew that he would not have long there, that he would of course be drawn into some branch of the military effort. In fact, he was granted two years of intense study, of rather more esoteric matters such as Alpha/Beta theorems.[3] By this stage, Dyson – an angular young man with large, penetrating eyes – was reading Aldous Huxley's *Ends and Means*, published in 1937, a series of philosophical essays concerning nationalism, religion, war and cycles of aggression. 'We insist that ends which we believe to be good can justify means which we know quite certainly to be abominable,' wrote Huxley. 'We go on believing, against all the evidence, that these bad means can achieve the good ends we desire.' He also noted the 'extent to which even highly intelligent people can deceive themselves in this matter'.[4]

Freeman Dyson was called up for duty in 1943; recognizing his brilliant intellect, the authorities sent him to Bomber Command HQ, a 'redbrick' structure on the Chiltern Hills just outside the Buckinghamshire town of High Wycombe.[5] Dyson was billeted near to the town, and every morning would get on his bicycle and ride five miles uphill to Bomber Command HQ. Sometimes he would be passed on his way there by a large government limousine, in the back of which would be sitting Sir Arthur Harris.

Dyson was selected to work with Bomber Command's Operational Research Section; he arrived at the point when the raids over Hamburg – spread over eight nights in July 1943 – had succeeded in raising an extraordinary firestorm over the city, almost a mile high. Dyson's section dealt with statistical analysis of all the bombing missions, in terms not of the buildings hit or the infernos started, but of the mortality rate of the aircrews and of what might be done to ease the horrifying rate of attrition that hung over every pilot and crew member's head as they took off into the darkening night skies.

Could there be a factor linking the bombers that were either shot down or blown up in mid-air? At the time, Dyson recalled, pilots and crews were assured that practical flying experience brought greater safety; that the more sorties a bomber accomplished, the more adept the crew would be in avoiding all the hazards that the brilliant German defence forces could muster. Dyson analysed the statistics of the planes that had not returned. He and his colleagues faced the bitter truth of the matter: experience made absolutely no difference to chances of staying alive.[6] A crew that had flown twenty-nine sorties deep into the heart of enemy territory was every bit as likely to become a flashing orange fireball as the crew that was just starting out. By the time they reached thirty sorties, this crew would have only a 25 per cent expectation of survival. On any raid it appeared that an average of 5 per cent of planes were lost, so after many hundreds of raids overall, the number of fatalities rose ineluctably.

Geometric propositions, once confined to blackboards in Dyson's world, were now matters of life and death. It took Bomber Command a long time to fully comprehend all the hazards that their crews faced in the air. It was assumed for some time throughout 1943 and 1944 that crews in exploding planes that had not been hit by enemy fire had fallen victim to mid-air collisions. The tightness of the bombing formations, the requirement to sweep in en masse surely meant that such contact was sometimes inevitable.

But there was another element of mortal danger about which Bomber Command was as yet unaware. Pilots sometimes returned from missions with the sinister impression that the German fighters were somehow invisible. Dyson speculated that the Germans might have achieved what had once been a theoretical dream: not invisibility, but on-board weaponry for their night fighters that could be fired upwards at an angle – optimally between sixty and seventy-five degrees – as the enemy planes flew beneath bombers unseen. He was correct. The Germans had perfected the technique, which they dubbed *Schräge Musik* (crooked music).[7]

Dyson was not confined to his stark office; there were times when he took to the air himself, flying high in the summer skies, conducting aeronautical experiments. There was no sense that he was unhappy about his personal position, or that his support for those young bomber crews was anything other than resolute. But in 1943 and 1944, as Arthur Harris selected larger numbers of German cities to be targeted for high-explosive and incendiary drops, Dyson found himself questioning the ethics of the bombing war.

He was later to confess that, as he had entered the conflict, his intellectual position had been very broadly pacifist. Yet he could also see very clearly that the Nazis were a regime that no one could allow to survive. The questions then began to come back to Aldous Huxley's ends and means. Many decades later, Dyson summarized his moral difficulties:

Since the beginning of the war I had been retreating step by step from one moral position to another, until at the end I had no moral position at all. At the beginning of the war I . . . was morally opposed to all violence. After a year of war I retreated and said, 'Unfortunately nonviolent resistance against Hitler is impracticable, but I am still morally opposed to bombing.' A few years later I said, 'Unfortunately it seems that bombing is necessary in order to win the war, and so I am willing to go to work for Bomber Command, but I am still morally opposed to bombing cities indiscriminately.' After I arrived at Bomber Command I said, 'Unfortunately it turns out that we are after all bombing cities indiscriminately, but this is morally justified as it is helping to win the war.' A year later I said, 'Unfortunately it seems that our bombing is not really helping to win the war, but at least I am morally justified in working to save the lives of the bomber crews.'

But, he concluded: 'In the last spring of the war I could no longer find any excuses.'[8]

Bomber Command had from the start been following a particular line of logic in its campaign: the belief that the conflict could be won decisively from the air. It was very persuasive: enemy tanks and ships targeted from high above and yielding; sprawling industrial plants and factories naked before the pathfinding pilots, defenceless against agile raids; vast dams, ghostly grey in the moonlight and towering over German valleys, marked out for destruction by the brilliant 'bouncing bomb' invention of Barnes Wallis. The enemy's defences grew ever sharper, swift night fighters pursuing larger bombers through the clouds, the tight organization of the anti-aircraft lights and guns. But there would always eventually be a technological response.

The literary critic and novelist David Lodge, whose father had been in the RAF during the war and who himself was obsessed with planes as a boy, was later alive to another element that somehow lightened the dark nature of the bomber crews' missions: the image of them (portrayed in films) as knights embarking upon a Grail quest,[9] travelling far into an unknown and dangerous new world in pursuit of their noble aims, many of them meeting death along the way, and those who did eventually return being imbued with a melancholic sense of having seen the darkness.

This was not how Freeman Dyson saw it; what Bomber Command was doing was laying down a clear road that led to Hiroshima and the deployment of nuclear weaponry. Dyson had arrived in his new role as the aerial photographs of the Hamburg bombings were demonstrating what destruction might be wrought upon a civilian population. The raids had been labelled Operation Gomorrah. The effects rather transcended the Old Testament inspiration. It would have been too soon for the eyewitness accounts of that 1943 raid to have filtered back, but the technicians of Bomber Command already knew what they had done.

In part, they knew because of the newly adjusted nature of the bombs: as well as high explosives and sticks of incendiaries, here were weapons that deployed burning corrosion: bombs with jellied petroleum and magnesium. Unleashed on bricks and mortar, these would create fires that could not be extinguished; this was also true of human flesh. Anyone touched by these searing substances would find no escape, not even by jumping in rivers or canals.

That volcanic firestorm, started on the night of 27 July, had increased Hamburg's fatalities to ten times the expected number for a bombing raid. Later, the figure was estimated at around 37,000 people, a death toll simply too large to comprehend. It was known the Germans had been very organized about protecting civilians, either in specially constructed shelters or, as in Dresden, in adapted basements and cellars, but although these shielded their occupants from blast, the wild firestorm still penetrated the depths. For those in the cellars, death resulted either through asphyxiation when the oxygen was sucked out or by roasting in the unendurably superheated air.

The Hamburg raids succeeded in swallowing large numbers of industrial concerns into that inferno; factories converted to wartime production. They also consumed transport arteries and made so many people homeless that the infrastructure of the city creaked on the edge of complete collapse. From the point of view of the Air

Chief Marshal, further similar missions would play a vital role in securing victory in Europe: with morale battered into blankness, and familiar, much-loved cityscapes erased as though they had never been there, surely the enemy would soon be forced to admit that the conflict was unwinnable.

Yet it was Winston Churchill himself who advised Bomber Command never to guess or assume how an enemy would respond to a vast and terrible attack; their reaction could never be predicted.[10] And he was proved right. The Hamburg raids had not resulted in anything resembling surrender or indeed despair. The immediate response from the devastated city's authorities was to attempt to organize the many thousands who had been left homeless and who had, in a kind of fugue state, wandered out past the city perimeter into the woodlands beyond. Police and medical authorities followed the trails of zombie-like people out into the forests and the fields; the survivors seemed to have become completely disassociated from time.

The farming communities who saw these wandering citizens – some in pyjamas, others barely dressed – were bewildered by their abstraction. With some gentleness, the authorities started to corral the survivors, having arranged for them to be transported to towns across the country. Some were sent by train to Bayreuth, which was in the middle of its annual Wagner festival. There were grandees in full opera dress who found themselves mingling in the streets with catatonic walkers, clothes still torn.[11] There may have been a few among the sophisticated opera-lovers who allowed themselves to think that this was indeed Götterdämmerung – the twilight of the gods.

Despite the horror, many survivors soon gathered their senses and were overwhelmed by a desire to return. Back in their obliterated neighbourhoods some could hardly orientate themselves; not only their apartments but their entire streets had vanished. Others were to be found desperately picking through rubble, turning over mummified corpses in their effort to find the bodies of their loved ones. According to one contemporary report, 'rats and flies were the lords of the city'.[12] The devastation also demonstrated the cold pragmatism of the municipal authorities: the inmates of a nearby concentration camp, Neuengamme, were forced to sift through the ash and melted flesh to recover the thousands of corpses for burial. But the almost surreal spectacle of Hamburg's working-class residential district reduced to pale ash elicited not the slightest hesitation from the regime in Berlin; nothing seemed to deflect the Nazis. Here, instead, was a propaganda opportunity to be spread around the world: the revelation of terror bombing.

Air Chief Marshal Harris never entertained any doubts about the strategy, even as the Royal Air Force was being pushed by others in the Air Ministry in the later months of 1943 and throughout 1944 to aim for more specific targets: synthetic-oil plants and refineries and ball-bearing factories. The idea was optimistic: by consistently striking at fuel sources and armaments manufacture, it would be possible to bring the German war machine to a halt, its tanks and planes emptied and starved of petrol. One objection to this was the question of efficacy: reaching and pinpointing such targets was one thing, but to damage them so severely that they would be permanently out of commission was another. So many other factors – cloud cover, flak, defensive fighters – meant that such highly specific missions would carry the double risk of a low success rate and high mortality among British airmen.

For Harris, these were what he had long termed 'panacea targets'. But in addition to this, the USAAF's targeting of infrastructure such as railways and refineries still created numbers of civilian casualties: the difficulty over precision aiming, combined with the fact that such industrial features were frequently sited well within the built-up areas of cities, meant that houses and flats were bombarded, and the civilians who had not been able to reach shelters were subjected to blast waves, fire and white-hot shrapnel.

With D-Day and the invasion of Europe underway in the summer of 1944, there were senior figures in Whitehall who were once more starting to think like Harris, and it was Sir Charles Portal who in August 1944 drew up a confidential document setting out the case for a dramatic, if not apocalyptic, bombing raid upon the city of Berlin. There had been attacks in the autumn of the previous year – termed the Battle of Berlin – that had met with only very limited success: the

long distance combined with strong German defences and poor
weather meant that, even though buildings and parks burned, the
practical effect of the raids was negligible. The administrative
machinery that held the Nazi empire together continued to function,
but now – with the Allies and the Soviets pushing from opposite directions through towns, across heaths and through forests – here was a
chance to launch a different sort of mission. The bombers, this time,
would not be looking for specific buildings. The target would quite
simply be the city of Berlin and all of its people. The code name for
this proposed mission was Operation Thunderclap.[13]

The term 'thunderclap' implies a moment of pure shock or fright,
as opposed to damage; a reflexive start as the heavens boom. But
there is also the distant resonance of divine intervention: the angered
gods sending forth punishing storms. 'This paper,' wrote Charles
Portal in the introduction to the confidential memo circulated within
the War Cabinet, 'proposes the renewal of area attacks on Berlin as
the most effective attack on German civilian morale that can be suggested.' The idea was to await the golden hour, the moment when 'a
sudden catastrophic area attack on Berlin offers prospects of inducing
the immediate and organized surrender of the Nazi regime, or alter-
natively of precipitating the collapse of its authority'.[14]

The paper posited that, although American attacks on specific
factories and plants had been a success, there had been little impact in
terms of undermining the confidence of the German civilian population in the Nazi regime. Thunderclap was, conversely, aimed directly
at the bodies and souls of the ordinary people to achieve 'maximum
moral effect' – a hefty euphemism for fear and insecurity. 'The attack
must be delivered in such density that it imposes as nearly as possible
a 100% risk of death to the individual in the area in which it is applied,'
the paper continued. The attack should 'produce an effect amounting
to a national disaster'. And more: the bombs had to hit places and
landmarks that were absolutely central to the identity of Berlin. Such
notable targets – governmental, cultural – would involve 'the maximum associations, both traditional and personal, for the population
as a whole'. This was not just about the destruction of civic symbolism; it was also very much about the deliberate targeting of human

life. The aim was to 'embrace the highest density of population', and to hit it repeatedly to give citizens the impression that there was nothing that their government could do to protect them. This was about much more than morale; it was about regarding those civilians – the mothers, the elderly, the infants – as being as legitimate a focus for the incendiaries as the Nazis who governed them.

'To the German High Command, defeat must seem inevitable as disasters grow day by day,' wrote Portal.[15] The trick was to strike with shocking ruthlessness when the confidence of the authorities was already sufficiently shaken; that way there could be a speedier collapse of the regime and a swifter end to the war. The carefully blank language and imagery of Thunderclap give the impression of smooth rationality, and the theory that a sudden burst of pure terror and destruction would induce Nazi inertia and surrender made superficial psychological sense. But under the technocratic terminology – the repeated use of the word 'maximum' – lay something that went rather beyond scientific strategy. Defeating a regime was one thing; but what sort of long-term future lay ahead for a nation whose old people and children had been specifically targeted at the moment when the nation was at its most vulnerable? In Thunderclap, there was an underlying assumption that the virus of Nazism lay deep within the flesh of German society as a whole; this was no longer simply a military force to be vanquished but an entire people.

In the event, Operation Thunderclap was set to one side in the long, gruelling autumn and winter of 1944, when the German army fought back with a terrible intensity. However, as the year drew to a close, the principles of the operation began to look extremely tempting once more, even as Air Chief Marshal Harris was being pressured to make more effort with his 'panacea targets'. There was a great deal of friction between him and Portal; the author of Thunderclap was by now conflicted and had swung back in favour of Bomber Command targeting the mechanical rather than organic heart of the Nazi regime.

Just weeks before the attack on Dresden, the two men engaged in a fiercely forthright exchange of letters about the goals of the bombers. The view of the War Cabinet, and of Portal, was that the focus of raids should once more be very much on Germany's oil plants, and on the railways transporting their products across Europe. But Harris was angrily sceptical and wholly convinced that the way forward was quite simply to raze more cities. His superior noted his reluctance coolly and wrote detailed letters explaining why he thought he was wrong.

In one of these, Portal tried to impress upon Harris the effectiveness of oil-plant targeting: he had 'a dossier of "Ultra" information' (decrypts from the British Government Code and Cypher School at Bletchley Park) gleaned from the aftermath of attacks. 'My dear Harris,' Portal wrote, using his habitual salutation, 'If cities, once attacked, were entirely destroyed, the chances would be better; but as you yourself admit, cities recover their industrial output . . . in four or five months.' After all those months of hitting cities, 'there is no evidence she [Germany] was [sic] near collapse'.[16]

Harris was hurt, especially as he was convinced that decisions were being taken in the Air Ministry that he was not party to. What especially rankled with him was the idea that some of those figures in the ministry were junior to him; this, he argued, was about experience. And underlying his irritation was the prickling and irrational sense that he was the outsider: despite his Devonian upbringing, Harris self-identified as what he termed a 'colonial', by implication outside of the inner rings of the establishment.

He wrote back to Portal on 18 January 1945, complaining that there was no precedent for policies laid down 'without prior reference to the Commander in Chief'. He was, he said, being handed target lists and bemoaned the fact that 'little I do now appears to meet with approval'.[17] Harris's view was that even some of the most spectacular targeted bombing coups had had scant effect, be it on oil plants or even vaster structures. 'The destruction of the Möhne and Eder dams was to achieve wonders,' he wrote, adding sharply, 'It achieved nothing compared with the effort and the loss. Nothing that is but a supreme display of skill, gallantry, devotion and technical ingenuity.' 'The material damage,' he went on, 'was negligible compared with one small "area" attack.'

And so, he argued, it would be equally ineffective to simply hit 'replaceable' oil targets ad infinitum. Moreover, Harris was anxious that the order signified an entire change of strategy. 'The main factor which I fear is the abandonment of priority for area attack,' he wrote. There were other difficulties: the year had turned and the nights were beginning to shorten – extra hazard for bomber crews in twilit skies. 'The enemy,' he continued, 'is neither a fool nor an incompetent.' And it was at this point that he made his direct plea that cities such as Dresden should now be targeted.

'The next three months will be our last opportunity to knock out the central and eastern industrial areas in Germany,' Harris wrote, going on to list them: 'Magdeburg, Leipzig, Chemnitz, Dresden, Breslau, Posen, Halle, Erfurt, Gotha, Weimar, Eisenach and the rest of Berlin. These places are now the mainspring of German war production and the consummation of three years' work depends upon achieving their destruction.' The next passage in the letter was underlined: 'It is our last chance; it would have more effect on the war than anything else.'[18]

As a parting shot, Harris expanded upon his sense of hurt: that Portal had suggested that in terms of orders about targets, Harris had not been wholly loyal. 'I will not willingly lay myself open to the charge . . . of not having really tried,' he wrote. In his anger, he flourished the threat of resignation: 'I therefore ask you to consider whether it is best for the prosecution of the war and the success of our armies, which alone matters, that I should remain in this situation.'[19]

Portal replied to 'My dear Harris' a day later, his letter a symphony of soothing notes. Yet underneath it was the clear message that he and the Air Ministry were not going to be gainsaid. On 20 January, Portal was still insisting on the importance of tackling the oil plants, adding that the Soviets had indicated how impressed they had been thus far with the effects of such missions. Portal was keen to share his own praise: 'I would like to say how pleased I was with the success of your recent attacks on oil targets.'[20]

He also tried to persuade Harris that – successful though he had been – Harris alone could not be expected to know exactly which targets would be most effectively destroyed, that some decisions had to be taken at the Air Ministry with full access to all intelligence. This meant from the codebreakers of Bletchley Park onwards. 'No commander

of a large strategic bomber force can possibly have time to study and
appreciate the enormous number of military and economic factors
involved in the selection of the best policy,' wrote Portal. 'He has
more than a full-time job running his Command.'[21]

And at this point, Portal's emollience was aimed at forestalling Harris's furious exit. 'I yield to no one in my admiration for the work
of your Command,' he wrote. Yet Harris was going to have to fall
into line; he could not be allowed to form his own strategies. 'You
apparently believe in putting all your effort into area attacks,' Portal
continued. 'We recognize that area attacks have been extremely valuable but we are convinced that in order to be decisive in themselves . . .
they would require a very much larger force than we possess . . . I willingly accept your assurance that you will continue to do your utmost
to ensure the successful execution of the policy laid down,' Portal
added, with a trace of steel. 'I am very sorry that you do not believe in
it but it is no use craving for what is evidently unattainable.'[22]

By 24 January Harris had stepped away from the brink of resignation, but he felt impelled to write to Portal once more. This time
there was almost a note of yearning. 'I am still, I must confess, of the
opinion that, in this hard winter – beset as they are on all fronts – a
determined effort could not fail to destroy most of the major towns I
mentioned and that that . . . would be the end of Germany,' he stated.
Harris conceded that there remained one problem: 'There is of course
the difficulty of getting the Yanks to come in on the area bombing.
But I am certain we could achieve it ourselves. It is for that reason I
am personally so upset at this sudden change of horses [by which he
meant the oil targets]. The bomber is the prime offensive weapon.'[23]

Yet even as Harris wrote, different cogs in the innermost war
machine were beginning to turn; the Joint Intelligence Committee,
the Ministry of Economic Warfare and the Air Ministry had been
studying with interest the vast numbers of German refugees pouring
out of the east, fleeing the terror of the oncoming Red Army. Here
was a chance to cause both severe disruption and confusion. The fact
that it would involve the most desperate and vulnerable of human
collateral seemed not to resonate in any way; Arthur Harris was by
no means the only senior Allied figure who had apparently passed

beyond regarding German civilian life as having any intrinsic value. Nor were decisions concerning targets entirely in his hands.

Winston Churchill was impatient to hear more of the possibilities. Was a vast raid on Berlin possible? And what of these other cities in the east of the country? Thus it was that Dresden – as well as Chemnitz and Leipzig – were added to the potential hit list. In Paris, at the Supreme Headquarters Allied Expeditionary Force (SHAEF), the HQ of the US and British in Europe, RAF Air Marshal Arthur Tedder – Eisenhower's deputy – also drew up a memo concerning joint American and British air attacks on east-German cities. Although ostensibly more about concentrating on hitting transport links, power plants and telephone exchanges, in cold reality this meant essentially the same as Sir Arthur Harris's approach: that is, the annihilation of the entire target city. Harris received these orders, with the list of potential objectives, very shortly after writing to Portal. When the wintry atmospheric conditions were right, then the bombers would fly out deeper into the east than they had ever been before.

And in airbases around the country, British pilots – and American pilots too, along with others from Canada, Australia, New Zealand and Poland – who had adjusted to a life in which the likelihood of imminent violent, terrible death was ever present were now being asked to push themselves further yet. They would have to find a form of disassociation, for how otherwise would they find it possible to fly deep into the darkness of Germany again and again?

9. Hosing Out

They were intelligent young men; and as some surviving correspondence shows, they were often very sensitive too. The shadow of their fear could be discerned in exchanges of letters with loved ones that started effusively and then began – with each successive letter, week after week – to tighten and become less expressive, more staccato. That was an age when such things could not be spoken aloud. The crewmen of the bombers were all afraid, yet all were taught to believe that such emotion could very easily tip them over a moral line into cowardice and official disgrace. This prospect held its own terrors. So these young men affected wide smiles and ludicrous acronym-based banter even as the empty beds on airbases on the days following missions spoke of the proximity of death.

Back at those bases in eastern England, the authorities ensured that days free of operations were filled with all the distractions high-spirited young men might want: foaming pints of beer, trips to the pub with the concomitant possibility of romance with local girls ('popsies'), variety shows featuring comedians essaying their more daring material. Yet none of these things could ever realistically have made the crews of the Lancaster bombers forget what they had been through, or what they had yet to face.

Contrary to the popular image, many of these young men were serious and reserved and preferred to take their pleasures quietly. One airman was genuinely delighted by the generous allocation of severely rationed oranges; and wrote to his wife about his longing for strawberries.[1] These were men who enjoyed serious authors and serious poets. Poetry was popular throughout Britain during the war, but many in Bomber Command eschewed the lighter works in favour of T. S. Eliot and similarly demanding artists. Miles Tripp, the young airman we encountered in Chapter 6 and who was to find himself at the forefront of the worst of the Dresden bombing raids, became a novelist after the war. He reflected deeply upon his experiences, both while serving and in the years after. His fiction perhaps acted as a lightning rod to protect him from the more violently frightening and traumatic memories, but he did not shy away from those either. What he and his fellow airmen endured now seems wholly inconceivable.

When crews were stood down from planned operations owing to adverse weather or one of a hundred other potential obstacles, this simply screwed the tension and the fear tighter, heightening the anticipation of horrors to come. Sometimes Tripp and his colleagues were taken by bus into nearby large towns for recreation, or to Cambridge to hear lectures, an aural diet more nourishing than the patter of music-hall comedians.

Admiration for the crews' achievements was not universal. By 1945 some political and religious hostility towards them and their role in the conflict was becoming more evident, not only in pained interventions from the Bishops of Chichester and of Bath and Wells but also in the literature of the Bombing Restriction Committee, a group that featured an array of figures such as the Labour MP R. R. Stokes, the philosopher C. E. M. Joad and the actress Sybil Thorndike.[2] In 1944, the committee's leading figure, author Vera Brittain, published *Seed of Chaos*, a passionate denunciation of the moral corrosion to civilization caused by the RAF's area bombing.[3] There were a few who thought that the airmen themselves would simply, finally, refuse to carry out such missions. But these critics, no matter how solid their ethical objections, did not understand at all the nature of life on those airfields, something that went beyond simple duty.

Among the prized attributes the RAF was looking for in recruits was an innate orderliness, both in physical approach and in temperament. The nature of those hours on board the Avro Lancaster bombers required an intensity of concentration and focus and more than this: an ability to react quickly and calmly to the unexpected. What now seems difficult to imagine is how all these thousands of young men were able to carry out operations that they knew very well could see them violently killed while still maintaining that steady gaze.

No one was conscripted into serving with RAF Bomber Command, or indeed with the US Army Air Force. In the case of the

R AF, all those many thousands of young men, broadly aged between nineteen and twenty-six, had volunteered. But this was a very different proposition to Fighter Command, where individual pilots in Spitfires soared through the clouds and had a measure of autonomy when it came to the pursuit and destruction of the enemy. Obviously, any form of combat flying was extremely hazardous – while death was the most obvious hazard, the mutilating burns suffered by survivors could be almost as bad – but there was an unquestionable romanticism attached to individual fighter pilots. When, after the war, Fighter Command's former chief Lord Dowding attended seances in Wimbledon to make contact with the long-dead young men, it was as if he imagined them still flying through the clouds. They had already been halfway to Heaven.[4]

It was different for the bombers: theirs was an industrial form of warfare. Those who volunteered had, from the start, the iron conviction that this was the way the enemy would be defeated: how else could the fear be endured? But there was none the less a stubborn and distinct sense of the metaphysical among many of the aircrew. In the Imperial War Museum, among diaries and correspondence, are many examples of poems written by pilots. There were those who would muse about the euphoria of flight, 'playing hide and seek with the clouds'.[5] The training period held its own range of dangers: fatalities and crashes were common. But these young men were initially caught up in the exhilaration of seeing their world from unfamiliar heights. This sensation occasionally suffused dreams: one crewman, Canadian navigator Frank Blackman, had a recurring and terrifying nightmare that he was flying of his own volition, unable to touch the ground, and that he was being drawn further and further up, the earth disappearing beneath him.[6]

A Lancaster bomber had a crew of seven. Some of these crews had coalesced during training, bands of young friends who knew that they could implicitly trust one another throughout flights of seven or eight hours' duration. There are innumerable photographs of such crews standing beneath their aeroplanes in the benign blue light of English afternoons, their faces seemingly free from strain. Yet as they left the pale sunlight and climbed into the dark, uncomfortable interior of their bombers, the reality was quite different. In his memoirs, Miles Tripp wrote about the 'Eighth Passenger' that accompanied the seven-man bomber crews, the invisible and ubiquitous presence to be found in every aircraft: fear.[7]

Bomber crews frequently formed extraordinarily strong friendships, a result of having to understand and intuit the thoughts and impulses of their crewmates at moments of dire stress. In command, no matter what his rank on the ground, was the pilot. In times of emergency it was his voice that would be listened to foremost. In front of him, in the nose of the plane, was positioned the bomb aimer. He would be staring down through a bubble of clear perspex, ready for when the blank silver darkness of cloud suddenly gave way for the deeper darkness far below, which he would seek to interpret. Like Britain, Nazi Germany operated very strict blackout regulations. Throughout the war the RAF had been developing new electronic navigation aids and target finders: beams bouncing up from the earth, blips on cathode tubes. But the bomb aimer was also reliant on his own judgement. It was hard to avoid being gulled by fires blazing in the cities below; very often these were decoy fires positioned on the edges of suburbs, far from built-up centres. Miles Tripp was a bomb aimer, and at the crucial point in a raid, when the plane was almost over its target, it was understood that for these few moments the aimer took over from the pilot as the dominant voice. It was his course corrections — 'starboard a little, a little more'[8] — that would be acted upon in the immediate seconds before the markers — brilliantly bright coloured flares to provide aiming points for following planes — and incendiaries and bombs were dropped.

Working a few feet back from the pilot — and behind a curtain — was the navigator. The curtain was needed, as the navigator required light and the plane could not afford even a glimmer to be seen. Like the pilot and the aimer, the navigator needed all his powers of concentration: any misreading or misinterpretation of the speed of a headwind or the path of a railway line could result in the bomber veering hundreds of miles off course. There was no let-up throughout the entire operation. Even if it stretched on for seven, eight, sometimes nine hours, the navigator not only had to get the plane to the target but also then get it safely back across Germany and across the Channel to its own airfield.

Close by was the wireless operator. In some respects, these young men were like today's computer experts, devoted to the technology. Although they were not trained to fly, the Lancaster wireless operators had all been through selection processes as rigorous in their own way as those used for pilots. The young volunteers had to be blade-sharp on mathematics, and also extremely articulate. They also had to be proficient in Morse code: an exacting enough discipline to translate and transcribe at high speed while on the ground, but high in the frozen air, in oxygen mask, gloves, bulky flying suit, and all the while contending against the muscular hum of the Lancaster's four Rolls-Royce Merlin engines, the rarest of skills to master.

Wireless operators had not only to deal with all the message traffic in flight but also to field weather reports and help the navigator by identifying the sources of other signals. Added to this, they were expected to man the Lancaster's guns whenever the mid-upper and rear turret gunners had to vacate their station. Immobile in their even colder positions, the gunners needed to take breaks both for the obvious reason (each plane was fitted with a chemical toilet) and literally to stretch their legs. Staying still in a plane that only had the most primitive heating could lead to frostbite, and certainly to a kind of frozen paralysis: they needed a chance to get the blood pulsing again.

The gunners in the perspex bubble turrets were faced with a paradox. On the surface, theirs was the most dangerous and terrifying position, with full view of enemy fighters closing in, the searchlights from below and the night air around exploding with flak; conversely, they at least could see what was coming from all directions and in theory could prepare themselves to meet it. The turrets were fitted with a seat, and the gun barrels poked through the metal fuselage. Even after many adjustments, and late in the war, these turrets still admitted the freezing air. The gunners therefore had to wear the most extraordinary range of protective clothing: Sergeant Russell Margerison recalled how the first item to be donned before an operation was a pair of ladies' silk stockings.[9] Then came more conventional long underwear. There were electrically heated slippers, which were worn inside fur-lined boots: there were also trousers and a tunic that were fur lined. The all-in-one flying suit was similarly electrically heated. Before getting into the turrets, the gunners' faces were completely smeared with an oil preparation to prevent frostbite, and as the operation unfolded, it was the gunners, with that panoramic view, who judged whether to open fire on enemy fighters in the dark who may not have seen them. It was the gunners who watched as incendiaries and then explosives landed on cities far below: mass destruction as glittering light display.

Training was hard, and dangerous; many young recruits found the combination of the aircraft's violent motion and movement of the turret made them impossibly nauseous. But the reality for these young men, who were both warriors and witnesses, went far beyond any normal description. Quite apart from taking aim and picking off enemy fighters coming in at extraordinary angles, the gunners in their turrets saw the fates of so many bombers flying along nearby. It was they who would watch as other planes glowed a deep cherry red, or burst into flame and blinding sparks before dropping out of the sky.

The seventh crew member bore the prosaic material responsibility for the aircraft, and yet he was also closest to its heart. The flight engineer was required to be an expert in matters mechanical, hydraulic and electrical. He would help with take-off, and fuel monitoring while in flight, and he would be sharp on fault corrections and understanding the root of any malfunctions. In addition, the flight engineer would sometimes aid the bomb aimer and he would also be prepared to take over gunner duties to give other crew members a break. But the flight engineer had an important role on the ground too: liaising with the maintenance crews who were looking after the plane. He would have intimate knowledge of any of the craft's aches and pains, or indeed worse problems that it might have developed. The flight engineer tended to the plane when it was at rest and coaxed the best out of it when it was active.

Some four out of ten bomber airmen were either killed, seriously injured or taken prisoner. The crews who were assembling for raids involving a thousand or more bombers towards the end of the war will

not have known of the precise statistics but equally there were no delu-
sions of invulnerability. The diaries of the time feature the leitmotif of
superstition. There were airmen who developed what would now be
termed obsessive-compulsive disorder: men who had to rub their faces
in a certain way just before they boarded; a gunner who had a very
particular order in which he had to get dressed, from the socks up; a
flight engineer who had become manically attached to a certain tweed
cap, and who would not contemplate flying a mission without it.[10]
Because, of course, the sort of courage needed to carry out such lethal
work over and over again could not be – would never be – innate.

There were particular bomber crews whose control and determination seemed so superhuman as to be bordering on the automaton.
These were the Pathfinders, and they were seen as the specially
selected elite of all the Bomber Command personnel. Unlike other
crews, who would face the prospect of thirty operations, these men –
precisely because of their experience and expertise – were required to
fly forty-five. That was not the only factor that would press on raw
nerves. The job of these crews was to lead the mass raiders and – when
over the target – begin to throw down the night-dazzling marker
flares. 'H-Hour was bombing time,' recalled Flight Lieutenant Leslie
Hay.[11] These men were the first to face enemy gunfire from the
ground; the first to be caught in the ghost-white beams of searchlights. The master bombers were the last to leave, circling the area
continually as the following bombers swept in and aimed for the targets that had been marked. Even though this was area bombing, they
still strove for precision, working with maps annotated with munitions factories or ball-bearing works, and seeking to identify these
shapes in the murk below.

The initial wave of Pathfinders would first drop deep green flares
within a mile of the target. These would be followed by what Hay
called 'lights' – a cascade of bright white incendiary sticks;[12] the city
below illuminated, the next planes would release red flares, which
were intended to mark precise targets. There were further colours
yet – orange, blue, pink – denoting different targets. These gaudy
illuminations, nicknamed 'pink pansies' and 'red spots',[13] were easy
marks to release monstrous 'Cookie' bombs upon, designed to crash

through entire buildings, peeling them wide open to receive the fire of the incendiaries. Once the bombs had been released, the suddenly lightened planes lurched into higher altitudes, then banked and pointed the way home towards the Channel and thence the sanctuary of eastern-county airfields. Meanwhile, the master bombers subjected themselves to a doubling of jeopardy. They flew over the roaring, burning cities in order to ensure that targets had been hit. These were airmen who knew that they were prime targets for retribution; the ones staying in the enemy sky the longest, always resisting the most fundamental human temptation to fly away.

It is difficult to imagine how these crews could have found any form of psychological respite back at base. Having seen bullets and flak tear through the outer skin of their planes, having seen faults develop, wings be hit, engines fail, having made it back through the lethal blank of Channel fogs, how was it possible for an airman to contemplate doing the same thing again just a few nights hence? There were those who went for meditative bicycle rides through the flatness of the fens; others who went to the bar. But these were only temporary releases; aircrew sharing rooms on base would frequently wake each other with nightmare screams.

One strand of this life seems even more difficult to contemplate now: the ice-shard ruthlessness of the authorities when it came to dealing with traumatized crew members. The accusation of 'lack of moral fibre' was one that might have found approval from the Nazis, for it suggested not merely a disgraceful inbuilt cowardice but something also possibly genetic: cowardice in the fibre of one's being.[14] Anyone tarred with this description was effectively denounced as a lesser type of man. The concept had been present in the RAF since the start of the war. Air Chief Marshal Keith Park of Fighter Command, for example, had considered such harshness essential at the time of the Battle of Britain: if a pilot was refusing to carry out duties, or displaying obvious signs of fear, then the reasoning was that he should be separated from his fellow airmen as quickly as possible, for it was believed that fear was contagious.

In the army, the aftermath of the First World War had deepened understanding of what was termed 'shell shock'. But curiously, in the RAF the idea that pilots and crew could be the victim of similar breakdowns was – for a time – not acceptable. Any bomber crew exhibiting such symptoms with no obvious medical cause would be removed from base and taken to a special centre. In some cases, the airmen's wings insignia would be cut from their uniforms. All previous service would be disregarded. The idea was that depriving a man of such a proudly won identity would be a deterrent to any other airmen refusing further missions.

It was argued by many that in a time of existential national crisis, such measures were wholly necessary; that if entire squadrons of crewmen were to be infected with the cowardice shown by the odd airman, then the RAF would be left with only inexperienced young novices to fly and navigate and defend the bombers. But as the war developed, RAF psychiatrists at last began to see that the flinty mercilessness of the policy – haunted bombers returned to ground duties and humiliated and scorned by their superiors – was hardly going to change the reality of how men reacted to flying through fire and seeing their comrades incinerated in the sky. When planes returned, Rose turrets (open perspex bubbles for rear gunners fitted to Avro Lancasters specifically designed by the Rose brothers) sometimes had to be 'hosed out', as one ground-crew member put it:[15] not the result of gastric upset, but rather the blood and flesh of crew who had fallen to enemy fire, with pilots steering their torn corpses homeward. Some RAF medics tried to soften the 'moral fibre' policy, pinpointing psychiatric breakdowns and prescribing appropriate treatment in retreats around the country, after which the afflicted pilots would have a chance to return to airborne duties.

It seemed that most bomber crews had, or knew of, someone who either had been removed smartly from duty or was visibly incapable of carrying on. Others, meanwhile, remained adamant that they were fit to continue when clearly they were anything but. A navigator called Bill Burke recalled how, after returning from each tour, having avoided being shot down by anti-aircraft tracer and having faced skies glowing with fires and colliding bombers, he developed the classic aviator's twitch.[16] To all intents and purposes, standing in the saloon bar of the pub, he would be fine; but when he came to light a cigarette, his crewmates would note with sympathy the uncontrollable judder of his hand as it tried to raise the match. In this, he was fortunate: such twitches in others tended to involve the head or even the entire upper body, and were utterly debilitating socially.

For others, physically and mentally shattered men who by continuing to fly were placing their crewmates' lives in even greater jeopardy, the official policy – the RAF's equivalent of handing out white feathers – made withdrawal in effect impossible. 'Since all aircrew were volunteers, no one could be forced to fly,' recalled Miles Tripp, 'but the humiliation and ignominy which followed the confession of a stricken man were such that some men continued to fly long after their nerves were in shreds rather than go LMF [lack of moral fibre].'[17]

By February 1945, however, the psychiatrists were more skilled at diagnosis: the authorities now no longer placed such emphasis on moral fibre. At this stage of the war, they did not need to. In any case, as Bill Burke also observed, there was an opposite (and presumably equally dangerous) psychological problem, which he termed 'flak happy'.[18] There were, among these young men, those who despite their twitches and their screaming bad dreams found themselves morbidly addicted to the adrenaline of their tours. These individuals – even having completed all the operational sorties they were due – craved to fly more.

This was the curious mental landscape that airmen inhabited in February 1945. Even as the Allies were moving steadily east, and the Soviets closed in, the air war saw a new kind of intensity. But it was not only British airmen – and their comrades from around the world, including Australia, Canada, Poland – who were being asked to draw from deeper wells of fortitude for the raids to come. American airmen – some of whom shared the philosophical doubts emanating from their own high commands about the efficacy and ethics of area bombing – were preparing for their own missions in parallel. The USAAF still favoured attacking by day; the fact that they were to end up following the British with a further raid on Dresden would colour the propaganda rising from the bombing for decades afterwards.

10. The Devil Will Get No Rest

The bomber crews of the US Eighth Air Force were far from home, and from familiar comforts. In the famous pamphlet entitled 'Instructions for American Servicemen in Britain', the men were told that their host nation was 'smaller than North Carolina'.[1] The consideration of cultural differences was good manners, but cannot have been of much help when it came to the raw fear of bombing missions. In those extremities, the US airmen had only one another to turn to. And although the mortality rate did not match that of their British counterparts, none the less, by the end of the conflict some 26,000 American airmen had died on European missions – and a great many of those who lived had seen close friends hideously killed. For some, that was even more frightening than the prospect of their own death. When these men returned from operations, having been subjected to ferocious anti-aircraft fire and sub-zero temperatures, and sometimes having been starved of oxygen and suffering from frostbite, they were obliged to try to recover physically and mentally under unfamiliar skies, and in dark-soiled countryside, flat and fretted with ditches and black streams. Lincolnshire, Rutland, Norfolk and Suffolk were rich in pubs with a thickly accented clientele, but came up short on the urban neon lighting and comfortable movie theatres that were the signifiers of their own land. Such details, so trivial sounding when Europe was awash with blood, were actually of great importance. On around 200 airfields across England, great efforts were made to ensure that the near half-million American airmen and their ground crews who had been sent to aid the Allied war effort felt at home.

Among those who would find themselves carrying out a daylight swoop over Dresden just hours after the British bombardment were young men like Morton Fiedler, who was twenty years old.[2] Fiedler was born and brought up in the tough steel-producing city of Pittsburgh, Pennsylvania; he had signed up as an aviation cadet and by the age of nineteen was a second lieutenant. Serving with 18th Bomb Squadron, 34th Bomb Group, Fiedler found himself transplanted from the thick industrial air and clamour of Pittsburgh to Mendlesham, a tiny village in Suffolk. The tour of duty was originally to be twenty-five missions; Fiedler was to fly thirty-two. It was his own free choice.[3]

Gordon Fenwick was born in 1923 in the small city of Sault Ste Marie at the northernmost tip of Michigan, just across the water from Canada and more or less in the middle of the Great Lakes.[4] This was a town dominated by shipping, and the 1930s Depression had hit it hard. As a boy, Fenwick took himself out into the country to hunt and fish to put food on the table. He was bright, and after he left school he studied engineering at the University of Michigan before he, like Fiedler, signed up for the war. His eyesight was insufficiently sharp for the role of pilot but he was snappy with Morse, and so it was that he came to England, based with 401st Bomb Group at Deenethorpe, Northamptonshire: a thatched pub, a grand stately home and small loamy fields bordering the base and its wide, flat concrete runway. From his very first missions, Fenwick understood immediately the proximity of death. On one flight, he recalled, 'a piece of flak sliced through the radio room and missed my head by about a millimetre'.[5] On another, his plane, *Mary Alice*, was so ferociously attacked by enemy fighters, with so many parts of the fuselage shot away, that it barely managed to cough its way back over the English Channel and make an emergency landing just a little beyond the white cliffs of Dover. He would also be called upon to serve as a nose gunner; in the B-17 bombers, the nose gunner occupied a transparent blister at the very front of the plane, equipped with either guns or auto-cannons. Like the pilot situated above him, he could see the defensive storm that the plane was flying into. Possibly this position made each mission a tiny fraction easier in psychological terms; on those daylight flights, a view of what one was flying towards rather than the view from a position on the side or at the rear of the craft could give a small illusion of agency or traction. The nose gunner would sometimes also conduct navigation duties.

And there were so many other serious young recruits: men such as Wendell Tague, twenty years old, born and raised in Iowa; Willmore Fluman, twenty-two, who hailed from Virginia. They came from a wide range of domestic backgrounds across a vast continent; sharp, smart and deeply committed. Yet 'commitment' is hardly adequate as a description, for these men, and their British counterparts, must also in a sense have felt themselves to be sacrificial warriors who had pledged their very lives to the cause. How else could it have been psychologically possible for Morton Fiedler, among others, to complete his tour of duty and then challenge death directly by volunteering for more?

After America came into the war in December 1941 following the Japanese attack on Pearl Harbor, the initial build-up of American air power on British soil was slow, but by 1944, and the tumultuous days following D-Day and the invasion of Europe, there was an entire parallel culture to be found among the villages of eastern England. The ubiquity of the American presence led it to be dubbed 'the friendly invasion'.[6] There was also, unmistakably, from the start, a sense that the Eighth Air Force was perhaps a shade more considered and careful in its approach when compared to Arthur Harris's Bomber Command. There was, at least for the aircrews, the feeling that their missions were highly specific; rather than area bombing, they were instead concentrating on knocking out particular factories and railway junctions. The fact that such raids caused what was then termed 'spillage' and today would be called 'collateral damage' was seen as regrettable but inevitable.[7]

The morning briefings at all those airbases were times of silent tension. The airmen awoke early, had a good breakfast and then assembled for their meeting. Behind a blue curtain was the map that would show that day's objective. When the curtain was pulled back, any operation involving a surgical strike on German movements within France or the Low Countries was greeted with a sense of relief; when the unveiling revealed an operation deep into Germany, there were groans from some, while others were too depressed and too frightened even to make that small protest.

Continual efforts were made to ease this psychological stress by creating a happy and relaxing on-base atmosphere. The aircrews were always well fed, and on some bases there were specialized bakeries providing them with the varieties of bread that they were used to back home.[8] Many airmen took to the village pubs with a mix of lively curiosity and good humour, while in the larger towns there were attempts in dance halls to bring seriously enthusiastic jazz to the local and by then largely female patrons. In the village of Lavenham in Suffolk – an absurdly pretty half-timbered vision of medieval English architecture, complete with a fourteenth-century church – the residents had since the start of the war been accustomed to RAF officers in the local pub, the Swan; by 1943, with the base one of the first to be turned over to the Americans, this bar, with its low ceilings and open fireplaces, had become the haunt of fascinated USAAF officers instead.[9] Here was an England that seemed almost defiantly caricatured: warm ales instead of cold lagers, whiskered locals, darts. It became a tradition for the US visitors to sign one of the bar's white-washed walls. Their signatures remain today.

There were some reports from the Mass Observation project (civilian participants in which submitted regular diaries to the relevant department) that these new arrivals were considered to be brash and boastful, and that they seemed neither respectful towards nor inter-ested in local matters or people. Yet this is possibly an impression created by a generation gap: the older inhabitants of east-coast vil-lages and towns might have resented what they saw as boorishness and vulgarity, but for many younger people it was a source of hyp-notic fascination. Children were gripped not only by the sight of B-17s and B-24s taking off and coming in to land; they were also mesmerized by the ephemera that these airmen were supplied with – the bottles of Coca-Cola, the tubs of Brylcreem. All these children had been raised on Saturday-morning cinema shows: westerns, science-fiction serials, films with gangsters. Here was an impossibly distant and exciting world somehow made real.

Similarly, when the band leader Glenn Miller came to play for American airmen, young British women who had volunteered for the Women's Royal Navy Service (Wrens) scrambled to attend these concerts too.[10] Of course, there were innumerable romances and not only, as was so waspishly observed by many then, because American airmen could procure invaluable silk stockings and mouth-watering tinned chicken. For young people, wartime always carries a sharp-ened erotic edge.

Away from their missions, US airmen were sometimes granted three days' leave. London was the obvious lure. Gordon Fenwick recalled travelling down from Northamptonshire not just to gaze upon the soot-besmirched landmarks but to sample the capital's pubs. Its antiquated and cramped saloon bars appear not to have dismayed him, and he remembered with some pleasure the friendly joshing from English soldiers at the counter repeating that familiar line about the Americans being 'oversexed, overpaid and over here'. The Tommies were amazed, Fenwick remembered, when they heard the American comeback about the English for the first time: 'Underpaid, under-sexed – and under Eisenhower!'[11]

In some cases, the lightness of their demeanour masked a rather more reflective outlook. American airmen were often more religious than their British counterparts and represented many different Christian denominations as well as having a sizeable Jewish contingent. Among the serving chaplains at the US airbases was the fondly remembered (and distinctively named) Major Method Cyril Billy, known to the airmen as 'Brother Billy'. Navigator Eugene Spearman recalled: 'We . . . taxied out to the end of the runway and awaited our signal for take off. Standing there during most of my missions even in rain or snow [was] Bro Billy, holding a Bible. His being there was such a blessing for me. Just knowing someone was praying for me made me feel better.'[12]

As with their British counterparts, an unquantifiable amount was being asked of the US airmen, and on-base psychiatrists were closely examining all the most common symptoms of combat stress. This was partly compassionate and partly practical, the authorities anxious that it might become progressively more difficult to ask, persuade or force men into battle. One airman recalled watching a plane disintegrate in mid-air and pieces of what he assumed were fuselage hitting the windscreen in front of him. With horror, he realized that he was seeing not metal but flesh; fragments of a dead airmen, blood and muscle, which became fused in the freezing air with the glass, meaning that those in the cockpit had to gaze upon these mortal remains all the hundreds of miles back to base.

It was such events that prompted the nightmares: airmen dreaming that they were trapped in burning planes, thrashing desperately, and even injuring themselves as they fell out of bed. Doctors monitored crew members as they neared the end of their tour, noting how these young men had aged in the space of a year to look fifteen years older or more. On the days when they were not flying, some were silent; others were prone to lightning outbursts of intense anger. Others exhibited a feverish desire for sex. As with their British counterparts, almost all were united by the greater fear of not being able to go on; of letting down their country and their fellow crew members.

The actor James Stewart – the most famous of those Americans who made a new home in Tibenham, a tiny community deep in the heart of rural Norfolk – was the commander of 703 Squadron and flew many B-24 missions over France and Germany, always with very specific targets for the bombs. Although remarkably fortunate himself, his plane yawing back and forth amid the red-hot ferocity of anti-aircraft guns but getting through, Stewart saw a number of other planes atomized and often returned to base to learn of the fiery deaths of friends.[13] For a time, he later revealed, he went 'flak happy' and was sent to a 'flak farm' to recuperate. He, too, visibly aged; after the war, upon his return to Hollywood, he was obliged to start portraying older men, and in the Hitchcock psychological thriller *Vertigo* (1958) he gives a powerful performance of a man in deep trauma. But despite all the mental turbulence, there was no change in Stewart's determination to fight the war to the end.

In a curious way, it is possible that American pilots and crew were shielded by a stronger sense that their actions ultimately were a moral good. Since the 1930s, as Americans set to work building up a more powerful air force, there had been certain orthodoxies established, one of which was the belief that 'daylight precision bombing' could be mastered to such a degree that collateral injuries and fatalities could be kept to a minimum. Pilots learning their skills at the Army Air Corps Tactical School in Montgomery, Alabama, were still being taught that 'terror bombing of civilians would provoke public outrage'.[14] Similarly, by 1940, it was understood by all within the US Air War Plans Division that there was 'no historical evidence that

aerial bombardment of cities, towns and villages has ever been pro-
ductive'.[15] They would have been watching, among other examples,
the British in the 1930s using such bombing techniques in Trans-
jordan and Palestine in efforts to quell local insurgencies.

However, by the winter of 1944, and the Battle of the Bulge, some
layers of fastidiousness had been stripped away from the USAAF.
Though there was still the conviction, in contrast to Bomber Command, that a mass raid carried out over a city in broad daylight would
allow for very specific targeting, there were now occasions when
the city itself would be the target. The reason was this: it seemed –
bafflingly to many in senior command – that the Germans, who
ought to have been on the edge of collapse, were somehow managing
to regroup. That they were largely spent was clear to see, yet the Nazi
leadership seemed to have inspired a terrible tenacity in those forces
they still had. There were senior American commanders who feared
that the war could go on for another year. This meant that the targeting of certain German cities had a practical purpose other than simple
Vergeltung, or retribution. In the early days of February 1945, US
bombers launched a daylight attack on Berlin: it did not aim for
factories or railways but for the city centre itself.

Broadly, General Carl Spaatz, who had overall control, and General
Ira Eaker, who oversaw all squadrons, tried to resist the gravitational
pull exerted by Bomber Command when it came to targeting civilian
districts. As the American ambassador to Tokyo had put it a few years
previously: '*Facilis descensus averni est*' – the descent into Hell is easy.[16]
None the less, like their British partners, they believed that the most
effective way to decapitate resurgent German forces was ever more
ferocious attacks from the air.

Dresden had earlier been identified by the USAAF as a useful
location to hit not long after D-Day, and on the afternoon of 7 October 1944, a tight formation of B-24s had flown deep into eastern
Germany with a very specific aim indeed: Dresden's main railway
marshalling yards, north-west of the main station. This raid was about
causing deep disruption: not only severing the railway artery running all the way from Berlin to Prague but also setting scarce
industrial materials ablaze. The raid was considered a success, yet it

also says something about the nihilism of that late stage of the war that the figure of 270 Dresden citizens killed somehow seemed unremarkable. Indeed, the Nazi-run newspapers – local and national – did not even mention the death toll (or, indeed, the bombing).

On 16 January 1945, the Americans flew over once more. One of the intended targets that day was a synthetic-oil plant about forty miles north of Dresden in a little town called Ruhland. There were innumerable difficulties; many of the bombers ended up striking an industrial plant at the nearby town of Lauta. This, however, was considered highly advantageous as well: the plant in question was producing aluminium. Once more, however, Dresdeners that afternoon realized that the air-raid sirens were no longer howling out only false warnings. Many of the bombers, having missed all their targets, made for the clearer certainty of the designated secondary aiming point: those Dresden railway marshalling yards. This time the death toll from the raid was 376 people. In among the high explosives dropped were 18,000 incendiaries: this was a foretaste of the fires to come.

At the time, 'miracle weapons' were a frequent topic of conversation among German civilians, and they were an idea that was genuinely feared by the Allies. The summer and autumn of 1944 had seen the Nazis aiming their V-1 flying bombs and V-2 rockets at London (the V stood for *Vergeltungswaffen*, 'reprisal weapons'): automated death whispering across the Channel. But there had been intense speculation in the Air Ministry about even more apocalyptic armaments. There was a real anxiety, for instance, that the Nazis would refine the technology further to deliver not just explosives but lethal poisonous gases such as Sarin. The Americans were anxious too: they suspected that it would not be long before a feral Führer launched biological warfare, raining down toxins that could cause fatal embolisms among thousands within hours. In addition to all this was the development of the Messerschmitt Me 262, Germany's first fighter jet.[17] How long would it be before these extraordinary aircraft – which had a flight endurance of up to ninety minutes and streaked through the firmament at unmatchable speeds of almost 550 miles per hour – were refined further?

This was why the American focus on any German industry – and especially that buried deep within the east of the country – had a genuine urgency. Draining the morale of the civilians below might have been counted as a bonus but the real aim, in fixing upon everything from aluminium works to railway lines, was to try to draw some of the venom of an unceasingly ingenious Nazi war industry.

The crews on these raids were sometimes airborne for close to eight or nine hours; many were simply blasted out of the sky, others developed engine troubles and had to crash land in or bail out over enemy territory, facing the prospect of permanent injury and disability or worse if they made it to earth alive. For all the careful images of insouciance and bravado – young Americans grinning and shrugging next to the nubile women who featured almost invariably as their nose-cone art – the reality was that sometimes crews returning to eastern England would descend from their planes and find themselves helpless with tears.

When the British bomber crews were briefed on the afternoon of 13 February 1945, and when their American counterparts saw behind that blue curtain the following morning what their target was to be, the first reaction among many was about not the city of Dresden itself, but its location so far east, further than most of them had ever flown before. Even targets in the west of Germany invoked dread; this one sparked a trepidation that was deeper yet. All these young airmen – Leslie Hay and Miles Tripp with the RAF, Morton Fiedler, Wendell Tague and his colleague Howard Holbrook with the 'Mighty Eighth' Air Force – contemplated their own deaths: men who knew that their blazing destruction might be necessary for victory.

The name Dresden may have meant as little to these men as Pforzheim or Magdeburg – they were just cities, after all, with Nazi soldiers and armaments factories. This was a form of warfare so relentless, and so nihilistic, that even the most thoughtful and sensitive airmen became numbed to their targets. As Gordon Fenwick recalled: 'There was a today, maybe a tomorrow. That was it.'[18]

PART TWO
Schreckensnacht

11. The Day of Darkness

In the thin cold wind of winter, this was – by tradition – a day of the brightest colour: green wool, purple and pink silk ribbons, gingham and rich embroidery, scarlet devil horns, huge yellow bows. In the eyes of the adults, the costumes for Fasching – the festival that marked Shrove Tuesday, the day before Lent – were both aesthetically cheering and also evoked the warmth of memories of celebrations in previous years. By contrast, the youngsters who wore this rich array of fancy dress treated it with full gravity and seriousness. In the chilly damp of 13 February 1945, with Dresden and its buildings and gardens and trees a uniform grey and smudged brown, and its adults and elderly people looking tired and drawn with anxiety, the city's children were insisting on dressing-up boxes and trunks being hauled out of attics and sheds and basements. Their mothers were happy to oblige.

For young Georg Frank, this indulgence was widespread in his street: the children 'fooling around in colourful carnival costumes' and adults, looking on, 'forgetting their worries about the increasingly serious state of the war'.[1] This little boy was very excited about his own costume: 'a colourful clown's bow' and a 'wide white collar'.[2] Elsewhere, the grave teenager Winfried Bielss noted approvingly 'the costumed and painted children'; he observed that, while 'total war had stifled almost all public amusements', there was still 'this glint in the calendar'.[3] Even the older citizens were temporarily diverted: Georg Erler and his wife Marielein remembered how previous Fasching festivals had coincided with 'the most grim cold', but this day, by contrast, was blessed with some 'serene sunshine and mild weather'.[4] They saw children out in the terraced streets of Neustadt, perhaps not as boisterous as in other years, but cheerfully playing in their fancy dress none the less. In the Altstadt on the other side of the river, seven-year-old Dieter Elsner, whose father was verger of the Frauenkirche, had been most insistent on being allowed to wear his prized American cowboy costume, complete with a tomahawk – presumably and imaginatively a trophy of battle on the plains. Despite Germany having declared war on America in 1941, Wild West iconography was remarkably persistent. The hugely popular cowboy novels written by German author Karl May were still read by Dresdeners.

Fasching was and is marked across the whole of Germany, but in subtly different ways. In the more westerly cities it grew out of medieval traditions invoking the spirit of misrule and for a long time had a distinctly pagan flavour: costumes evoking the Green Man or the masked personifications of the winter season as a desiccated, cackling old woman. In Saxony, the celebrations had more of an element of the world turned upside down, clownish fools elevated to the high halls of power. But there were still the evocations of darker forces: people dressed as imps and demons, manifestations of the forests. Linked to this were the ceremonies on hills that culminated in vast fires, symbolizing the defeat of the cold and the advent of spring. A sophisticated and intellectual city such as Dresden could never quite abandon itself freely to such rituals: here instead simply was a festival before the days of abstinence that preceded Easter. Tuesday 13 February 1945 was a day of drinking and socializing, and it was the children in their costumes – including miniature devils – who provided that sense of occasion.

That occasion was to come a little later though; this was, after all, still a school day for those pupils whose schools had not been requisitioned by the military or to shelter refugees. Thirteen-year-old Helmut Voigt, who lived in the well-to-do south-western Dresden suburb of Plauen, was set a task by his teacher near the beginning of his day. The school authorities had noticed that some doors were insecure and needed new locks and bolts. Helmut was given some money and asked to find and buy some; this was a simple-sounding task, but in a time of chronic material shortage, such items were elusive. The local ironmongers had none. The idea that Helmut eventually hit upon, necessitating a visit to the Altstadt, would shape the trajectory of both his day and his life.[5]

★

The city's schools had been assiduous in teaching their pupils about emergency measures in the event of an attack; young Dieter Haufe and his classmates had been instructed on how to smother burning phosphorus with sand.[6] Elsewhere, at Müller Gelinek school, the teachers were quick to issue bombing alerts to their pupils. The building had had a very near miss in the American raid on the railway marshalling yards of Saturday 16 January, an occasion described to them as 'a terrorist attack on Dresden'. Ursula Skrbek recalled that at her own school, the authorities sent children home early almost every day in this lethal time.[7] Other pupils were drilled in trooping down to improvised basement shelters.

By now Dresden's children regarded the city's improvised shelters as part of the texture of everyday life. Georg Frank, who lived with his family in an apartment block, recalled the steep staircase that led down beneath it, and a brick-lined main cellar corridor, off which were smaller cells, each with its own wooden door. The Frank family had enhanced their little space with a table and one or two wooden chairs; other seats were made very simply from wooden boards. Georg remembered that the old brickwork was crumbling in places, with gaps in the mortar.

Dieter Haufe's family had been forced out of their previous accommodation by bomb damage. The shelter in their new apartment in Pieschen – a suburb to the north of the Elbe on a hill overlooking the Altstadt – was actually a converted workshop. This semi-basement had narrow, horizontal windows high up on the walls through which the sky could be seen.

Other shelters were rather more sturdily appointed; the basement of the Taschenberg Palace, opposite the Zwingergarten and the Catholic cathedral, featured concrete flooring and steel doors. The palace was being used by Wehrmacht officials and municipal and police figures; this was not a refuge intended for the general public. Yet just a few streets away lay an underground space which was open to anyone who might have considered it; the mighty edifice of the Frauenkirche, standing in the open square of the Neumarkt, had a crypt. This was a low-ceilinged labyrinth of arches and ancient tombstones. The Frauenkirche crypt was not actually consecrated for burials; the old headstones set into the thick walls had been placed there centuries earlier following the destruction of another church nearby.

The Frauenkirche was surrounded with a busy mix of cafes and small shops in tall nineteenth-century buildings that contained innumerable apartments above ground and warrens of equally venerable cellars below. The one concession that Gauleiter Martin Mutschmann had made towards providing the city's population with practical, viable shelters was to allow work to be carried out underground. Instead of remaining as separate cells, brick walls were knocked through so that all the cellars along a street were connected. The end result was a tight subterranean labyrinth, cellars running beneath one street linking up with the passageways beneath others. As well as having access points from the private premises the cellars serviced, the tunnels emerged at two open-air destinations: the stone embankment of the River Elbe was in one direction, while the other took a route that once more saw the light at the Great Garden park in the city centre.

Some families, conscientiously following official advice, had taken the precaution of prepacking suitcases with necessities, including gas masks and blankets. Ten-year-old Gisela Reichelt, whose family lived in an apartment block just two streets away from the bustling main railway station, had been through the drill many times and had become quite used to the musty darkness of the building's basement.[8] Lying as it did on the south side of both the railway tracks and the Altstadt, this was a rather more modern cellar that connected with no others. The apartment building was at the foot of the gentle incline that led up towards the southern suburbs. In this district, there were wider avenues, and tree-filled courtyards. Gisela recalled that that afternoon, she and her friends had played out in the crisp cold air. Their shouts and laughs would have bounced and echoed off the tall walls.

A little to the west of the city, sitting in a small rocky valley, was a business concern that had its own, pre-built shelters. The owners of the Felsenkeller brewery, a construction dating back to the late nineteenth century, had been innovative about using the landscape around it, and tunnels had been bored deep into the rocks adjacent to the main buildings. Now, like most other factories in Dresden, Felsen-keller had been turned over to intricate and technical war work; the lighting company Osram now occupied a large part of it, producing instruments in tungsten. Seventeen-year-old Margot Hille, who had started working at the brewery the year previously immediately after leaving school, was on the morning of 13 February preparing for another day of a job that she occasionally considered wearisome.[9]

That February, one recurring annoyance had involved Fräulein Hille's working hours. She started very early, just after dawn, and was supposed to finish at 4.30 p.m. But the director of her department 'often came in just before closing time and started dictating letters to the secretary'. As a result, Fräulein Hille had to wait around as the secretary then typed the letters up, had the finished copies approved by the director and then placed them in envelopes for Fraulein Hille to take to the large post office a mile or so away in Plauen. The result, she remembered, was that she 'often did not get home until after 6 p.m.'.[10] On the morning of 13 February, Margot was tired; she had had a run of restless, sleep-broken nights.

There were workers all over the city who, themselves facing drear-ily long hours, somehow managed to not quite see the forced labourers around them. Dieter Haufe's fifty-three-year-old father had been engaged in local construction projects, including the digging of tank pits. Now he was, as Haufe observed, compelled to take on duties at the enormous Goehle-Werk plant just to the north-west of the Alt-stadt, up in the green hilly suburbs.[11] Here was one of Dresden's centres of slave labour: in this complex dedicated to the manufacture of instrumentation for aircraft and submarines worked Jewish women selected from concentration camps for whom the factory had become their world: intense hours, insufficient sleep in crowded dormitories, then the return under artificial light to complicated assembly lines. Dieter Haufe's middle-aged father might himself have been tired, but his life was still largely his own.

In addition to all those factories that ringed the city, there were also, on that February morning, hundreds of people engaged in the wide variety of civic duties that kept the city's blood pulsing through its veins. As well as the extensive tram network – the rails and wires criss-crossing at busy road junctions – there were public buses, a few of which were, remarkably, being driven by prisoners of war. Dieter Patz recalled that his school bus was driven by 'a young man with a dark complexion and black hair'.[12] The passengers, with perfect civility, greeted him as 'Alex'; he was a French soldier captured long ago.

Early on that Shrove Tuesday morning the city's railways were already a tightly packed mass of humanity. The central station was receiving innumerable men, women and children disembarking from trains that had come from the east. The rails and the platforms were elevated; beneath lay the station concourse and below that were subways and cellars. Extraordinarily, despite the chaos, there was still a wide range of facilities on offer at the station. For soldiers who were passing through there was a small laundry at which they could drop off their kit bags to have their uniforms cleaned as they spent a couple of hours in the town.

The station also had a number of city policemen on duty; not for fear of disorder but rather to forestall confusion among the countless refugees that might have gridlocked the entire place. The railway workers, too, needed their wits about them to cope with the many platform and timetable changes as they informed tired and sometimes traumatized families which trains they should take when and from where. Even for experienced railway workers such as Georg Thiel, the semblance of order in the station dissolved with each arrival.

And outside, in the streets leading north, that fragile sense of trying to maintain cohesion in the face of teeming chaos persisted; here were refugees on foot, pushing north towards the Altstadt, the river, the new town and the leafy suburbs and countryside beyond. Dresden's tram routes were becoming increasingly congested and awkward, horses and carts dolefully moving across the rails, pedestrians crowding one another off the pavements. The streets around Prager Strasse had always been busy in peacetime; now there was an edge of incipient anarchy to the sometimes directionless throng.

Just a quarter of a mile away, close to the bulk of the grey stone municipal offices, the even more severe stone of the Kreuzkirche held out the prospect of calm. On that day before Lent, in the sombre dark of the great church, the choir were preparing for the following day's services. The people outside, pushing and dodging their way through the human tide of winter coats, will have heard the occasional crystalline notes of sopranos and altos pierce the air. Such disconnected snatches of familiar devotional hymns can have the effect of stopping time; a moment of dislocation. But reality could never be held back for long.

Also struggling through traffic and crowds throughout that day was the philology professor Victor Klemperer. That morning, before 8 a.m., he had left his lodgings in one of the Judenhäuser facing the empty site of the old synagogue – the cramped, cold accommodation that he and his wife had been forced into, along with so many others, near the Frauenkirche. His instructions for the day from the municipal authorities were to deliver swiftly a circular letter to seventy of the city's remaining two hundred-odd Jews, in addresses scattered around the city. All those who received it were required for 'out-of-doors-work duties'.[13] The letter instructed them to pack clothes and emergency provisions to last three days. They were to report the next morning to an address near the municipal offices. Clearly, they were being taken somewhere.

Professor Klemperer was informed that he and his wife Eva would not be required to report for such duties. Instantly, he told his diary, he felt the distance open up between him and those he was handing the letter to.[14] Unusually, to complete his task, the authorities permitted him to travel by tram: a mode of transport forbidden to Jews. The order to report for 'outdoor work' duties seemed to take no account of age or, indeed, ability to work. Klemperer was in no doubt what the letter meant to the recipients: a train journey, the silence of a railway siding, death. In hushed evening discussions in the Judenhäuser, rumour and dark speculation had been shared. The dread was all the worse for being so rational.

Professor Klemperer was convinced that his own apparent reprieve was extremely temporary, and that he and his wife would be facing the same prospect within a week. He dutifully made his tour of the Judenhäuser scattered around the city, delivering the summons to addressees ranging from ten-year-old girls to women in their seventies to mothers with small children. The mothers seemed stoical, but as soon as their doors closed Klemperer could hear them weeping uncontrollably.

The professor had seen so many years of accumulated cruelties, large and small, but even with so much experience of so much viciousness, the pain never diminished, and nor was it ever blunted. He and Dresden's other Jews had endured both the sadism of the Gestapo and the blank indifference of their fellow citizens. But now – at a point where he and so many others had spent the evenings speculating about the rate of the advance of the Red Army, and about the state of the German defences – this seemed like a final effort to rid the city of every last individual Jew just as it seemed that the world was about to be transformed once more.

And because their community had been ruthlessly forced into its separate state, so Professor Klemperer and his Jewish associates looked at the fears of their fellow citizens with an almost dispassionate curiosity: whereas, as he wrote, Jews feared most of all the Gestapo, gentile Dresdeners were terrified of the Soviets.[15] There were, he noted, rumours circulating that Soviets dropped in by parachute were infiltrating the city, pretending to be German. There were also rumours that Gauleiter Mutschmann was preparing to flee Dresden. A friend of the professor told him that he had seen German soldiers attaching explosives to the Carolabrücke, the main bridge over the Elbe, presumably in preparation for delaying the ineluctable advance of the Red Army.

The story was corroborated elsewhere by sixty-seven-year-old Georg Erler and his wife Marielein. On that day, they too had been in a state of some anxiety, which found its outward expression in elaborate schemes to protect all the beautiful heirlooms that they had accumulated across the years. Herr and Frau Erler lived to the east of the city, in a smart apartment with a large garden, in a street full of grand villas. Alongside their paintings and porcelain, they owned a quantity of silverware; the previous day, 12 February, they had put as much as they could of it into an improvised strongbox, placed it in their car and driven some twenty miles south to an acquaintance in

Dippoldiswalde. Herr Erler felt that in the event of the Red Army marauding through the district, there was a chance at least in this more rural corner that their treasure might be missed.

But on 13 February neither he nor his wife had been able to shake off the prickling sense of anxious insecurity. Their son and daughter lived in the northern city of Lüneburg, so they had no vulnerable dependants in Dresden, but their elegant apartment seemed more than just a home; everything they valued about life seemed contained within those walls. Georg Erler recalled with sensual vividness the beauty of their Biedermeier mahogany table, covered with green silk; the armchairs and sofas; the oil paintings depicting distant members of Marielein's family, including one eye-catching portrait in which Friedrich Cappel and his wife Louise were depicted in costume, he in the hunting clothes of the forest and she in more sumptuous finery. In addition to this was a no less striking fantasy study in oil of Aphrodite rising from the waves, by an artist called Boyen, whom Erler noted had succumbed to 'mental annihilation'.[16] Some of their paintings had, like the silver, been packed up. A few were in the coal cellar; others had been sent to their daughter in Lüneburg. There was also a 'sonorous' piano, which Marielein played; Herr Erler had bought sheet music 'for some of Beethoven's sonatas' in the hope that some of their cultured guests might care to try it, but few had.

Herr Erler was especially protective of their extensive collection of beautiful Meissen porcelain. There were Copenhagen vases, decorated with cyclamen and dandelions;[17] gold-rimmed vases; a coffee service, also rimmed with gold leaf; there were bowls and plates daintily decorated with cornflowers and coffee cups that were souvenirs unique to the Erler family, adorned with specially commissioned silhouettes of long-dead relatives.

'There were always fresh flowers from the garden in vases,' recalled Herr Erler, proud that the apartment spoke of refinement and taste.[18] There were modern accoutrements too, from the white-tiled fireplace to the standing electric lamps to the gramophone player kept within its own cabinet. There was a strong sense, from Herr Erler's recollections, of a domestic world that was perhaps unusually self-contained and unusually aesthetically pleasing. On the early afternoon of the

13th, the couple decided to go out for a walk; for both had heard the rumour about the Carolabrücke being primed with explosives. The twin itches of curiosity and unease were too strong to ignore.

Marielein Erler had believed that the city would be safe quite simply because of its renowned beauty, but doubt must have crept in as she and her husband crossed the bridge heading north, towards the Neustadt, and saw the soldiers at work. 'We wanted to see if it was really like that,' remembered Frau Erler. 'We had heard that dynamite was being prepared to blow up the bridge. Yes, it was like that! Soldiers kept watch at several places on the bridge. We asked them if it was true about the dynamite. "It's true!" they answered.'[19] As they reached the opposite side, they turned back to look at the Altstadt. 'We looked into the Elbe,' recalled Frau Erler, 'and gazed at the beautiful panorama of Dresden.'[20] Georg Erler was the air-raid 'block warden' for their street. He was to be on duty that night.

Someone else who had spent a lot of time speculating about the Soviet advance – and about the terrible firepower that the Red Army would bring to the city – was also moving through the streets that day, near the functionalist buildings of the university. Mischka Danos was planning a party for that evening in his bedroom back in the large old guesthouse he was living in. He was hoping to serve his guests a Russian delicacy called Kissel, a form of sour jelly mixed with berries, although there were certain ingredients that he still needed to procure. Other than that, the Latvian's day had been filled with work for Professor Barkhausen in his electrical research laboratory. Given the general circumstances of the war, Danos had had the most remarkably relaxed few weeks: he had only recently returned from a winter vacation, spent partly at Innsbruck.[21] It was as though the young physicist was moving in some parallel dimension to all other civilians; a life where pleasant travel and buoyantly intellectual conversation were still perfectly possible. The very idea of serving his guests a Russian recipe that coming evening was itself remarkably insouciant, given the thunderous proximity of the invading Soviet armies.

Almost a thousand miles away, under a sky that was clear and chilly, Miles Tripp had left his RAF base that afternoon on his motorbike.[22]

He knew that he and his crewmates would not be receiving their briefing until the late afternoon, so had taken the opportunity to roar through the country lanes that bisected small green fields and clumps of woodland on his way to Bury St Edmunds; the motorbike had an irksome fuel leak that he wanted mending.

Tripp and his crewmates had recently received the news that their tour of duty was being extended; they were now required to fly forty missions over Germany before they would be released from bombing duties. As Tripp saw it, this was the crossing of the border into another realm, a moment of transformation when profound fear became something more metallic. He and his crewmates were all very well aware of the mortality rates, yet there were still sparks of hope in their souls, expressed tangentially in a reluctant belief in the supernatural. Tripp and his fellows were easily spooked: their crewmate Harry, a Jamaican airman, had developed an uncanny ability to predict – hours before they were told – exactly which city in Germany they would be targeting next. Was he getting privileged inside information or was there something else, a form of preternatural premonition, going on? Harry had told Miles a while back that he had had a dream: he had been friends with another airman in Canada who had died in a crash. Harry told Miles that his friend had visited him in that dream, holding his hand out in greeting. 'I don't like that sort of dream,' Harry had told Miles.[23] Miles could not have agreed more.

But on that afternoon of 13 February Miles Tripp was seeking out dull normality in Bury St Edmunds, the busy little timber-housed town under the sky of pale blue and white, leaving the motorcycle with a mechanic and then, on some impulse, making a visit to the local library. Tripp sat and watched the sun shafting through the great windows before selecting several volumes of poetry from the shelves, with which he returned to his desk. The poetry, he later recalled, 'was an unconscious effort to establish a connection with an earlier, safer existence, because I was reading the poems that I enjoyed at school'.[24] Yet the works brought no ease. Instead, Tripp, sitting at that library desk, found himself feeling increasingly nervous. It was time to pick up the repaired motorcycle; and as Tripp returned to base, the sun was low over the western horizon.

In Dresden, by the late afternoon, the crowds in the streets of the Altstadt had grown denser; the railway station and the roads had brought in uncountable numbers of new arrivals. There was an urban rumour that had spread with some speed: that among these thousands of milling refugees were furtive army deserters, doing their best to avoid official attention. It was understood that the authorities would show no mercy to any who were caught, and it was estimated that in Dresden on that day there were at least a few hundred, possibly a little under a thousand such men, dodging through the shuffling families gazing at the elegance of the Prager Strasse shops.

Also moving among them, from different directions and with different purposes, were two schoolboys. Winfried Bielss had gone home from school and changed into his Hitler Youth uniform ready for his evening duties. The clothes spoke of hyper-aggressive authority (the brown shirt with swastika armband, the shoulder straps, the imperial coat of arms in the form of the eagle, and the motto 'Blood and Honour'),[25] but this boy's mind could not have been further from war. He had instead been thinking of the fine collection of Erzgebirge toys – richly painted wooden folk-art dolls and marionettes – that he had recently seen in the study of his uncle. More particularly, he had been daydreaming about his uncle's stamp collection. Bielss too had a deep enthusiasm for philately. Even in the depths of war there were dedicated stamp dealers in Dresden, including a shop called Engelmann that stocked collectibles. Bielss found himself wandering there to stare at the window display. One other shop lay on his route: Bohnert. This had a more unusual display: rare stamps that had been charred and burned at the edges. This, thought Bielss, 'was an indication that in the event of an air raid, even a vault is not protection enough for them'.[26]

At around the same time of day, teenager Helmut Voigt was in the large square of the Altmarkt. A few months beforehand, much of the space in the middle of this cobbled square had been requisitioned and dug out for the construction of a large reservoir, the size of a swimming pool but deeper, with smooth concrete sides; this was intended for emergency use by the fire service in the event of an air raid rather than to augment the town's supply of drinking water. Helmut – together with his cousin Roland – was on his quest for bolts for his school. Travelling in to the city centre from the suburb of Plauen on an unusually busy tram, Helmut was certain that the still-functioning department store Renner would surely have something approximate to his needs.

The cousins had noted the unusually crowded streets, their tram stopping and starting, progress halting, with innumerable human obstacles. The department store itself, though, was relatively calm. The young Voigt approached an elderly salesman in the household-goods department; he went to check the stocks at the back, but without success.[27] The pair left the fancy store empty-handed and once more traversed the busy square and its reservoir.

The afternoon was giving way to twilight. Voigt boarded a bus pointing homewards, but the crowds made the journey fraught. As well as the endless slow-moving mass in Prager Strasse there was drama too; at one point, a pedestrian collapsed; the bus conductor had to help get him out of the road to safety.

Voigt's path was crossed by Lothar Rolf Luhm, a young soldier on leave following convalescence from an injury. Luhm had managed to meet up with a soldier friend called Günther Tschernik. He had originally planned to spend a few days in Schneidemühl, a town in occupied Poland (now called Piła), but it was by then 'a fortress'.[28] Luhm had been wounded during the Ardennes offensive in late 1944. He had then been sent to spend some weeks in a sanatorium in a snowy Silesian town then called Schreiberhau. He was in Dresden pretty much by chance; Luhm was simply making his way back to his unit. Now, awaiting transport connections, he and his friend Günther had a little time to explore this unfamiliar city.

Also unfamiliar with Dresden – but extremely pleased to be there – was Norbert Bürgel, a boy refugee who had left Silesia with his family in order to join relatives in a suburb to the north-west of the city, on the hills looking down over the Altstadt. (In this respect he was unusual; the majority of displaced people were passing through on a journey further west.) By 13 February, Bürgel had been in Dresden for a week, staying with his uncle Günther.[29] The idea that Shrove Tuesday should feature festivities had not been forgotten, and the Bürgels were set on enjoying dinner at a restaurant at the far

end of the tram line in the suburb of Gohlis, a smart enclave where
the city touched the countryside.

Back in England, in the deep twilight green of Suffolk, Miles Tripp
and his crewmates – among whom were the skipper 'Dig', the navigator Les and the sharply intuitive Harry – were now on base, in the
canteen eating their preflight meal.[30] They still did not know what
target had been fixed upon for that night; they would find out very
shortly. But this was one occasion when Harry's strange powers of
insight failed him. He had, he told his crewmates, 'no hunches' about
this one.

When the curtain was drawn back on the map pinned up in the
briefing room that evening, as they sat at tightly arranged tables with
the other crews in their squadron, all eyes were drawn to the red
ribbon marking out the route across the Channel. The ribbon's line
stretched across France, past Stuttgart, Frankfurt and Mannheim,
further and further east. Tripp recalled that 'nobody had ever heard
of Dresden being raided before'.[31] Indeed, it seems his own immediate thought was not about the immense distance, or the huge amount
of time their plane would be vulnerable to German fire – some nine
hours in the air; it was that the city would not have the 'black belt' of
defence that encircled Berlin and the industrial cities of the Ruhr.
Miles Tripp already knew that Dresden was, as Victor Klemperer
later described it, 'a jewel box'. In fact, there was a defence force;
although the city's anti-aircraft guns had been moved in January, sent
further east, there was a small squadron of Messerschmitt fighters
stationed at the Klotzsche airfield, built in 1935 as an airport befitting
a sophisticated destination and which stood on a northern plain above
the town, some five miles from the centre.

The USAAF had been due to fly a raid over Dresden that day,
but this had been postponed owing to adverse weather. In terms of
coordination, the shared targets were by now routine; lists of cities
and industrial plants were agreed at the Combined Strategic Targets
Committee. It was General Ira Eaker who, eighteen months beforehand, had outlined to Churchill the proposition of 'round the clock
bombing' – the Americans aiming (in theory) for industrial targets in

daylight, the British then swooping over at night. Unusually, on this occasion, the RAF was to be the first to attack. The tables before the pilots and their crews in that briefing room were covered with maps, and the airmen, many smoking, with the rich haze of tobacco building in the room, studied them intently. The advance of the Red Army – Tripp and all his fellow airmen in that room were told – had created chaotic conditions in Dresden, with so many thousands fleeing before them. The aim was not explicitly to bomb civilians, but instead to create an atmosphere of panic. The effect of this would be a general paralysis of communications, railways and roads, to strike at the efforts of the German military to mount an effective defence in the east.

Tripp later confessed that the briefing disturbed him;[32] the plan clearly involved igniting alarm among displaced people and he remembered from 1940 the distressing newsreels of French rural refugees desperately seeking to escape the Nazi invasion of their landscape, and of the open sadism of the Luftwaffe in swooping down on these helpless people and firing machine-gun bullets into them.

And so the bomb aimer left the smoky briefing room and went to stand outside in the sharp evening air. He recalled that the sky was 'tangled with stars'. Tripp at this point started to think about the duration and distance of the mission, and his anxiety became more straightforward. That night 796 Lancasters and Mosquitos would be carrying some 5,500 airmen to bomb Dresden in two huge waves. Tripp's plane was to be part of the second wave, hitting the city as it was still absorbing the shock of the first attack. Tripp was joined by his crewmates, who seemed similarly apprehensive. The Australian pilot 'Dig' had been given the crew's regular sweet rations for the mission – chewing gum, barley sugar and chocolate. The chocolate, it was noted, was the milk variety: a rare treat. One of the crew members nobly forwent his portion of chocolate, insisting that it be put aside for his crewmate's much younger brother, a child who in those severely rationed days lived for such elusive delights.

Small tokens of generosity had still been evident in everyday flashes throughout the civilian populace of Dresden too. Victor Klemperer, although crushed into a state of exhausted, depressive dread by his day spent making those terrible deliveries, recalled how just a week or so previously, when the assistant in a grocery shop had been reluctant to serve the rations he was entitled to, a woman in the queue behind had offered to help him out with her own allowance. She had seen the yellow star; she knew what she was doing. For the past few years, interspersing the creeping fear, the random outbreaks of official violence, Klemperer had always noted the fleeting but significant kindnesses; the neighbours and passers-by who told him that they thought what the authorities were doing was awful.[33] He was not the only figure to be surprised by surreptitious warmth and sympathy.

Near the wide-flowing Elbe, the waters high with the melted winter snows, in the west of the city stood an enormous abattoir complex. In the section that had formerly held pigs in pens waiting to be butchered and cold stores in which to keep their carcases, a group of prisoners of war were being held, their closely guarded dormitory a few feet underground. Among them was the American novelist-to-be Kurt Vonnegut. Captured some weeks previously, he had seen the more bestial elements of the German military – his guards were sadistic and fanatical, always twitching for the opportunity to slam rifle butts hard into stomachs or cracking across heads.[34] Yet during the days, when the prisoners were marched along the street to the malt-syrup factory, Vonnegut caught shafts of light.

The syrup was derived from barley; thick and brown. Vonnegut and his fellows, who were existing on ever-thinner broths with specks of meat, tough black bread and ersatz coffee, were driven almost mad with temptation by the fat vats: the promise of filling sweetness. Also working at the plant were numbers of local women; Vonnegut recalled piercingly when – unable to resist any longer – he waited for the guards to look away and plunged his fingers deep into the forbidden sticky warmth of the syrup, and then brought it back up to his lips. As he swallowed the syrup, he caught the eye of one of the women workers who had seen him; and instead of denouncing him angrily, she smiled.

Vonnegut had a sense that he was in what his narrator Billy Pilgrim would later describe as 'the most beautiful city in the world'[35] but he could only ever see the most tantalizingly small fragments of it. The same, it seemed, applied to the humanity in those around him. Apart from those hours in the syrup factory, he and his fellow prisoners were simply locked away in the abattoir bunker. Work started early and finished in the late afternoon; then the men would be marched back to the slaughterhouse for another inadequate meal of broth.

Elsewhere, the authorities had lost none of their implacable vengefulness: in the police headquarters not far from the Frauenkirche was another disparate group of prisoners of war, all under arrest. One of these was Victor Gregg, the young Englishman who had just a couple of days previously been sentenced to death for sabotaging the machinery of a soap works. With his execution due to take place the following morning, on 14 February, Gregg had no choice but to await his fate in the middle of that crowd of condemned men, in a room used as a temporary cell with a high ceiling and glass cupola, its lavatory comprising two buckets in a corner. Gregg's co-accused Harry was still blithely insisting that something would turn up.[36]

And as he and the other men stared at the walls, just a few hundred yards away, the children in the nearby residential district of Johannstadt, with its tall apartment buildings, neat little squares and proximity to the Great Garden park, were continuing to run around in their Fasching costumes. Ursel Schumann was 'dressed as a little gentleman in a suit and a hat'.[37] It clearly gave mothers and grandparents some comfort to see the children free of anxiety; and perhaps the extra comfort of seeing the old tradition that they too had enjoyed persisting even in these most desperate days.

At around 6 p.m. in England the first wave of Lancasters were ready to fly, sitting on airfields in Lincolnshire and Suffolk in the winter darkness, awaiting the green signals from control vans. The airmen, in their electrically heated suits, had a carefully calculated extra item: a piece of cloth with the Union Flag and stitched with the words 'I am an Englishman' spelled out in Russian.[38] In the event of being shot down, they needed a means of establishing their identities instantly in the face of Soviet troops, because the Red Army was known to operate with violent impulsiveness.

Dresden was not the only target that night; there were to be feints elsewhere, raids on Magdeburg and Nuremberg and Bonn. The idea was to sow confusion in the Luftwaffe control centre, to deny them a focus for their defence. There was also a scheduled raid on a hydrogenation plant that lay north of Leipzig, not very far from Dresden. This was to involve over 350 planes. In total, the RAF was sending around 1,400 planes over Germany that night. This was to be the most extraordinarily choreographed aerial ballet: meticulous timings, smooth order. Other crewmen, such as pilot Leslie Hay, had received similar close briefings on the nature of the target and the reason for it. Industry, he recalled, was hardly mentioned, although the intelligence maps, colour-coded, did show the various manufacturing works that ringed the Altstadt. And again, there was a regretful reference to refugees; and the need to spark fear and chaos among them on the roads in order to bring German materiel transport to an effective halt.

By the time the first of the Lancasters was airborne, a little after 6 p.m., the sky in the east was black. The planes flying down south from Lincolnshire were joined, fifty miles west of London at Reading, by more squadrons; the coordination required to keep so many hundreds of aircraft in an orderly formation was extraordinary. The bombers, their crews attending to their tasks of navigation, of preparing to scatter 'Window' into the night skies to confuse the enemy's radar, of defending the craft with machine guns against the predations of German fighters, approached the Channel, which under the stars had the faintest lustre, then swung down across the French coast before setting their courses for their multiple missions. The flight to Dresden would be roughly four and a half hours.

And in Dresden itself, the sun was long gone; the early evening winter sky, intermittently cloudy, touched for a time with sapphire. The River Elbe darkened; above it, in the wide sky of that valley, tiny stars materialized. The middle-aged men who had spent the day working in what their small sons assumed were 'scissor-making' factories and the like were not quite free to return home at the end of their shift; yet to come were compulsory meetings of the Volkssturm. Many among them simply wanted a decent supper – fried potatoes were often cited as a craving – and beer.

All the while under the darkening sky there were no city lights to be seen in the strictly enforced blackout. And so the refugees who had just arrived by train, or by wagon, were now faced with the prospect of navigating a strange city in utter darkness. By now, the children in their cowboy and devil costumes had been rounded up by their mothers; time for supper, time to get ready for bed. But the older children, in the shape of the Hitler Youth, their regulation necker-chiefs tied in triangular fashion, were very much out on the streets: not to bark orders, or to menace, but to guide refugees to temporary accommodation for the night in requisitioned public buildings. Even in that murk, the organization of the city was meticulous.

12. Five Minutes Before the Sirens

The guides had done their work: more families escorted back onto train platforms, or carefully led through lightless streets to the rectangular outlines of municipal buildings, where they found themselves in halls with makeshift beds, facing other families in identical circumstances, every future moment overcast with uncertainty. Fifteen-year-old Winfried Bielss, in his uniform, had received orders from a Nazi official and had been helping a family of six – 'women, children and elderly people'[1] – who were deposited, bewildered, at the main railway station. They were to be billeted in a school in the Neustadt on the north side of the river; this necessitated a tram trip and he escorted them (helping with the great quantities of luggage that they had managed to hold on to) on this journey which took them across the Albert Bridge and into the elegant nineteenth-century terraces beyond.

For these and other selfless acts, Bielss was given one mark. He and his friend Horst Schaffel ensured that the refugee family were received in the school building that they had been assigned to. The streets of the Neustadt were still busy; in the sharpening late-evening air, Bielss and Schaffel started to think about the prospect of home; for Schaffel, this lay on the other side of the river. They just had a few more refugee arrivals to help.

Despite the bustle and chaos, there had been nothing to provoke unease either in the city's routine precautions or on the early evening news. Close to where the boys were working was the Sarrasani circus: on this day of carnival, great numbers of Dresden families (some with rural refugee relatives) and soldiers too had queued for admittance to its circular theatre. With all the cinemas now darkened, this was the only form of escapist entertainment left in the city. There was no sense that the circus was threadbare or starved of resources; rather, it was still a brightly lit spectacle of trained tigers, gaudy clowns, elegant performing horses and the newly formed 'Bob Gerry Troupe': 'Aryan' acrobats who had mastered forming unusually tall human pyramids, as well as other tightrope and flying-trapeze tricks.[2] In addition, the refreshment facilities were impressive: there was an underground cafe and an underground bar. These, and an adjoining network of sub-terranean passages, had been modified so that when the air-raid sirens cried, which they did almost every night, the performance could be halted and the audience calmly directed to safety until the danger passed. The circus was valued by the authorities as it provided amuse-ment and colour for factory and munitions workers who had almost been turned into robots by the nature of their daily tasks. Closing the cinemas – establishments hugely popular with the workers – had been a very serious step, but the Sarrasani name had been associated with Dresden even longer than the lure of film.

Quieter diversions were taking place elsewhere. That evening, the city's most distinguished medical practitioner, Dr Albert Fromme, was at a small drinks party for a neighbour, Frau Schrell, who had celebrated her birthday the day before. The friends were gathered in an apartment.

Elsewhere, similarly set on seeing friends was the artist Otto Grie-bel. The last few years had seen Griebel's fortunes ricochet violently, from the menace and harassment that he had received from the Gestapo in the 1930s to the official condemnation of his art by the authorities to his drafting into the Wehrmacht, bringing technical drawing skills to the eastern front. Griebel's world must have seemed to him, at times, blackly Dadaist. He had been back in Dresden for several weeks, reunited with his young family in an apartment to the south east of the city.[3] On the evening of 13 February he was on his way to a private party in a tavern in the Altstadt, not far from the Kreuzkirche. He caught a tram from that southern suburb into the city centre, and navigated through the darkened, cobbled maze of tight old streets to find the carefully blacked-out pub. There the artist stepped in through the tavern door to see, among other faces, a musi-cian friend called Scheinpflug. The beer and the schnapps seemed in good supply; but what was also striking was not merely a sense of old friendships withstanding the grim twists of war, but also the sense of this social group enduring in the face of the authorities' loathing, the knowledge that those same authorities had spied on them in the past and would be minded to do so again in the future.

To the south were more revellers, although rather quieter and more discreet than the tavern drinkers: these were the party guests of Mischka Danos, all standing in his boarding-house bedroom, some enjoying their Kissel. Danos had made imminent plans to depart; to travel to Flensburg and there meet up with his mother, who would have made her own separate way (the idea being that if either of them experienced any difficulties en route, the other would not be pulled into whatever trouble it was). Present in that room was a young woman that Danos recalled knowing simply as 'the Karl May girl': because she had a terrific enthusiasm for the 'cowboys and Indians' Western novels that the author had written decades earlier.[4]

In an even smarter suburb in the east, Georg and Marielein Erler were in their living room; they had had a modest supper that evening, and were listening to the radio.[5] Herr Erler, as the air-raid warden for this part of the street, was perpetually ready, yet he and his wife were not anticipating any attacks from the air. They were focusing much more on the fast approach of the Red Army. They had a car, and even at this time of severe fuel rationing, sufficient supplies to get them away from the city, and to stay ahead of the brutal invaders.

There were many others around the city who lacked the Erlers' economic freedom: working mothers and frugal grandparents who – even if they had relatives in other cities – could not guarantee that those cities were any safer, or could provide the means by which they might support themselves. Poorer families had suitcases packed too: but only with gas masks and blankets, to be taken to their cellars, in the event of an air raid. A couple of years previously, Gauleiter Mutschmann had made strenuous efforts to persuade parents to evacuate their children to new billets in distant rural villages. He and the authorities had gone so far as to try to end daily lessons at schools, but the parents did not want their children to leave and the children wanted to stay at home. And so in apartment buildings that ringed the Altstadt, there were many children who had had their Faschingnacht suppers, and were now snugly in bed.

Older children were also preparing for bed. Thirteen-year-old

Helmut Voigt, back home after that halting journey from the department store, had had his supper and had also assiduously packed his school bag in readiness for the following day.[6] Closer to the centre of the city, ten-year-old Gisela Reichelt was already in her bed, her dolls Monika and Helga by her side. Like other children, she remembered her mother listening to the voices on the radio.[7] In innumerable apartments those radios murmured, the lights in the living rooms pale, the ticking of coals in the fireplaces, mothers mending clothes while listening, the elderly sitting with them, eyes grave. Even in peacetime, Dresden was not a city where there was much activity on the streets after a certain hour; away from the industrial concerns and the busy tram junctions, children settled in quiet rooms under thick blankets to keep out the cold.

Yet in the heart of the Altstadt – where horse-drawn carts were still moving in some numbers through its narrow streets – there were brief flickers of teenage romance. Hans Settler was a nineteen-year-old soldier back in his home city on leave; his family lived in the north-western suburb of Radebeul and he had a girlfriend who lived almost in the centre of the city. His had been a patchwork war. Previously an apprentice toolmaker at the Dresden firm of Böhme KG, he had been conscripted aged seventeen. In the rip tides of the conflict he had found himself swept, as a flak operator, from Holland, down to a chateau in France and thence to Poland and the eastern front.[8] He had sustained an injury – not serious, but enough to have him repatriated for recovery. And on this evening, Hans Settler was enjoying being back by his girlfriend's side. They had spent the evening among the little cafes of the Neustadt and now, around 9 p.m., it was time to walk her home to her family's apartment just off the Altmarkt. He recalled that, as they parted, the bell of the Kreuzkirche rang out across the vast market square.

These bells were the constants of Dresden: the deep resonance of the Kreuzkirche contrasting with the lighter tones that rang out every quarter hour from the Frauenkirche; and just several streets away from that, the rival discordancy of the bells from the Catholic cathedral. The music of these spires was sombre, yet just a short distance from the Catholic cathedral, at the baroque entrance to the

Zwingergarten, there was an exquisitely light variation on all of these: a set of bells fashioned from ceramic that – when they sounded the hour and half hour – tinkled with high, amused, sophisticated music. The bells of the Zwinger were there for those who wanted assurance that light and happiness were perfectly natural to this world. But it was to the more reflective, darker notes resonating from the church bell towers that Hans Settler and his girlfriend said their farewells.

13. Into the Abyss

The noise had an industrial quality; an urgency but also a practicality. Unlike the air-raid sirens in England – the high pitch of which was faintly other-worldly, a banshee cry in the dark – the *Fliegeralarme* in Germany were set at a lower octave. They rose and fell as did all sirens, but it was like an alert or even an end-of-shift signal one might hear in a factory compound: workmanlike, as if to say that everyone should move sensibly, and there was no prompt for panic. Across Dresden the sirens were set on rooftops and walls, and by February 1945 their notes would have been regarded by many as simply dreary: night after night of false alarms had drained them of their original potency. At 9.40 p.m. on the 13th the city's sirens were activated once more, and as the drone filled and echoed down the narrow streets of tall blocks, and pierced the air of the wider avenues and the wealthier suburban streets, many citizens were already resigned to making their way to the shelters yet again, for there had also been an update on the radio: the presenter interrupting the programming to tell listeners that a line of enemy planes had been detected flying towards the city.

Dr Albert Fromme was still with the small band of friends celebrating Frau Schrell's birthday. The urgent alarm came without warning.[1] As they listened to the throaty wail outside the window, one of the party turned the radio on, to find out whether there was anything to worry about. 'I immediately felt that something significant was going on,' wrote Dr Fromme later.[2] The announcement on the radio was that bombers were indeed on the approach to Dresden. The party was swiftly concluded as he and his neighbours gathered their 'air-raid kits' and took them to the shelter in the basement.

Such studied calm was possible for the adults, but not so easy for the smaller children. Georg Frank, who had spent the day in his colourful clown's bow and collar, was in his bed; his father had returned home from the meeting of the Volkssturm and his mother had warmed up some supper for him. He was already listening to the radio, as was the boy, half-waking in confusion, when a rather more emphatic announcement was made: 'Attention! Attention! Anglo-American bombers in approach to Dresden! Seek the air-raid shelters immediately!'[3]

And Herr Frank could not later remember whether he, as a little boy, was still half-asleep when hauled out of his bed by his mother. The memory had the power of a bad dream: 'Was it just the fright of being pulled out of bed that caused the tears?' And with this rupture came the noise of the sirens which to the little boy were 'ghastly'. He was wrapped in a blanket and, carried by his mother, rushed out of the apartment.[4]

Their shelter was the cellar; the long brick corridor with the little cells leading off from it. On the way down, he was conscious of 'the faint stairwell lighting' and the total blackness outside the staircase window. His father had brought down a few family belongings and now they all moved into that vaulted cell, with its simple table and home-made chairs, and the little boy watched as his father stowed their small treasures away in a corner. The few simple provisions they had brought were laid upon the table.

Just two or three blocks south of the main railway station, on Schnorrstrasse, was the apartment where ten-year-old Gisela Reichelt lived with her sister and her mother, Frieda, who was eight months pregnant. Gisela later remembered that the air-raid sirens had simply become an accepted part of life in Dresden; she did not associate them with horror, because the night-time alarms had all proved false. Even as a ten-year-old, though, she was aware of what the war had brought to others; she knew from the radio and from newspapers that Allied bombers had effectively destroyed other German cities such as Hamburg and Mannheim. Indeed, before 1945, in the earlier days of the war, when Bomber Command had been relentlessly attacking cities such as Frankfurt and Hanover, Dresden had been the sanctuary for so many refugees coming not from the east but from the west, from towns and cities and streets that had been transformed into smoking rubble. But, she later remembered, there was some form of general psychological block among Dresden's citizens. 'No one could ever imagine that our city would be the victim of a cruel and senseless bombing.'[5]

Gisela was in bed, though not asleep, when the sirens began their cry. 'We grabbed our suitcases which were always to hand and went down to the cellar,' she later remembered. Gisela also managed to pick up her dolls Monika and Helga. As she and her mother reached the cellar, anxiety set in almost at once. Gisela's father was a soldier; where was he at that moment? The sorts of worries that even ordinarily could keep a child from sleep were hugely magnified in that enclosed space. There was no optimism now that it was a false alarm, for Gisela could see that her mother was also drawn with anxiety. Into that cellar came neighbours and latecomers, and all the while the sirens outside continued to cry.

One cellar with a very distinctive savour was that into which the American prisoner of war Kurt Vonnegut and his fellow captives had been escorted: what he described as a meat locker lay beneath the converted barracks of slaughterhouse number five.[6] This cellar was accessed by means of an iron door and down an iron staircase. The room was very large and very cool; here and there slabs of animal carcases – sheep, pig, horse – were impaled upon hooks that hung from the ceiling. There were a great many other unused hooks dangling. The space was whitewashed and candlelit. In that cold February, electric refrigeration had not been deemed necessary for the meat; the air was sufficiently cold as it was. For the next eight or so hours, this was to be the physical limit of Vonnegut's world, as his imagination was galvanized by the echoing noises from above. Many of the guards who usually stood watch over him and his comrades came off shift and returned to their nearby homes. The American POW was safer than his Nazi jailers.

Across the river, the sirens could be heard within the Sarrasani circus box office and the entertainment in the ring was instantly halted. That evening's ringmaster, plus some of the attraction attendants, told the audience that all the shelter they needed was just down the stairs. There might have been a few soldiers in that audience who would have relished the prospect of a compulsory visit to the establishment's subterranean bar. With no fuss or agitation, from the elderly to the young, row upon row stood and slowly made their way towards the exits indicated by their ushers. The circus animals, meanwhile, were led to their special enclosures in a vast yard at the back of the building.

On a smart street in the east of the city, Marielein Erler and her husband Georg had understood very well the meaning of the radio announcement: the wording, from the 'bomber approach' to the invocation of all necessary precautions, had been used on Herr Erler's warden training courses: it meant that this was a serious emergency. And yet the Erlers felt that they were properly prepared. The house in which they lived had a cellar, and they were joined by their fellow residents. They had packed not two but six suitcases in readiness: as much of their clothing as they could manage.

Also in that cellar, Marielein recalled, was 'a big box with the best porcelain – noblest Meissner'.[7] It also had some items of crystalware. It would not be fair to interpret this as irrational materialism; rather, it was clear that these and other pieces were infused with memory. The pleasure the Erlers derived from these treasures was not greedy but delicate and subtle. There was also a sort of charmed optimism about the idea that such objects would be safe even deep in a cellar during a bombing attack. But Marielein wanted to offer comfort to others too. The neighbours who had gathered in the cellar included one small family, with two very young children: a girl called Elizabeth and her even smaller younger brother. As they adjusted to the low lighting amid the musty brickwork, Marielein tried to soothe the children. The girl, she noted, was trembling and she put her arm around her.[8]

Some cellars were more accommodating than others. Helmut Voigt, together with his mother and his older cousin Roland, had to leave their apartment building south-west of the railway station and make their way along the street to the entrance to an industrial basement beneath a local brewery (a rival to the Felsenkeller, which was not far away). This modern shelter – concrete stairs down, bare lightbulbs and pale walls – was several flights underground. Voigt estimated that it had room comfortably for about a hundred people.[9]

But as the sirens cried that night, the teenager noticed with a little discomfort that something new was happening: the cellar was filling with
not only familiar neighbours but also a continual line of strangers whose
footsteps could be heard descending those concrete stairs.

'Many people came in who had never been there before,' he later
recalled. 'Some were the passengers from a tram on line 6'[10] and others
were refugees; in other words, people out on the streets who understood suddenly how much danger they were in, and who had followed
a line of other citizens making for the shelter. As each new arrival
came down the stairs there was a palpable sense of shifting. Usually
quite roomy, the cellar now no longer had any more seating free; each
new entrant had to stand. There was an anteroom too, and a short
corridor, but conditions in these were becoming cramped as well.

Through all of this, these citizens across Dresden who took shelter –
thousands of people, moving in as orderly a fashion as they could – had
no idea how much time they had before the raid would begin. The
sirens and the radio announcements spoke of imminence, but what
did that mean? Seconds? An hour? There were a great many who
tried, above the incessant klaxons, to discern the approaching hum
of aircraft. Indeed, in the heart of the Altstadt there were many still
out in its streets and narrow alleys, ignoring the bellows of on-duty
police officers and looking up at the sky.

One such was the soldier who had so recently recovered from his
wounds in the snowy east. Lothar Rolf Luhm had become separated
from his soldier comrade as he wove his way through the baroque
lanes that wound around the castle and the Catholic cathedral. He
found himself on the square outside the cathedral, overlooking the
Augustus Bridge. There were stragglers running in all directions.
Without quite realizing the futility of the question, Luhm – a stranger
to the city – quickly grabbed one person and asked where he was.

Footsteps on cobbles, the endless undulating wail echoing off walls
of thick stone. Luhm spotted people hurrying towards a grand structure that lay beyond the castle: an eighteenth-century building
fashioned to look like a chateau. Setting off at a run, the soldier followed these figures in and was directed towards a staircase.[11] As well
as the bare concrete and pale wall lights, there was a feature that set

this shelter apart: heavy steel doors. One other element immediately caught Luhm's eye: the heavy presence of what he described as 'Golden Pheasants'. This was slang for Nazi Party dignitaries: the colours of their uniforms – the browns and the reds, and the gold tassels – inspired the term.

Luhm was now underneath the Taschenberg Palace, for a long time a bureaucratic centre for the Wehrmacht. It had originally been built by Augustus the Strong as a residence for his mistress, the Countess of Cosel. Luhm found himself among a jostling, heterogeneous crowd, notable for a number of 'well-fed burghers' and police officers who were in radio communication with officers elsewhere.[12] He was near the heart of the municipal Nazi establishment, and it transpired that his friend Günther had also made it down there. They were, Luhm recalled, the only soldiers among all these civilian personnel; and no one seemed to question their presence.

That little world beneath was very far away from the cobbled lanes above; aside from the continual complaint of the deep-throated sirens, the road outside, which turned on to the richly ornamental entrance to the Zwingergarten and then led, a few yards further on, to the cheerful classical structure of the Semper Opera House, was now quiet. Further on, past the Catholic cathedral and up the steps to the promenade of Brühl's Terrace, with its flagstones and balustrades, the last stragglers were making their way to less secure cellars. Along that terrace lay the elegant facades of the Academy of Arts and the Albertinum; the latter institution, the base of the civic authorities and services, had its own extensive cellar, which was filling from the street side with a mix of public officials and citizens caught some distance from their usual refuges.

And just a few yards along from this lay the Judenhäuser. After a harrowing day delivering deportation notices to fellow Jewish citizens, Victor Klemperer was drinking coffee with his wife when the sirens sounded. A neighbour, Frau Struhler, exclaimed bitterly that she hoped the bombers would come and smash everything up.[13] Clearly, this was the only escape that she could envisage. Klemperer did not seem at all shocked by the bitter nihilism.

There was a separate 'Jew cellar'; Jewish people were not permitted

to seek shelter among Aryans. Like many other cellars in this part of
the Altstadt, this was a space of crumbling brickwork and not wholly
underground; there was a window at pavement level. As in neighbouring streets, they contained only rudimentary facilities: chairs,
buckets of water, blankets. Klemperer, his wife and all those others
who resided in the old wooden structure made their way down the
stairs. In such spaces, and such circumstances, there was little anyone
could do but sit silently.

A few hundred yards south of this, the choirboys of the Kreuzschule had been ushered down to their main school building's cellars.
Beneath the February night sky, the neo-Gothic Kreuzschule, with its
strong vertical and triangular lines, looked a little like a vast church
organ in silhouette. The boys gathering under this structure were, in
contrast to the inhabitants of the Judenhäuser, among Dresden's most
cherished souls: their intense musical talent far removed from the
everyday squalor of war. On ordinary days, theirs was a rarefied life,
and yet now they were in no more a privileged position than their
Jewish neighbours. And with them in those cellars was the choirmaster, Rudolf Mauersberger: he was certainly keenly aware of
the menacing dissonance in the city's sirens. As a composer, he was
acutely sensitive to the music of everyday life. Just weeks beforehand,
his choir had been performing songs that he had written inspired by
Saxon folk tales and melodies, delicate interweavings of rural
history and Christianity.[14] These compositions were a determined
counterpoint not only to the war but also to the martial nature of the
Nazi regime; they spoke of a Dresden heritage rooted in a more spiritually nourishing world. In those minutes of silence and waiting,
Mauersberger was absorbing the tones and rhythm of the warning
wails. The music of war was painful to him; a pain that he was determined to condemn, and to share.

Even in the unknowable chaos of an air-raid warning, the boys of
the Kreuzschule had structure; an institution that was there to look
after them. But some half a mile south, at the city's main railway
station, the situation was noisier: a vast crowd being hustled down
the stairs into the underground spaces that lay beneath the platforms,

a tumult of voices and footsteps echoing on stone. There was shuffling, scuffling; elderly people, small children, bewildered and directionless and moving where they were told by the station officials and railway police. The uncertainty here, perhaps, was stronger. With the air filled by sirens, these refugees would have had no sense of how much time they had to find themselves a secure spot in those corridors and tunnels, or even where the exits were.

Günter Berger was among the railway staff, with his colleague Georg Thiel. The crowds were even denser than on previous days and evenings because, for the past few hours, more steam locomotives than ever had been pulling up to the platforms. 'In addition to the daily scheduled traffic, there were many specially scheduled trains coming in from the east,' recalled Berger. 'There were drivers and passengers who had covered immense distances in a day; and the train carriages were packed with refugees.'[15]

The unceasing sirens and the urgency of the radio announcements meant Berger and his colleagues had to act with single-minded efficiency if they were to get all these people to shelter; there was clearly no time to think of alternatives. 'What we feared had now arrived,' remembered Berger. 'With heavy hearts, we had to act swiftly and with care.'[16] He knew his main duty was to remain within the station precincts, and in those dark minutes he and Thiel met a train that had just pulled in. Careful not to spark panic, they disembarked the frightened refugee passengers as quickly as possible, instructing them to leave their luggage in the carriages and get down the stairs as swiftly as they could.

As Berger recalled, 'A considerable mass of people had accumulated,'[17] yet the new arrivals remained calm as they complied. Some corridors beneath the platforms made a cruciform shape; Berger and his colleagues briskly choreographed individuals along its arms. Some young helpers belonged to the League of German Girls, who had been instructed to tend to any wounded soldiers arriving by train, but many of those men were too badly injured to be moved easily from the station's underground corridors.

In another train that was approaching the city in those minutes was the great-uncle of Margot Hille. 'Uncle Hermann', as Margot called him, was among those fleeing the lower Silesian town of Głogów. This quiet, pretty place had been transformed into a Wehrmacht stronghold, a line that the Nazis were determined that the Red Army would not cross. The Soviet troops responded to that with a terrible onslaught that destroyed the town centre stone by stone. Uncle Hermann's train had been travelling through the countryside for the best part of the day, and at a few minutes to ten was nearing the darkened centre of Dresden and its glass-roofed main station.

A little to the north, where the railway tracks curved across the River Elbe and into the more modest station at Neustadt, there was also a jostling mass of refugees awaiting instructions. Winfried Bielss and his friend Horst were a few streets away on their Hitler Youth duty, having settled another refugee family into temporary accommodation at a commandeered school. They had been on the street and some distance from their homes as the sirens started. They had to decide very quickly what to do.

Among the elegant nineteenth-century houses and apartment buildings on Katharinenstrasse they found access to a shelter. It was little more than a simple cellar, and uncomfortably if understandably crowded. Extraordinarily, though, the boys were told that they could not stay; there was no room for them; they would have to find somewhere else. Seconds later, Winfried and Horst were back on the street, with the sirens echoing around them.

What to do? Should they return to the Neustadt station? Bielss was reluctant; there was no room there either. Horst suggested sprinting across the bridge and through the streets of the Altstadt to his family's home near the Kreuzkirche, but it was a good mile away and Bielss did not think that they had enough time.

As the boys debated under that black sky, they were approached by two hurrying policemen and taken to another cellar a few doors along. It was too dangerous for them to remain out in the open air, one of the officers told them.[18] But some curious quirk made Bielss demur. He felt an inexorable pull towards his own home, regardless of time or jeopardy. This too was a mile away, but on this side of the river, past the Neustadt.

Bielss talked Horst into leaving and they slipped out of the cellar past the police officers who were trying to maintain order among its many other occupants. The boys walked briskly along deserted residential back streets, the large villas and terraced apartment buildings blank, the darkness complete and the only noise to be heard the interminable rise and fall of the sirens. When they were stopped by more police officers, Bielss coolly reassured them that he lived only one street away and was nearly home. This was not true, of course, but the police were satisfied and they hurried to their own shelter. 'I just wanted to walk home through quiet neighbourhoods,' Bielss later recalled.[19] Perhaps because the streets were empty, Bielss curiously remembered the atmosphere as calm – though navigation was slightly difficult because in the absence of any street lights the city before him was simply shapes in the dark.

They were now passing a small park, darker even than the street, and the boys were alone. They were on Alaunstrasse, which is halfway up the gentle slope that rises to the north of the Elbe, and from this point, they could see the silhouetted domes and towers of the Altstadt and the clouds above. It was now that they became conscious of the hum. 'The sound of aircraft engines became audible,' remembered Bielss. But neither he nor Horst was anxious; indeed, that deep note prompted them instead to speculate on the city's air defences. They both assumed that there would be fighters taking off from the Klotzsche airfield, which lay about four miles to the north.

The boys' faith in the city's defences was ill founded. Some dozen or so Messerschmitt fighters had belatedly been scrambled, only just becoming airborne as the bombers began their sweep along the Elbe. There was a sense of exhaustion and resignation in this token response, the Luftwaffe either tragically underestimating the size of the incoming raid or simply accepting it as a force that could not be met in kind. It is possible, too, that the squadron was under orders to conserve fuel for the more terrible battles with the invading Soviets to come. The impotence of this force, simply circling around, was to be made clear a few minutes later; one Messerschmitt visible from the ground amid the haze of initial bright silver and green marker flares dropped from above.

This was what the boys down below, hurrying through those

streets, were about to see. When Winfried and Horst reached the wider avenue of the Jägerstrasse, that hum intensified, the deep note resonating more powerfully, and quite unconsciously the boys found their pace quickening further. Here was something that sounded directly like a threat; a noise with an almost primal quality. The boys turned on to Zittauer Strasse, which was a little closer to the river, and it was at this point that they now began to sense what was coming: the prospect of many, many bombers, thousands of feet up, almost invisible against the darkness but the ever-louder hum now carrying a distinct edge of implacable aggression. The boys looked to the horizon and saw two balls of bright red falling from the sky above the Ostragehege, or city sports stadium. Following the illumination of the green and silver flares, these red falling stars were among the more mesmerizing of the 'Christmas trees', as they were termed: the glowing target indicators, dazzling in the darkness of blackout, thrown down from the lead Mosquitos in order to provide an aiming point for the bombers following close behind.

'Now we started to run,' remembered Bielss.[20] The boys were close to Bielss's home. They were at once mesmerized and horrified by the way that the sky and the city seemed slowly to be brightening. Out of the black clouds and the darkness were falling countless Christmas trees; the marker flares being scattered widely now, from the Altstadt to Johannstadt. Bielss recalled seeing other flares in different colours, brilliant blue, intense green and even a very bright orange, which turned the clouds above a sickly yellow. It might have been tempting from that viewpoint on the gentle hill on the opposite side of the river to stop and watch, at least for a few seconds. But the boys understood, perhaps prompted by the cacophony of the approaching bombers, that they had to sprint for sanctuary.

That macabre sense of wonder at this light show was left for others in the Altstadt itself. There were some 300-odd people, in the heart of that old city, who had fixed upon the crypt of the Frauenkirche for their shelter, hurrying across the dim cobbled square to the entrance at the side of the church. As they walked down the narrow stone steps and found places to sit amid the subterranean tombstones, the church above them was empty. In the darkness, in the main body of the church, it was still possible to see the golden glint of the altarpiece. The interior of the church's dome, painted in unusual shades of pink and pale blue, always found new delicacy on nights when the beams of the moon streamed through the clear windows. But now, instead, the intense red falling stars outside cast their lurid moving light, and their fiercer colours, upon the faces of the painted saints.

14. Shadows and Light

Dresden's attackers were young men who had been granted the most extraordinary power, although it did not feel like that to them. They were undertaking a mission where both the advantageous weather conditions and the lack of any meaningful defence meant that their target was wholly vulnerable beneath them, theirs to incinerate, theirs to demolish. Yet they did not see themselves as avengers. Perhaps after flying so many missions and facing so much enemy fire, and inexplicably surviving where so many friends and comrades had been consumed in molten explosions – perhaps after all that, the capacity to imagine all those people thousands of feet below as living individuals had simply been cauterized. The bomber crews of the RAF might for once have had the almost unchallenged power of Norse gods, but they carried out their instructions without emotion. In operational terms, those at the head of the storm were almost preternaturally abstract about what they were soon going to do.

The war had acquired its own ever increasing velocity of airborne destruction. The Germans had some months previously subcontracted the task to blind machinery: the V-1 missiles (known as 'doodlebugs', the incongruously innocent-sounding nickname a reference to the insect-like whirring noise they made) and the V-2 rockets launched from the Low Countries at Greater London and towns on the east coast. The V-2 rockets were as tall as houses; the geometrically perfect parabola they described in the stratosphere before pointing down to streets, to homes, and then, with their impact, flattening, killing, deafening and blinding, had a particular edge of pure anarchy. Who needed pilots and crew when the most advanced technology, launched from another country across the sea, could deliver death so randomly? Well over a thousand of these rockets were launched at Britain. They killed over 3,000 people. A few days before the Dresden raids the east London suburb of Ilford had been

hit by one such projectile that landed in a street of semi-detached
houses, children playing in gardens while being watched by tired
mothers. The impact atomized one house, demolished several others
and took many lives. This was a recalibration of total war: civilians
murdered by remote control.

But this Allied raid on Dresden had not been prompted by a desire
for retaliation; not even by desperation. For the airmen, this was just
another fear-filled night; and Dresden was just another target. In the
sparse, comfortless aircraft interiors – dark greens, cold metals, utilitarian seating – there were countless distractions that somehow
prevented minds from settling on what they were about to unleash.
For some the cold was biting beyond discomfort, a result of the electrically heated flight suits malfunctioning. For others, there was the
simple tight flutter of tension; the sense of having no agency on such
an intensely lengthy mission. As the 244 Lancasters that made up the
bulk of the first stage of the attack were propelled across the German
skies, they had been overtaken by a small formation of eight Mosquitos, the nimbler aircraft there to help with the process of marking
targets in the city far below. These Mosquitos in turn were catching
up with an advance party of Pathfinder Lancasters; it was from these
planes that the Christmas trees were dropped, hypnotically bright
markers betraying the shape and contours of the target city with such
lurid beauty.

In earlier stages of the war, the inaccuracy of RAF bombing raids
had given cause for concern as synthetic-oil refineries escaped demolition while explosives landed in open country. As bomber pilot
William Topper recalled, this was due in part to 'scanty' or indeed
non-existent markers,[1] but the guidance technology was improving,
and by the night of 13 February 1945 target indicators, as they were
known, were extremely effective. The unearthly light of a marker
flare was carried in a bomb casing in the form of sixty magnesium flares; when ejected from the aircraft, the casings opened and each
flare was fused to ignite in the air shortly afterwards. When falling to
earth, these sixty incandescences would, according to Topper, look
from a distance either like a bunch of grapes, or a magician's bouquet,
or more frequently an inverted fir tree, hence the 'Christmas tree'

21. Air Chief Marshal Sir Arthur Harris of Bomber Command, seen at the board in the centre, was of acidic temperament, but was gregarious and inspired loyalty.

22. Bomb aimer Miles Tripp, far left, together with his bomber crew. This author-to-be wrote later of his crew's friendship and dreams as they flew night after night through enemy fire, death an iron-cold expectation.

23. The American novelist Kurt Vonnegut was taken prisoner in the icy winter of 1944. On 13 February 1945 he and his fellow captives were being held in a Dresden abattoir. That night would inspire one of the most abiding novels of the twentieth century.

24. The conditions over Dresden on 13 February 1945 were unusually clear; vast 'Cookie' bombs were dropped, smashing through rows of buildings and instantly fragmenting entire streets.

25. Bombers carried cameras that photographed the destruction. One bomb aimer described the lattice of light that the fiercely burning streets had become.

26. Terrified people sheltering on the ground below listened intently for the abrupt change of note as a plane's bombs were released and the lightened craft suddenly gained altitude.

27. The firestorm generated temperatures that caused clothing to combust, tar to melt and cobbles and lamp posts to sear uncovered flesh. As the night wore on, the storm became an infernal tower of fire reaching almost a mile into the sky.

28. In the aftermath, the bombed city was almost impossible to negotiate. Rubble seethed with heat and once-familiar streets could no longer be identified.

29. Emergency teams were summoned from Berlin to deal with the corpses. Desiccated and mummified on the surface, there were thousands more in brick basements beneath, chambers which had become ovens.

30. The American raid of 14 February was launched against an already pulverized city.

31. The most famous photograph of the devastation, taken by Richard Peter, depicted not a stone angel but a statue representing Goodness on the roof of Dresden City Hall, overlooking the unthinkable destruction in the south of the Altstadt.

33. Thousands of bodies were burned on makeshift pyres in the central market square. The threat of pestilence amid the decay meant there was no time for conventional burial or cremation.

32. Given the dismembered or otherwise mutilated state of so many thousands of bodies, the authorities often had to rely on possessions to identify them.

34. Prisoners of war had to dig bodies out of basements. Kurt Vonnegut later wrote that moving through these shattered streets was like walking on the moon.

35. Amid the charnel-house horror, authorities also had to contend with many thousands of refugees, including great numbers of small children, who had to be fed, hydrated and found billets in villages around the city.

36. Already disoriented from trying to negotiate the city's fragmented streets, survivors also had to cope with the noxious smell of burning materials mixed with what one survivor remembered as the 'terrible sweetness' of death.

37. As the Nazi regime fell and the Soviets overtook Dresden, the labour of clearing the streets began. Tracks were laid for railway trucks to bear away the vast hills of rubble.

38. There were some volunteers for clearing, but Russian soldiers found means of pressing other less-willing citizens into labouring duties, including finding their identity papers 'faulty'.

image. When these fiery flares landed, they would continue to burn and glow, throwing their light all around on the ground. Afterwards would come further target indicators – heavier illuminations of brightest red – dropped with even more precision from smaller Mosquito bombers. For the raid on Dresden, Topper was the lead target-indicator pilot. He and the other Mosquito pilots – their planes and their loads lighter – were able to race across the darkened skies to reach the east of Germany within about three hours. They knew next to nothing about the city's defences; intelligence had not been able to penetrate that far. Their one feinting manoeuvre was to first point towards the nearby industrial city of Chemnitz and only at the very last moment bank towards Dresden. For Topper, the only unusual thing about that night, apart from the intense cold, was the distance they had to fly.

He was twenty-nine years old and a journalist by profession. Born in Lancashire, he had volunteered for the RAF instantly at the declaration of war in 1939. He proved so proficient as an all-rounder in training that he in turn became a flight instructor. The later years of the war had then seen him flying bombing raids over a variety of German targets – cities, factories and refineries. He remembered one occasion in the autumn of 1944 when the cloud cover was so low that, as his plane finally dropped beneath it, he found himself suddenly confronted with the prospect of tall refinery chimneys racing towards him.

Then he and his colleagues were briefed for Dresden. 'We all knew it was a lovely city,' he recalled. His assigned target was the Ostragehege sport stadium – one of three stadia in the city, as he recalled from the maps. Topper also knew, as did his colleagues, that the city 'was full of refugees, it was full of art treasures', adding, 'We were told [that] it had been the Russians who asked for it.' That briefing, he remembered, was explicit in setting out why the Soviets wanted Dresden to be targeted – the Germans, they were told, were sending vast quantities of supplies through the city to the eastern front. Topper also remembered that they were warned very cogently on no account to fly any further east if their planes ran into difficulty. They were left to draw their own conclusions, said Topper. He knew that the distance involved would be stretching the Mosquito to its outer limits, and there was also a precise choreography that had to be followed. The Mosquitos had to get out of the way fast so that the Lancasters following a matter of minutes behind could sweep through smoothly. Adding to the tension of precision timing, the Mosquitos had to follow a different course on the return to Britain, leaving space for the vast phalanx of second-wave bombers.

The weather conditions were by no means certain. Topper recalled that the Meteorological Office had seen the development of a serious cold front that would freeze the land and the skies from the east all the way to Britain. They could not be certain about the depth of cloud cover that night. Fortunately, not long before Topper and his colleagues were set to climb into the night there came reports of a favourable break in cloud over eastern Germany, a window of opportunity that would open after 9 p.m. From Topper's point of view, the mission then became 'almost a doddle'. There was little opposition as they flew at 30,000 feet; then, after three hours, and after the feint towards Chemnitz, the dramatic bank to Dresden and, suddenly, there it was. The river was visible winding through the city, which itself simply looked 'cold and grey'. But the first of the Christmas trees were twinkling: green and silver.

Topper and his fellow Mosquito pilots had descended fast and were just a few thousand feet above the ground; they would drop further to not very much more than the height of a modern office skyscraper. Topper had an impression of the bridges over the river being busy with refugees. Then he saw the stadium and he knew it was time to begin. As well as the target indicators, each Mosquito was now also fitted with the latest in high-speed camera technology on the underside. When markers were dropped, the camera would take six photographs in fast succession, together with almost preternaturally bright flashes. Those flashes would cause several pilots a moment of blood-quickening fear, the certainty that they had been hit, and then the heavy pulse of relief upon remembering.

The phrase used over the radio between the planes was 'Tally ho!'; part morale-boosting, part ironic, this cry was the preserve of country hunts, the riders in red coats pursuing the fox across green fields. Thought to have originated in the late eighteenth century, a corruption of the French '*Taïaut!*', which was a cry to the hounds in deer hunts, it became associated most strongly with the rural English upper classes; an unthinking full-throated shout pitched with the hunting horn. By the 1940s, the phrase had been expropriated by working-class music-hall comedians in mockery; for the young men of Bomber Command, whose social backgrounds on the whole were not exalted, it was part of a rich and expansive self-conscious lexicon of RAF slang that made light of death.

Into the cold grey went the fiercely burning target indicators. A 'large pool of red appeared in the middle of the stadium', recalled Topper. The other Mosquitos were now dropping their own indicators, which spread out a little from the stadium and into the narrow streets of the Altstadt; their work done, they could now depart. Topper, though, as lead marker, was de facto deputy for the mission; he and his co-pilot instead turned away before circling, supervising from a distance. He watched as into that shallow valley of spires and domes, bridges and narrow lanes, ever more glittering lights fell from the sky.

In the streets of the city, a few allowed themselves to be captivated by these lights, even though they understood the danger very well. Norbert Bürgel was with his uncle, just outside the city centre; they had been on a tram heading back to the suburbs when the sirens began. According to Bürgel, the electric current was suddenly cut off and the tram came to a halt.[2] The handful of passengers, on a street about a mile out of the city centre, watched as in the distance the sky lit up with white and green and red flares. Instinctively, Norbert and his uncle ran to the underside of a railway bridge, thinking that this might give them some cover against what was so clearly coming.

To the east of the city, Georg and Marielein Erler were sitting in their cellar beneath the grand apartment house they lived in. Some of their neighbours were present, but there were still a couple missing, even as the faint vibration of the first planes could be felt in the air. The Sieber family, who lived on the third floor, eventually materialized at the door of the cellar and took their places. They told the Erlers and the others that they had been looking at the descending lights from their windows. 'This observation,' recalled Georg Erler, 'left no doubt that Dresden's fate was set. For a defence by German flak against the impending attack was out of the question.'[3]

Young Dieter Haufe, to the north-west of the city, was looking out of the pavement-level window of the half-basement/workshop that he and his family were using as a shelter. Despite imprecations to come away from the glass, he could not stop staring at the red and yellow falling from the sky.

Closer to the centre, Winfried Bielss and his friend Horst could see that they were moments away from terrible danger and were running the last few yards to his apartment building in Sanger Strasse. 'When we arrived back at home, it was almost like daylight,' he recalled of the luridly lit city. 'The cloud cover was yellowish coloured and . . . orange Christmas trees fell through the clouds.'[4] When they arrived, Bielss found his mother more distracted and harassed than panicking; she had been working at her sewing machine and was determined before the attack began to get it and as many finished pieces of clothing as possible down to the basement shelter. She had heard the alert on the radio and had herself been mesmerized by the coming of that gaudy night, but now, with supreme practicality, she directed her son and his friend to grab all the pieces of clothing they could from the apartment and take shelter in the cellar. By this time, he recalled, the noise of the bombers was deafening.

The target indicators had been dropped over the Ostragehege by Topper, the first intense spot of red burning within the stadium and others fanning out like the spokes of a wheel, so that the bombs that followed might not all be concentrated on one small area. The angles of so many centuries-old streets were thrown into a terrible and lurid relief by the unnatural light. The deepening hum told all the sheltering citizens what was to come.

15. 10.03 p.m.

The blasts were felt as much as heard; booms that jolted through the chest. 'The house shuddered,' recalled Dr Albert Fromme, who had been sheltering with friends, neighbours and children in a cellar to the west of the city. 'The children were very excitable.'[1] The neighbour Herr Schrell, whose wife had just been celebrating her birthday, proclaimed: 'I think we have been hit.' They had not; they would have known nothing about it if they had.

The first wave of the attack on Dresden had started with the target indicators at 10.03 p.m., a little ahead of the schedule that the controllers had anticipated. Just moments later, the following planes roared out of the distant black sky; citizens of Dresden might have been expecting the bright beams of searchlights from the hills, the crack of defensive firepower as teenage gunners aimed flak at the invaders. But all such firepower had been moved east, and there was no resistance. Georg Frank was in the cellar of his apartment block with his parents. He was still wrapped in the blanket that he had been sleeping in. 'From afar you could hear the muffled hum of aircraft engines and the first detonation of bombs.'[2]

The Lancasters, flying 10–13,000 feet above, were dropping, in the main, two forms of lethal weapon: incendiary devices, intended to start fires in and around the wood-filled buildings, preceded by high-explosive 'Blockbuster' or 'Cookie' bombs, mostly 4,000lb in weight. These bombs were about the size of three men standing in a huddle. When the plane's bomb aimer pressed the release mechanism, they dropped through the sky nose-first. Primed to detonate on contact with any hard surface, they delivered simple annihilation, the term 'Blockbuster' signalling their capacity to bring down entire blocks and terraces. A direct hit from such a bomb would simply take the architecture of a building apart with a shock wave that would radiate with such strength that even an aeroplane a few thousand feet up would be buffeted. The incendiaries, bound together in clumps, were more insidious. These were intended to capitalize on the dislocations caused by the bombs, dropping down through gaping roofs and catching fire, flame gradually joining with flame across the fresh ruins of even the grandest institutions.

In the boarding house where Mischka Danos was hosting his leaving party, he and his guests were, almost incredibly, ignoring the warning sirens, perhaps through the insouciance of youth, perhaps because they had simply heard them too often. The get-together continued until one moment of utterly surreal fright when, with no warning, Danos's closed bedroom door came off its hinges and appeared to 'slowly keel' into the room.[3] For a few seconds, Danos and his guests simply gazed at this phenomenon. Finally, they understood it was time to go down to the basement. The distant bass booms became gradually more distinct.

For those in other cellars, the nausea of claustrophobia was now increasingly difficult to suppress. Margot Hille was sitting with her mother in the communal shelter 150 yards from their apartment block in the south-west of the city. This too had a window; the pavement and the street outside were as 'bright as day' with the flares.[4] And then came the approaching crashes, each one delivering its own individual shock. The Hilles' neighbour, Frau Fischer, who had been sitting beside them, collapsed. It was assumed that she was having a heart attack.[5] What help could there be as the booms grew louder? Margot's mother tried to comfort and calm Frau Fischer as best she could.

Margot Hille was not to know that already, just moments into the attack, her cousins who lived close to the city centre were dead. Their apartment building near the Ostragehege had been torn apart. Even in their shelter they had been dismembered and burned almost instantaneously, yet their mother, in that same shelter, was somehow still alive, horribly seared by what was later presumed wrongly to be burning phosphorus. If this cellar, like so many others, had had a pavement-level window, the force and the heat of the blasts would – in a blink – have shattered it into hundreds of thousands of superheated shards, as it had innumerable others around the city.

For Gisela Reichelt, sitting in an ill-lit basement to the south of the railway station, just a few minutes after 10 p.m., there was not just her own fear to cope with; her mother too seemed absolutely paralysed, and the ten-year-old girl had no idea what to do. She remembered how a 'Hitler Youth boy' had come running down to their cellar to announce that the entire city was glowing with Christmas trees; and that the air-raid warden 'told us in horror that it was probably going to be a terrible night'.[6] The first bombs were deafening and came, she said, 'blow by blow'. The air itself seemed to ripple. 'Everyone in the cellar began to pray,' she recalled. 'Even those who did not believe in God.'[7] Although she had taken her two dolls with her, she now felt too old to be comforted by them, so she joined the grown-ups in praying. 'I was scared and I did not know what to do, the fear took control of me,' she later recounted.[8]

Just to the north of the Elbe, overlooking the Neustadt and the Altstadt, Winfried Bielss, his mother and his friend Horst were sitting in the basement with the other residents of their apartment block, looking upwards towards the low ceiling. Bielss recalled that as well as the shocks, there was almost a musicality in the sounds of destruction. It produced a state of near terror in everyone. The air pressure generated by the first detonations was so powerful that the floor shook.[9] There was also a poltergeist effect: doors on floors above rattling with frightening violence and being slammed open and shut, as though by a compulsive demon. 'Paint and plaster came off the wall and there was dust,'[10] Bielss recalled. The dust became pervasive, so that as well as claustrophobic unease there was a sudden unspoken concern about whether they could breathe the air itself. But above all this was the satanic music: the deep hum of all the passing aircraft, in counterpoint with a 'swelling singing and whistling' created by the falling bombs. 'The light was still burning,' he remembered, 'but we became very quiet and looked up in alarm' at the pressure of another nearby explosion. There was more spasmodic rattling agitation from doors above; then the silvery clangour of the house's windows shattering.

Awful as they were, these effects were minor compared with what was happening in the close-built dwellings in the narrow streets of the Altstadt that had either been partially demolished by falling explosives or were now being eaten by climbing flames sparked by the sticks of incendiaries. And in the cellars beneath – those that had not collapsed or fallen in – huddled elderly women and men, mothers with infants, small children, sitting on floors or makeshift chairs, motionless. In some, the lights were flickering. In others, the air was growing harder to breathe. In the heart of the Altstadt, the brick-work of the underground maze of connected cellars was shaking; walls bulged inwards, doors jammed.

Many had equipped their cellars with buckets of water and blankets; moist blankets would be their only armour if they had to fight through intense heat. But these small brick chambers were beginning to seem more like tombs than sanctuaries. Those within who were not praying may have started to notice a curious pressure in their lungs. This might have been psychosomatic for some, but whatever the truth it required extraordinary effort of will not to listen to instinct: that impulse to get out into the air and run, far into the dark cold night and beyond the crashing and the inhuman whistling. But the instinct would have been wrong; those who were outside in the Altstadt were beyond all hope of such rational escape. One soldier cycling down the street was blown off his bicycle and in that split second of detonation his limbs were neatly removed, his torso coming to rest on the road. The bellowing fire of the explosions instantly charred anyone in their path and burned off all their clothing, leaving them both dead and naked.

For those below simply listening helplessly – those whose homes lay under the flight of the bombers – this was an exercise in mental endurance. Georg and Marielein Erler were tested to an extraordinary degree. 'Apparently the first bomb exploded some distance from our house,' recalled Herr Erler. 'Immediately afterwards came the second one, the third one and, by degrees, the noise grew more and more thunderous. It became so furious that it seemed it might turn the house upside down.'[11] He and his wife together with his neigh-bours and their children sat rigid in helpless silence. 'Every moment, we were preparing for the eventuality that the next one would hit this room, that there would be a sudden end. Then, suddenly,' Herr Erler continued, 'the next explosion came in really terribly close.'[12] Then several dreadful things happened at once: a brick in the cellar wall that had been deliberately loosened on a previous occasion to allow greater circulation of air suddenly shot out and flew across the cellar; the blast of hot air that caused this also instantly snuffed out the candles that they had been burning and the electric bulb failed. The Erlers and their neighbours were in instant darkness. 'The walls shook and the house seemed to collapse over us,' remembered Herr Erler. 'A terrible bursting and shattering sound was heard.'[13]

Lancasters were flying over the city at the rate of one every five to ten seconds; the relentless hum high above was a source of intense psychological distress but also – to those either under it or observing from a slight distance – a cause of black wonder. To the north-west of the city, Norbert Bürgel and his uncle were still under a bridge, having watched the spectacle of the Christmas trees. It was as if the boy and his guardian were taking shelter from a rainstorm. But it was from this vantage that both found themselves hypnotized by the skyline before them; the distant booms and echoes, and the macabre brightening of the sky above the old spires.

They were mercifully removed from the raw spectacle of panic among other refugees, not least those who had sought safety beneath the central railway station. The station itself had not been marked out as a target, it lay just a street or two outside the radius of the glowing, fizzing markers, but the geometry of the raid – the intricacy of the calculations to ensure maximum impact – meant that bombs and incendiaries were being released to rain down destruction upon an ever-wider area. Those gathered in the echoing tunnels beneath the station were beginning to feel the full effects of the Allies' savage assault.

There was a train on one platform that had been due to leave, pointing along the silver rails to the western night; the passengers who had rushed to board now found themselves sitting targets beneath that vast glass-vaulted roof. The stairs that led down to the concourse and the tunnels were still crowded when, with shattering detonations, the monsoon of superheated glass from the station's roof combined with the searing flare of fire on the platforms and at the stairheads to create a primal surge of panic-fuelled strength from the top of the stairs that pulsed down to crush those below. People at the bottom suffered the lethal asphyxiating weight of dozens upon them while those above were burned, disfigured and torn open by shrapnel. Screams were superfluous, or at least not remembered by witnesses. Somehow, in the midst of so many people acting wholly on terrified impulse, the railway police elsewhere in the sheltering tunnels were able to persuade other passengers to remain still.

The majority of the high explosives were falling in the streets north of the station. The nearby hotel used by the vicious bureaucracy of the Gestapo – the Continental – had been bisected with such a bomb. The incendiaries were quick to start gnawing at its highly flammable innards: the wooden furniture, the textiles. In two other Nazi strong-holds, however, the defences were holding firm. There was a shelter beneath the Albertinum which was being used as a base for the city's civilian defenders – the firefighters and the police. Gauleiter Martin Mutschmann was to be found neither here nor in the smart shelters beneath the Taschenberg Palace half a mile west, so he was probably taking cover in the private shelter constructed beneath his own com-mandeered residence. No one appears to have missed him.

Other Nazi officials were on view, though. In the cellars of the Taschenberg Palace, soldier Lothar Rolf Luhm and his comrade Günther Tschernik were observing the 'well-fed burghers in brown uniforms'[14] who appeared to be in radio contact with other Nazis around the city. But ten minutes into this rhythmically jolting onslaught, they were clearly as helpless as all their fellow citizens, if rather better insulated. The impact of the detonations could be felt but this cellar seemed secure. There was one focus of clear anxiety: the idea of a fire starting above, flames taking possession of the palace and creating an inferno directly above their heads, cutting off the exits. Even as the bombers continued to fly over, Luhm and Günther noticed 'the men with golden tassels' looking at them, and Luhm guessed that the two soldiers in this shelter would very soon be sent out into the dark on fire-watching duty to ensure that any rooftop flames were extinguished, regardless of the danger.

Even in this cataclysm, some were a fraction more relaxed than their fellow Dresdeners. Otto Griebel was still in the brick-lined cellar of the Altstadt tavern with his friend Scheinpflug. They had been drinking spirits before the attack began and it seemed – as a heavy blast shook the foundations of the cellar and caused the lightbulb to go out, leaving all the guests sitting in perfect, eye-pulsing darkness – that they were managing to control their panic. They were not yet to know that they were at the heart of the catastrophe; even after only ten minutes of bombing, there were streets around them that were deformed beyond any recognition. Perhaps there was a belief that this had to end; that the Allies would not spend the entire night sending plane after plane over. Perhaps also too there was the first inkling – which was to be reflected across the city – of a hideous curiosity. If only the cellar could withstand the next few minutes – and when the bombers were swooping away into the distance, back to their own country – what then would the friends see outside? What would their world look like?

It was around that point that the angular Gothic construction of the Kreuzschule was hit, the bomb punching straight down through it, stone and wood offering no resistance. That moment brought annihilation to eleven boys and three priests who had been in the shelter. The fires took hold quickly afterwards. The other boarders, together with their choirmaster, Rudolf Mauersberger, escaped the building into the stinging, cindery air outside; the boys were corralled eastwards, across the burning forecourt, in the direction of the Great Garden park a couple of streets away. The pulse of the blast on the Kreuzschule had forced out every window, every pane of glass, every door.

Nor was there was any comfort for anyone taking shelter near the dark stones of the Kreuzkirche, which stood close to the Renner department store. Part of the roof of the Kreuzkirche was hit, and the nave of the vast church was fragmented in the shock waves. The church was now open to the sky; and to the seemingly endless cascade of magnesium incendiaries. The fires were fed with splintered pews. In the ear-shattering pandemonium, the mighty bell in the tower of the Kreuzkirche tolled violently with the repercussion. Just yards away, Renner, the shop that represented the modern secular life of the city, was penetrated in a flash, the vast bomb unravelling in an instant the complex structure of its impressive escalator. In every department the fabrics, the furniture, the clothes, the household goods, the bedding, the linen immediately caught fire.

In the streets around it there were still substantial numbers of rural refugees and terrified horses. Even those who were not pulverized or shredded by metal and stone shrapnel, or simply burned alive, could not escape the lethal effects of the high explosives. The bombs changed the very air itself, replacing breathable oxygen with a momentary supersonic shock that could either dismember a human body in under a second or leave its internal organs squeezed, lungs drawn almost inside out. Hearts would be violently contracted and expanded; innumerable blood vessels and veins and arteries would burst at once. As the blast radiated out, the composition of the atmosphere was elasticated, expanding and instantly compressing as though the sky itself was struggling to breathe.

Those standing under the low stone ceilings of the crypt beneath the Frauenkirche a few streets further north experienced the attack as a series of almost subsonic booms, so deep they were more a visceral than an aural experience. Like Gisela Reichelt in her cellar, many that night surely prayed with a passionate faith that they had never before acknowledged even to themselves. Perhaps there was a sense that the Frauenkirche would be spared; that such a sacred space could never be a target. The pillars of the church, mighty blocks of sandstone, might have afforded a more immediate stability; unlike all the brick cellars in which the walls were beginning to crumble, the temperature was rising and the atmosphere was becoming more and more airless, the crypt of the Frauenkirche and the cold flagstones of its floor might have seemed comfortingly serene.

But outside, the studied elegance of Dresden was being mutilated; several streets down, the upmarket shops of Prager Strasse and the smart apartments of the wealthier citizens nearby were crushed, the glass of window displays shattering. Boutiques, perfumiers, jewellers: the exquisite ornaments and fragrances scorched to their base constituents. Elegant hotels were punched inwards; silk curtains shredded and flaming, marble floors cracked, beds and linens and carpets eaten – slowly at first but with fast-gathering strength – by more fire. A street of once haughty grandeur was now hissing and spitting with burst pipes, dissected pavements, the crackle of tables and chairs in exposed restaurants as the flames met. The people sheltering in basements directly beneath these smart shops now found exits blocked with burning rubble; they knew they were buried alive.

Then there was the landscape that was shared by all, the common cultural and religious focal points that between them seemed to contain the different shades of the city's soul. The Zwinger Palace and Pavilion and ornamental gardens were hit. Although the art works contained within the palace had long since been removed to safety, the building itself – in part a baroque fantasia – was one of the city's most cherished landmarks, a signifier of a light-hearted, droll sensibility that had been advertised to a wider world. There was little here for the flames to get a grip on, but the finely ornamented pavilion was instantaneously made gaunt and hollow. Just a few yards away from this was the even greater splendour of the Semper Opera House; that night, its reception rooms, gilded boxes, the vast auditorium of velvet and fine-grained wood, were opened up and incinerated. Like the Zwinger Palace, this completely incidental target was one that struck at the city's heart, its entire view of its own ethos and special place in modern civilization.

Yet the historic soul of the city lay some yards to the south east, across a cobbled square: the Catholic cathedral, an eighteenth-century baroque construction, in the crypts of which were contained the remains of Saxon kings and princes. It also housed one of the city's more extraordinary relics: when the great elector Augustus the Strong died, his heart was removed and buried within the cathedral walls. Sacrilege comes in various forms; the high explosives that fell nose-first through the roof of the cathedral were tokens of pure nihilism.

This was not a factory producing optical equipment, or spare parts for planes or tanks. This was a holy place that had held on to its own unique life even throughout the coming of Hitler and the Nazis. The effect of its destruction – upon those left to see it – would be that of simple despair and fury as opposed to crushed morale. Of course, while those hundreds of planes filled the sky, no one was giving consideration to heritage; in the small brick cellars of the Altstadt, the elemental need to protect flesh and bone was almost the only conscious thought among so many thousands, recoiling at every crash. The roar of the cathedral collapse was part of the cacophony that a few streets to the east had made the occupants of the cellar beneath the Judenhaus inhabited by the Klemperers hold increasingly close to one another. Victor Klemperer recalled hearing – above the sudden repeated shocks of explosions – the small sound of whimpering.[15] He and his wife Eva found themselves, by impulse, lowering themselves to the floor and putting their heads under the chairs. Another deep impact, and suddenly the back window of their cellar was blown in. To Klemperer's horror, the courtyard outside was as 'bright as day'.[16]

The light was coming from a hideous combination of magnesium flares and fire. Another of the cellar's occupants was fast-witted enough to perceive the hazard from spreading flames and remembered that the cellar had a stirrup pump and some water. There were frantic efforts to douse and moisten the incipient blaze, and as the explosions continued all around Klemperer recalled that he lost any objective sense of time. It was as though the people in the cellars had been part-hypnotized by the ordeal; that in the act of anticipating the instant blackness at any moment, free will was held in a state of suspension.

Gisela Reichelt recalled that in her own cellar, through the booming tumult, everyone was quiet. Her heavily pregnant mother could not bear to sit; instead, in what appeared an attitude of perfect terror and despair, she was simply lying on the floor.[17]

What none of them could know was that this was only the beginning. Victor Klemperer remembered that even if it had ended there, with the first raid, it would have been understood as a horrific and unparalleled disaster. The fires, beginning to flare into greater strength, as the smashed roofs, doors and windows caused eviscerated buildings to act like giant chimneys, were starting to eat not only thousands of homes, shops and businesses but also shared and collective memories. In the space of just a quarter of an hour, that first wave of 244 bombers and nine markers had dropped some 880 tons of bombs on Dresden, 57 per cent high explosives and 43 per cent incendiaries. The 4,000lb air mines and other assorted explosives had displaced architecture; the hundreds and thousands of incendiaries, primed to ignite with different triggers and delays, were fuelling the flames that grew obligingly amid floorboards, furniture, wooden beams and

clothing The bass hum of the first wave of bombers was now reced-
ing into the night, leaving not silence but the cracks and crashes of
structural collapse. The cruellest noise of all, however, might have
been the lighter notes of the all-clear sirens that echoed from distant,
as yet undamaged streets around thirty minutes after the first marker
flares had been dropped. This was the signal to those in the cellars to
emerge. It was unintentionally cruel because the civic authorities
were telling the people of Dresden that the worst had passed.

16. The Burning Eyes

For those who were unhurt and unharmed, apart from their racing hearts, the curiosity had a dreadful unmoored quality: what did the world outside now look like? Then there was the fear: for family elsewhere, for friends, for homes, for cherished belongings and keepsakes. Had any of their material possessions survived the onslaught?

To the south of the city, Gisela Reichelt was preparing to emerge from her shelter with the grown-ups. 'Now the door of the basement was opened after what seemed an endless time,' she recalled. 'No one could imagine what to expect! The city burned brightly and it was so hot you could hardly imagine it.'[1] The road on which she lived, Schnorrstrasse, was close to the railway station; and beyond that, under the mix of low cloud cover and a widening pall of smoke, the sky was an odd shade of amber, reflecting all the flames below. The girl and her mother walked slowly along the road until they faced their own section of the apartment building. It had been torn asunder. That was when the horror came. Their home had taken a direct hit. To emphasize the implosion of their ordinary lives, mother and daughter then gradually understood that the rubbish lying around them on the street was in fact what remained of their possessions, the debris blasted out of their flat. All their belongings lay in gutters. 'We could not cry,' remembered Frau Reichelt, 'we were just glad.'[2] But mother and daughter now thought of the girl's aunt Trudel, who lived in another neighbourhood. Was she all right? How – late on this burning night and amid the human chaos – could they make contact with her?

As they, and so many others, were now stricken with helpless anxiety for loved ones, the civic authorities – even in the continued absence of the Gauleiter – were already organizing their response to the emergency with impressive speed and coordination. Fire engines and crews, many of whom had in the last few minutes come in from the suburbs around the city, were navigating volcanically hot rubble – stone, paving, concrete, collapsed tram lines, smashed pipes – to get as close in as possible to the wildfires in the Altstadt. The reservoirs in the Alt-markt had been constructed there for this very eventuality; a plentiful supply of water to douse the fires. Yet despite their willingness, the crews found themselves facing an already daunting proposition: ever-climbing blazes stretching out over a vast area from the river down to the railway station a mile away – a landscape of fire.

A little to the south-west of this, Margot Hille and her mother had emerged from their basement. The suburb they lived in, although not directly beneath the main wave of bombers, had still received some stray blasts and incendiaries and Margot, a member of the League of German Girls, was anxious to do her duty. She decided to make for the centre of the city and give first aid to all who needed it.[3] Her mother, staring at the livid sky and taking in the distant deep noise, was frightened by the idea. In any case, they first had to check that their own home was still intact.

Frau Hille's apartment was on the third floor of their block. They took precautions: as part of their emergency kits they had goggles to protect their eyes from flames or falling debris. As they climbed the stairs, it seemed at first glance that – despite fires in neighbouring blocks, and a larger blaze at a nearby textile factory – all was in relatively good order. There was a 'large, crescent-shaped' skylight window above the third landing and Margot Hille made to open it.[4] The percussive effect of even distant blasts had wrought its damage. The frame had been shaken loose and both it and the glass swung inwards, striking Margot hard on the head, the window smashing at her feet. She had taken the weight of it on her nose. 'Thank goodness I was wearing the goggles,' she recalled.

After taking a few moments to recover, and finding that otherwise the property seemed relatively undamaged – the young woman was even more determined to head into the Altstadt to perform her civic duty. But her mother now held her back by telling her that she had very possibly suffered a concussion from the falling window, and that if she went she would be in as much jeopardy as those she sought to help. 'That's how she saved my life,' recalled Margot.[5]

She also unknowingly saved her daughter from the distress of seeing injuries and mortal wounds that lay quite beyond her imagination.
The firefighters trying to manoeuvre through the narrow streets of
the Altstadt, down tall alleys framed with bright flame issuing from
blank, broken windows, continually encountered corpses as they
went – people who, it might only be presumed, had been crazed by
the claustrophobia and increasing heat of the narrow brick cellars and
had thought fatally that they would fare better in the open. Many
simply lay on pavements as though asleep; as if all that had happened
was that they had succumbed to peaceful fatigue. And all around, the
heat pulsing against the cold night air, and the different scents of
smoke from various sources – wood, fabric, tar, paint – filled the
lanes behind the squares.

Near the castle, itself burning from a hit, was the Taschenberg Palace,
in the well-built shelter of which Lothar Rolf Luhm and Günther
Tschernik now understood from the 'Golden Pheasants' that they
were expected to do their duty outside. The Nazi officials were
also ready to act: the first thing was to ensure that the palace itself
was not burning. Luhm and his new fire-fighting comrades left
the cellar, climbed the stairs of the building, opened a hatchway and
made their way onto a flat section of the roof. They extinguished
several small fires caused by thermite incendiaries, which all present
mistook for what they termed phosphorous sticks,[6] but they could
also taste the heavy smoke drifting over, and at the back of the building, looking down to the cobbled road below, facing the Zwinger
Palace, they were shocked not merely at the smouldering stones, but
also by the sight of the inert fire engines and the corpses of their
crews. Luhm had been at Normandy in July 1944; now, on the roof,
he found himself thinking of that bombardment, and how even that
had 'not been as a bad' as the prospect he now faced.[7]

The flames were a source of wonder to the young refugee Norbert
Bürgel, and his uncle, who had watched that first raid from under a
bridge. Uncle Günther, perhaps traumatized, was gripped by some
extraordinary imp of the perverse; he thought that if they could get

to the railway station, then perhaps normality would have resumed and they might be able to get home – he lived a little out of the city – by rail. A glance at the skyline might have told him otherwise, but there was also a sense of awe as the middle-aged man and the young lad now walked towards that brightly burning centre. In their view was the former cigarette factory, turned ammunition production line, which at the beginning of the century had been originally and whimsically built to look like a giant mosque; against the black night sky, the flames leaping out of it were dazzling. They walked under the main railway line that pointed across the river, and towards the Taschenberg Palace, the Zwinger Palace, the Catholic cathedral and the castle. All had fires burning. The boy and his uncle, while aware of all the hazards, could seemingly not stop their march, as though they were hypnotically drawn. To the rear of the Taschenberg Palace were a few small courts, and then Wilsdruffer Strasse, upon which stood some of the city's smartest shops. The whole road was now bathed in dancing, searing light; from both sides of the wide avenue, fires shot out and upward from the shattered windows of smoke-blackened buildings. The pair veered to the right, southward, in the direction of Prager Strasse and thence the central station. Through the side streets, recalled Bürgel, they had been able to see the burning Altmarkt.[8] Carefully they picked their way down several more streets of tall, smoking buildings; but they could see that it was probably impossible to get to the railway station. Fires erupting behind windows above them and roofs ablaze from dropped incendiaries, not to mention the thickening smoke and ever-increasing heat, forced them to change direction, and so they pointed themselves north once more, moving slowly in the direction of the River Elbe.

At around 11 p.m., some thirty minutes after that first wave of planes had finished their work, there were tiny corners in the Altstadt – corners so far free from fire – where a few people gathered, dazed and beyond ordinary language. The uncle and the boy came to a small bar, relatively unscathed, that was affiliated with the Würzburger brewery. Several people were inside and Uncle Günther decided that some refreshment was in order before their extraordinary odyssey continued. He ordered half a litre of beer. 'The bombed-out had

already made themselves comfortable,' observed Bürgel.[9] The respite
was to be brief.

In another bar, a few hundred yards away, the drinkers had responded
to the all-clear with some caution. The shock suffered by Otto Griebel and his musician friends in the cellar when the lightbulb had
suddenly gone out had been offset by a corresponding moment of
relief when, a short time later, it began to glow uncertainly again. On
hearing the faint cry of the all-clear they had gingerly left the cellar
and climbed the stairs to the bar to discover that, although the buildings all around were either smoking, smouldering or aflame, their
own establishment was serendipitously largely untouched save for a
smashed window. That alone called for further refreshment: a drink
to survival. The landlady produced a flask of schnapps and some
glasses.

The streets around them were heavy with the dissonance of
silence and sudden grinding noise, the collapse of stones and bricks.
Emerging from this curious atmosphere came the wife of one of the
musicians who was drinking there, entering through the still-intact
front door wearing an air warden's helmet. With tears pouring down
her face, she told her husband that they had lost everything.

For the others, that strong liquor was welcome, but Otto Griebel
was now extremely anxious to get back to his family apartment in the
south-east of the city. He had no way of knowing if his wife and
children had come through the attack unharmed, or whether the raid
had been concentrated on the centre of the town. Near 11 p.m., he
made his shaken excuses to the landlady and his friends and stepped
outside into a changed world.

The thickly heated air was becoming uncomfortable to breathe;
Griebel watched firemen all around aiming jets skyward at high windows. Because of the fires, the centre had become a maze filled with
dead ends of masonry and burning timber. The artist instead pointed his
way towards the river, perhaps reasoning that he would be able to circle
around the worst of the damage and weave back through untargeted
streets. Reaching the river, with the fires to be seen roaring in the
municipal buildings on its far bank, Griebel gazed at the curious

spectacle of the Carolabrücke: around the structure, before it spanned the water, there issued ghostly blue flames.[10] It took him a while to realize that this was the result of gas pipes somewhere having been hit. Griebel continued to stare; and then angled eastward.

On the other side of that bridge, the audience and the staff of the Sarrasani circus were emerging from the theatre's basement, the staff checking anxiously for fires. There were small conflagrations in the straw near the stables and other parts of the permanent structure had been hit, but the building was intact. The impresario Trude Stosch was nevertheless anxious; her instinct, shared by so many other Dresdeners in the Neustadt, was for everyone to assemble on the meadows by the waters of the Elbe. In particular, she wanted the performing horses and their handlers and riders to make for the open air. (The circus tigers obviously had to remain in their cages at the back of the building.) Illuminated by the nearby flames of the shattered Japanese Palace, the elegant horses were guided onto the street, and thence to the gentle grassy slope that led down to the river, where they moved among huge numbers of terrified refugees; and they all faced the fiery spectacle of the Altstadt, the glow reflected in the black waters of the Elbe.

Mischka Danos recalled that as he and his friends cautiously left his boarding-house basement after the first raid, there was initially a remarkable absence of fear. On that gentle hill near his university electronics laboratories, and overlooking at a distance the old city, he was hypnotized by the kinetic spectacle of fiery eruptions: on the wide avenue where he was standing, apartment blocks suddenly exhaled flame; down the hill, those flames near the railway station were more intense and beyond that, into the old city, it was becoming difficult to see. His own research building close by had just caught fire; the blaze was in one of the topmost storeys. Given that the planes had passed, Danos like so many others assumed that it was now safe, and he began forming plans to escort his friend, the 'Karl May' girl, home. But his curiosity about the fires in the city was overwhelming; he craved a better view. So Danos fixed upon climbing a little further up the hill. He remembered that in a stretch of open ground, there had been an anti-aircraft battery position. He also knew that it had been abandoned a while ago. This, then, would serve as his vantage point.[11]

In some cases, the bombers had managed to hit pertinent targets: the factory compounds of the Zeiss Ikon works, although constructed to withstand such a raid, were none the less very seriously damaged. The slave labourers – inmates from concentration camps brought in to engage in specialized technical tasks – were not on site but in barracks a little north of the city. Under the weight of the bombardment, even reinforced modern structures were forced to bend and snap. Also overwhelmed by the conflagration was the bulk of the Seidel und Naumann works. Closer to the river, that vast cigarette factory, recently converted for the manufacture of bullets, was now exhaling flame. The same was true of many other converted munitions works that were to be found outside the Altstadt. One slave labourer in a camp on the edge of the city that night was a Czech Jew called Michal Salomonivic; he recalled looking out at the rich amber sky and feeling a wave of exultation: surely this was a sign that the war was almost over.[12]

Closer to the centre of the city, a teenage girl called Erika Seydewitz had spent the last half an hour or so frantically fighting the conflagrations started by the incendiaries.[13] Her family lived in a fourth-floor apartment very close to the Rathaus. Like countless others, they had experienced that first wave of bombings as a series of sonic shocks in a small brick cellar, from the walls of which dust had cascaded. An especially loud crash was heard just before the all-clear sounded, which the girl's middle-aged father was convinced was the noise of their apartment block being hit. He made for the cellar stairs and his spirited daughter signalled her intention to go with him. He did not demur.

Her father ascended first, beckoning her to stay on the ground floor, and then he called for her to come up. Astonishingly, given that they had been directly in the bombers' path, the damage appeared to amount to one shattered window in the living room, burst skylights on the landing and cracks in the ceiling looking up to larger apertures in the apartment-block roof. They tried the electric lights and found to their amazement that they worked. However, it was clear that the pair were not safe; embers and sparks from incendiaries and other fires were beginning to swirl around in a strange, strengthening wind, falling through the skylights and the ceiling cracks and flying through the gaping window. Father and daughter could see the danger from these 'fireflies' and 'glow-worms', as they described them.[14] They had some rudimentary emergency equipment: a large stirrup pump and some buckets of water. The aim was to rescue as many of their valuables as they could and get them out of the apartment. Erika and her father now went down to fetch her mother and sister. The family gathered in the apartment. Through force of habit stemming from years of blackout observation, the mother switched off the light. The father switched it back on again so they could see what they were doing as they fetched their possessions. The mother had to be stopped from switching it off again. 'We just could not convince my mother that the little light that was produced from the fitting did not really matter compared to the stronger light that was coming from outside,' recalled Frau Seydewitz.[15]

The family were aware that they had to hurry. As the eldest daughter worked the water pump, squirting at the 'glow-worms' onto the rugs and near the curtains, her mother grabbed a large bag. Into this she threw some items from the kitchen, then some more valuable belongings from the bedroom: a camera, some shoes and even a hat. Through the cracked ceiling could be seen a spreading fire up on the roof caused by a glowing thermite stick. They had to get out.

The family's most expensive domestic item was their new, state-of-the-art sewing machine, and it was Herr Seydewitz who took charge of carrying this downstairs as mother and sister hauled the big bag filled with the other domestic bric-a-brac. The level-headedness shown by them all was remarkable, for outside in the Altstadt it was obvious that the flames were brightening and the eerie and stifling hot breeze was intensifying. There were other residents in the building who had ventured out of the cellar; some were elderly, and now seemed paralysed on the stairs. The Seydewitzes had planned to return to the cellar to see out the night, but now it became clear that, despite all their firefighting efforts, the building was going to burn.

Erika saw the thickening smoke on the fourth and third floors; very quickly it began to billow. The family was gathered in the ground-floor lobby, but now it looked as though they were trapped as the land on every side became a wall of flame. Close by was the grand department store Böhme; and it was engulfed. The flaming wreckage was falling from the sky. The family had a car, but had they left it too late to flee? At the back of the apartment building was a water barrel, and they swiftly soaked all their coats, and some rescued blankets too. Erika, keeping a lookout from the front, told them that the flames from neighbouring blazes no longer seemed to be licking at their walls. There was a chance.

But what to do about the elderly neighbours? One old woman 'sat on the stairs in the hallway [and] gave us no answer'.[16] Fortuitously, her son arrived at the apartment block, and she was happy to move for him. But there were two other older residents, a husband and wife, who seemed similarly incapable of movement. The smoke was deepening and the pervasive heat from outside made it obvious that staying was impossible. The Seydewitzes were desperate to get out but they could not abandon these two. Erika's father found the answer, delivering his order to the old lady 'in a sharp tone'. 'There was a blazing glow on the street,' Erika recalled. 'The overhead line of the tram hung down.'[17] And here was something she had never observed before: the tarmac on the road was searingly hot. Everyone was loaded into the car, but within a few yards it was clear that it would not get very much further. The tar was bubbling. The family and the old couple would somehow have to find some shelter on foot, sticking to cobbled pavements as opposed to the treacle of the road. The cobbles were hot; and all they could find by means of cover was an archway over a passage near the Rathaus.

Down in the cellars, that bare-bulb-lit brick warren of interconnected small chambers, narrow corridors, makeshift wooden doors, there were elderly people, and mothers with prams who were reluctant to move, thinking it better to see the night out in comfortless safety. The cellars were not still. Through various passages that ran beneath the lanes that led down to the river and its meadows opposite, and to the open air of the Great Garden, other people were picking their way in multiple directions. Some were leaving, some were returning. At the larger entrances to this subterranean maze the effect of the outer doors being constantly opened and closed to let people in and out was funnelling the increasingly hot and acrid air into the tunnels. These were not purpose-built shelters but extemporizations, and so their ventilation was unplanned. The depth of the cellars varied, too, according to the ages of the buildings above, which added to the problem of free air flow. It had been loosely assumed that the cold wind from the river and from the large park would gust through, with a supplementary breeze coming from the innumerable smaller entrances dotted around the old city. That might have been the case in normal circumstances, but the physics of that night were far from normal and the complex pattern of twisting, turning brick passage-ways leading to that large river exit was beginning to act as a flue, sucking hot air through the chambers towards the cold Elbe outlet.

Even so, this increasing discomfort – accompanied in some cases by a growing drowsiness in the tainted air – was clearly felt by some to be worth risking. In others there was a psychological factor at work, an exhausted passivity, a sense that legs would no longer obey the impulse to move. This phenomenon had been documented in other bombings, and was observed by Erika Seydewitz as affecting her elderly neighbours.

At street level, the shops, the restaurants, the older apartment buildings, the hotels were now burning with a ferocity that was changing the physical characteristics of the atmosphere. The fire was reaching up into the sky, consuming oxygen at an ever-increasing rate, and the cold, drizzly air in the Elbe valley was rushing ever faster into that vacuum. In the cellars, the chemistry was changing too as invisible fumes began to whisper from brick chamber to brick chamber, though so gradually that those who noticed a shortness of breath, a curious feeling that even the deepest breath could not fill their lungs, might have attributed the symptoms to stress or fear.

A short distance away from the Altstadt, those who had emerged from their own basements looked with awe at the vividly flickering, ruby-red sky. For Helmut Voigt – who had spent what seemed to the boy an 'endless time' in the concrete shelter of the local brewery – there was astonishment that, in his suburb, everything seemed to be intact.[18] As he stared at the burning horizon, the worst problem he could see was that his journey to school the following morning might be more difficult than usual. When he and his mother returned to their apartment they found not one window broken. Indeed, all was so normal that he returned to his bed.

Voigt was lucky. When Dr Albert Fromme emerged from the basement in which he had been sheltering he saw immediately not just the carnage that had already been wrought but also the illimitable mortality that would follow. Just to the west of the Altstadt, near his hospital in Friedrichstadt, large houses and businesses were pulsing with the intense heat of fire. His own home – although damaged – was not burning at that stage, though scorching sparks were floating and falling in the shimmering sky. He raced inside to fetch water and douse fabrics that were vulnerable to the floating embers fluttering towards the building's shattered windows. His own survival backpack, assembled some time beforehand, was an exercise in carefully thought-out precautions; as well as including the recommended goggles to protect his eyes from fire, of which he would make great use in the hours to come, Dr Fromme had anticipated, for instance, that walking on hot rubble along melted-tarmac roads would require the thick leather padding of large ski boots.[19] Added to this, he also carried a razor and a sponge-bag, knowing he would need to live at the hospital in the event of a disaster such as this one. He realized that the next few days were going to be the most extraordinary ordeal medically, but his immediate difficulty was finding a route to the hospital that did not involve passing through an inferno. For Dr Fromme, the longest night had barely begun.

In the east of the city, elderly air-raid warden Georg Erler and his wife Marielein emerged from their bunker to find that, although all the windows had been blown out and the chandelier had been shattered, the house in which they lived seemed – so far as they could see on that glowing night – unscathed. There were fires elsewhere in properties down the street though, and a curious contrast between the chilly drizzle moving in from the Elbe and the waves of heat that Erler felt against his face as he paced up and down the road, assessing what he might be able to do. There were neighbours to help, people of a similar age to him whose apartments no longer had windows and who were anxiously moving all flammable furniture and possessions – curtains, rugs, desks, silk-covered sofas, paintings, much-loved books – as far back as they could from the window frames and the treacherous 'glow-worms' that were starting to fall like luminous snow.[20] The Erlers then walked back into their own apartment. Books had been hurled to the floor by the force of nearby detonations; vases were shattered. It was difficult for them to carry out a more detailed inventory of damage to their oil paintings and their furnishings because the electricity supply in this part of the city had failed and, in the rising wind, they could not keep a candle alight.

'We quickly removed the curtains,' he recalled, 'which stretched through the open windows like flags waving to the ever more numerous sparks, as if they wanted to catch the sparks and kindle them into flames.'[21] The wind seemed to be growing stronger. 'After getting rid of the glass fragments on the window-sill, we then tried to close the shutters, which, despite their iron bars, barely withstood this storm-like draught.'[22] All the Erlers' neighbours were comparing notes on the damage done, yet perversely the mood was almost helium-light. Partly this was due to sheer relief; here they all were, alive and unhurt. But there was also that sense of the familiar becoming unmoored, and a sort of dizzy excitement – a form of adrenaline-boosted elation – at navigating this new world. 'We were all happy,' recalled Georg Erler, citing the fact that their treasured homes also seemed relatively unscathed.

Satisfied that the immediate area seemed safe, Herr Erler set off on an inspection of the neighbourhood; part of his duty as an air-raid block warden. One house in a neighbouring street was on fire, but the caretaker and a few other residents were rushing to and fro with water, and appeared to have the blaze under control. He walked on a little further; but as he reached Striesener Plaza, the prospect was more shocking. This was one of the area's more elegant spaces;

late-nineteenth-century houses and villas overlooking gardens dominated by an ornate fountain. Herr Erler could immediately see that
the building housing a large bookshop had taken a direct hit to its
north-eastern corner. Fellow fire wardens told him of the immense
air pressure that the bombs had created, the deep and extraordinary
craters and the even more extraordinary fact that so many of these
buildings had actually survived that mighty explosive downpour. The
organization could not have been more meticulous: wardens operating on grid systems had instituted fire-watch stations, and even as the
clocks crept to twelve they were going about their business tirelessly.
The wardens were also comforting local residents who were still 'terrified in their limbs' a good hour or more after the bombers had flown
off. Herr Erler bumped into a local lawyer, Dr Thor, who himself
was still very badly shaken after the attack. There was also another
warden whose own home had been hit; in the face of this, he was
trying to organize residents of the damaged block to take refuge in
the apartments of neighbours nearby. Despite the fact that their
homes were seething with smoke and wreckage, there were some
elderly people who could not be persuaded to walk even a few yards
to temporary shelter.

Even those who were willing faced difficulties. The elderly mother
of one resident, Frau Richter, was ready to go but was finding the
jagged, smoking rubble difficult to negotiate on frail legs. Adding to
the hazards were nearby buildings so damaged that they might collapse at any moment. Herr Erler pointed Frau Richter and her mother
to alternative accommodation in a different direction; he never
learned their fate. 'It probably would have been the same [as if they
had stayed],' he recalled, because the following events would turn all
their lives inside out once more.[23]

Meanwhile, his wife Marielein had been trying to find out what had
happened to some of their local friends. She had been shocked to see
the state of their apartment – the fragment of chandelier hanging
down from the ceiling 'like an icicle',[24] the crunch of broken glass, the
infernal glow of the flying embers whistling in through the open window, the efforts to get the shutters closed – but stepping out once more

on the streets and surveying the damage seemed to bring a wave of another kind of emotion over her. She found her friend Michael and a few others in a neighbouring street, and in that moment, she recalled, 'I experienced the most reassuring thing that people can experience – being with friends who had suffered the same pain.' There was, once again, that curious uplift of happiness. Everyone hugged each other, feeling intensely grateful. 'All in all,' she recalled, 'the joy was that we still lived.'[25] Yet the fires dancing high into the heavens from the Altstadt, seen from this genteel suburb, were as stark as they were from other vantage points. And still the prodigiously strengthening wind was rushing towards the inferno.

On the other side of the river, the Bielsses and the other residents of their apartment block who had been sheltering in its basement had in the wake of that first raid checked the property thoroughly for incendiary sticks. Unlike nearby properties, the building had not been hit. 'The sky was fierce,' remembered Winfried,[26] but there were blazes close by as well. A few streets away the great complex of the Waldschlösschen brewery was enveloped in flame. The all-clear had been heard howling in the distance. There was a dedicated 'flak' radio station that broadcast from Berlin and which detailed on nights such as this the areas that had been hit. It also gave warnings of further bomber incursions. (The authorities had issued a map of Germany on which the country was divided into squares. Each city had code letters and numbers that the broadcasters would sometimes use; Dresden, Bielss recalled, was designated MH 8.) Frau Bielss tried to tune in but the radio now seemed to be dead. One of their many concerns was for the family of Winfried's friend Horst. They asked their neighbours if they could use their telephone to contact them but the number appeared to be unavailable. The boys returned to Bielss's apartment, where they all 'cleared the shards' from the floor; it was a twitchy displacement exercise. As Bielss recalled, they 'didn't quite know what to do about the excitement'.[27]

With the night sky outside glowing with a rose-red light, the immediate requirement seemed to be for food, and Frau Bielss went into the kitchen to prepare them all a light meal. But Horst, gazing at the infernal sky, was increasingly anxious; he was desperate to get back to his own home. Bielss and his mother knew they could not let the boy go on his own, and in any case they too had relatives and friends south of the river whom they wanted to check on, so they all set out together. Underlying all this was a curious kind of exhilaration. As Bielss observed: 'We were not able to think of sleep after this excitement.'[28] They also understood that many other people would be twitching with the same impulse on that night: both to check that loved ones had come through unscathed (seemingly few contemplated the possibility that they had not) and to satisfy that magnetic desire to explore the burning city. It was not a morbid motivation, more an expression of the feverish energy created by the sensory assault of the bombers. Sitting still while their hearts were still skittering did not seem possible. Yet just a few steps outside in the acrid air brought the reality of that night into focus.

The trio walked towards the river, and after several blocks came to the wide Bautzner Strasse, where two grand houses were burning lustily, the occupants doing what they could with pails of water and garden hoses. Some of the more valuable furniture had been retrieved from living rooms before the flames took a grip, placed on the pavement and in the road under the bright night sky that was painting everything a surreal apricot. A little further along a more pungent fire raged in and around the brewery; stone flagstones smouldering, wooden beams crackling. The flames were illuminating the whole area, recalled Bielss.[29] Close by was the once-elegant Heidehof Hotel. It too had been hit, and the air was now so thick with smoke and floating ash that it became difficult to see across the river. It was clear that the city below was burning ferociously, but that unsettlingly strengthening breeze, plus the increasing difficulty of trying to see through eyes half-shut to avoid those burning 'glow-worms', started to impress upon this small party that getting across the river might not be as easy as they'd imagined.

Then there emerged from the ashy haze a spectral group of shuffling, limping, foot-dragging men in nightclothes: wounded soldiers who had been recovering in the Deaconess Institute – a hospital a little further along the river. The institute had been caught by explosives and incendiaries, forcing its evacuation, with the walking wounded helped from their beds and those who could fleeing the grounds. 'Everything was burning in the city,' recalled Bielss, but the smoke was now too thick to make out any sort of detail at all.[30] The wounded men had shocked Bielss and his mother more profoundly than anything else; they realized that it might be best to turn back and at least fetch some goggles from the apartment.

Horst agreed to the change of plan, but it became apparent that even the route to relative safety presented new and unexpected hazards. 'Our eyes were burning with the biting smoke,' remembered Bielss. In that short time, other large buildings had caught fire and in some of the narrower streets flaming debris was crashing to the cobbles below, throwing out sparks. Retracing a journey that just a few minutes before they had taken for granted now became a matter of anxious calculation. They eventually got back to the apartment via a rather circuitous route and once more tried unsuccessfully to make contact via their neighbours' telephone. Horst was clearly now becoming quite frantic about his family, and what was happening in that ochre haze across the river. With goggles at the ready, they once more left the apartment building, their idea this time to forge a route along the banks of the Elbe, especially the stretch of meadows that faced the Altstadt on the opposite side. They could all feel that something in the air was being transformed; the pale frontages of the villas and apartment blocks of the Neustadt were being whipped with 'strong sparks',[31] the sinister embers now flying almost horizontally. As they reached the Jägerstrasse, a road that led down from a park, the wind seemed more of a burning gale, the bright orange embers filling the air with such ferocity that the road actually appeared impassable.

It seemed more obvious than ever that this was not a conflagration that could be countered. The trio passed a building that was used by military administrators: the fires were devouring it, yet no one was making even a token effort to douse the flames. It was obvious that there was simply no point. Moreover, the very air was becoming hostile, the ashy particles that made it so painful simply to keep one's eyes unshielded also irritating windpipes and lungs, provoking hacking coughs and a frightening sensation of raw discomfort and black aftertaste with every breath drawn.

Then some more people emerged from the fervid haze who seemed to have no official designation but none the less offered a single message: 'Do not try to go any further into the city.' They were, as Bielss recalled, 'strongly advised', though in truth, looking at the infernal prospect through their ash-flecked goggles, it was advice they scarcely needed. The jittery excitement was giving way to leaden tension.

A little earlier, near what was fast becoming the golden, volcanic heart of that inferno, Victor Klemperer and his wife Eva had – like everyone else – instinctively responded to the departure of the bombers by trying to restore a semblance of domestic stability. They left the cellar and immediately noted the curiously strong wind: Klemperer wrote that, even at that point, he wondered whether it was natural or foreshadowed a firestorm.[32] But for him and his wife, there was none of the nervous, excitable springiness felt by younger citizens, rather an awful weariness. The cobbled ground beneath their feet was covered in shards of glass; as they opened the door of the Judenhaus, it became apparent that there was glass everywhere indoors as well. All the windows had been blown in, both those facing the Altstadt and those facing the Elbe. Trudging upstairs together with a fellow resident, Frau Cohen, they discovered yet more glass and a view from one of the windows of the distant bank of the Elbe and the municipal buildings on the north side of the river bright with fire.

Inside the frayed house, the lights were not working and the water supply had been cut off. Frau Cohen, assessing her room in the rich glow of the fires, told the Klemperers that the bomb blasts had shifted her furniture. The Klemperers moved into the kitchen, where Eva found a candle and lit it. There was some coffee from earlier, now cold, which the couple drank, and a little leftover food too, which they ate. The couple by now seemed largely oblivious to any clamour or noise from the surrounding streets, or even the sounds of nearby buildings crackling and creaking, weakened by the flames; indeed, Klemperer and Eva now seemed overwhelmed by fatigue. Extraordinarily, heedless of the danger from spreading blazes or collapsing buildings, they entered their bedroom and lay down upon their twin beds. Eva rose again immediately, exclaiming that her bed was full of glass. She removed it as best she could and lay back down again. Her husband observed her almost disinterestedly, and before he knew it he was fast asleep.[33]

The Klemperers' intense fatigue might have been caused in part by the invisible fumes that were fast becoming pervasive; the chemicals and gases produced by the multitude of burning materials in innumerable apartments and grand shops nearby. But Klemperer's sleepiness seemed to find an echo in many other of the city's elderly residents that night, something that was possibly a traumatized reaction to that colossal assault: old hearts made to race unwillingly followed by a bitter recovery that left limbs feeling inert and unresponsive. For so many of a certain age elsewhere in the city, swift flight was impossible. But Klemperer had spent years under the malicious Nazi administration not simply accepting what was happening. In the hours to come, he and thousands of others would be driven into the most extraordinary fight for their lives.

17. Midnight

Professor Heinrich Barkhausen's laboratory was now open to the night air; great gulping flames exulting amid what was left of the delicate glass instruments, the wire coils, the electrodes and the diodes. The exquisitely calibrated means of controlling and directing certain frequencies, the sonic technology that had been the professor's specialized life work, had been splintered and reduced to an elemental level. Dresden Technical University lay to the south of the Altstadt and had been hit with incendiaries and high explosive. The fire had been slow to take hold, but when it did, it fed avidly. This was an example of the 'wild bombing'[1] that, 10,000 feet above, the RAF master bomber had cautioned every crew about as they made their passes over the city – off target, not part of the mission.

Very close by was the striking structure of the city's Russian Orthodox church, with its blue onion domes; those wanton random explosives had not touched it, whereas just yards away, the university was consumed. It is not clear precisely where Professor Barkhausen was at that hour, but his protégé Mischka Danos was not far away, a little further up that hill, having stationed himself and the 'Karl May' girl at an abandoned anti-aircraft battery position, from which both now gazed at the vast infernos before them. Danos recalled – to his own discomfort – that he felt like Nero, the emperor who watched Rome burn.[2] Many others remembered that odd and guilt-inducing blend of emotions: shock shot through with a wonder at the terrible spectacle of it. The fire in the city was transforming into a new kind of destructive force. The air was turning inside out.

There were many in the ill-lit brick cellars under the Altstadt who had registered the change in atmospheric composition: the increasingly oppressive pulses of heat; the effortful thinness of breathing, of the sort experienced in nightmares; the dizziness that came with standing; a rising sensation in the diaphragm of nausea. The result was a sudden overwhelming desire to get out, to stand under the open sky. Some remembered that the brick tunnels led eventually to the bank of the Elbe, and were making for what they thought would be its clean, cold air. Others were intent upon reaching the Great Garden park, perhaps envisaging frost-twinkled trees and long cool groves. But the narrow passages and extemporized doorways that comprised the labyrinth were not made to cope with large numbers of people attempting to move in opposing directions. In addition, many of those sheltering were elderly, old men and women in winter coats, no longer nimble. One man in a constricted passageway stumbled, fell and then was slowly crushed as the uneasy queue behind him surged irresistibly forward. Two people became wedged into a doorway as people on either side tried frantically to push past.

The combined fires above – flames leaping and jumping from building to building, road to road, now rising higher than the spires of the stricken churches – were also beginning to be felt beneath the surface. The intensity was radiating through the stone and the brickwork. It was obvious to many that whatever lay outside was worth risking, in order to escape these dim and toxic overheated tunnels. But there were other instances of unforeseen terror: a passage that turned through ninety degrees had a suspended wooden fire door that panicked shelterers on either side, moving fast, in a tightening crowd, unaware of each other's presence, were trying to push open. Of course, with the force balanced, the door would not yield and the panic intensified, with others then trying to move back only to find themselves firmly trapped in an unmoving mass.[3] Bodies pressed against warming brickwork as people breathed ever deeper in their attempts to remain calm even as their hearts somersaulted with fright.

A great many of these sheltering Dresdeners were feeling increasingly unwell as listlessness combined with worsening headaches and muscles and joints began to protest. In the absence of adequate ventilation in the cellars, the oxygen was slipping away by stealth and gathering in its place – without odour, invisible – was carbon monoxide. The very elderly and small infants were the first to feel the effects, but before long men and women of any age would have closed their eyes. Sleep would be followed by unconsciousness and then in some cases heart attacks, in others simply a cumulative suffocation. Fourteen-year-old Ursula Elsner, sheltering with her family and younger brother Dieter in a cellar near the Frauenkirche, recalled that her own moment of panic came not through any of these symptoms, but when she saw, in that low glow, flakes of ash beginning to flutter in through the passageways, at first a sprinkling, but then more, horribly suggestive of an oncoming avalanche.[4] She cried out to her family, and she and her little brother hurried down those rough-walled passages, to the steps to their exit. The Altstadt by this stage seemed composed purely of flame and sparks. She and Dieter ran in the direction of the wide Elbe. Many of her family remained behind in that cellar, perhaps by that stage simply unable to move, their limbs weighted by the poison in the air.

A little further east were streams of Dresdeners joining refugees and entering the darkness of the Great Garden park. The surviving boarders from the Kreuzschule and their teachers held back on the fringes. Those making their way into the dark groves near the park's zoo heard the agitation from the caged animals, as they looked back at the Altstadt, and the extraordinarily coloured flames: from deepest orange to a curious sapphire where a nearby gasworks had been hit. Here, among the oaks and lindens and chestnuts – punctuated by the odd crater, earth scattered wide – was for many almost transcendent relief: the ice-kiss of that February drizzle, eyes adjusting to blessed dark after squinting and peering through molten yellows and reds. More than this, the taste of pure air, breathed deep down. Perhaps a few worried that there could be a further swarm of bombers that night but even for them this vast tree-filled space, which covered roughly the same area as the Altstadt itself, must have seemed intuitively safe, an anti-target, a substantial rectangle of darkness contrasted with the scorching spectacle to its west.

Another intuitive sanctuary was the wide patches of green that lay on the north side of the Elbe, the 'meadows' that led down to the water's edge. Although some riverside municipal buildings, including the exquisite baroque Japanese Palace, had sustained serious damage and were still billowing flame and smoke, they were sufficiently far from the banks of the river to allow people to congregate on the grass in front of them. Doctors and nurses from hospitals half a mile away had contrived to get patients here, shuddering in the night air among the horses from the Sarrasani circus. It also became a form of auditorium; from this vantage point, the biblical conflagration across the river could be comprehended on something like its proper scale. The glass dome of the Arts Academy was still somehow intact; through it, and on either side of it, could be seen the towering fires. It is conceivable that from a distance, and separated from it by a wide, cold river, the sight was as compelling as it was terrifying, but the pervasive wind prevented the accompanying range of piteous noises registering with the spectators. The sounds of individual anguish did not carry across that distance over the underlying deep roar of innumerable flames.

Even then in the Altstadt there were some open spaces where it was possible to seek refuge, in particular the nine-foot-deep concrete reservoir that had been built in the Altmarkt square. Some struggling out of the increasingly asphyxiating cellars had clearly recalled it, and in that extremity many were desperate to drink and douse themselves. Men and women, overlooked by the burning Renner department store and the smoking ruins of the Kreuzkirche and other blazing buildings, began climbing over the waist-high wall of the reservoir and dropping into the cold pool. The shock, after the pervasive heat, would have been extreme, but growing numbers of people had the same idea and the large reservoir was now filling with bobbing figures.[5] The fact that the water was not intolerably, limblockingly cold on that freezing February night was in itself a sign of the inferno's fundamental strength. The firefighters were still present but seemed increasingly helpless. There were other reservoirs, and other districts of the city that were not yet past saving; but the Altmarkt was beyond their powers.

Just two streets away, Erika Seydewitz, with her mother, father, sister and elderly neighbours, was still crouching in a stone archway near the Rathaus. Her father was thinking with a kind of manic energy: he was convinced that they might yet be able to save the family car and possibly even some of the more valuable items from his photography shop. Tentatively – to the disbelief of Erika's mother – father and daughter ran out into that white-hot rain of falling embers. The car was not yet on fire but it obviously would never move. And then, jumping at ear-piercing reports from the roaring apartment buildings, Erika slipped and fell. 'The cobblestones were so hot that I burned my hands,' she remembered. 'My only thought was: even if you end up breaking your arms and legs, get up quickly.'[6] She heard the creaking from above transform into a darker bellow: a house somewhere behind her collapsed in on itself.

In those few minutes, the world had changed. There was 'a storm on the street'; a strong, searing wind, blowing embers and sparks. Erika was aware of just how dry their coats were now, despite their earlier soaking. They fought the firestorm that was tugging and twitching at their limbs, pushing their way back through those streets towards the uncertainty of the stone archway where the rest of the family sheltered. These impulses to protect belongings of both real and sentimental value seemed to have a degree of irrationality, even to those who acted upon them, but perhaps it was natural to try to cling to any symbols of certainty.

While Dr Fromme was making his way to the hospital, his family and neighbours in the west of the city saw the fires spreading unstoppably street to street, house to house, and their collective instinct too was to rescue a range of domestic items and take them into the street. Among the Frommes' treasured items were, understandably, a wedding photograph and Dr Fromme's beloved typewriter and, perhaps less accountably, an armchair and some coats. There was some debate about taking the most valuable bottles from the wine cellar; this was decided against. The idea was possibly for them to load as much as possible into the car and drive away. Yet the biting orange embers in the air were floating down and bringing their fiery touch everywhere: one neighbour's suitcase, sitting out on the pavement, burst into flames. A radio hauled from the house had 'to be defended from the sparks'.[7]

In the Altstadt, in the shadow of the smoking Catholic cathedral, Nazi officials remained in the cellars beneath the Taschenberg Palace. Lothar Rolf Luhm, back down from the roof, looked on as the mothers in that shelter pushed their small children close to the 'Golden Pheasants', as though somehow proximity to those in power would offer talismanic protection. It was a gesture of superstition that, as Luhm recalled later, made the young soldier suddenly yearn to be back in his tank, out in the field.[8] There was more certainty offered by that sort of warfare than there was in this darkness. Having spent the earlier part of that night clambering on hot tiles, spotting the luminous, fizzing incendiaries and throwing them clear, there seemed nothing more that could be done; the torture of the uncertainty was the fact that he had no idea whether another attack would be coming that night or how long those cellars would continue to remain inhabitable.

In other cellars, less well appointed, mothers sat on bare chairs, staring into the eyes of strangers, the random shelterers caught in the storm. There were other women, heads back, eyes closed. One witness recalled desperately trying to wake her mother, who was proving very hard to rouse. A cry of 'The fire is burning here!' at last seemed to penetrate her slumber and she and her daughter got up and moved through the passageways, edging back and back to find another place to stop and rest beneath a flickering light.[9] Already there were uncountable numbers in that maze of cellars whose sleep had become death, either through suffocation or heart failure. The earth above was baking. No rest was possible for anyone. Yet through all the fearful movement, the instinctive ideas of which way to turn, the oldest impulse of all, to remain close to loved ones, prevailed.

Up above, the sumptuous shops of Prager Strasse were charred shells; the interior of the Central Theatre, with its plush auditorium and rich red seating, was now blackened, the stage open to the fiery sky. The restaurant and bar that lay in a deep cellar under the theatre had hosted a meeting of the Volkssturm that night; at first, when the bombing had started, the bar must have seemed a congenial shelter for the men who had stayed on late, perhaps a chance for a few extra steins of the local Radeberger beer to see them through the attack before they made ready to perform their civic duties. But here the fumes from the fire were swifter and more insidious than in other quarters; all those drinkers were now dead.[10]

The flames that rose above Prager Strasse were met at the cross-roads by blazes that had gutted the clothing stores of Wilsdruffer Strasse, the fires criss-crossing, filling every small street and passage so that from above, it looked as though the roads of Dresden were a dark mould into which molten gold had been poured. On the edges of the Altstadt, just beyond the city's inner ring road, the darkness of the Great Garden park, stretching for a mile, was still drawing refugees with carts. The horses pulling them must surely have been alarmed by the animal noises echoing from the zoo as the elephants bellowed and the gibbons chattered in wild distress.[11]

From the hill to the south of the railway station, at the abandoned anti-aircraft battery, Mischka Danos was almost immobilized, not from fear but from a blend of high tension and intense curiosity. There was a form of lookout tower close by; he ran up its narrow steps to gain a wider view of the pulsating storm. He watched as fire joined with fire, as explosions sent up mushroom clouds filled with sparks and incandescence. He was fascinated by the strengthening inrush of the wind, by the sound of apartment-block rafters creaking, the throaty roar of collapsing roofs. And he watched as down in the Altstadt, just under a mile away, individual orange glares fused and merged, a wall of light climbing into the dark sky. It resolved, he recalled, and became more like a tower of flame,[12] a vast cylinder of fire fed by a roaring gale, all other flames and sparks pulled irresistibly towards it. This fire tower started to burn over the very centre of the Altstadt. Indeed, it was now the city itself; thousands upon thousands of fires that had melded to become one incandescent entity, filling every street. This biblical pillar of light must have been an appallingly ir-resistible spectacle, but for Danos it was somehow too abstract at this stage for him even to begin imagining its effects on those close to it, or in its eye, or to contemplate what traces of flesh or bone could possibly be left after such a visitation.

Neither could he have known that there was no immediate prospect of peace for any living thing in the wider city. The civic authorities, in their bunker near the Elbe, had received the communication over the radio. There was another formation of bombers approaching.

18. The Second Wave

At roughly the same time as the initial wave of 244 bombers were beginning their flight back to England, the next wave – very much larger – of 552 bombers were already reaching up into the dark over England, above the silver clouds, crossing the Channel to the continent; their stream of planes would come to form a line some 120 miles long.

Bomb aimer Miles Tripp recalled the discomfort of his own position on board his Lancaster; he was surrounded by 'Window', the packets of metallic strips that would later be dropped out of the craft to blind the German radar.[1] At the start of their flight, minutely calibrated to join up with all those other bombers leaving from bases all over the east and the south of England, there had been an unsettling incident when Tripp had looked out into the darkness only to recoil in sudden panic as he saw another Lancaster making straight for them. He shouted with alarm and, equally suddenly, 'the Lancaster vanished'. It had been an illusion, or an hallucination. He recalled his relief that his intercom was not on, and that his fellow crewmen had not witnessed his momentary fright. There had been enough disquiet already about fellow crewman Harry's apparent gift of premonition. Death was inescapable and pervasive; superstitions and sudden visions were perhaps to be expected. As they crossed the Channel, Tripp noticed the starlight, the way it made it possible to just see the English coastline. Then he focused on his own task of monitoring the H2S radar and navigation system, the beams of which pulsed down to the earth and back up again.

His senses were on high alert in the near-darkness of the Lancaster interior, monitoring the steady bass line of the engines and, as they crossed battle lines, sightings of flak. A spat arose between Tripp and his crewmate Ray, whose job it was to jettison the thousands of strips of 'Window' through the perspex aperture; Ray complained that Tripp's duties were light compared with those of others and Tripp irritated him by affecting a languorous aristocratic drawl to proclaim that, on the contrary, he was working terribly hard. Another crewman's electrically heated flight suit was malfunctioning; as a result, 'Junior' was extremely cold. Throughout the four-and-a-half-hour flight there, they saw the thin glowing lines of flak aimed at other aircraft. The H2S guidance system, which seemed to have been playing up, now started into life, searching for their target, yet as they neared their objective it became apparent to the crew that it would hardly be required. The gold and red fires of Dresden, clamouring ever higher into that night sky, were visible from some forty miles away. Tripp wriggled his way into the bomb aimer's compartment at the front of the plane and gazed down, noting that there was no cloud. Still a few miles away from the city, some half-dozen Lancasters were visible ahead, perfectly silhouetted black against the rosy glow. At a height of around 10,000 feet, Tripp found himself looking now at 'a fantastic latticework of fire', the 'fiery outlines of a crossword puzzle'. He gazed down at 'blazing streets . . . from east to west, from north to south, in a gigantic saturation of flame'.

Tripp was in charge of giving the instructions for the plane's positioning as they neared the city, and it was at this point that he made a conscious decision not to add to the firestorm. He told the pilot, 'Dig', to veer starboard, and it was only when the plane was clear of the heart of the inferno that Tripp pressed the mechanism to release his explosives. He hoped, he later recalled, that the bombs would land in open country. It is most unlikely, however, that they did; it is much more probable that they detonated in peaceful streets on the outskirts, simply sparking yet more fires. The gesture was human (and possibly widespread – there were accusations of explosives being deliberately offloaded in the North Sea), but the fact remained that few bombs that night were going to land harmlessly. This second wave was to bring with it many more 4,000lb 'Cookies' and other varieties of explosives and incendiaries: in total, an additional 1,800 tons of bombs were to be dropped by the second wave, and many in areas that were not yet throbbing with that lethal light. Several miles away, on the Klotzsche airfield, the Messerschmitt fighter pilots sat poised, but no orders came to scramble. Their commanders no doubt understood very well how futile a gesture any attempt at defence would have been.

Of course, the bombers above were not to know this, and in Tripp's Lancaster the curious, nerve-tautening structure of every raid was present once more: after a flight filled with hazard, the actual act of bombing lasted no more than a minute and then there was the fresh, quiet tension and fear of the flight back through that dark enemy territory: the red lines of tracer fire, bright white globules of fighter flares – 'flaming onions', as Flight Lieutenant Leslie Hay referred to them[2] – falling in their flight path; distant fires in distant cities; the moment of nausea when another Lancaster was 'coned' by powerful searchlights, the plane blossoming in flame against the starlit sky. In Tripp's plane there was a sense of compressed hush; a Thermos of coffee, and the lighting of (nominally forbidden) cigarettes, flavoured with menthol.

About the bombing itself, there seemed among other crewmen a sense of disassociation; but from so many thousands of feet up, with the 'enormous bowl of rosy light' arising from below,[3] it would have been truly remarkable for any of these crews to have felt genuine empathy; for how could anyone imagine what it was like on those streets below? Miles Tripp recounted his feeling of squeamishness, but given the atmospheric phenomenon he was witnessing, he clearly did not allow himself to dwell on any idea of individuals caught in that horror. Among the other crews of those 552 second-wave bombers that swept through that astonishing storm there seemed an unwavering sense that this was something that had to be done; a mission that simply had to be completed.

There is a film sequence, taken from the underside of one of those Lancasters, that shows in black and white the fires across the city, pulsating points that sometimes flare up into lines of pure white, the sudden blooming of more huge conflagrations. Yet the film does not convey the most hypnotic element, as recalled by Tripp and others: the colours in that inferno. The bomb aimers in that second wave sensed from the most cursory glance at the city below that it was fast burning to destruction already, but for the most part they tacked close to their instructions. As Warrant Officer Harry Irons (later awarded the

Distinguished Flying Cross), a rear gunner, later put it: 'We didn't realize how big it was going to be.' Nor was there any idea of guilt: 'We were very young and we lost so many boys ourselves,' he added.[4] What all these thousands of crew members had been asked to do, in mission after mission, became an implacable routine. The fact that their own lives were so fragile added another layer to the complexity of their emotions.

Thousands of feet below, almost a mile away from the centre, as this fresh wave of bombers began its sweep through at just after 1 a.m., Mischka Danos made a move that would have been counterintuitive to many but perhaps natural to him as a physicist: he pulled the 'Karl May' girl across that patch of green space and into a bomb crater that had been left by the previous raid: another badly aimed projectile. Danos knew that, under a fresh attack, the crater would afford them cover – not, of course, from a direct hit, but from all other explosions. There was still not quite fear in his breast but instead a tight high tension, as he listened to the 'hissing' and the 'whirring' of the fresh incendiaries that were falling out of the sky.[5] Over the lip of the crater they watched as, against the deep ruby and billowing black of the city landscape, the air was once more lit up as plummeting incendiaries opened and released rods of pure white.

For the citizens closer to the centre of the city, this second wave was greeted with not only terror but a sort of moral disbelief: how was it possible for anyone to inflict this abomination? The authorities had tried to reactivate Dresden's air-raid sirens; but few were still functioning. The growing firestorm had melted most of the city's electrical systems, rendering them as useless as the tram lines lying in the road.

In the Judenhaus on Zeughausstrasse, in a room whose shattered window admitted all the noise from the city outside, Professor Victor Klemperer slept – a measure of the seriousness of his heart condition, but also perhaps a traumatized reaction not just to the bombing but to the day beforehand, that tour of the city effectively handing out death warrants to most of its remaining Jewish population. He was woken suddenly by his wife. Because most of the city's air-raid alarms were out of action, the civic authorities were sending officials with hand-held sirens out into those streets that were still negotiable. Faint but unmistakable, the noise was just about audible to Eva, who explained to her husband that there was no electricity.[6] Now the couple had to prepare to flee back underground.

The professor had a rucksack containing some manuscripts and a bag with some of Eva's 'woollen things'. He also had a blanket, which he wore around his shoulders. Putting his hat on, he hurried with his wife downstairs and into the street, which was suffused with an intense and lurid light. In that corner of the Altstadt, near the Frauenkirche, Klemperer observed that the roads seemed empty, and now he and Eva made their way to the courtyard that held the entrance to the 'Jews' cellar'. Before they reached it, there was a vast explosion. The professor crouched, clutching a wall; a few moments later, with the booms of detonations elsewhere, he moved, turned, looked up – and could not see his wife. Assuming that she had gone down into the cellar ahead of him, Klemperer found the entrance, walked down the steps and took in a crowd of frightened faces. He scanned the dark cellar for his wife; but he could still see no trace of her. A moment later there came a crash and a flare of brightness and once again there were figures ready with water and a stirrup pump. The professor was desperate to find his wife; he started to back out of the cellar and into the courtyard. He recalled that he did not actually feel afraid at this point, more exhausted. And he speculated that it was because he was anticipating the end. Another vast crash and he felt a searing pain above his eye. His immediate impulse was to feel for the eyeball itself. 'It was still there,' he stated simply. But alongside the pain and the disorientation was now something new: as he looked at the streets, he no longer recognized them. The fire and the colossal damage were such that the city appeared to have been disassembled.

For Lothar Rolf Luhm in the Taschenberg Palace shelter, this fresh bombardment was worse than the first. 'Again and again, we heard the cracking,' he recalled. 'Again and again, the walls trembled, even the ground under our feet seemed to tremble.' A bomb landed closer. 'The fire was so strong that it blew open a steel door,' he remembered. 'It got very hot and the air became scarce. My eyes burned. I couldn't recognize anything. I thought that we were all going to burn.'[7] And even in this comparatively well-built shelter, there seemed to be a sense of the clean air disappearing. Luhm, his vision dimming, recalled moving around, trying to find places where he might breathe more comfortably. The lights were on, but because of his painful eyes and gradually occluding vision, he seemed more aware of darkness. In the corners of the cellar were others who had managed to get in before the larger fires had filled the streets. At his approach they looked up but said nothing. Luhm found that he could not speak to them either; all just stared mutely as the frequent crashes from above shot through every nerve. Luhm found himself holding his breath, and the bombardment seemed to him without end. He and his fellow shelterers were now existing in a separate corner of time; unable to distinguish seconds, minutes, hours. The grand building above him had been all but annihilated.

In one of the cellar tunnels near the Elbe, Norbert Bürgel and his uncle had found shelter just a short while before the second raid began; their ordeal had a sensory violence. 'The floor rose,' he remembered, as bombs fell nearby; mortar was shaken from the walls and from the ceiling. There were frightened calls for sand; an outer shelter door, smouldering with thickening smoke, needed to be extinguished before the fire took a serious grip. In the pale yellow light of the ceiling bulb the grey fog of choking smoke spread to fill the room, leading to a number of people trying to push back into the cellar beyond, fearful that the oxygen was running out. They were met by others emerging from those passageways having themselves been pushed from the opposite direction, for deeper in that maze the air had in places been almost completely sucked out. The brickwork itself was beginning to smoulder with the heat radiating from the vast infernos above. And so it was, with bombs booming outside, that Bürgel and his uncle now found themselves caught in a brick chamber between those trying to get to the river and those trying to retreat from it. The chamber was, he recalled, very crowded. Yet somehow the infection of panic did not spread: he and those around him managed to stay calm.[8]

★

Just before those emissaries with the hand-held sirens had hurried through the passable streets, Gisela Reichelt and her mother had left their shelter south of the railway station and were surveying the hot rubble in the street outside their home when they were greeted by Gisela's grandfather, Herr Thieme. Her grandparents lived near the city centre and, in the reverberating aftermath of the first bombing, Herr Thieme had manoeuvred his way past the burning station and up the gentle incline towards their apartment block. Even before that second wave of bombers, the chances of survival in that furnace citadel had been poor. He simply wanted to know that they were alive before turning back to the cathedrals of flame that were dominating the skyline to be with his wife. Thieme returned to his house near the Kreuzkirche and joined Gisela's grandmother, sheltering in the cellar as the air filled with the deep choral music of the new approaching attack. And then their house was 'hit hard'. It seemed to the old couple that the entire property was going to collapse in on them, perhaps trapping them in that brick chamber beyond rescue, so even as the raid continued they now scrambled up the cellar steps, energized by terror, desperate to get outside. On the threshold of the street, Gisela's grandmother was hit by some falling burning material that her granddaughter was convinced was phosphorus.[9] The flaming substance was more likely to have been an incendiary stick, or jellied petroleum from another sort of incendiary, or wood, or some other material, or fabric, but whatever it was it clung close to the old lady and set her clothes alight. Gisela's grandmother burned to death. Herr Thieme, who had been a matter of seconds behind his wife, similarly fell victim to some other flaming debris and was blinded.

Some impulse made the old man walk away from the burning corpse of his wife. Stumbling through the intensely hot rubble, he used the muscle memory of his local area to move sightless through those flaming streets. Such a situation is difficult now to envisage or even comprehend; the wind rushing into the central inferno – suffocating, sparkling with bright embers – would have been soughing at over a hundred miles per hour; even those who were fit were finding it difficult to stay upright, let alone move. Some felt themselves being pulled by a hideous and implacable force towards the vortex, having to crouch down and brace themselves against its lethal attraction. Along narrow streets of tall buildings, their windows blank, brickwork blackened, tumbled burning debris in the fast-moving wind – the remains of domestic furniture, fragments of rubber and wood from cars, burning branches from fallen trees all being sucked into the great onrush. There were citizens in the midst of this trying desperately to hold on to lamp posts in order to escape the inferno's anti-gravitational pull, but the lamp posts themselves were scorching to the touch. It was into this burning wilderness of night that the newly widowed, newly blinded old man walked.

Gisela would discover all this only very much later; her own immediate ordeal was also harrowing. Mother and daughter were back down in the apartment-block basement with their neighbours. 'No one could imagine coming out of this hell alive,' she recalled. 'What did a ten-year-old girl think about such terror? It's hard to imagine what was going on inside me. But like the first attack, I was thinking: "How can you be so cruel?" I was full of fear and could not imagine that we would emerge from that cellar alive.'[10] She and her heavily pregnant mother held each other tight, and they prayed. Yet the bombardment continued for so long that they gradually found that they could no longer speak; a form of torpor had gripped them both.

On the other side of the Elbe, Winfried Bielss, his mother and his friend Horst had been considering making another attempt to cross both the bridge and the city, to establish that Horst's family was safe, as well as checking on Winfried's cousins. Then came the hand-held warning and once again the trio withdrew to the basement, from where, just a few minutes later, the renewed noise of distant explosions could be heard. The boys – as with the first attack – initially imagined that the explosions were at last evidence of the city's anti-aircraft defences coming into play: mighty guns trained on their airborne enemy, but they swiftly and with leaden hearts realized that that was not the case; that these bombers were in fact flying over with insolent ease.

There was a difference this second time, though: the bombers had widened their angle of attack slightly. The explosions were coming very much closer. Winfried was preternaturally attuned to the sinister symphony of the attack. 'The explosions came closer and closer and louder and louder, the floor began to shake more and more perceptibly,' he recalled. 'Before the explosions we heard again the hissing of the falling bombs – the metallic beats that may have come from flying bomb fragments or from the effect of firebombing on stone. In our area, many incendiary bombs either burned out without danger or became deeply stuck in the ground.'[11] He was interested in the 'small propellers' on the incendiaries that would have given them a rotating motion and a distinctive sound. This, however, was only the start. The larger explosions grew closer yet.

The basement area had a sort of hallway, where they were crouching, and now they looked up as a mighty force smashed remaining windows and battered doors. Bielss recalled that, in the case of their own apartment, they had left the doors deliberately ajar, thinking it might mitigate the effects of the surge in air pressure and the destructive blast waves. But now the impacts were so close that the pressure of these waves could be felt compressing his eardrums and, even more distressingly, pushing down on his lungs. Dust cascaded from the basement walls; the air became immediately stuffy and breathing became noticeably and increasingly difficult. 'The electric light flickered,' recalled Bielss, 'but it did not go out.' And now the incendiaries and the bombs acquired a new quality of music; from that basement, it seemed that the night air was 'singing', 'whistling' and 'hissing'.[12] The explosions that followed were so deep that it felt as though his ears had been cracked. The aural effect completely surrounded the three of them; they sensed not only the bombs nearby, but those far away too. As for many others sheltering in basements throughout the city, time became an impossible abstraction; the passing of it could not be perceived. There was another extraordinary aural recollection: as they flew closer the baritone hum of the bombers was transformed into a high-pitched 'howl', and the sound of their engines changed register as soon as the heavy ordnance was released; suddenly the note sprang higher as the lightened planes likewise shot forward and upward.

Another shattering crash: it was clear that the apartments next door had been hit. The boys listened to doors and glass crashing down the central stairwell; the building seeming to undulate on its foundations, and from the next-door basement came the increasing sounds of panicked occupants convinced that the structure was about to implode in on them. The door in the wall between the two basements – installed, as in the Altstadt cellars, as a precaution – was tried and then opened. And as the neighbours peered through, with them came the heat: the block above was open to the burning sky, and to that lethal wind that now came rushing through the base-ment. The boys and the other residents took fright at the prospect of white-hot incendiaries landing on and setting fire to their own roof, and it was decided – even as the bombers continued to roar overhead – to make a fast search of the floors above. According to Bielss, the claustrophobic basement now started to look like a welcoming alter-native, but it had to be done. The floor beneath crunched with glass, and as he and his neighbours moved up the stairs through the darkened block, they closed any windows that weren't rendered completely beyond repair by the blasts. And as they did so, the fire in the distant sky grew higher.

The temperature change was apparent even inside the fast-moving planes above as the conflagration centred in the Altstadt rose an esti-mated mile into the sky. The bomber crews were flying through an extreme phenomenon of physics: an electrically charged firestorm. It was so far beyond any human capacity to assimilate that it is little won-der that later, back in their bases in the cool grey of morning, so many airmen could not find words to describe what they had witnessed.

Below, the oxygen was being pulled into the heart of the inferno, sent skywards with the shrunken, desiccated body parts and the pul-verized debris. The roads were melting and burning; the cobbles were seething. Even a mile away, the great inrush sucked insistently at Marielein Erler as she searched for her husband Georg; when the second air attack came, he had been inspecting properties a couple of streets away for damage and was forced to take cover in the nearest shelter he could find. His anguish at being separated from his wife was possibly more acute than any other anxiety he felt during the bombardment. He knew that she had been checking on friends in their immediate neighbourhood; had she found shelter herself? Herr

Erler was in a narrow cellar with some refugees and local residents.[13] He had thought that this part of the city could never have been a target for anyone: there were no important strategic sites or factories or railway stations among these smart villas. But still the bombs came and the masonry 'quivered'.

His wife Marielein was, in fact, nearby, having managed to get underground just in time. She had thought the worst was past, but now she sat rigid as the hammer blows struck again in relentless repetition. One mother sitting amid the bare bricks was holding her toddler tight and crooning reassurance: 'Steppi, be calm, they will not hurt you.' Frau Erler recalled her wonder at this sentiment as the walls around them threatened to burst. Then, as happened in so many other places, the interconnecting door – the breakthrough – that connected with the maze beyond suddenly slammed open. Through it flocked a panicked throng, fleeing from a cellar a little further along the way that had been filled with winter fuel. As the fires hungrily licked through, the store of coal and wood was billowing smoke, heat and sparks which followed the crowd through the breakthrough, making the air in Frau Erler's shelter unbreathable. No matter what was happening above, they all simply had to get out; there was no chance of survival down there.

Through an exit framed with flames they emerged into the night air as the bombers above continued to fly towards the unearthly light. 'This sight!' recalled Frau Erler. 'This hell on earth!' She looked out on what had once been an upmarket neighbourhood: now it was a prospect of blazing houses, falling walls and torn roads. It was 'a mad firestorm'. But worse was the obscenity of the corpses: the streets were littered with the dead. As the minutes passed and the bombers flew off into the night, Frau Erler and her friend Frau Jung, rather than retreating into darkness, felt impelled to walk up the road to the street in which they lived, holding each other for support both physical and moral. She recalled being 'full of fear' before, in one curious heartbeat, she was suddenly alive with elation as she rounded a corner and happened across her husband, who had left his own shelter at around the same time. That moment was, extraordinarily, one of the happiest of her life. 'I was not alone any more,' she remembered. 'I was able to cry out my grief and shed my tears with my husband, who was in deep shock with me.'

They moved on to Striesener Plaza, now pitted with fiery craters, many houses around them glowing wrecks. She described the very air in that once handsome residential square as 'terrible' and 'brittle', and what was now 'a howling storm' blew in their faces, with all the hideous eye-burning hazard of sparks and embers. There were 'wailing people, crying children'. The Erlers were sitting on a tree that had collapsed earlier; near them was 'an old couple from Silesia'. The Erlers made a movement to get up and the refugees begged them to stay: they 'did not know Dresden' and 'did not know where to go'.

Were it not for that second wave, Helmut Voigt might have spent the night simply staring at the changing colours in the sky. Before that attack had begun, he was with his mother back in their apartment in the south-west of the city, gazing out of the window in silence, and it was he who heard the faint sound of the hand-held siren. 'My mother did not believe me at first,' he recalled.[14] He made her listen; the howling was being ineffectually amplified by a speaker mounted on a nearby water tower. Quickly they gathered themselves, left the flat, and went to alert their neighbours. The landing was illuminated in the reflected glare of the fires. Their designated shelter in the cellar of the nearby brewery was a few hundred yards away. Even as the residents hurried, they could hear the resonant low note of the approaching bombers. Everything 'went very fast', recalled Voigt.

The bombs began to fall as they were starting their descent into the gloom; the cellar was dimly lit only by emergency lighting. More and more people were running in off the street and trying to push their way down into the shelter. Young mothers trying to bring prams down the concrete stairs had to resist the weight of the people pressing behind them. The cellar had two levels and people were having to squeeze into the lower one to make room above for the frightened new arrivals. Voigt and his mother were among them. He remembered the emergency lighting 'flickering', threatening to plunge them all into darkness. From above came the hollow booms;

the sense of the ground shivering. Yet as they moved into that deeper cellar, the higher floor now packed, Voigt experienced a curious sensation. They were now cut off from the noise of the world outside. He and his fellow shelterers felt oddly detached as they spread out in that industrial semi-darkness.

Then the light went out. The darkness was total, and there was little to be done but to endure. There was no panic, more a sense of helpless suspension. Then the light flickered back on again. Perhaps, however claustrophobic the conditions, these deep cellars seemed to many a comforting sanctuary, for when an air-raid warden made his way down the stairs unexpectedly and told everyone that they had to leave, and quickly, there was, Voigt recalled, a sense of astonishment which now had the effect of 'rousing' people from their positions. The shelterers were directed to a secondary stairwell and told they had to get out of there fast, for their own safety. But a swift evacuation was impossible at speed. Those mothers with prams and infants, the frail elderly with their clutched luggage, all slowed progress to a crawl.

Again and again the crowd halted on the concrete steps; no one could edge forward, no one could see anything beyond the heads up front. Still, though, there was no sense of panic, more a form of silent stress. When eventually they reached the top, they saw the reason for their evacuation. The shelter was next to a large coal store; if incendiaries had set the coal ablaze, those below would have been slowly and certainly suffocated as the smoke poured in. Under the pulsatingly bright sky, and with the planes apparently having all passed over, Voigt and his mother hurried to inspect their apartment block; it had suffered damage and small fires blazed in several of the flats. The residents made their way indoors, determined to extinguish them. Helmut ran to fill their bathtub, intending to take buckets of water up to the roof to extinguish the incendiaries there. With their sole safe shelter now deemed too dangerous to use, this practical activity might have kept their minds off the terrible possibility of yet more bombs falling.

Near the university, Mischka Danos and his companion had left their sheltering crater as the bombs fell closer and closer. The nearby abandoned anti-aircraft emplacement had a concrete bunker attached.

After a struggle to get the doors open, the physicist and his friend found cool shelter. They were quickly joined in that darkness by others, all strangers and all women, mothers and teenage daughters who seemed to have arrived there quite casually, but who must in truth have been walking through burning streets in shock. One young woman complained that she had left many of her favourite gloves behind. Another was anxious about a diamond ring that she had failed to take with her.[15] Danos was outraged, later recalling that he was stunned by the number of conversations he overheard concerning the loss of expensive stockings. But perhaps these comically tiny miseries were being voiced as a means of shutting out deeper shock, since he also noted that there were many others who did not utter a word during the bombing or its aftermath. The horror had overtaken them.

The very idea of minor materialistic complaints lay far beyond the reach of countless other Dresdeners. Before the sky had been criss-crossed with more bombers, the fires had already forced great numbers of both citizens and refugees alike from the choking streets, past the Hygiene Museum and into the sylvan cool of the Great Garden, walking deeper into the shadows cast by the eerie artificial sunset. In the centre of this vast grand park stood the rather beautiful baroque Summer Palace, an eighteenth-century construction. Here too was an exquisite and scientifically important botanical garden containing rare plants in small greenhouses and, inside its main build-ing, a scientific library holding many antique manuscripts. Past this building walked the strange, silent, ghostly procession of forms mov-ing as far into the woods as they could. Some tree-tops and high branches were already burning; floating, questing embers from the Altstadt having come to rest on dry bark.

When the second wave of bombers came over, all those below in the Great Garden were completely exposed. As explosives and eye-dazzling incendiaries fell in all directions, the dark air suddenly filled with the bright white flowers of detonation. Manicured parkland became peppered with great bowls of smoking earth, hundreds of them, stretching a mile back, containing smashed bone and flesh and viscera; people were either physically annihilated on the spot by direct hits or transformed into flickering torches by the savagely burning timber around them. The Summer Palace received some of the heavy bombs; it was demolished in a frenzy of sparks and flames as bright as the sun. And those refugees who had instinctively turned to this inner-city woodland for protection were now trapped in a savage forest fire, the air a new cocktail of carbon monoxide, carbon dioxide, benzene and nitrogen oxide.

The zoo also received direct hits. The animals suffered atrociously: there were gibbons whose paws were sheared off, leaving them with bloody stumps; hippopotamuses in their pool, hit by falling debris, were pressed under the water and drowned. The elephant house caved in, the blast wave and the sharp debris knocking one animal onto its back, its stomach torn open. The other elephants were 'screaming'.[16] The lions were for now unharmed, but the zookeepers understood that the risk of further bombs freeing them and driving them in a frenzy into the night meant they would have to be shot. A giraffe had already escaped from its bombed enclosure and galloped off. The screeches from the zoo sounded nauseously disorientating to those in the burning woods beyond; who was to tell which cry was animal and which human?

There was similar distress on the other side of the river, both on the banks of the Elbe and in the compound of the Sarrasani circus: in the open air, as the bombs and incendiaries fell, some of the performing horses were torn terribly by shrapnel. And the main Sarrasani theatre, which had survived the first raid almost intact, was now hit squarely with explosives; the great dome was penetrated and the supremely combustible material within – the plush seating, the matting, the wooden struts, the curtains – was brushed by the falling incendiaries and caught light instantly. Those who had retreated once more to the theatre's underground bar no longer felt safe with the structure above so gravely damaged, but they at least had alternative exits. The circus animals in their compound had no chance to escape the flames. The tigers' keepers looked on with horror as they realized they could do nothing but let their beautiful charges burn alive.

The implacable inferno in the Altstadt was now claiming victims who just a short while beforehand might have thought that they would be spared; those nine-foot deep reservoirs in the central Alt-markt square were already bobbing with corpses. The water level was well below the edge and there was no purchase to be had on the steep concrete sides to enable anyone to haul themselves out. No access ladder was provided, nor anything else that could have helped the exhausted water treaders to pull themselves up. Some of those who drowned had – in their scrabbling desperation – tried to hold on to others, but had only succeeded in dragging them down too. And among those who held on, repeatedly and fruitlessly reaching up that vertical stretch of concrete, the struggle cannot have continued for very much longer. In other reservoirs nearby, the hazards were even more unexpected. In one, so many people had jumped in that they had now become somehow immovably wedged together. In another, the violent heat of the firestorm and the debris made the water hotter and hotter; those who had lost consciousness could not have hoped to survive this braising of their organs.

And there were still those who, having found the poisonous, swel-tering cellars beyond endurance, emerged at street level into a vast smelting furnace: a fire that was now wrenching at anything that could be pulled up high into that fast-swirling tornado. One young woman saw a mother struggling down a blazing street with her baby; and watched how the baby was snatched in a split second up into the white-hot flames. There were others now condemned to death by their shoes, which melted or simply caught fire in the bubbling black tar of the roads, leaving their feet unshod, blistered and swiftly scorched; they fell to their knees and hands, which also instantly burned, immobilizing them.[17] Some died where they were, others were drawn upwards by that preternatural wind. Still others died on the spot; already comprehensively starved of oxygen, they had suf-focated as they tried to walk.

A few thousand yards could be the difference between death and sur-vival. There were tall, gaunt alleys – windows belching fire – where the heat was now so concentrated that clothes self-combusted, yet just beyond the Altstadt, along the slightly wider, newer roads that pointed to the suburbs, there were still stragglers walking, some with more purpose than others. A few were making their way towards medical help, with the additional hope that the hospitals themselves might offer sanctuary. Within the large Friedrichstadt hospital – which itself had been damaged – conditions were continually teetering on the edge of shutdown.

Dr Fromme and his team were doing what they could to bring relief to those who had been hideously burned. He recalled that one doctor went missing, never to be seen again.[18] On the wards, the power failed, making it very difficult to work in the semi-darkness of emergency lighting. There were problems with the water supply too, which was becoming intermittent. Fires that had broken out in the cellars had to be contained and sectioned off. The lack of power and fresh water left instruments unsterilized and wounded patients literally parched. The bombers had dissolved back into the night, but they had destroyed the world outside the hospital grounds, leaving it in the most acutely vulnerable position. Where were fresh supplies to come from? Not merely the ordinary items of sustenance, but medicines, and in particular, painkillers. In a letter to his family written soon afterwards, Dr Fromme did not say precisely how he and his colleagues were able to alleviate the agonies of his patients. The walking wounded, by some accounts, were in an almost robotic state, pulsing with adrenaline. It seems that the nurses and doctors were too; Dr Fromme related how everyone worked all through that terrible night.

In the early hours, he could not yet know how many friends he had lost; how many neighbours. He was certain that the family's dog, Elko, had perished, after the animal had run off into the night, barking at the bombs, never to be seen again. 'I hope he had a gentle death,' he said later.[19] Dr Fromme also knew that his home was in ruins. There were family portraits, disintegrated by the flames; gone too was his extensive medical library, of which he had been extremely proud. In addition, the manuscript of a new medical monograph that he had been working on had burned. He – and everyone around him – had had their lives reduced to raw constituents: homeless, with the precious tokens of their pasts dissolved. Yet amid the fundamental uncertainty they were alive.

In a hospital on the other side of the city, conditions and cases were more extreme: the Johannstadt hospital had an extensive maternity wing. The second wave of bombers had dropped many of their explosives shy of the city centre and they had landed here, in this inner eastern suburb. The hospital itself had received serious hits; yet now, as the firestorm rose, it was one of the few buildings in the area left standing.

This hospital, like all other Dresden institutions, had underground shelters, to which many patients had been evacuated with the first warning. As the night had developed, however, there were some, mothers with newborn babies among them, who had the uncontrollable compulsion to get out of the hospital altogether. A few of them, wrapped in nightgowns, blankets, coats had already swaddled their newborns and hurried out of their wards and into the open, towards the Carolabrücke, crossing to the Elbe meadows where the air, even though thick with floating fingers of ash, at least had oxygen that could be breathed. The accompanying keen drizzle was an insignificant discomfort in comparison.

Back at the hospital, people moved like somnambulists towards the gates in the wake of the second wave; refugees who had been trying to find shelter. Dorothea Speth, one of Dresden's tiny community of Mormons, recalled how one couple had been walking up the road with the fires dancing around them. Suddenly, it was as though the man had spontaneously combusted; he collapsed, enveloped in flame.[20] Frau Speth attributed this extraordinary death to a form of invisible phosphorus that caught light as soon as anyone trod upon it, but the real explanation was somehow even ghastlier: just the accident of wearing dry clothes, with the air dancing with the orange orbs of embers, was to invite immolation.

As at Friedrichstadt, it is hard to conceive how doctors, nurses and orderlies were able to continue functioning with water running dry in taps, lights waveringly uncertain and burned people arriving from the blazing streets looking for sanctuary as much as treatment. A pervasive smell of scorched fabric, the raw, dark colours of scalded flesh, the multiple layers of pain. Margot Hille had a great-aunt who lived close to the Altstadt who somehow survived when everyone else in her shelter perished. She had severe burns; again attributed to 'phosphorus'.[21]

In Johannstadt, as in much of the city, the landscape had been violently rearranged. Roads had been obliterated, familiar shopping streets reduced to stumps like grey broken teeth, the ashy ground around littered with bodies that were either whole or dismembered, clothed or naked. Yet even this diorama of death did not convey all that those 796 bombers had achieved across those two raids. There were Dresdeners still, at some distance, who were now witness to an apparent upturning of the laws of physics.

One of these was Victor Klemperer. With the second wave of bombers, and the wound to his head, which bled great gouts, he had lost sight of his wife Eva in the crowds near the trees of Brühl's Terrace overlooking the Elbe. All was elemental confusion; at one point he stumbled into a public telephone kiosk in an effort to be free of the flying sparks that were making it so painful to see; then he was recognized by an acquaintance. Some brilliant quicksilver instinct had told the professor to cover up the yellow star on his coat and then taken him on to the historic riverside terrace forbidden to Jews.[22] All Klemperer could think about was Eva: how had he lost her, and what had become of her? Those milling on that stone-flagged terrace appeared to be on the frontier between two worlds: the Dresden of night, with its rippling river and cool drizzly wind and, not more than a few hundred yards away, the airless, pitiless, unsurvivable landscape of fire. For Klemperer, time could be neither felt nor calculated. His acquaintance, seeing his bleeding head, extemporized a bandage for him; the professor did not seem aware of pain. Behind him, the creaking of rafters, the sharp percussion of cracking stone. In the Neumarkt, upon which stood the Frauenkirche, gutters and pipes had melted, the liquid metal joining with the viscous boiling tar. The church itself had somehow not been hit, but, already, its eight sandstone foundation pillars were radiating heat.

On the other side of the river, Horst Schaffel looked across at the city and the shimmering column of light. His friend Winfried Bielss still had his mother, at least; Horst had no idea if any of his family, who lived in the midst of that ghastly light, were alive, or whether he still had a home. The boy ran down towards a burning municipal building near the Carolabrücke; the few soldiers that were still in the area told him flatly that the bridge was a ruin and could not be crossed. Similarly, Margot Hille and Gisela Reichelt in the south of the city were aching with worry about relatives living in and around Johannstadt. Thousands of Dresdeners were taking comfort, however small, in the fact that this dreadful night must surely soon be at an end. But thanks to the colossal quantities of grey and black smoke that filled the valley of the Elbe, there would be no proper dawn over Dresden that morning.

19. From Among the Dead

As the night drew to its close, ever more people lost — or were losing —
their sight. For Marielein Erler, itching became pain, almost fittingly
at the point when, having spent her entire adult life surrounded by
objects of beauty, she was now obliged to gaze upon the most extraordinary obscenity. Long after the last repercussions of the bombs
had been felt, and with the air still dense with flecks of matter, she
and Georg picked their way along shattered pavements past the
scorched structures of burned-out houses, some still issuing flames.
They saw along the way 'large numbers of dead people'.[1] The corpses
were mostly naked and burned beyond recognition. Twice they saw
the bodies of pregnant women whose bellies had somehow been
opened to reveal their unborn children.

Of course, their own home was almost unrecognizable too; some
odd compulsion made the pair go into the garden, where their carefully
tended flower beds were buried under debris. At the back was a wire
cage in which the neighbours had kept pet rabbits: the creatures were
now simply 'charred lumps'. Marielein Erler's eyes were now seriously
troubling her. She and her husband decided that they were going to
walk to the home of her elderly aunt Else, who lived a little way out of
the city centre in a suburb where the firestorm had not reached. They
did so under an iron-dark sky, filled with the hot dust of charred debris,
and along roads upon which ash had fallen like snow. They moved out
into air that flowed more cleanly, and gradually away from the sight
and the smell of burning. As they got there, they saw that the old lady's
house had been hit too, but it was not on fire, and Aunt Else herself was
perfectly unharmed. 'She greeted us with tears and hugs,' recalled Frau
Erler.[2] By this time, she could hardly bear to open her eyes. 'I asked for
a handkerchief and some water,' she remembered. 'I had to cool my
eyes.' But a water pipe somewhere must have been shattered; none was
coming from the taps. In some desperation, Frau Erler went to ask a

neighbour, but all the woman had was some dirty water in a large pan. She tried to rest her eyes by sleeping, but they were no better for a short rest. She and her husband decided to return home. Hopefully they and their neighbours could band together and help one another.

Something similar was happening to the vision of Lothar Rolf Luhm. He and the others had emerged from the cellar of the Taschenberg Palace; miraculously, its entrance had not been blocked by the wreckage of the building above. It was difficult for them to know whether the sun had risen, as thick smoke filled the sky. As he and several companions explored the still creaking, cracking city, there were flames suddenly breaking out of house ruins, turning shards of glass into flying blades, the glow of fires in churches and the silent, pale rubble of what once had been narrow roads that were now wholly unrecognizable. Luhm's unsteady steps, his ever-blurring sight, would have made this walk slow. Yet the group managed to find the wider avenues and cross the remnants of the Altstadt towards the Great Garden. They would have passed the Altmarkt, the bodies within the reservoir now discoloured and beginning to bloat. Luhm and his party picked their way through snaking tram cables, long severed; there was the wreckage of a tram in the road amid other debris. Luhm recalled that it was full of 'women, children and soldiers' who all 'looked as though they were asleep'.

They reached the Great Garden, the clumps of the oaks and the lindens stretching for a mile, blasted and split and felled and blackened, the craters deep and decapitated bodies and torsos flung everywhere. It might have suggested to a scientifically inclined observer some kind of multiple meteorite strike: the grass and the soil and trees punched and wrenched and scattered by vast forces. As Luhm observed, there was an illusory and chilling peace about many of the corpses: women and children who at first glance seemed unharmed. Yet this was where his own vision was faltering badly; his eyes were darkening. Luhm did also notice, though, that they were not alone among the living; moving around the bodies were people who seemed intent upon giving aid, even in this haunted landscape. 'Volunteers were everywhere, helping where possible,' he recalled.[3]

Among his companions were his soldier friend Günther and a mother and daughter who had been with them in the palace basement. It was decided that the men would go with the mother and daughter in search of their relatives who lived a few miles away, in the countryside. But Luhm was functionally blind and none of them had any idea which direction to head in. A volunteer medical orderly checked Luhm's eyes and proclaimed that he was suffering from nothing more than a temporary form of 'smoke poisoning'. The daughter took Luhm's hand and began to guide him as the little group now picked its way through rubble in search of an undamaged bridge across the river, and the road out into the chill, open landscape beyond.

At around the same time, Mischka Danos was also drawing close to the burning timber of the Great Garden; he'd felt at first when he'd left the sheltering bunker as though he was walking in his sleep. The wider avenue near the central railway station was easy to negotiate – strewn with brick and rubble and glass, there was none the less a path through – but with the narrower streets of the Altstadt, everything changed; here were hot boulders that had to be climbed. Danos at one point saw a little boy, no more than five years old, lying by a fence, looking as though he was sleeping. This was the first entire corpse that he had encountered. Other glimpses had been fragments of humanity: a leg and a foot jutting from under bricks, a mass of hair attached to an unseen head that was submerged beneath blackened stone. There was a kind of cumulative effect in all of this; the young man, who had originally been impelled by curiosity to see what had happened to the city, was now at last beginning to feel fear.[4] The reaction might have been delayed but that did not diminish its intensity. It was there, deep down, like a flickering fire taking hold. His walk continued, taking him, directionless, towards the river and the Neustadt beyond.

Not far from where Danos had been sheltering, the grandfather of ten-year-old Gisela Reichelt was walking in that twilight morning; with the streets and alleys he had known all his life reduced to their constituent stone and dust, navigation would have been difficult enough, but now he was also entirely blind. Yet he still walked. Miraculously there were others, able-bodied, moving through the coagulating dust, who saw and came to his help. Slowly and carefully the old man with his streaming, sightless eyes was taken to the Johannstadt hospital. None there would be able to cure him but there he would at least find comfort and reassurance. His granddaughter and her mother, meanwhile, were some distance away. The nerve-stretching stress of the night had not ended for them as the last of the bombers echoed away: first, the main entrance to their cellar was blocked with intense flames and a pavement window had to be broken to allow all the residents to climb out. Gisela's mother was two weeks away from giving birth. Then, having successfully climbed away from these flames, they were greeted, on that dark street, with an unending prospect of fire.[5]

Their own home was destroyed; there was no possibility of return. All that could be done was for the pregnant woman and her daughter to negotiate the still-sticky tarmac, the collapsing wreckage from tall residential buildings, the throat-clinging dust. On top of this, some-how Gisela's mother had to find means of distracting her daughter from the twisted, naked mummies, coated with ash. The answer was to run, or at least to move as fast as they could. There was an aunt who lived a few streets to the south, in a rather smart suburb with elegant apartment buildings; these were in flames, but the aunt was safe.

They all went to check on Gisela's other grandparents, on her father's side, who lived close to the university, again on a tree-lined street with villas and apartment blocks in a style suggestive of France. Now, every property was either ablaze or simply gutted. But her grandparents, having emerged from their own basement, were also safe, and they decided to move on as a group. There was no coherent plan; their volition seemed mainly based on fear. They all moved 'without actually knowing where to go'.[6]

They were not alone. Other figures were moving through the broken streets, the underlying impulse clearly to get out into the fields and woods beyond the town. They and Gisela's family were as cut off and as vulnerable as any medieval inhabitants of a long-besieged village. They had been bombed out of the twentieth century, and out of the modern age.

As Horst set out with Winfried Bielss and his mother from their base-ment just before dawn, the boy still had no means of knowing the fate of his family. The teenager left his companions and pointed himself east, in the direction of the Loschwitz crossing some three miles upriver, a turn-of-the-century suspension bridge colloquially referred to as the Blue Wonder. This symbol of Dresden's engineer-ing genius still stood. But as the boy crossed, and picked his way through the eastern suburbs towards the shattered remains of Johannstadt, this was his last trace of reassurance. He reached his family home to find simply a burned-out void. There was no trace of his parents. He had with him a notebook, and he left a brief message wedged into what remained of the house's front porch. Then Horst retraced his steps through the skeletal streets to the Blue Wonder. Cross-ing back to the east side, he climbed the hill and entered the clean, rain-laundered darkness of Dresden Heath, the forest that lay on the edge of the city. He picked his way through miles of trees and even-tually reached the home of some relatives who lived in a small village.

Some knew precisely how horrific the sights would be, including civic officials, railway personnel and indeed Dr Fromme's fifteen-year-old son, Friedrich-Carl, who was approaching the ruined railway station under that dark morning sky.[7] The glass roof and the proud glass dome had been shattered; platforms, and the trains standing at them, had also been hit. Fires still burned; heat continued to radiate from the concrete of the platforms. There were a few bloodied, dis-membered bodies on this upper level. It was also obvious that the lower levels, the darkened tunnels and corridors, had become a mass tomb. Some bodies were crushed, victims of panic, others had split open. And there were more yet of people who had found their way into the sta-tion's bomb-proof air-raid shelters and then simply run out of air and suffocated where they sat. Some had baked, as the ambient temperature rose ineluctably in the fires. If Friedrich-Carl had been hoping to

administer any kind of aid, it is difficult to know quite where
he would have begun; the initial horrified estimates of mortality
were numbered at 3,000. All these people, many of them rural refugees, had died in and around one tunnel. But such numbers, in any
case, could only be understood on the most detached level; what
could quantification have mattered to those who gazed upon those
underground passages stuck fast with corpses?

Friedrich-Carl reported back to Dr Fromme, who was still
working at the hospital. There were now more soldiers in evidence
too; after the anarchy of the fire, the compulsion to restore order was
strong and indeed, at the hospital, the military were proving to be
of solid practical assistance to the doctor, providing trucks so that
patients might be transferred to smaller, undamaged clinics and
hospitals in the suburbs and countryside around the town. This was
critical; without reliable supplies of electricity and water – and with
finite stocks of painkillers, dressings and sterile instruments – there
was only so much Dr Fromme and his large team could do. On top of
this, some outbuildings, including the laundry, the dental clinic and
the gynaecological unit, had been irreparably damaged by the bombs.
As soon as he could, Dr Fromme requested a lift from a military
truck to go and inspect the facilities of several small clinics in the
surrounding area; this would also be a chance to give staff at
these establishments an idea of the challenges they were going to face:
the wet flesh around the discoloured burns, the smoke inhalation,
the widespread damage to eyes.

Elsewhere in the city it was as though ghosts had returned. Margot
Hille's great-uncle Hermann had been on a train approaching the
main station just moments before the first wave of bombers came
over. Now in that ambiguous time before the feeble first light, Hermann presented himself upon the doorstep of his brother, Margot's
grandfather. Great-Uncle Hermann was wearing a suit that was not
his and unfamiliar shoes. He explained that 'the burning train had been
driven out of the station'.[8] There were few details, other than that in the
fires of that night Hermann had lost his clothes, yet had somehow
found the wherewithal to acquire more. His brother, who had emerged

from the sheltering cellar to check that his bombed house was not being ransacked, agreed to take him in; faced with this surreal sight, it is difficult to imagine how he might have done otherwise.

Yet thousands of others suffered the opposite of that consolation. Margot Hille's aunt, who lived quite close to the Altstadt, had lost contact with her daughter in the panic of that night; now in the dusk that should have been day, she was walking through the seething ash and still glowingly hot scattered bricks and stones of those ruined passages and alleys, in the hope that somehow she might chance across the girl. Margot joined her repeated, neurotic sorties, and this was when the teenager glimpsed the true visceral impact of the attack upon the city: the burned corpses lying in the melted roads; far-scattered limbs; severed heads lolling on seared earth. All these were, at least, identifiable – not that this would have offered any comfort, but Margot Hille's aunt could see no indication of her daughter either alive or dead. The air was not still; there were the reverberations of cracking, creaking, collapsing structures both near and in the distance and continual movement from others who had either come to claim the dead or to help those who miraculously still lived.

Elsewhere, having crossed the river, Mischka Danos delivered the 'Karl May' girl to the home of her family in a wooded suburb, a large house that still had windows intact. The girl's parents showed an exhausted Danos upstairs and invited him to lie down upon one of the beds. He did not sleep long, and on waking felt compelled to return to the ruins. Near the rubble of Johannstadt he was confronted with what at first he thought was some sort of vision: walking down the broken street was a giraffe.[9]

On Brühl's Terrace, Victor Klemperer, his eye and temple still painful from the shrapnel, was gazing as though hypnotized at the fires in the Altstadt behind him; before any suggestion of morning light, he had the impression of a tall tower glowing dull red, as well as all the 'theatrical' fires elsewhere.[10] He himself was numbed, save to reflect occasionally that, having survived the night, it would be awful now to meet with some form of accident. Where was his wife? They had now been separated for hours. He trudged a little further towards the Elbe, to a small copse at the end of the terrace that overlooked the river and there, sitting on a suitcase, was Eva. They embraced hungrily, knowing that they had lost every material possession and that it did not matter.

Klemperer was desperate to know where she had been. In the bloody confusion of that second raid she had been pulled down into an 'Aryan' shelter. She had left quickly and then, once more in the smoke-billowing street, set out to find her husband. The force of the fires and the threat of falling debris – she too was hit on the head by some fragment that had detached from a burning building – forced her into shelter once more, this time beneath the Albertinum, which was housing the civic authorities. Eva was underground for some time, but again she could not bring herself to stay. She was a committed and determined cigarette smoker, and as she had emerged into the haze of that unnaturally hot night, facing the smouldering Arts Academy, she was twitching for tobacco. She had a packet of cigarettes on her; but no matches. Seeing something glowing on the black ground, she bent forward to light a cigarette from it. The glowing object was a burning corpse.

After this, she had moved off in the vague direction of the cooler air from the river; now she was reunited with her husband. In that semi-darkness, the exhaustion was so deep that they seemed not even able to recoil with full fright from sights that in normal circumstances would have made anyone start. Professor Klemperer recalled walking past a man who had had the top of his head removed, the interior of the skull 'a dark bowl'. There was also a severed arm, with a perfect pale hand, untouched, as though made from wax. The elderly couple watched as, in that uncertain grey morning light, a sort of procession formed on the road that ran alongside the Elbe. Locals and refugees had become indistinguishable. There were people with handcarts with miscellaneous household items, others who were carrying boxes. Klemperer's yellow star had long been removed. The couple met another resident from the Judenhaus, Herr Eisenmann. He had his small son by his side, but he told the Klemperers that he could not find his other loved ones. His eyes filled with tears as he indicated his little boy and told the Klemperers that the child would soon be asking for breakfast, and that he did not know what to give him.

Across the river, on the wide Elbe meadows, individuals – some in coats, some still in nightwear topped with blankets – walked to and fro, gazing at the burning fires pouring yet more smoke into the blackened sky. They were bewildered by the amputation of so many familiar towers and steeples; the dark-stoned Catholic cathedral, now imploded; the grand opera house, disfigured and levelled beyond recognition; the baroque Zwinger Palace, much of its delicacy annihilated. Among the dislocated citizens were the teenagers of the Hitler Youth and League of German Girls, who had rushed in from the relatively unharmed suburbs, anxious to help wherever they could. Of the Nazi hierarchy there appeared little sign. Naturally, there were soldiers and firemen and medics attempting to organize people who scarcely knew that they were still alive, but the senior Nazis were nowhere to be seen. Most especially, there was no appearance from the Gauleiter of Saxony to rally his people. Martin Mutschmann was notable by his continued absence as the city's civic servants now tried to bring some measure of rationality to this shattered world. Neither, of course, was he present when just a very few hours later a renewed humming resonance sounded in the distance.

20. The Third Wave

The doubts and the qualms – and then the quiet, reflective horror – came later. The young American was a nose gunner; a staff sergeant who had already completed twenty-seven missions across Europe. His position in flight inside a transparent bubble of perspex, gun in readiness, enabled him to see approaching enemies and their fire, and also the daylight glitter of rivers far below, snow-topped hills, the built-up rectangles of city and industry, smoke and fire rising from the bombed streets and plants. Howard Holbrook would later recall, in a tone intended to be light rather than laconic, that he had seen many 'life and death situations'.[1] Given the mortality rates among American as well as British airmen, this was a deliberate understatement, though he added that he received no injuries. This was quite remarkable: among USAAF bomber crews, it was later calculated, the average life expectancy was fifteen missions; not even a full tour. Like their British counterparts, American airmen were shot out of the skies in colossal numbers.

Now, on the morning of 14 February 1945, as the dark skies over the east of England became greyer and lighter, Howard U. Holbrook was among hundreds of American airmen staring at the freshly revealed map, with its red-coloured thread denoting route and destination. If he was dismayed by the distance to this city deep in Europe, he would not later recall it. 'At briefing, we were told we were going after railroad yards,' he remembered. 'But my plane was loaded with firebombs.'[2]

Holbrook was twenty-four years old; he had joined up three years previously. He had been born in Coeburn, Virginia, a tiny town deep in the Appalachian countryside, on the Lonesome Pine trail that was almost as far from the ethos of the big city, geographically and psychologically, as it was possible to be.[3] Holbrook was among some 450,000 US airmen who had volunteered from across the United States, men representing a wide tapestry of backgrounds and beliefs, many with names that spoke of German or Italian heritage. Holbrook was a member of the Baptist Church. He was a man of strong faith. Yet within just a few hours of that morning briefing, Holbrook and his fellow airmen would be regarded by the people of Dresden as a demonic force motivated not by moral fervour but by some darker malice. Their attack would be seen as unfathomable; with the streets deep in human dust, cellars filled with the dead, and the survivors, traumatized, wounded, already seeking to match body parts to the identities of loved ones, how could the 'American gangsters', as they came to be known to post-war Dresdeners, possibly justify swooping in once more? But these Americans had, like the British the night before, been told of troop movements, and of the need to sever communication and transport lines. And was not daylight bombing a means of at least giving civilians a chance?

The US Strategic Air Forces Intelligence Office in early 1945 considered that the Luftwaffe had 'rebounded to a degree not considered possible by Allied Intelligence';[4] the Nazis were fighting back with real venom and energy. Nor had the fighting on the ground become any less intense; quite the reverse. In the cold of that European winter, during the bitter slog through forests and rivers, the number of US soldiers killed or seriously injured was increasing dramatically. Perhaps the resolution of the conflict seemed predetermined: but even with the knowledge that the Allies and the Soviets were between them ineluctably closing in from either side, Hitler's Nazis were clearly not going to consider surrender. As veteran and literary critic Paul Fussell wrote years later: 'We knew the Germans had lost the war, and they knew it too . . . It was the terrible necessity of the Germans pedantically, literally *enacting* their defeat that we found so disheartening. Since it was clear that we were going to win, why did we have to enact the victory physically and kill them and ourselves in the process?'[5]

In the higher reaches of both British and American bomber commands, the gravity of war blunted any lingering concern for civilians. Although Sir Arthur Harris was the most brutally straightforward of them all when articulating what he saw as the necessity of deliberately bombing cities, his superiors and their American counterparts were by 1945 philosophically close to his position. The commander of the US Strategic Air Forces, Carl Spaatz, had, at the beginning of February, come to agree that attacks on Berlin, Leipzig and Dresden were both justifiable and desirable. This was not malice, nor was it quite the ruthless urge to eradicate all traces of the enemy. But there was a decisive cognitive shift, the turning of a blank face to the civilians who would endure the full pain of these raids. The aim, as stated, was to create 'disruption and confusion';[6] these words are kinetic, suggesting chaotic movement, ungovernable crowds making life impossible for ordered civic authorities. What they do not suggest is corpses sitting in cellars with melted, fused organs.

In addition to all this, for airmen such as Howard Holbrook, to fly over Germany bathed in full sunlight required as much courage as night-time bombings: the planes, silver and flashing in the sky, were very much easier for the Germans to target. In the early weeks of 1945 Holbrook and his fellow B-17 crew members had flown missions that targeted synthetic-oil plants and railway lines, dropping bombs over Mannheim and Lützkendorf. The US missions were always presented to the aircrews as against infrastructure and fuel supplies, as though smashing a machine rather than its operator. However, the truth was that the B-17 bombers were never as scalpel-sharp accurate as they might have believed or hoped. Many of their bombs fell literally miles off target. In the case of vast industrial plants surrounded by scrubby country, this mattered little, but in the case of railway marshalling yards close to city centres, precision was paramount if accompanying terrible civilian casualties were to be avoided.

Holbrook and his fellow crewmen in 384th Group were stationed at Grafton Underwood in Northamptonshire. Though the airfield was as bleak as all the others, the village itself was very pretty: thatched houses composed of milky-brown stone, a brook running alongside the main road. This quiet remnant of English rural life must have offered some peace away from the mayhem of war. During several recent missions, Holbrook's plane – which the crew had named 'Danny' – had run low on fuel and had had to find alternative airfields to land on, once in the (now Allied controlled) Low Countries.

That morning of 14 February, Holbrook and his comrades felt no sense that the war was coming to its close. Like their countrymen, they were reading not merely about European casualties, but also about the toll of the war against Japan, which had its own intensity. As the flock of B-17 bombers took off from airfields around England that morning, their bomb bays were stacked with both explosives and incendiaries. Not all were destined for Dresden; there were to be simultaneous attacks on Chemnitz and Magdeburg. Yet underlying these general aims was little precision. Cloud cover was making navigation difficult that day, and of the twelve divisions of bombers that traced their contrails above German skies, three tacked too far south and ended up accidentally bombing Prague, then in the Nazi-controlled Protectorate of Bohemia and Moravia.

But Holbrook's plane steered its course effectively, and he recalled many years later that, as they flew closer to Dresden that lunchtime, the smoke visible from many miles away, it became clear that the city was defenceless. It was just a few minutes after noon when they arrived at their target. A total of 311 American bombers were rushing through the clouds towards the still-burning city. Their focus – the railway marshalling yards in residential Friedrichstadt – was almost wholly obscured by the toxic smoke rising from the seething ruins. There was no possibility that any of these bomb aimers were going to be able to release their payloads with complete accuracy. It was for this reason that this fresh wave of bombing was viewed from below with a horror that for many turned gradually to hatred, and indeed had a direct effect on the way that Dresdeners recalled their own personal experiences on that day. For those who were not wounded, or related to fatalities, the impact was not immediate; it was an epilogue to the trauma of the night. In time, and with growing anger, collective memory would change.

Before the Americans came, fatigue had crept over both Winfried Bielss and his mother; despite all he had seen and felt, the boy was overpowered by the need to sleep. His eyes closed, and the next he knew, his mother was waking him several hours later.[7] The hand-held sirens had once more been sounding through the city. The bombers were coming back. In his recollections, Bielss seemed to register neither surprise nor shock nor outrage at this, but he clearly felt keenly the pain of those who had suffered through the night. Bielss recalled noting with interest the musical timbre of the approaching force; the slightly lighter note that suggested they were fewer in number than the night-time raiders. 'This air attack lasted thirteen minutes,' he said. From the ground, there was little indication that the target was the railway marshalling yards. Bombs were falling on streets already strewn with cadavers, and on the distraught grandparents, aunts and uncles who were scrambling through still-smoking ruins in the mad and desperate hope that they would find loved ones alive and whole. In the Bielsses' apartment, the power suddenly failed as an American bomb hit one of the city's major power cables. Remarkably, the electricity supply was restored after twenty-four hours; the determination of those city workers to see that the entire town was not reduced to a primitive state despite the primordial assault was intense.

A neighbour of the Bielsses, Frau Wack, had earlier gone to the Altstadt, where her daughter Margot lived; the last she had heard was a telephone call the previous night that Margot had managed to make from a police station. After that, she had made for one of the innumerable cellar shelters. Frau Wack located the shattered block that was her daughter's address; the cellar had not withstood the bombardment or the poison air and she was told that all its occupants had perished. Such was Frau Wack's distress that the fact of a fresh daylight raid appeared not to have entered her conscious thoughts. In some terrible way, she herself had become inured. She later told the Bielsses that, according to the rescue teams, the entire inner city was burned out.

Some friends of Frau Wack arrived at the Bielsses' apartment block from the bombed-out neighbourhood of Johannstadt. They had survived in their basement even as the buildings on their street were battered, fragmented and eaten from within by the incendiaries. Again there was little if any mention of this new air raid, or of the bombs that were dropping upon still open wounds. The people were simply too exhausted. Bielss recalled that they 'smelled smoky' and were extraordinarily dirty. Their immediate desire was for water to quench their terrible thirst. All their local supplies had been cut.

Fortunately, the Bielsses' water was still running. The Johannstadt refugees slept for the rest of that day and all through the night that followed; the extremes of physical terror could only be borne consciously for so long.

For Helmut Voigt, 14 February and the attack from the US planes had in a sense been prophesied. He had heard it from local soldiers, aware that the British bombed by night and 'the Americans will come in the day'.[8] Just after noon, he heard a warning whistle; heads jerked upwards to scan the muddy clouds. He did not remember hearing the approach of the planes at all, but he did recall seeing at a distance the little black dots falling and then hearing the first detonations. Then he suddenly became aware that other planes were coming in their direction. He and the neighbours ran for the cellars – a return to the sooty darkness and then the noise from above of repeated beating. Voigt's apartment block was hit and several bombs crashed into the communal gardens. No one could quite believe that the Americans had returned to strike an already gravely wounded city. Voigt and his neighbours were fortunate still to have shelter. Many others did not.

Georg and Marielein Erler, walking the cracked streets of Johannstadt that late morning, their eyes flickering over the stray body parts, had met up with a few familiar neighbours; these included Frau Zaunick, who, like Erler, was an air-raid warden. She had managed to gather a few residents together and she and Herr Erler made a plan that they should leave the city and find a village for badly needed sustenance and rest. Like so many other Dresdeners, the yearning for sleep was extremely powerful. Herr Erler wanted to round up some more of the residents under his charge, and it was decided that they would rendezvous near the Great Garden park. Marielein elected to stay with Frau Zaunick as her husband walked off.

Weary and nerve-stretched, Frau Erler sat down on the fringe of the park: here were flower beds and bushes that had somehow evaded the bombs and the fire, splashes of green and pale blue in a city limned with grey. After five minutes there was a rush of feet and a cry: 'They're coming back!'[9] The drone from above was sudden; and Marielein experienced the cold horror of being out in the open air with no possibility of reaching shelter. Instinct impelled her to push her way into the heart of a large rhododendron bush. She knew as she did so that it was 'ridiculous'; yet what else might she have done? And now, with hideous speed, the bombardment started again. Marielein Erler, crouched in that bush, recalled that it was like boulders falling from the sky. All around her were screams; then there was the flash of an explosion nearby. Frau Erler was hit in the head with a shard of shrapnel. 'I felt the warm blood on my face and neck,' she remembered, surprised to find herself still alive.

The attack passed over, leaving fresh casualties in its wake. Marielein emerged from her hiding place to the sound of 'children screaming'. Other children, she recalled, lay dead. She made her way to a bench and sat down; all she could think was that she must wait for her husband to return. To the west of the city, fresh plumes of smoke rose. Marielein, immobile on her bench as all around her people moved back and forth, was approached by a man concerned at the blood streaming from her head. He insisted that she should seek medical attention, but she had no intention of moving until she was reunited with her husband. Impatiently, the man seized hold of her, pulled her up from the bench. With some vehemence she extricated herself from his grip, and returned to where she was sitting. The man – a rescue worker, perhaps – told Marielein that he would give her five minutes to wait for her husband, but it could not be more because she was bleeding to death.

The man walked off, presumably to help elsewhere, and time for Marielein Erler became disjointed. She looked on impassively, her eyes still fogged and painful, as volunteers began lifting corpses, gathering them together on that road. She was aware of other injured people around her, knew they were being led away. Still she sat, immobile and immobilized.

Above her, a British plane was circling through the dirty clouds, a Mosquito capturing on film the extent of the damage wreaked by the Americans. The 311 Flying Fortresses, in their efforts to target the Friedrichstadt marshalling yards through dense brown smoke, had had some success: rails were buckled and snapped, sheds and carriages burned. A number of the incendiary bombs, however, had fallen elsewhere: four-storeyed residential buildings that had escaped the fires and the sparks of the night now had their roofs punctured, their inhabitants forced once more into cellars where the air was fast becoming toxic. Hit too in greater numbers were the factories that before the war had produced so many sewing machines and typewriters and bicycles. In that sense, the raid was effective: these converted armaments works, industrial fortresses filled with precision-instrument production lines, had essentially been demolished. The nearby Friedrichstadt hospital sustained some minor damage too, yet it was into these wards that the freshly wounded would be brought: bloody wounds to dress, the acute distress of the more seriously maimed and mutilated, and the efforts to somehow dull the fires of their pain.

In a matter of minutes, the American crews were returning above the white cloud base to England. The next day they and British bombers would take off once more, reaching deep into Germany to attack other targets: Chemnitz, Magdeburg. Dresden was, for them, unexceptional; simply another objective. Only very much later did some of them reflect on the deeper import of that raid; one ball-turret gunner, Harold R. Nelson, accepted that 'the bombing of Dresden was really nasty'. But he was also quite sure that, in its own way, the raid had helped to 'shorten the war'.[10]

The people of Dresden, though, were already beginning to form their own interpretation of what had happened. For Margot Hille, the American raid was a 'crime against humanity';[11] many years later, she recalled hearing about how 'low-flying' aircraft had deliberately shot at the assorted refugees – rural and local – who were gathered helplessly on the Elbe meadows. This was to become a recurring leitmotif in the city's story about itself, but it was not true. Although there had been fighters escorting the bombers, they were not 'low-flying', and no such strafing had taken place. (Similar stories would emerge from Britain: children who distinctly remembered not just German planes swooping down, but even, and impossibly, the faces of the pilots.)

This might have been an instinctive and subconscious means of channelling anger against an attacker that was otherwise faceless and blankly impervious. Better a remembrance of vengeful sadism than the almost industrial and passionless production-line process of death.

In Dresden, such 'recollections' were painted even more vividly. For example, Gisela Reichelt and her mother had been in a horse-drawn cart out in the countryside, part of a procession of exhausted citizens hoping to be billeted on farms on the uplands, when she saw the planes once more approaching the city behind her.

What could they want? The city was 'already broken'.[12] There was more: she remembered the human convoy being attacked 'again and again' by low-flying aircraft, the planes shooting at anyone not under cover. But memory can play false, and it is possible that what she actually saw were in fact Luftwaffe reconnaissance planes trying to assess the damage; and that the gunfire was an illusion produced by the terrified and panicked reactions of the adults around her. If the child was surrounded by grown-ups who were understandably agitated by the sight of any aeroplane, then she would have been certain, as she flung herself down, that this was an attack. Certainly, she recalled no one being hit; the group all reached their ordained village later that day.

Others had the most explicit memories of being dive-bombed out on the meadows by the Elbe; and so closely that they could describe the malicious American pilots. One person was adamant that they had been attacked by a black pilot – an unlikely identification, given not only the blurring speed and altitude of fighters but also the fact that their pilots wore oxygen masks.

Such stories spread rapidly among the thousands of displaced Dresdeners who, late that afternoon, were still almost catatonic with shock. People who, amid the still hissing pipes and the loud creaks of near-demolished flats and shops, searched single-mindedly for their loved ones, alive or dead. Whatever terrible abuse their bodies might have suffered was seemingly of no matter. They had to be gathered up properly. More practically, the civic authorities knew that this landscape of illimitable corpses had to be cleared before it brought lethal infection to the living population. There was no time for fastidiousness. And as the salvaging of mutilated and fragmented bodies began properly that afternoon, so too did many other Dresdeners begin dazed, dream-like journeys out into the country, wafting like dandelion seeds and with seemingly as little agency. It had been only eighteen hours since that first wave of bombing.

PART THREE
Aftershock

21. Dead Men and Dreamers

Once the Americans had departed, some could not resist the urge to explore and examine the ruins more closely; there were those in search of the missing and others impelled by a form of horrified fascination. Winfried Bielss and his mother wanted to know what had become of cousins across the river in devastated Johannstadt, but perhaps unconsciously they also wanted to prepare their own inventory of the wider devastation. As they walked through the Waldschlösschen area that overlooked the river, the boy and the mother gazed with some intensity at bomb craters. They saw a 'bent bicycle',[1] and near it, the limbless body of a man. They walked on, passing the Deaconess hospital complex, parts of which were still burning. Once-smart villas were now ruins. The boy noted – perhaps with some proprietorial hubris – that his own school seemed undamaged. Many other pupils might have felt a surge of disappointment. Now they passed more villas that seemed simply to have burned down rather than having been demolished by bombs. Here too were more schools, and municipal buildings, gaping and knocked through. At the river it looked as though the Albertbrücke, which crossed to Johannstadt, had been damaged. The meadows in front of the water were, despite the heat of the city on the opposite bank, rimed with pockets of ice.

On crossing the river, mother and son were able to take in the panoramic sweep of destruction. On Sachsenplatz, tall residential blocks and shops were now jutting, fractured remnants. A road that led between two such blocks was impassable: electric tram lines, fallen, were twisted like spaghetti on the streets in all directions; trees had been wrenched out by the roots and lay across the avenue; there were burned-out cars, and a burned-out tram as well. Bielss and his mother picked their way carefully around these obstacles, to the main thoroughfare of the Lothringer Strasse, upon which stood the court building. This fearful symbol of authority, with its courtyard guillotine, was still standing, but had been deconstructed by fire, leaving exposed its blackened insides and, in that chill air, the sharp tang of burned wood and fabric. On what remained of the pavement before it lay bodies and detached limbs, still clothed. Mother and son moved on.

This was a landscape that had been turned into a puzzle; it was very difficult to orientate oneself along former roads of shapeless boulders, to discern where streets had once been, with apartment blocks smashed to the ground, villas now simply consisting of two or three walls, their domestic innards indelicately exposed to all. The boy noticed that his mother stooped a little to examine each corpse that they passed. Any one of these bodies might have been family. There was still worse to see. A little further south, the middle of one road had been smashed to form a giant bowl, around which on the gravelly rubble lay twisted, naked corpses. The blast, and the inrush of oven-hot air, had sucked the clothes from their bodies as it toasted their flesh. This was the succinct degradation of organized civil and aesthetic society; a manifestation of physical force and a manipulation of physics that had comprehensively desecrated the dead. On they moved, Frau Bielss having checked the undressed cadavers.

On a narrow street near the hospital was a wall of dusty, sharp debris, three feet high, spanning the entire width of the road and topped with more corpses. As they reached the corner of another smoking street the boy suddenly thought of their family tailor, Wenzel Lupinek, who lived and worked in this area. Just the previous year Lupinek had fitted him for his first suit, intended for his church confirmation. How could he have survived among these collapsed buildings?

The pair went to check on some relatives who lived close by. With trepidation they looked at the buildings that seemed relatively undamaged, and at those that were now skeletal. The boy found one reason for a sliver of hope: unlike many of the older buildings in the inner city, these apartment blocks had been constructed with girders and supports made from steel rather than wood. This meant that the cellars were more likely to have maintained their structural integrity.

The dark stairs and passages that led to them were still too hot to descend; heat radiated from them as if from a baker's oven. A little further on they discovered a minor miracle: their relative Horst Poppe was on the cracked pavement outside the exoskeleton of an apartment block. Winfried was bemused by the quantity of valuables Poppe had apparently saved; here, out in this dense, savoury, smoky air he had created a small mountain of rescued glass ornaments, porcelain and handicrafts. And he had news: two of Frau Bielss's other relatives had gone to the apartment of his sister-in-law and were safe. The only person he had not yet been able to account for was his mother-in-law. Even as the three of them talked in this eerie landscape, that same mother-in-law suddenly came walking around the corner; she had been forced to seek shelter elsewhere. There was the reunion; and then the mother and the boy – having established these survivals – were now anxious to get back to their own home, and indeed to a district that still felt alive.

As they walked back through the maze of demolished buildings, the boy and his mother breathed in the burning wood, mixed with the smell of scorched clothes and seared rubber. There was a new element too: a rising smell from the multitude of corpses, a 'disgusting sweet mixture' that, Bielss recalled, he could still summon even at the distance of fifty years.[2]

The boy and his mother were, relatively speaking, extremely fortunate; they had found the people they were looking for, and discovered they were alive and unhurt. Nearer the Altstadt, elderly men and women searched for missing spouses, children for parents and parents for children. In the alleys near the Kreuzkirche, they too were climbing on rubble that was still hot. On the main stretch of Prager Strasse the concrete and stone debris in the middle of the road was piled almost at head height, and could be clambered upon only with the greatest difficulty, in the process dislodging individual stones that might reveal clumps of hair or disembodied hands. It would be like disturbing a grave. A little further south, soldiers, nurses, doctors and volunteers worked by the ruins of the railway station. Those who had died on the platforms and the ground-floor concourse were now arranged there in neat rows. Dresdeners scanned the macabre display to see if they could identify loved ones, many of the bodies with skulls so extensively damaged and faces so burned that identification was possible only by what they wore. Efforts were being made to retrieve the corpses from the darkened lower levels, but people had been packed together so tightly, and the atmosphere was still so hot, airless and toxic, that so far very little progress had been made. Rumours spread with extraordinary speed; Dr Fromme swiftly heard from one of his staff about the speculation that 3,000 people had been down in those dreadful tunnels.

Even though many cellars were still too hot to enter, the authorities were anxious about the possibility of pestilence. Mere minutes after the American raid, soldiers and volunteers, firemen and medical staff were directing the aimlessly milling crowds of refugees and bombed-out citizens firmly towards the city's arterial roads, telling them that if they kept moving, out of the suburbs and into the countryside, further volunteers would guide them to villages and farmhouses where they would be well fed and billeted in large barns filled with fresh straw. The Gauleiter of Saxony had finally emerged from his own private shelter and was now ordaining that anyone caught looting would face certain execution.

Such a declaration would have meant nothing to those who, badly hurt and silent with shock, were being gently ushered from the streets to makeshift field hospitals erected with startling speed around the town. There was a small military medical unit at Arnsdorf, among the tall trees of the heath. Dr Fromme had led the efforts to ensure that the facilities were sufficiently robust to take more patients. Private cars were pressed into service; Dr Fromme's own vehicle – which unlike so many others had not had its tyres liquefied or its engine melted – was jolting back and forth along country roads as patients were ferried to temporary accommodation. Beyond the conflagration, winter had retained its grip, making the rural evacuations treacherous with snow. Dr Fromme also had to contend with a telephone system that was only partly functioning. Remarkably, health care was something that many Dresdeners somehow knew would be available. Margot Hille, who had the previous day been twitching to volunteer for the League of German Girls, despite having sustained a blow to the head, was the next day still being held back by her fearful mother. But Frau Hille, regardless of the American raid, was also insistent that afternoon that her daughter instead go to a clinic that had been established at a school near to where they lived. The mother was convinced her daughter had suffered a 'concussion to the brain'[3] and a broken nose.

Margot was examined and pronounced fine, following which the pair hauled their packed suitcases to the complex of buildings that comprised the Felsenkeller brewery. They, along with a few other employees and their families, had decided in the aftershock to relocate to the safety of the brewery's tunnels, dug deep into the rock of a hill and secure against further attack from whichever direction. The chilly tunnels had earlier had proper lighting installed, and the Felsenkeller management had presciently even ensured that there were bathroom facilities for use in the event of the shelter being occupied for prolonged periods. For a while, these tunnels would become a sanctuary.

For Marielein Erler, sitting stunned on the bench by the Great Garden park, her temple bleeding after the American attack, there was also efficient help. After having pulled herself away from one potential saviour, she was approached by another man, who managed to coax her into standing and led her to a car. She was driven some ten miles south to Kreischa, an area high on the plateau above the city. Here was an impressive hospital, sanatorium and spa facility. Marielein was taken straight to casualty, where three doctors were attempting to tend to a great crowd of patients. Her temple wound was of concern, but it was quickly decided that it could simply be cleaned and stitched. A greater problem, said the doctor who had pronounced her lucky, was her eyes, which were still painful and dimmed and causing her distress.[4] Eye drops were administered. Then Marielein was led away to one of the clinic's wards, where a bed waited for her. Naturally, she was anxious about her husband, not having seen him since minutes before the American attack, but no sooner had she been helped into the crisp bed than intense fatigue overcame her. Like so many others, she plunged deep into a blank sleep.

While so many thronged the city's outer roads and bridges in their quest for safety, others barely moved. Professor Klemperer, reunited with his wife Eva, had spent part of the day at the Jewish cemetery, which had been nominated as a meeting point for the city's remaining

Jews in the wake of catastrophe. Finding no one there, he had returned to his wife at Brühl's Terrace. The exhaustion was so great that even an explosion caused by one of the American bombers – though creating a moment of terrific fright – appeared very quickly forgotten. Indeed, Klemperer seems to have been largely unaware of – or perhaps simply dulled to – the third raid. By the late afternoon the city was filling with medical personnel and ambulances summoned from nearby towns and cities, and even from as far away as Berlin. Like Klemperer, many on the terrace seemed to be having painful difficulty with their eyes.[5] Young medics were moving among them with eye drops and thin spatulas with which they tried to clean away a little of the dirt from the corners and beneath the eyelids. Klemperer heard the jocular command from the medics of 'Hold still, Dad!'

He and Eva moved into the bulky black edifice of the Albertinum, in the cellars of which she had taken shelter. The roof had been hit but the structure of the lower two floors was perfectly sound. This civic fortress had vast rooms with very high ceilings; electricity was being provided using a hand-operated generator. And in one of these high rooms, the medics had set up as many makeshift beds as they could, and guided their often elderly patients to lie down on them. Some were Jews; no one seemed to be checking, and certainly no one was turned away. Klemperer had heard from a friend outside that everyone in the professor's building had survived.

That cold February evening in that echoing room was both uncomfortable and curious. Despite the best efforts of the medical teams in attending to their charges, there was next to no food or drink to sustain them because emergency supplies had yet to be assembled. The medical workers shared their own rations – largely bread and sausage – with their patients, but water was the biggest problem. There had initially been enough in the taps to allow patients a mouthful of tea each, but then the water supplies gave out entirely and some on the rickety makeshift beds were now tormented by dusty dehydration. Klemperer recalled that one old gentleman had awoken suddenly in deep distress, having apparently been dreaming that he was drinking deep draughts of cooling water. Klemperer himself recalled that he fell into a near mesmerized state in the lengthening shadows; he watched as two men started to crank at the manual generator, the emitted light throwing their own vast shadows against the wall. They must have seemed like images from one of the expressionist films by which Dresdeners had once been so hypnotized.

The ruined city in twilight; the flickering orange of the still-burning fires within buildings; in the Altmarkt, the discoloured bodies floating in the water of the reservoir; nearby, the sudden groans and cracks from the blackened Kreuzkirche, the roof open to the starry night. Near the Kreuzkirche, in the now completely demolished blocks and alleys and passages leading to the Frauenkirche, a young soldier named Hans Settler stood like a ghost, still and watchful, gazing at the absence that had once been the block in which his girlfriend had lived. Around him were figures moving like somnambulists. These he later termed 'death-men, dreamers'.[6]

Beyond that now empty space, towards the Neumarkt, amid the vast piles of masonry, one great structure still stood, newly silhouetted against the velvet sky. The Frauenkirche, with its huge dome, its stolid octagonal structure, appeared untouched, an unspoken symbol of defiance. Those who had taken refuge in its crypt, having passed the night and the morning safely, had left to try to reach family and friends, leaving the building unattended. But the fires that had washed through the city had not yet finished with the Frauenkirche, and as dusk fell the soot-blackened sandstone could in places be seen glowing with a dull ruby light. As without, as within, there was a sound like that of an old ship creaking and yawing, as though swaying in the night. Despite its apparent invulnerability, in the earlier bombings one of the foundational pillars holding the tiers and the galleries and the great dome hundreds of feet above the ground had shifted under the enormous impact of detonation. Another explosion had created a symmetrical effect in another foundation which had the benefit of balancing the first dislocation, but the gravitational pressures that had been captured and held by the architect two hundred years earlier were slowly becoming unharnessed.

There were few people that evening to witness it. Even the prisoners of war were far from this place now. Kurt Vonnegut had spent the larger part of 14 February being herded by guards and corralled into organizing carts and wagons and wheelbarrows; the 150-odd prisoners were being transferred from their slaughterhouse quarters to Gorbitz, another camp just a little outside the city. Later that day the prisoners were still painstakingly manoeuvring their primitive conveyances through the maze of blocked streets and sticky roads. By the time they reached the hills that climbed out of the city, the wheels were claggy with melted tar. Like so many others, they had both seen and not seen the bodies of children, the bodies of mothers. They were soon to inhabit a necrotic nightmare. It was to fall to these men – among other prisoners – to excavate the city's buried dead, starting the next morning.

22. The Radiant Tombs

In the strange noiselessness that now lay across the obliterated city, any sudden snap, any grinding girder was magnified in the still air. Where just a couple of days before had been the bells and rumbles of trams, the hubbub and bustle of commerce, thousands upon thousands of different conversations, families in apartments, assistants in shops, waiters in bars and cafes, there was simply a desert and the absolute vacuum of silence under a weirdly darkened sky of smoke.

On the morning of 15 February, the structure of the blackened sandstone in the Frauenkirche had at last been decisively transformed by the searing heat, and the building, over 200 feet high, was buckling and swaying on its mighty pillars. In some parts, these pillars were still glowingly hot, in others they were cool; the building was latticed with instability. And now, with a gathering thunder that echoed across the surrounding grey ruins, the pillars fractured and collapsed inwards, taking with them the vast dome that had dominated the Dresden skyline since the eighteenth century. The church imploded, a rushing roar; the exquisitely painted inner dome, the great bells, the delicately carved galleries, the vast clear windows, all pressed and crumpled down upon the marble floor and on the crypt below. Gravity sucked the church inside out, and chunks of masonry the size of cars were flung outwards onto the cobbled square beyond. The spiritual heart of Dresden had been shattered. Few were there to grieve it.

In the Altstadt, some 75,000 apartments and other housing had been either demolished or at best rendered uninhabitable. Amid the sudden movements of ragged brick structures on the point of collapse, isolated men and women clambered over rubble obsessively; in that uncanny grey, eclipse-like twilight, these were people who had no idea whether to hold on to hope or start mourning. Mothers peered intently at clothed, disembodied limbs; siblings picked their way through the stones and stared at the corpses that lay as if at peace. A family friend of Winfried Bielss fell into a routine: walking into the devastated old city, much of the architecture so levelled that she could see streets a quarter of a mile away; searching in vain among so many others for a sign of her daughter. In sick hopelessness she would return to her apartment in the Neustadt before, not long after, distractedly setting out again. Similarly, an older female relative of Margot Hille, injured and taken in by the teenager's mother, walked constantly alongside every flame-gutted ruin near her home in the hope of catching even a glimpse of a familiar garment. In this way, so many citizens were forced into a form of suspended grieving.

That sense of fragility, of imminent collapse, was present not just in traumatized survivors and the fragmented remains of the tall buildings but also in the actual fabric of the city's administration; the web of infrastructure – roads, power, water – had been effectively torn apart. All, from the minor officials to the senior dignitaries who had sat out the bombings behind steel doors, now gazed helplessly at a burned and bloody wilderness. The civic authorities drafted in all the civil servants they could muster, and SS men were dispatched from Berlin. They began their work quickly, for they knew that the broken threads of this society must swiftly be retied. If not, one result of many might be pestilence arising from the unburied dead. Coming in to oversee the general administration was a senior figure called Theodor Ellgering from the Inter-Ministerial Committee on Bomb Damage. Ellgering – who was close to Goebbels – had gathered a great deal of experience in other burned cities from 1943 onwards: Cologne, Hamburg, Kassel. The proficiency – especially at this stage in the conflict, with the fighting east and west depleting resources – with which he and his retinue acted was quite remarkable. Given that electricity and water in some parts of the city were either nonexistent or intermittent, there were three priorities: first, feeding and hydrating survivors; second, carrying out the immediate execution of looters and anyone felt to be peddling rumours or lowering morale; and third, in the mild conditions, finding a means of speedily identifying and meticulously cataloguing thousands of corpses before their disposal.

Ellgering might have been aware that one of his colleagues had visited Dresden just a month previously to check on the provision of shelters, that such provision had been found seriously wanting and that Joseph Goebbels had demanded the dismissal of the mayor, Hans Nieland.[1] Somehow this notification had not come through to Nieland; he was now simply a mayor of ruins. In fact, he was not even that; faced with this devastation, Nieland was already making his plans to leave the city far behind him and also somehow to evade both responsibility and disgrace. His superior, the Gauleiter Martin Mutschmann, was in turn making plans to assume full mayoral authority. It is difficult to know how far Mutschmann had managed to convince himself that the Nazi regime could hold on to power, and that Dresden could be defended. Whatever his opinion, Nieland and his family were already packing. One Dresdener, in conversation with another at a temporary shelter, claimed that she had glimpsed Mutschmann; her interlocutor replied that if she had seen him, she would have smashed his mouth in.[2] But such seditious talk was still unusual.

Theodor Ellgering saw to it that some roads were cleared and that others, whose half-collapsed buildings presented an obvious hazard, were blocked off. This was the easy part of the job; harder was commandeering supplies of food and coffee from undamaged suburbs and outlying towns and villages, and ensuring that the survivors gathered in school buildings and halls were given hot soup and sandwiches. As for looting, there was little in the blackened hollow shells of the Altstadt that would have been worth even the most desperate thief's time, but there was always a possibility that grocery shops and similar outlets on the other side of the river might be targeted by the younger, fitter refugees and deserters.

There were serious difficulties, though, in the gathering up of the dead. Not from a shortage of labour for the hideous task: the city was still replete with 'workers' – in reality, slaves – who were based in camps in the suburbs. In addition, there were also large numbers of soldiers, and prisoner-of-war parties such as the one to which Kurt Vonnegut was attached. But the nightmarish hurdles they were going to have to overcome were twofold. First, above ground there was the practical problem of trying to establish the identity of bodies from a collection of detached limbs and heads; in the Great Garden there were body parts hanging from the branches of the trees that had survived the fire. The second was to extract the corpses entombed underground. A colleague of Theodor Ellgering recalled how soldiers had managed to dig through the ruins of a building in the Altstadt, and had found the buried entrance to the cellar. The door was opened and a terrible wave of heat pulsed out.[3] The smell was not described. Whoever went down into those hot catacombs to begin retrieving the corpses – torches flashing, gas masks ready – would be left with images that they would see for the rest of their lives.

This was the prospect that lay before Kurt Vonnegut and other POWs of a variety of nationalities: a descent into unimagined depths. They were led in lines from their new barracks in the suburbs to hills of boulders in the Altstadt; apart from the barked orders, they too were listening to ear-pounding silence, punctuated by the rhythmic picking of steel tools into grey stone. At the very beginning, the task seemed fruitless, for all the various search parties could do was choose piles of rubble at random and begin digging into them. The architectural infrastructure of the Altstadt had been so comprehensively scrambled that former landmarks – cinemas, restaurants, theatres, wine bars, shops – could not be identified with any certainty. Sometimes rubble would be pulled away only to reveal yet more rubble. Nor were the routes through the subterranean maze leading from the Elbe and the Great Garden guaranteed to be passable; collapsing tunnels were always a possibility. Eventually, though, these digging parties began to find, beneath tangles of twisted metal and baked brick, little staircases leading down into the dark. Vonnegut described the first contact with seated corpses as being akin to entering a wax museum.[4] But with the opening of these warm tombs came the chemical change that brought forth the stench of the dead, which was like 'mustard gas and roses';[5] and he described all these cellars as 'corpse mines'.[6] All of this would form the dark bass line of his 1969 novel *Slaughterhouse-Five* – the narrator Billy Pilgrim flitting between different time streams, as the horrific past seeps into the present – and the prose did not need exaggeration.

Vonnegut and his fellow 'corpse miners' all saw the varieties of death that had been visited upon those in the cellars. By torchlight, they made their way down into the stifling brick recesses and a great many of the bodies they found looked as though they were simply practising meditation, having suffocated where they sat. Other cellars contained more terrible prospects: collapsed walls had crushed some bodies; others when moved became separated from their heads. One man's detached head was still wearing a hat. The flies had been swift to materialize. The unidentified intact corpses were laid along the roads in lines in the hope that family members would be able to recognize them. In *Slaughterhouse-Five*, Billy Pilgrim recalls that he was digging with a Maori prisoner who became so violently sick as the work progressed that the ceaseless gut-wrenching retching actually killed him. There was a more generalized fear of miasma and illness and rats. Urban legends from other bombed cities featured accounts of rodents that had dined so royally that they had become obese.

A further difficulty was that in many cases the brickwork of these black cellars was still searing to the touch. Some corpses had been roasted so completely in the darkness that they had shrunk to the size of marionettes. The body of one old woman was recalled as having a much reduced, wrinkled face, but her silvery hair was still lustrous. Where the decaying corpses could not be extracted from collapsed cellars, soldiers equipped with flamethrowers had to try to cremate them in situ. In terms of logistics, there was something remarkable in the response organized by Ellgering, especially considering that it relied upon forced labour: the methodical efficiency with which the rubble came to be excavated over the coming hours and days and weeks did not immediately seem to speak of a dying regime.

Nor, from the point of view of the Allied forces, did there seem any sense that the survivors should be left in merciful peace to recover the remains of the dead. Also on the morning of 15 February, a formation of American bombers had taken off from RAF Deenethorpe in Northamptonshire intending to target a hydrogenation plant close to the city of Leipzig. They were instructed that if the cloud cover was too heavy to make accurate bombing possible, then their secondary target was to be Dresden. This became the case. The bombers set course for the city. But it is possible the filthy airborne debris from the previous attacks played a part in shielding Dresden, for the skies above were too murky that day for the US bombers to discern their perpetual target of the Friedrichstadt railway marshalling yards. Of the bombs that were dropped, a large proportion were wildly off the mark, landing in outlying small towns like Meissen and Pirna. In the south of the city, the notorious courthouse received a hit. Other than this, the ten-minute American raid appeared not to have even entered the consciousness of many citizens. The business of attending to the dead occluded all other considerations.

Families with undamaged homes in the wooded suburbs, their uneasy nights disturbed further by the distant howls of distressed ownerless dogs, made their way into the heart of the Altstadt to view the lines of bodies in those ruined avenues. Relatives, friends, colleagues were identified, sometimes simply by their clothing, a handkerchief, a watch, a ring or some distinctive jewellery. These orderly identification lines were sometimes joined by horribly irregular additions as old men pushed barrows and carts upon which had been placed the mangled, torn, bloodied remains of those that they believed to be their loved ones; one elderly woman was seen negotiating the dusty roads with a heavy sack which was found to contain a shrunken body. Where were these broken people going? What curious plans had they formed as they pushed and carried these grisly burdens? Some accounts were filled with recollections of how soldiers in and around the city were generally straightforward and kind; perhaps these victims of the most extraordinary trauma were treated gently too.

As many as 10,000 bodies, according to some accounts, were carefully catalogued, placed in trucks and taken to a cemetery to the north of the city near Dresden Heath, where spaces had been cleared in the woods for vast communal graves. Yet even the most meticulous planning was at a loss to cope with the truly horrific scale of the problem: if all the thousands of remaining corpses yet to be exhumed were dealt with in the same way, the process would take too long; they were fast becoming noisome. There was one other possibility, which would leave little room for mourning but which would be none the less effective: to subject those bodies to one final fire in the city itself and then bury the massed ashes among those trees. On the devastated Altmarkt, the reservoir now cleared of its bloated contents, the authorities had found a central location that would serve as an outdoor crematorium; once the bodies had been catalogued, the paperwork on each individual collated, there was no time to lose. The department store Renner – a shattered husk, its sales floors open to the sky – had one final contribution to make. The store's steel shutters were the only part of the building's structure to have come through the bombing relatively unscathed. To burn bodies requires a good air flow, so it was necessary for the heaped corpses to be raised from the ground. Accordingly, around the smashed and scattered cobbles of the Altmarkt, punctuated with singular brick walls and angled collapsed girders, metal rods of the shutters were arranged horizontally across the open spaces, and boards placed on top. Onto those boards were thrown the first of many thousands of bodies to burn, towering heaps of human mortality, a medieval vision unfolding on an industrial scale. Ashes and bones were removed; more bodies were brought forth; flames were rekindled.

The civic authorities did their best to be accurate with the accounting, and for those corpses found indoors or in cellars there were at least addresses that they could be checked against. But others found lying broken in the open air, especially around the Great Garden, were harder to attach names to. Unknowable numbers of these victims, from children to mothers to elderly women, were undoubtedly rural refugees, their documentation in cinders, who had either failed to find shelter or been too frightened to stay in the shelters that they had been directed to. Here too, on the edges of the park, vast pyres were built. And still, among all the blasted trees, the deep craters, there were people walking absently, peering, staring, moving on.

Across the river, and in the city's suburbs, residents were making their own discoveries about fatalities. Winfried Bielss and his mother, walking around their own neighbourhood of apartment blocks and villas in the Neustadt, soon discovered that Winfried's great schoolfriend Klaus Weigart had been killed along with large numbers of his family, including the respected Dr Wilhelm Weigart.[7] One of Bielss's schoolteachers, Walter Liebmann, was also dead, together with his wife. They had been in the basement when their house received a direct hit with high explosives. The only part of the structure that still stood was the music room.

Bielss and his mother also adopted the method used – as though transmitted by morphic resonance – by thousands of other residents in those dazed hours and days for leaving messages to be seen by those who might have escaped: notes written on card or paper and propped up against or wedged in familiar doorways, or what remained of them, simply addressed to the absent loved ones and friends who had lived in these places with pleas to get in touch.

There were also messages left for the searchers by those who had been evacuated to countryside billets. Mischka Danos left word for his mother, whom he understood to be travelling from Prague to Dresden by train; within hours, he would find himself with a great many others in a rural barn, with a single lightbulb and a great deal of straw. Elsewhere, the condemned British soldier Victor Gregg – who had escaped from his captors out onto the streets when his temporary prison in the police station received a bomb through its glass cupola, only to witness women with their hair on fire and their children being drawn up into the firestorm – was still managing to evade the military authorities.[8] His instincts pointed him to the roads leading east, towards the hillier regions through which the Soviet forces were moving unstoppably.

The Hille family remained terrified – not without cause – that the Allied bombers would be flying over again. They had not been alone in making for the sanctuary of the Felsenkeller brewery's rock-face tunnels. (They might have been less sanguine had they known of the concealed Osram precision-instrument factory that the complex also housed.) The tunnels, she recalled, were dank and soon became insanitary; conditions were basic, and especially uncomfortable for two pregnant women who had joined the shelterers. But they were determined to stay, especially overnight.

Elsewhere, having marched out of the city, Gisela Reichelt and her mother were finding the countryside disorientating and strange: they had been billeted on a farm and the stress upon Gisela's heavily pregnant mother was understandably taking its toll. She was, her daughter recalled, 'exhausted by the events and fearful for the future'.[9]

For others, though, there were outbreaks of gratitude and relief: the artist Otto Griebel, whose studio had been comprehensively destroyed in the firestorm, was reunited with his sheltering family. His son Matthias, aged eight at the time, was later to recall how their own shelter had been swept by fire, and that outside 'was a vision of hell'. 'The bombs had thrown people into the trees . . . the water mains were broken. The gas pipes were on fire.'[10] The larger questions of responsibility and guilt were to inform the boy's future career path in the city. That same gravity and perplexity was shared by a number of Dresden's children, some of whom were to become writers and journalists and who would also later ponder the moral questions. Was it at all possible that the city itself had helped to invite its own destruction? Matthias Griebel was later to point at a swastika flag and say: 'A fire went out from Germany and went around the world in a great arc and came back to Germany.'[11]

At the city's centre, Professor Klemperer, having established for certain that some forty of the Jews in those allocated Judenhäuser had survived, took the advice urgently offered by a friend: to pass himself off as Aryan. He had already felt giddy with an odd tension merely by walking up and down Brühl's Terrace, forbidden to Jews, but he and Eva reasoned it out: in the conflagration, huge amounts of paperwork and records had been incinerated, and if they were to join other evacuees – the army was terrifically well organized at taking citizens to prearranged farms and barracks – then there was every chance that he would not be recognized. In any case, the alternative was to continue to acknowledge his religion and face being murdered there and then. Just because the city had been destroyed did not mean that the Nazi regime had suddenly abandoned its plans for extermination. Professor Klemperer and Eva thus joined the city's evacuees and were driven five miles north, to the airport, where temporary living quarters had been arranged.

Here there was water, and some incredibly satisfying noodle soup that Professor Klemperer devoured, although the herbal tea was less satisfying.[12] And, as he confided with such winning frankness to his diary, he was less than thrilled with all the other people that they had been billeted with: working class, coarse, materialistic and, in a couple of cases, childlike. Klemperer pondered whether all Dresden's intellectual class had been incinerated. The professor's focus wavered extraordinarily between the unsatisfactory nature of their companions – one night Eva found that the woollen cardigan that she kept under her pillow had been stolen by a roommate, whom she had to shame into returning it – and the possibility that he might be recognized and denounced to the authorities as a Jew. He had been walking that tightrope of death for so long, and he understood that only getting away from Dresden entirely would lessen the chances of discovery. He and Eva could find lodgings in another city and simply start anew. For very different reasons, other Dresdeners were reaching the same conclusions, for as well as bombed-out houses there was still the threat of the oncoming Soviet forces.

The elegant Marielein Erler, who was having her eyes regularly treated with drops in the hospital in Kreischa, was told flatly that she would have to vacate her bed now that she had broadly recovered her sight and her head injury would soon heal; the need of others was greater. And so this demure lady in her fur coat, one of the last things of value that she owned to have survived, found herself discharged with several other Dresden citizens. They were pointed in the direction of a school in which to sleep that night. The 'beds' were simply chairs pushed together, and Frau Erler and her new companions spent the night 'half-sleeping', and quietly talking, reliving their experiences.[13] Frau Erler still had no idea what had become of her husband. The next day she was able to hitch a lift from a military truck heading for the city. She simply wanted to see her home, but on arrival she was confronted with a prospect worse than she could have anticipated. The streets 'smelled horribly', both of fire and of death; they were 'silent and extinct'. The bodies 'had risen to mountains on the roadside'.[14] She watched as men in white suits picked bodies up from the gutters and with a swift exclamation of 'one-two-*three*!' threw them onto trucks, which would then head off towards the Altmarkt. There were also, she remembered, soldiers with flamethrowers: ad hoc cellar cremations.

In the cases of both Frau Erler and the Klemperers, departure from the city was complicated but possible; the Klemperers had to hitch lifts, and walk for miles along flat country roads, but they eventually reached a railway station; similarly Frau Erler, driven back to Kreischa, also by means of a hitched lift with the military, managed to make her way to the railway station of a nearby town. Extraordinarily, given the damage wrought by both the British and Americans resulting in burned rolling stock, snapped rails and holed bridges, the regime was managing once again to run trains at least near to the city, if not through it, even though services were sporadic, and liable to unexplained delays of several hours. The outlying railway stations might have been a cacophony of refugee and soldier voices, but there were trains running west, to Leipzig, Chemnitz and beyond, away from the advancing Soviets.

At Dresden's main railway station the labourers and the soldiers were still working to retrieve the bodies from what had become the catacombs beneath the concourse, lining them up on what remained of the platforms. Dr Fromme was taking a strong interest because his son, on civic duties, had 'set up his mission' at the station.[15] Fromme himself was overseeing other casualties from around the city, taken to medical facilities in nearby towns like Arnsdorf, and was reconnoitring the area in his car, trying to get a sense of the scale of the human damage that had been wrought. At the station, Fromme's teenage son could not calculate how many corpses he saw, nor would he dwell on their condition. But meanwhile, a little over half a mile away, engineers had already set to work on repairing the tracks that ran north to south on the main Berlin–Dresden–Prague line. It would be a matter of only days before a limited number of trains were once more running through the centre of the city.

Churchill had once counselled his senior commanders against trying to predict the effect of firebombing upon a population, and the citizens and civic authorities in Dresden were demonstrating that Allied 'morale bombing' induced neither the expected terrified immobility nor a hoped-for rebellion against the Nazi ideology. Instead, there seemed to be an overwhelming, almost detached urge to set the city in order and bring sense and meaning to a catastrophe that could not yet be comprehended except in its most singular details. It was also at this point that the wider world came to hear of what had been done, and reacted in some cases in such a way that Joseph Goebbels in Berlin scarcely needed to add his own embroideries.

23. The Meanings of Terror

The women and men in towns and cities across Britain who sat down at kitchen tables with their morning newspapers on 15 February, eating their strictly rationed butter and bacon, now knew that this had been an unusually large bombing raid on Germany: following brief final-edition headlines the previous day, all the papers now had fuller reports – and expert analysis. It would take a few more days before the attack was seen by some in starker moral terms; for the Nazis to fully capitalize upon the horror, for questions to be asked in Parliament and for the prime minister himself apparently to recoil.

At first, the raid was presented in terms of the logical progress of war; although Britain's press had to abide by subtle wartime censorship, there was no strong indication here that the reporters were being urged to hold back. On 15 February the working-class *Daily Mirror* declared that this was 'Germany's Worst Air Blitz', adding that '1,350 US heavy bombers . . . showered hundreds of tons of bombs on Dresden, which was raided for the third time in little more than twelve hours . . . They stoked up the fires raging from the 650,000 incendiaries and hundreds of explosive bombs, dropped by 1,400 RAF planes the night before.'[1] The numbers of planes had been puzzlingly inflated; but the attack was presented here squarely in the context of aiding General Konev and the advance of the Red Army; there was no emphasis on civilian casualties.

The more patrician *Daily Telegraph* the same morning betrayed more fascination with the effects of the bombing, and indeed with the responses from the Nazi regime. After the initial RAF raids, involving 'many 8,000lb and hundreds of 400lb high explosive bombs . . . flames could be seen 200 miles away. When the Americans arrived, the fires were still burning.' Strikingly, though, the newspaper tried to anticipate the propaganda battle that was just beginning internationally: 'The German reaction to the bombing of Dresden by 800

Lancasters was to label it a "terror attack", the *Telegraph* report continued, 'in which famous buildings were destroyed. The Berlin military
spokesman declared that the RAF "hit exclusively the centre of the
city".[2] Yet the *Telegraph* readers were to be reassured that the city was
'an important railway junction' with 'large ammunition workshops
and factories'. The railway was crucial: it was 'a meeting place of main
lines to eastern and southern Germany, Berlin, Prague and Vienna . . .
Dresden is desperately needed as a concentration area for troops and to
house administrative services evacuated from elsewhere in the Reich.'

The *Telegraph* also engaged its in-house RAF specialist – the
Military Cross-holding retired Air Commodore Ernest Howard-
Williams – to analyse the raids and their effects. He was not wholly
numb to the fact of dreadful civilian casualties, but context was all.
'The massive Allied raids on Dresden indicated that the plans made at
the Yalta Conference are being implemented almost before the ink of
the signatures is dry,' he wrote, suggesting that the attack was inspired
by the desires of the Soviets. 'A heavy strain had already been thrown
on routes to the eastern front, other than that through Dresden, by
recent raids on Chemnitz and Magdeburg which were again attacked
yesterday.' But Howard-Williams was thinking of more than railway
lines. 'It is estimated that troops and civilians in Dresden may have
numbered up to two million,' he continued. 'The normal population
is 640,000. Many Berliners and evacuees from the east had fled to the
city which had excellent rail communications with the capital and
had developed into a huge arms centre . . . The confines of the city
include over thirty miles of track and a huge marshalling yard on the
left bank of the Elbe, which is crossed by six bridges.'

As an 'Air-Staff Officer' told him, 'Give us a month of reasonable
weather, and we will paralyse the railroad system of the German
armies in the east and in the west.'[3] The emphasis was very much on
infrastructure; the term 'refugees' was avoided. But the retired expert
also mused about other aspects of the city's life. 'Dresden is the seat of
a technical academy and an academy of arts,' he wrote. 'I understand
that the more valuable art treasures have long since been put underground elsewhere.'[4] That indeed might have been the chief concern
among many of those middle-class *Telegraph* readers, a substantial

proportion of whom would have had a few pieces of Dresden porce-lain in their display cabinets. The newspaper's puckish gossip column 'Peterborough' that morning essayed a joke in very bad taste in the form of a mock headline: 'Air Raid on Dresden – New Version of a Bull in a China Shop'.

This unseemly description is unlikely to have been appreciated by the bomber crews returning from further missions: the targeting of benzol industrial plants from Essen to Cologne. For the airmen of Bomber Command, Dresden was already in the past, and according to the bomb aimer Miles Tripp there was little sense of the future. They were, instead, living purely in the present; fear remained deep in the marrow, but there was something else too: what seemed like an addiction to flying, and to adrenaline. The almost total lack of defences around Dresden had been unusual; the silver of the moonlit night sky was – over other German cities – still lined and scored with the orange fire of flak. In mid February the Allied armies below were yet to make their deci-sive advance through the German forests; and the flight crews each night were still aiming to destroy infrastructure as well as fuel supplies. Tripp recalled that the night after the Dresden raid, the order came through that they were to set course for Chemnitz, a town that lay a little to the west.[5] He, his crewmates and his superiors knew that there would be large numbers of refugees. The idea left Tripp momentarily reflecting on his own sudden absence of qualms. This bleakness was counterbalanced by the hypersensory awareness that he and his crew-mates experienced while flying through those skies, an overwhelming sense of aliveness. For the pilot of their plane, 'Dig', the missions by themselves seemed no longer sufficient to keep his heart pounding at the rate to which he had become accustomed; after the bombs were dropped, and the craft was turned back towards England, 'Dig' would put the plane into a vertiginous dive, Tripp in the bomb aimer's position staring down at the fast-approaching North Sea or gazing at cyclists on English lanes suddenly ducking and falling off their bikes as the plane dived at them.[6]

When Goebbels used the phrase 'terror bombing', it had no inter-national traction; when, however, on 16 February it was deployed in what seemed to be ill-thought-out error by an American Associated

Press reporter called Howard Cowan, it suddenly and unexpectedly acquired heft. Cowan, in Paris at SHAEF, had been at a press conference given by Air Commodore C. M. Grierson of the RAF. Grierson had spoken of how the purpose of targeting Dresden and other such cities was to create administrative chaos, and also to disrupt German transport links and communications. But that concept of targeting not specific factories or plants but the city itself, in such a way as to create insurmountable difficulties for the civic authorities, seemed to be a bland way of expressing the more ruthless truth. Grierson was asked about refugees; he sought to emphasize the railways and roads, and the proximity of the Soviet forces. But the indelible impression was left that refugees and civilians would form a part of this engineered chaos, blocking these roads in vast, panicked numbers. And the journalist Cowan, with enthusiasm, summarized the approach in his report's introduction, by stating: 'Allied air commanders have made the long-awaited decision to adopt deliberate terror bombing of German population centres as a ruthless expedient to hasten Hitler's doom.'[7]

His report also noted that an earlier attack on Berlin was upon a 'refugee-crowded' city. This was not to signify moral disapproval; indeed, Cowan wrote that there would be 'satisfaction' in those parts of Europe where thousands of civilians had fallen victim to the German Air Force and the V-1 and V-2 rockets.[8]

Somehow, the report – even after objections were raised – made it past the censors, and a couple of days later it received coverage in the American press. In Britain, newspaper editors were of their own volition more circumspect. This was not to say that the fate of Dresden was ignored; quite the reverse. Both the left-leaning *Manchester Guardian* and the right-wing *Daily Telegraph* carried reports in the days afterwards that conveyed the extraordinary extent to which it had been incinerated. On 17 February, the *Telegraph* relayed a line from the German Overseas News Agency: 'The Allies have turned Dresden . . . to ashes.' The city, it stated, was 'one great field of ruins'.[9] Some days later came a further dispatch for British readers: 'The Dresden catastrophe is without precedent . . . A great city has been wiped from the face of Europe.'[10] On the same day, the *Daily Mail* proclaimed that Dresden was 'a city of the past'.[11] It was not the facts that were suppressed but the interpretation. National editors were in agreement with Bomber Command and the War Office: this was not a new tactic of 'terror bombing' but the result of aiming for the transportation network of an enemy army. None the less, neutral countries such as Switzerland and Sweden picked up on the overenthusiastic phrasing.

Even then, there was not a great deal that Goebbels could achieve by promulgating it, nor by his swift decision to magnify the numbers of the dead by ten times, claiming that 250,000 had perished that night. Perhaps there was the chance that this would inspire newly recruited boy soldiers into more determined fighting against the Soviets, the Americans and the British, but he also surely knew that by suggesting that the Allies could kill a quarter of a million defenceless German citizens in one night, he was conceding that they were the dominant power; any talk of the Germans being close to deploying top-secret miracle weapons to gain a surprise victory was now notably sparse. There are hints from the private correspondence of Goebbels that he understood very well the reality of the Nazi position by that stage, and equally suggestions from eyewitness accounts and diaries from the German populace that victory was extremely unlikely, aside from a few who believed that on Hitler's birthday – 20 April – a new wonder plan or superweapon would be revealed.

The phrase 'terror bombing' *did* matter very much to the Americans, though. As soon as it was printed there was immediate disquiet, and great efforts were made to align future US news reports so that it would be made clear that the USAAF had been specifically targeting railway marshalling yards, not defenceless people. Colonel Rex Smith, a USAAF public relations officer, was anxious that the American public should understand that US crews were still engaged in 'precision bombing'.[12] It is possible that he and other senior figures still believed that such a thing was remotely achievable, given that their 'precision' targets were so close to residential housing and high population densities. But it was vital that the public appreciated that, no matter how barbarous the Nazi enemy, the Americans would never sink to that moral level. This was not merely for fastidious reasons of maintaining the morale of the aircrews, but also part of the preparations for the post-war power struggles to come: in order to carry authority throughout Europe, and indeed defeated Germany, the Americans had to be seen as the virtuous power, doing only what was necessary to remove the evil of Nazism with solemnity and regret and scientific calculation. In this, there was also a measure of distancing themselves from the British, though merely in terms of press presentation. The air war continued as before, and in the case of one particular town, with even more lethal intensity.

Pforzheim was known popularly as Goldstadt, the Golden City. This elegant town, a prospect of spires and turrets standing in a valley on the fringes of the Black Forest and close to the border with France, had long been a centre for both exquisite jewellery work and precision watch-making. It was a town of some 80,000 people; here were craftsmen in long-roomed workshops with large windows so that their delicate tasks with coils and springs, with flashing diamonds and glowing gold, could be bathed in light. Naturally, as with Dresden, many of these workshops were turned to new purposes for the war, manufacturing fuses and small ordnance and arms components. This was one justification for its appearance on the bombers' target list. Another was – again, like Dresden – that the town was a troop-movement hub. At this stage, the Allied armies had yet to cross the Rhine; that was still a month away. On the night of 23 February, Bomber Command raised another firestorm. The column of incandescent light rising from Pforzheim was said by some accounts to reach almost a mile into the sky.

As with Dresden, thousands sheltering in cellars were condemned, the superheated air becoming toxic, the oxygen vanishing. Proportionately, the casualty figures were very much worse than Dresden. In the space of a few hours, some 17,600 people were killed – almost a quarter of the population. In terms of fire and explosive damage, the impact was also seismic: an estimated 83 per cent of the town's central buildings and housing were destroyed. The idea of one in four of a town's population being killed in the space of a few hours is very difficult to comprehend; a massacre that ripped each and every family in Pforzheim to shreds, as well as tearing away homes and shelter, leaving a landscape looking like medieval ruins. This was the true gravity of war, the wild maelstrom that

somehow had its own impetus, divorced from serious tactical thinking. Aside from the phrasing of newspaper reports, the shocking
severity of the bombing of Dresden – like Hamburg, Cologne, Essen
and Magdeburg – had clearly not prompted any pause, or hesitation,
or doubt in the minds of the bomber commands.

And on the other side of the world, the American conflict with Japan
brought a night of bombing that in terms of scale and suffering dwarfed
Dresden: the 10 March attack on Tokyo. In the space of two and a half
hours B-29 bombers poured fire on the city, with Japanese defensive
fighters and the fire services down below powerless to beat back the
fury. The Americans had taken careful note of the natural catastrophe
of 1923: the earthquakes and tsunami that had summoned the whirling
tornadoes of fire known as 'dragon twists'; the bombers, which started
flying over at around midnight, now created their own inferno. The
sector of the city that lay in their sights was home to just over a million
people. Families sought vain refuge anywhere: canals, rivers, temples.
The roaring firestorm rose and fathers, mothers, children were burned
alive where they stood as the seething sky turned bronze. It was said
afterwards that American pilots had to pull oxygen masks on quickly
as they flew over, not for lack of air, but because of the pervasive stench
of roasting flesh. Curiously, though, this raid and others like it seemed
not to spark the same introspection that the European campaign was
inspiring; instead, it seemed to many that General Curtis LeMay's
bombers in that part of the world were simply seeking to bring an early
end to hostilities in order to avoid more bloodshed – an argument that
would be made more forcefully in the months to come with an even
more terrible and history-changing raid.

But as all this unfolded, there were those back in England who
were ever more profoundly troubled about the fate of Dresden
specifically, and about everything that this one particular raid appeared
to symbolize. Opponents of area bombing were now speaking ever
louder. The Bishop of Chichester, George Bell, was among them, as was
Vera Brittain and Alfred Salter, MP for Bermondsey West, a London
district that had itself been heavily damaged by bombing. Passionate
too was the Labour MP for Ipswich R. R. (Richard Rapier) Stokes,
who, early in March 1945, stood up in the chamber of the House of

Commons to attempt to challenge the apparent new orthodoxy of heavy firebombing. He was responding to a statement given by the saturnine Sir Archibald Sinclair, Secretary of State for Air, who had proudly told the House on 6 March: 'The strategic bomber offensive . . . remains the principal role of the British and American Bomber Commands . . . The arm of Bomber Command reaches across Europe from time to time and bombs targets in direct support of the redoubtable Red Armies in their advance from the East.' Sir Archibald also stated: 'Allied air bombing is on such a colossal scale that Dr Goebbels has had to admit that it can now hardly be borne.'[13]

Stokes – who was not in any other sense a pacifist – had listened to other questions in the chamber to do with lifting the blackout in England. His own interjection was rather more piercing. As reported in the *Manchester Guardian*, he said:

. . . reference had been made to the accuracy of our bombing. He [Stokes] did not believe in that humbug. Where strategic bombing was necessary, it might have to be put up with, but the Russians did not seem to think it necessary. He had been reduced to despair about the moral issue of strategic bombing and viewed with alarm the disease and poverty that would arise and which would be almost impossible to overcome. Was terror bombing now part of our policy? he asked. If so, why were not the British people being told what was being done in their name?[14]

This evoked a sharp response from Commander Rupert Brabner, undersecretary of state for air, who was addressing the House and who denied 'terror bombing'. 'Our job,' he said, 'is to destroy the enemy and this we are doing in an ever more efficient and ever-increasing way. It does not do Mr Stokes justice to try and suggest that our air marshals or anyone else are sitting down thinking how many German women and children we can kill. It is not true.' Stokes persisted: why then had one report referred to terror bombing? Sir Archibald rose with the answer to this. 'The report,' he said, 'was not true.'[15]

The Commons reporting meant that the phrase 'terror bombing' received its first airing in the British press; the following week, Stokes was involved in a further parliamentary controversy when in a slip, he used 'unparliamentary' language to accuse the War Office of lying.

The prime minister certainly paid close attention to Stokes's earlier comments, and it was Churchill himself, addressing the House a week later, who rose to challenge Stokes not on the point of 'terror bombing' but upon the accusation of parliamentary deceit; Stokes, flanked by Aneurin Bevan, gamely spoke up for himself but was forced to concede that 'misleading' would have been the more appropriate word. It is difficult to imagine that Stokes had not sparked unease within Churchill, or at least catalysed it. For within a fortnight, the prime minister was secretly to express his own moral fears and difficulties to the air chief marshal of Bomber Command.

But before that happened, that same air chief marshal was on insistently bullish form: his own view at the beginning of March 1945 was that his bomber crews were not receiving the praise and admiration that were due to them. Sir Arthur Harris had clearly also been stung by the phrase 'terror bombing', chiefly because he detected in it a pattern of unfriendly and unhelpful journalism. He wrote a passionate letter on the subject addressed not to Churchill but to General Dwight Eisenhower, Supreme Commander of the Allied Expeditionary Force. 'I ask for your personal assistance in a matter which is causing me and my Command great concern,' he wrote. 'As you are probably aware, we have virtually destroyed some 63 amongst [sic] the leading industrial towns in Germany, and vastly damaged a great many more, including Berlin, on a scale far beyond anything that we have suffered in this country.' But the bomber forces, he complained, suffered an 'almost entire lack of credit' among the war correspondents. Most woundingly, Harris asserted, journalists were going so far as to ascribe such destruction to 'the artillery'. As the armies advance, he wrote, would it be 'pardonable' if 'credit is given to us for our efforts' for the damage caused to those towns and cities beforehand? 'The present state of affairs is already causing considerable bitterness amongst my crews, a body of men whom you are well aware carried on this fight virtually alone for two years, and without any aid from the ground forces for four years . . . I know I will not appeal in vain to your generous nature in making this request.'[16]

And indeed the appeal worked. 'Dear Bert,' wrote General Eisenhower on 7 March (a curious nickname apparently derived from an old naval custom of referring to anyone called Harris as 'Bert'). 'I read your letter with the most sympathetic understanding and have been cudgelling my brain as to the best way to meet the situation.' Eisenhower's plan – apart from briefing the army press relations officers – was 'to write you and Tooey Spaatz each a personal letter which, if you so desire, may be published to your commands. If this action were taken the letter would naturally find its way into public print and would do something, I think, to accomplish the purpose.'[17]

General Eisenhower duly wrote the letter: he pointed out that 'city after city has been systematically shattered'; that the advancing armies saw all around them 'striking evidence of the effectiveness of the bombing campaigns' and that 'the sacrifices they [the bomber crews] have made are today facilitating success on all fronts . . . The effect on the war economy of Germany has obviously been tremendous; a fact that advancing troops are quick to appreciate and which unfailingly reminds them of the heroic work of their comrades in Bomber Command and in the United States Air Forces.'[18]

The contrast with the 'top secret' sentiments expressed by Winston Churchill at the end of March 1945, and conveyed in a letter from Deputy Chief of the Air Staff Norman Bottomley to Harris, could not have been starker. The moral questions that arose from the Dresden fires had been preying on the prime minister. There was no talk here of heroism or sacrifice in Bottomley's letter:

Dear C-in-C

At the instigation of the Prime Minister we have been asked to consider whether the time has not come when the question of bombing of German cities 'simply for the sake of increasing the terror, though under other pretexts' should not be reviewed. One of the reasons given is that we shall not for instance be able to get housing material out of Germany for our own needs because some temporary provision would ultimately have to be made for the Germans themselves . . .

Finally, the note [from the PM] states that there is need for more precise concentration upon military objectives, such as oil and communications behind the immediate battle-zone, rather than on mere acts of terror and wanton destruction.[19]

This was extraordinary: the prime minister accusing the chief of Bomber Command of 'mere acts of terror'. Bottomley included in his precis a further extraordinary thought from Churchill – that the morality of Bomber Command was in doubt: 'The note comments on the destruction of Dresden as a serious query against the conduct of Allied bombing and expresses the opinion that military objectives must henceforward be more strictly studied in our own interests rather than that of the enemy.' But the Air Ministry was with Harris; Bottomley in that same letter suggested that the PM's note 'misinterprets the purpose of our attacks on industrial areas in the past' and concluded that there 'has never been any instruction issued which gives any foundation to an allegation that German cities have been attacked simply for the sake of increasing terror'.[20] In other words: Churchill was mistaken. And the Air Ministry was anxious for Harris to see that.

In his flinty, contained reply to Bottomley the next day, Harris signalled his intention to bite his tongue, despite passages in the PM's note being 'abusive in effect, though doubtless not in intention'. But he was also adamant that his own philosophy be understood, for Harris did not conceive of himself as anything approaching a 'terror bomber'. He wrote that to 'suggest that we have bombed German cities "simply for the sake of increasing the terror, though under other pretexts" . . . is an insult both to the bombing policy of the Air Ministry and to the manner in which that policy has been executed by Bomber Command'. Harris argued that the policy was as much about aiming for the 'dislocation of transportation' as the destruction of buildings, and that 'Dresden was recommended by the Targets Committee as a transportation target as well as on other grounds'.[21]

For Harris, it was almost too obvious to be stated that 'the destruction of those cities has fatally weakened the German war effort and is now enabling Allied soldiers to advance into the heart of Germany'. 'We have never gone in for terror bombing,' he continued, 'and the attacks which we have made in accordance with my Directive have in fact produced the strategic consequences for which they were designed and from which the Armies now profit.' He was also piercingly bitter about the underlying suggestion from Churchill that even if in the

past, bombing cities was justified, it was none the less always 'repug-
nant'. Harris could not accept that. 'Attacks on cities like any other
act of war are intolerable unless they are strategically justified. But
they are strategically justified in so far as they tend to shorten the war
and so preserve the lives of Allied soldiers.' These lives were, he
wrote, of paramount importance, adding with a caustic rhetorical
flourish: 'I do not personally regard the whole of the remaining cities
of Germany as worth the bones of one British Grenadier.'[22]

But he wanted it to be understood that he was not bloodthirsty;
that if it was decided that the strategic bombing must now end, and
the bomber crews be stood down, then this 'last alternative would
certainly be welcome. I take little delight in the work,' wrote Harris,
'and none whatever in risking my crews avoidably.' On the face of it,
Harris's impassioned self-defence had an impact in the Air Ministry,
and upon Churchill himself. For Norman Bottomley wrote Harris a
very quick note a few days later to tell him that 'you will wish to
know that the allegations of acts of terror and wanton destruction in
the conduct of our bombing in the past . . . has now been with-
drawn'.[23] But the ill feeling was still there on both sides; Churchill's
later apparent reluctance to offer proper acknowledgement of Bomber
Command – together with Sir Arthur Harris's later fury at the perceived establishment dismissal of the achievements of his crews – was
venom that sank deep.

So even as the crumbling masonry of Dresden – the Altstadt eerily
silent on those early spring days – continued to collapse without
warning, and as its citizens tried to restore some form of familiarity
to a blasted landscape, they were not to know that their city had
already become a byword for the hideous, unthinking, reflexive
excesses of war. Arthur Harris had argued that all raids were a lottery
dependent upon weather conditions, and that it was near impossible
to plan or calculate their exact outcomes. But there were in Dresden
a number of people who did not understand it as a random blow, an
accident that grew beyond the initial intent; instead they were beginning to understand it as the ferocious consequence of the scourge of
Nazism.

24. The Music of the Dead

The fear was so pervasive and continuous among so many people that when, a few weeks later, the next attack came, it was met with fatalistic paralysis. The Dresden skies filled with silver in the early days of March: a new American raid on the railway marshalling yards. This was in the mid morning and, as ever with precision bombing, a number of the explosives landed elsewhere, including upon the already damaged police headquarters and in the meadows that lay by the side of the burned Waldschlösschen brewery. The response seemed to be one of traumatized indifference; later, it featured fleetingly in the collective memory.

Even in the midst of this general dread, however, nothing hindered the city's relentless efforts to restore a semblance of normality. Near where the central theatre had stood, and where just days previously hideously burned and shrunken bodies had been deposited from wheelbarrows, a temporary bureau for missing persons was established in one of the few buildings that remained stable enough to work in. Here, information and messages could be exchanged. Separated families, disorientated in the dust and dwelling in temporary shelters, could leave news of their whereabouts for loved ones.

Another cause for fear, especially among those billeted in the leafy countryside, were the rumours that Soviet soldiers had been spotted in the forests. In the woods around Dresden, evacuees saw ever-younger German soldiers – acned teenaged lads – who seemed curiously listless in the face of what appeared to be fast-approaching vengeance from the east. On top of all this was the anxiety inspired by the authorities' iron fist: the signs proclaiming that looters would be shot.

Middle-class refugees who had lived all their lives in suburban comfort now found themselves trudging across frozen agricultural plains. Marielein Erler, who had linked up with other well-to-do Dresdeners in the countryside thirty miles out of town, was curiously buoyant,

39. The destruction of the Zwinger Palace and gardens, amid the city's other treasures, presented an ideological dilemma for the Soviet authorities: should such bourgeois structures be restored?

40. The Soviets were swift to impose their will on Dresden. Here we see hastily erected road signs in Russian.

41. For Stalin, who refused Marshall Plan aid, the reconstruction of the city became a source of ideological pride. Propaganda posters emphasized the importance of 'learning from the Soviet people'.

42. Many found the ruins eerie at night, others worried that violent attackers might lurk amid the rubble, but some found poetry in the sunsets over those shattered streets.

43. While the nearby Kreuzkirche was restored in the 1950s, the Frauenkirche remained an amputated stump on the square of the Neumarkt. The Soviets had no interest in restoring it.

44. 'Hill and Ploughed Field Near Dresden', painted by Caspar David Friedrich *c*.1824, depicting the dome of the Frauenkirche through the trees. The city and its atmosphere coloured many of his more beguiling and unsettling works.

45. A detail from an epic mural gracing the wall of Dresden's 1960s Communist Culture Palace, entitled 'Way of the Red Flag'.

46. A tower block bearing, on its roof, the exhortation: 'Socialism wins'. The city remained a crucible of artistic and inventive endeavour but the aesthetics of the streets changed, becoming starkly modernist and severe.

47. The 'Procession of Princes' mural, gracing the exterior wall of the castle stable courtyard, was entirely created using Meissen porcelain tiles in the early twentieth century – one of the more remarkable survivors of the bombing.

48. Despite the rigid uniformity, there was an impressive scale to Dresden's 1960s housing constructions. Journalist Neal Ascherson noted 'the Stalinist style', although something similar was echoed throughout western Europe too.

49. The once-exclusive shopping parade of Prager Strasse was transformed into a modernist precinct with fountains and state-owned shops. On one occasion in the 1950s, a shortage of sought-after ladies' coats caused a near riot.

50. The futuristic flats of Prager Strasse commanded views to the surrounding hills. As the years wore on, Dresden housing schemes became noted for uncertain supplies of hot water and other maintenance failings.

51. The young KGB agent Vladimir Putin greatly enjoyed his Dresden posting in the 1980s, fifteen years before he became Russian president. He was said to have been especially fond of the local Radeberger beer.

52. The choir of the Kreuzkirche had, under the baton of cantor Rudolf Mauersberger, entranced audiences across Europe and America before the war. After it, Mauersberger composed the *Dresdner Requiem* and continued to lead his renowned choir until his death in 1971.

53. Even at the height of Nazi oppression, communist Elsa Frölich held her faith. When the Soviets took over, she immediately landed a civic role. The city saw many such astonishing reversals.

55. The eminent physicist Professor Heinrich Barkhausen had been pursuing his groundbreaking work in the city long before the Nazis rose. Having survived them, he stayed under the communists, who garlanded him with honours.

54. Novelist Erich Kästner, author of the much loved *Emil and the Detectives*, was born in Dresden. In the 1950s he returned and wrote a powerful eulogy to the city's ruins.

56. Under the Soviets, the gradual restoration of the Altstadt focused on civic rather than aesthetic priorities, but the Old Masters and other artworks were restored to the city from Moscow.

57. The rebuilt Frauenkirche – itself a feat of engineering ingenuity – was consecrated in 2005, sixty years after its destruction. The church stands as the emotional heart of the city.

58. The bright interior of the Frauenkirche today dazzles visitors with colour and light. It is a symbol of remembrance and peace, reconciliation, atonement and, above all, friendship.

even though the whereabouts of her husband Georg were still not known. Her plan was to travel north to her daughter in Lüneburg; there was a dauntless resourcefulness about her knack for hitching lifts with young German soldiers. She later recalled being alive to the piercing winds that blew across the plains; and to the simple but profound pleasure of a bowl of hot goulash.[1] Her route involved travelling via her parents' house in Schöningen, her progress a mosaic of hitchhiking, walking and train journeys on a German rail network that, although unpredictable, still criss-crossed the country despite the Allies' best attempts to destroy it. Frau Erler's parents greeted their daughter with huge relief, having heard the news of Dresden's fate. The family's happiness was complete when, after Marielein had spent a few days resting in these cosy surrounds, a knock at the door signalled the arrival of Georg. The reunion was ecstatic.[2]

Her husband recounted the nightmare of separation, the numberless bodies he had seen in the flames and his own meandering travels, via Leipzig, until mutual friends had told him where to find his wife. What seems even more extraordinary now is that Marielein, throughout her own ordeal, was able to continue writing to her mother and daughter: letters and postcards from the sanatorium in Kreischa and notes from the towns en route. The Saxon postal service was, like the trains, performing with remarkable efficiency.

The middle-class wanderers also included Victor and Eva Klemperer; they, along with so many others, were sent from town to town and even to tiny villages across the country in search of acceptable lodgings and rations, and their lives became a cycle of waiting for late-night trains and pitching up at village inns where the landlords were either movingly generous with food and space, or snarlingly hostile.

Little Gisela Reichelt and her mother remained unhappily billeted on their farm; conditions were not comfortable and it was here that Frau Reichelt gave birth to Gisela's little brother. There would be complications, and just a few months later the baby died. It was a fearful time to be pregnant.

In April, a band of young soldiers, none older than seventeen, were temporarily stationed in one of the city's grand villas on the hills that overlooked the Elbe. They were joined by even younger boys from the Hitler Youth. One teenager had found in the villa's attic an exceptionally fine electric model train set manufactured by Märklin, a firm that produced exquisitely crafted replica engines. A space was cleared in one of the downstairs rooms and the boys laid the rails quickly. Suddenly they were all completely absorbed in the movement of the model trains: boys kneeling and lying on the floor and taking turns with the controls to drive the miniature locomotives.[3] This was both a reversion to a curtailed childhood and a means of exerting at least some control over an imaginary world while knowing that they would soon be sent east to face a brutalized enemy.

There was a widening gulf between the citizens of Dresden and those who had power over their lives. In mid April, Gauleiter Mutschmann informed them, on the front page of the local newspaper, that their city was now a fortress. 'We are not willing to deliver ourselves to a cruel enemy without fight and without honour,' he declared.[4] Any suggestion either of defeatism or even simply of false rumours from any citizen would invite terrible punishments: anyone perceived to be 'advancing the enemy' by these means would be 'ruthlessly eliminated'. (Such elimination was already occurring in other cities such as Munich, where the authorities were hanging those perceived to be defeatist.) This was to be a battle 'for freedom' and 'for life', the article continued; the Führer himself had assigned a general to focus on the defence of Dresden, and Mutschmann would be staying within the 'fortress' to ensure that the party continued to support the population in those difficult days. Part thunderous threat, part exhortation, the declaration might have inspired a few resolute party loyalists. But another report in that Dresden newspaper the same day illustrated just how far from reality the authorities were drifting. Claiming that all the Germans needed to secure victory was more time, the report feebly suggested that, in England, Churchill's premiership was being threatened by attacks from Labour's Aneurin Bevan; that there was a 'highly dangerous power struggle' underway. Dresdeners were facing a rather more immediate and terrifying threat.

The previous day Arnhem had been captured by the Allies as the Red Army continued their advance to Berlin and a British division entered the Bergen-Belsen concentration camp, which the Germans had abandoned. There, among some 60,000 starving and desperately ill prisoners, they also discovered the great mass of corpses that the Nazis had not found time to dispose of: some 13,000 bodies. The gradual unveiling of this national psychosis, the Allied discovery of the scale of the Holocaust across Germany and Europe, was not easily appreciated by people in cities such as Dresden that remained under Nazi control, but there were a few there who suspected none the less. Mischka Danos, for instance, recalled how in 1944 he had struck up a friendship with a young nurse who was on vacation from an institute some distance from Dresden that she would not name; she was pale and haunted and Danos had wondered to himself if she had been corralled into helping with some of the live medical experimentation he had heard rumours of.[5]

For the city's artists – including those deemed by the regime to be 'degenerate' – the days and weeks after the destruction produced intense creative reflection. The ordeal of Otto Griebel and his family had been similar to that suffered by so many others; at first reunited, the family was separated again in the confusion immediately following the bombing, Griebel and some of the children being ushered to one billet, his wife and the other children to another. Eventually, via the formal and informal grapevine, the Griebels were at last reunited – all unharmed – and evacuated to a little place called Eschdorf. Griebel had lost the great bulk of his work, that which had not already fallen victim to the Nazi obsession with degenerate art. He recalled later that all this came around his fiftieth birthday, upon which it was 'customary' in more normal circumstances for such a milestone to bring celebratory exhibitions of an artist's work and public honours. 'All this has been spared me,' he wrote.[6] He did not feel that he could 'start again', that the impulse had been 'sunk with the city of Dresden that I loved so much and where at the same time my work and everything that I loved have disintegrated'. Yet the next few weeks – and an upturned political landscape – would bring an unexpected new development to his artistic life.

Similarly, another of the city's artists was brooding over his incinerated work. But for fifty-six-year-old Wilhelm Rudolph – a former expressionist who from the 1920s had reached back into some of the traditions of Saxon folk art to produce nature drawings and elaborate woodcuts – the bombing had instead sparked a compulsive pulse of fresh creativity. Rudolph, like so many others, had had difficulties with the Nazi regime's art monitors; though not wholly proscribed, he had had to move carefully. Now he became one of the more prominent figures around the city's ruins; scrambling through the dust among the fast-sprouting weeds that were forcing their way through the cracks in the shattered paving, Rudolph saw the need to capture all this on paper, with reed pen and black ink. He positioned himself before the splintered ruins of the railway station, meticulously capturing streets of hollow buildings, their now empty windows admitting sunlight and casting unfamiliar shadows.

He did all this in the face of official suspicion: the signs forbidding looting were prominent and the police scrutinized him closely. In addition to this was an unspoken accusation of morbidity: photography was one thing, ensuring that the atrocity was captured for history, but was this a place for art? Rudolph was as unheeding as the elderly men and women who daily haunted the rubble looking for lost loved ones. His work has a spare, unflinching quality.

'There was no time for mourning,' said Rudolph later. 'In 1945 no one mourned; it was survival. I drew, I drew obsessively. It was all still there, that's the unimaginable thing. Dresden still stood. The fire had left the sandstone of the buildings standing like skeletons. Only later did it all collapse or was blasted away.'[7]

And in a city that was renowned above all for the richness of its music, it was just weeks afterwards that the cataclysm began to be memorialized in the slow composition of a requiem. The Kreuzkirche cantor Rudolf Mauersberger had survived that night, sheltering with the boys of the choir not far from the charnel wasteland of the Great Garden park. In the days that followed, the memory of those eleven choirboys and three priests who had died in the raid preyed upon him intensely. Amid the general exodus, Mauersberger was billeted in the countryside, where he started to give thought to what would become the most important work of his life. 'How Desolate is the City' was the introduction to the requiem addressed to Dresden itself.[8] Among its lines were: 'How is the city that was so populous now so deserted? . . . How are the stones of the sanctuary scattered?' These were the questions that had to be addressed, in perplexity, to Heaven: 'We have lost our hearts, and our eyes have become dark . . . Lord, look at my misery, O Lord, look at my misery!' Unlike the prevailing fashion at the time for atonality, Mauersberger instead found moving echoes of old German hymns and wove them together with the deep chimes of the Kreuzkirche, a resonating choral baritone hum signifying the approaching bombers and episodes of intense percussion signifying the fire: 'Alas, that I was born to see the destruction of my people!' The imagery was apocalyptic: pale horses, angels in the sky, the earth trembling and fiery hail shooting down from above.

And as Dresden continued living its fever dream, the Nazi regime at last started collapsing inwards: Hitler turned the gun on himself in the Berlin bunker on 30 April 1945. Yet the war was not quite over; the Führer's chosen successor, Admiral Karl Dönitz, understood that surrender was necessary – but, as he saw it, only to the west. To the east of the country, it was imperative, as he and the remnants of the previous regime saw it, to continue to fight and resist the oncoming Soviet forces. If they did not, millions of German soldiers would simply be captured and marched to Siberia, and the women and the children they left behind would be at the mercy of men they regarded as barbarians. In Silesia and Pomerania there had been outbreaks of murder-suicide; young families in their terror choosing to kill their own children either by drowning or through poison to evade the approaching Red Army before ending their own lives.

In Dresden, where the nights were experienced as agonies of suspense, either in anticipation of further fire attacks or simply listening out for the ghostly booms of battle echoing from the distant hills, the population was apprised by the Gauleiter of his own intentions. Even as news of Hitler's death (the exact circumstances carefully omitted) became official, Martin Mutschmann was apparently at one with the new Dönitz government. Although the Americans had reached Leipzig, there was no prospect of their penetrating further into Saxony and reaching Dresden before the Red Army. Thus, in Mutschmann's view, the citizens would have to prepare to meet the Soviet invaders with ruthless resistance: the city – or at least those parts of it still navigable – was to be the battleground. Snipers would be stationed street by street on fire-blackened rooftops, while the swastika was to continue to fly on any civic building that had come through the bombing relatively intact. Yet even as these fierce directives were issued, the increasingly chaotic movements of the German army – many troops now being led far south of Dresden towards Bohemia in a futile effort to block the Red Army – told Dresdeners another story. Did Martin Mutschmann truly believe at any point that the people of this single city could prevail over the might of Stalin's men? Or that he could surrender to the Americans, but not to the Soviets? Such delusion is hard to imagine.

On 7 May Wilhelm Rudolph tried to ignore the rumbling of troop vehicles, the blend of disciplined soldiers and – in other corners – the deserters who were abandoning their weapons. 'The Russian artillery was already firing on the city; it was dangerous in the rubble,' he later said. 'There were also defensive positions in the ruins, which one did not see; Dresden ought to be defended. They could pick you off like a hare.'[9] Despite that, he continued his obsessive drawing. It was also on 7 May that Martin Mutschmann – giving the lie to all his furious Nazi fundamentalism – quietly fled the city. He secured transport, making for the Erzgebirge, about sixty miles south-west, where he planned to hide in the house of a friend. As the Red Army now captured thousands upon thousands of German soldiers to the south and the east of the city, Dresden was wholly defenceless.

Margot Hille and her mother had left the brewery tunnels and returned to occupy their broadly undamaged apartment in the south-west of the city. Having witnessed both the raids and their macabre aftermath, their lives would never again be truly normal, but when the Soviets marched across the Blue Wonder on 8 May – VE Day – the seventeen-year-old saw even more of the true pitilessness of war. The Red Army entered in triumph, and even though the soldiers were apparently ordered on pain of immediate execution neither to steal nor to assault, there was little sign that the threatened penalty acted as a deterrent. Almost immediately there were hideous stories of sexual assaults so serious that they caused lasting injuries. Close by to the Hilles was a villa where a number of Soviet soldiers were billeted. Opposite this house lived two friends of Margot, fellow female apprentices at Felsenkeller. They drew the attention of the billeted soldiers and, as Margot recalled, the Soviets went 'in and out' of their apartments and 'celebrated' with them. 'What followed then, I do not have to describe.'[10]

Nor would she have wanted to. After repeatedly raping the two girls, the Soviet soldiers were insistent that they wanted more women and it seemed only a matter of time before they came looking in Margot's apartment block. Margot's mother quickly hatched a plan to protect her daughter. There was a workshop at the back of the block to which Frau Hille obtained access, and then set about rearranging the machinery stored within to create camouflaged hiding spaces for her daughter and the other young girls in the building. When the Soviets came, Margot and her neighbours took cover in the dank, oily space and waited, not daring to breathe, as the men demanded that they be produced. The teenagers lay beneath rusted metal in the dark, listening to the harsh bellows, the commands, the fractured German. The soldiers, losing patience, turned their attentions to the next apartment block along. Margot heard later that one young woman had been forced to climb down the building from her first-floor bedroom window in order to escape. Another female colleague of Margot simply jumped out of her third-floor window as Soviet soldiers came systematically crashing into apartments in search of fresh prey. Margot recalled that her guardian angel must have been present; there was a lawn below and she escaped with only a few broken ribs.[11]

In those first few days after VE Day, the Soviets were very quick to consolidate control over the civic offices of Dresden, and were equally quick to issue communiqués concerning the welfare of the people; they also ensured that fresh supplies of potatoes and wheat were brought into the shattered city. While Dresdeners were being fed a little better, the speedy reordering of its courts, its schools, its university, its radio broadcasts, its cinemas, its bureaucracy, its shops, its cafes, its restaurants, its factories and precision laboratories and workshops was already underway. The 'Golden Pheasants' and other Nazi Party officials were arrested and imprisoned. Some would face transportation to labour camps in Russia, others chose poison. In their place were appointed citizens who were exultants about the new regime. Among them was the cigarette factory accountant Elsa Frölich, a communist sympathizer who had remained unswerving – if necessarily silent – in her opposition to Nazism. On 8 May she and a friend, Erna Fleischer-Gute, presented themselves at makeshift offices established on Taschenberg Square by Soviet officials who were restructuring the organization of the city. Frölich was made most welcome, and one of her first duties was to oversee the return of prisoners from concentration camps to the city.[12]

For Victor Klemperer and his wife Eva – who since the bombing had been on a seemingly interminable journey back and forth across the country, witnessing the coming of the American soldiers in the west and their wry generosity in little villages towards German civilians, who were by turns startled and charmed by the warmth of black soldiers – the return to their old house had the flavour of 'a fairy tale'.[13] To know once more after all those years in dread a semblance of security, to have the anvil weight of oppression lifted, was extraordinary, and at times fearful too, because of the anxiety that fast-switching fortunes might change once again.

In the midst of the general chaos were symbols of more profound confusion: in those days, Klemperer recalled, no one in Dresden was quite certain of the exact time. The reason was that Radio Berlin – which marked the hours – was in one time zone; Bremen, occupied by the British using GMT, was in another; and Dresden was on Moscow time. There were other tokens of change. Klemperer was hearing stories of Soviet expropriation: everything from precision factory equipment, loaded onto trains and taken east, to the human technical experts who engineered these marvels also finding themselves en route to Moscow. For Klemperer, though, any qualms about the forced egalitarianism of the new regime were balanced out by his own hopes that Dresden's university might be not only restored but also elevated to a new level by Moscow's requirement for intellectual excellence. Any anxiety he had that the new forms of coercion might produce a fresh outbreak of Nazi resistance were balanced by his own dazed pleasure at being suddenly treated with so much friendliness, warmth and respect by those who had previously shunned him.

The Gauleiter's whereabouts, meanwhile, were discovered in a matter of days by the Soviet forces, who took him into custody. Many of his colleagues and friends had chosen to kill themselves rather than fall into Soviet hands. Mutschmann preferred to protest his innocence, but if he felt that he had no crimes to answer for, the Soviets considered differently. He was taken by train to Moscow, where he was interrogated and imprisoned in the Lubyanka. His fate was deliberated with some care, for the final decision to execute him did not come until 1947. By this stage, the full, unthinkable scale of Nazi atrocities had been exposed and judged at Nuremberg. In contrast to Mutschmann, however, his former mayor Hans Nieland – who had also fled the city shortly after the bombing – was treated more leniently. After four years of internment in British facilities in West Germany, Nieland was found to have been merely 'marginally incriminated' in the crimes of the Reich. By 1950 he was a free man; shortly after this, he became a banker. Nieland died in 1976, aged seventy-five.[14]

In the spring and summer of 1945 the silent grey vista of the levelled Altstadt, from the river to the Great Garden, was a landscape that Dresdeners viewed with unease. At night, in humid lightning storms, with skeletal structures made stark in the flashes and rain teeming and hissing furiously in the dust, many avoided the ruins. Urban legends arose about what might happen in these wastelands after the sun went down: tales of malign figures lurking behind fragments of wall waiting to attack. Old men walked arm-in-arm for protection. Yet if cities can be said to possess their own spirits, then the coming years saw Dresden tentatively begin to regenerate and renew its soul, especially through art and music. Even as cattle were driven through the wilderness of stone that comprised the remains of the Neumarkt, the city's sense of itself as a place of culture and high expression was slowly reawakening. Meanwhile, the ethical debates about the ferocious destruction wreaked upon it began – in England and America especially – to find new force and bitterness in some corners, and to cement the view of the city as a treasure that had been brutally ravaged.

25. Recoil

If the destruction of Dresden was a crime, then who precisely was guilty? To begin with, the shock seemed too profound to allow for finely reasoned inquests. The famous Dresden-born author Erich Kästner – whose bestselling 1929 novel *Emil and the Detectives* had bewitched millions of children – was among those in the months after the cataclysm who returned to the city and walked down long canyons of haphazardly piled bricks and boulders, open to a wide and wholly unfamiliar sky, filled with horror as he tried and failed to locate sentimentally remembered spots in this weird wilderness. Later, he bitterly reflected on the futility at that point of trying to assign guilt for this atrocity.

Kästner was born in 1899: his saddler father and hairdresser mother (occupations old and modern, interestingly spanning the turn of the century) had made their home on the other side of the river, near the Neustadt station. Kästner's early childhood, before a move to Berlin, had been filled with expeditions to the grand streets near the Kreuzkirche, the dome of the Arts Academy and the bright colours of the flower stalls lining the Altmarkt. That day when Kästner returned to Dresden, he tried to find his old school but it had vanished. He walked across the grey prairie of grit that had been the Neumarkt and looked up at the remaining fragments of wall that had been the Frauenkirche, where he had once sung as a schoolboy.

For him, the years of Nazi rule had been personally fraught with hazard; in the early 1930s he had been implacably opposed to the rising National Socialists and described Goebbels as a 'limping little devil',[1] yet had chosen not to emigrate to safety. In 1933 Kästner's adult novels – one of which, *Fabian*, recounted louche sexual scenes in Weimar Berlin – were among the first to be publicly burned. The Nazi regime had ostracized him and he had to write screenplays under a pseudonym. Kästner was familiar with bombing, having seen the attack on Munich, where he lived, but the incineration of his beloved home city shocked him deeply. Some years later, he wrote:

Dresden was a wonderful city . . . history, art and nature intermingled in town and valley in an incomparable accord . . . And you have to take my word for it, because none of you, no matter how rich your father may be, can go there to see if I am right. For the city of Dresden is no more . . . In one single night, and with a single movement of its hand, the Second World War wiped it off the map.[2]

Kästner observed that among the Great Powers, there was mutual blame; in his view, there was a terrible purposelessness about this 'quarrelling'. That it would not bring Dresden or its beauty back to life.

And among those citizens who had lived through that infernal night, there similarly seemed no desire for either vengeance or even accusations; at least not initially. For Marielein Erler, reunited with her husband and daughter in Lüneburg and dictating her account of the bombing, while sitting on a bed, her eyesight perhaps permanently damaged by her ordeal in the fire, the responsibility arguably lay with 'that crazy man' Hitler.[3] Though she also thought that the will of 'a higher power' had to be considered as well. Conversely, for Gisela Reichelt, thinking back years later, there was something purely nihilistic about the attack; it was essentially 'senseless'.[4] She was looking at it from the point of view of her ten-year-old self, and all the other children of the city, so many of whom among the survivors were horribly injured.

This was a psychic wound inflicted upon the city that its people would never be entirely free of, but nor was there time in that immediate post-war period for inquests. The Soviets, who were tightening their grip on the Dresden civic infrastructure in offices where damaged roofs left rainwater in puddles on the floors, were paranoid about the intentions of the Americans, the French and the British ensconced in the west of Germany. There were no certainties anywhere in a nation that was split ideologically but not yet politically, and in the weeks and months after surrender Dresdeners were facing the most terrible food shortages and ever more frequent power cuts. Even bread was becoming scarce. All this left neither time nor energy either for public mourning or to address the moral dimensions of the bombing.

In certain circles in Britain, though, the subject of the bombing campaign was provoking wider unease, not so much from passionately outspoken figures such as the Bishop of Chichester, George Bell, who had pleaded consistently for the distinction to be drawn between 'Nazi assassins' and the 'German people', but more, in the wake of VE Day, among senior figures in Whitehall. Having proudly trumpeted British success in the Battle of Britain, the war in the desert, the campaigns in Italy, D-Day and the push through Europe, firestorms were not going to be woven into this national tapestry of gallantry and courage. Air Chief Marshal Harris was acutely sensitive to this, to the fact that Churchill had not explicitly mentioned the efforts of the Bomber Command members in his victory address and to the fact that the ground crews were not going to be awarded a special Bomber Command campaign medal. Harris himself had written proudly to his entire personnel, praising the efforts of all from the ground crews to the airmen who 'fought alone through black nights, rent only, mile after continuing mile, by the fiercest barrages ever raised . . . In each dark minute of those long miles lurked menace . . . In that loneliness in action lay the final test, the ultimate stretch of human staunchness and determination.'[5]

It seemed intolerable to Harris that such monumental courage should be so casually dismissed by Whitehall. The personnel of Bomber Command were to be awarded only the standard 'Defence' medal, which, Harris later wrote in his memoirs, was the subject of much 'bitter' comment among those ground crew and engineers. As Harris added acidly (and snobbishly), 'Every clerk, butcher or baker in the rear of the armies overseas had a "campaign" medal.'[6] As to the ethics of the bombing: 'I was called upon to attack Dresden,' wrote Harris. 'This was considered a target of the first importance for the offensive on the eastern front.' However, he went on, 'I know that the destruction of so large and splendid a city at this late stage of the war was considered unnecessary even by a good many people who admit that our earlier attacks were as fully justified as any other operation of war.' Harris understood himself to be the plain speaker, up against a hypocritical and squeamish establishment. Yet with all that said, he too seemed eager to place the responsibility elsewhere. 'Here I will only say that the attack on Dresden was at the time considered a military necessity by much more important people than myself.'[7]

Harris was made Knight Grand Cross of the Order of the Bath, an honour that came from the Palace, but he saltily declined any honours that would have been offered from Whitehall. If his aircrews could not have special recognition, then neither would he. He also expressed his desire to return swiftly to his colonial heartland as governor of Rhodesia. The position was not vacant. The silence of his superiors in the coming months and years became more marked; Churchill's history of the war failed to mention the Dresden bombing. There was an element of shame in that 28 March memo that the prime minister had sent concerning area bombing; a sense that he feared that the British had become, as he once warned, 'beasts'. Mixed in with this was some anxiety about the future of Germany itself; to be seen celebrating and honouring such destruction through specially struck medals would not have gone down well with the defeated population.

The Americans too seemed at best ambivalent on the subject, even though they held Harris in some regard and had awarded him their own Distinguished Service Medal. Harris, too, maintained a very friendly correspondence with figures such as General Ira Eaker.[8] (He later noted in his memoirs that the Americans 'used against Japan exactly the same method of devastating large industrial cities by incendiary bombs as was used in Europe by Bomber Command'. And this was before the even more terrifying weaponry that they were soon to deploy.) But there were some very distinguished Americans who seemed keen to separate the Japanese fires from that one specific inferno on the Elbe. One such figure was Telford Taylor. Taylor had spent part of his war deep in the most secret heart of the Allied operation: as a codebreaker at Bletchley Park in Buckinghamshire. After the war, as a lieutenant colonel, Taylor, who originally trained as a lawyer, was a prosecutor at Nuremberg. In February 1945 he 'was privy to some of the discussion about the proposed attack against Dresden'. The morality of the issue had preyed on him ever since:

What Sir Arthur Harris's purpose was, I do not know, but the British told the doubters that there was a German armoured division in or near Dresden blocking the Soviet advance from the east, and that the Russians wanted an aerial attack to clear their way.

However, the British decoders had produced information that the German armoured division was not at Dresden but in Bohemia many miles to the south. A senior air officer of the British intelligence group, based on this and other information, concluded that there was no military purpose to be gained by attacking Dresden. He so informed Sir Arthur's headquarters staff, without result.

The British air officer then gave his information to the staff of General Carl Spaatz, Commander of the US Army Air Force in Britain. General Spaatz concluded that the Dresden raid should be called off but Sir Arthur was adamant and General Spaatz was unwilling to stand aside if the British were insistent on going ahead.

And so both air forces joined in the attack with the much denounced consequences.[9]

There was, in this account from Taylor, a suggestion of something dark and cold in Harris, launching an attack which he knew to have no military basis. Yet Taylor ignored both the transport targets and indeed the element of Soviet involvement.

And there were those who had been at the heart of the USAAF who were brisk on the subject of ethics. Major General Robert Landry, who had been Director of Operations at SHAEF, was asked many years later about the Dresden raids and about the American bombers attacking a target that had already been essentially levelled. It was put to him that it was a 'terror raid'; he dismissed the suggestion instantly. 'I don't think there was ever any question of whether or not some civilians were going to get killed . . . because the Germans put a lot of factories right in the cities, and who was to determine whether there was a factory there or not?' he said. 'Nobody was going to take a load of these goddamn bombs back and drop them in the North Sea when they were fighting somebody like the Germans.'[10]

Elsewhere, the burgeoning debate was precisely coloured by the question of German temperament; many in Britain believed that, as a nation, Germany was especially prone to militarism, and to brutality in pursuit of conquest – that there was a specifically Teutonic impulse that had recently pulled the world into two devastating conflicts. And some worried that there was every chance Germany would do so again. The young scientist Freeman Dyson, who had worked in Bomber Command and who had come to feel a revulsion especially for the raids carried out towards the end of the war, found himself discussing the Dresden bombing raids with a 'well-educated and intelligent' wife of a senior air force officer. Dyson asked her if it was right that the Allies should be killing large numbers of German women and babies. She told him: 'Oh yes. It is good to kill the babies especially. I am not thinking of this war but of the next one, twenty years from now. The next time the Germans start a war and we have to fight them, those babies will be the soldiers.'[11] There was something quite extraordinarily primitive about this exterminating impulse that stayed with Dyson for decades. The sentiment would also have confirmed the worst suspicions of the Bombing Restriction Committee, which issued a pamphlet a few months after VE Day claiming that 200,000–300,000 people – some ten times the real figure, echoing the Goebbels propaganda – had been killed in Dresden.

It would be several years before the new president of Saxony, Max Seydewitz, decreed – with the blessing of Moscow – that the raid had been an act of 'Anglo-American terror bombing'; that the British and Americans had been 'brutal warmongers'; that the ruins of Dresden stood as a spur to 'fight against the imperialistic gangster war' and to combat 'the stranglehold of fascism'; and that this terrorist outrage should be marked with an annual commemorative silence, with all traffic halted.[12] With Germany divided, and the Americans and Soviets seeking to divine one another's intentions across the Iron Curtain invoked by Churchill, the bombing of Dresden would now be the subject not of reasoned inquiry, but of ever more shrill and venomous propaganda serving a variety of ugly political causes.

In England, not long after the war, Sir Arthur Harris was invited to give a talk in the Devon market town of Honiton, near where he had gone to school. The speech he gave, the notes of which are now among his papers, had a tone of defiance, and indeed compassion, for his airmen and the station crews. He placed special emphasis upon the vast sacrifice made by those flying through the relentless flak who had to fight 'with their heads' rather than their bodies.[13] They had shortened the war, he said, and by so doing saved uncountable lives. Out of 125,000 aircrew, some 55,573 had died: Harris made sure these statistics were known.

Elsewhere, there was, in transatlantic popular culture, one bitter-sweet moment for surviving flight veterans. The Powell and Pressburger film *A Matter of Life and Death* (1946) was a metaphysical drama about a bomber pilot – a poet called Peter Carter – who bails out of his burning plane without a parachute, having in those last few minutes fallen in love over the airwaves with June, an American wireless operator guiding him back to England. Carter survives thanks to a bureaucratic mix-up in Heaven, washes up on an English beach and ecstatically meets June. Then a heavenly emissary descends to earth to try to persuade him his time is up, even as he protests that he is now too deeply in love to leave life. This was the first ever film to receive a Royal Command Performance, attended by the king and queen. The film's spoken prologue – beginning in outer space, closing in on the earth and finally, from very far above, on Germany – talked of 'a thousand-bomber raid', but this was a drama that began with the return from that raid, over the foggy English Channel. And because it was a fantasy, it could safely suffuse the bomber pilot, played by David Niven, with an almost absurd romanticism without troubling the audience with ugly moral questions. The film was also about redemption and the importance of forgetting: with the war over, and the dead happy in Heaven, those on earth had now to steep themselves in all that was beautiful: from summer-evening trysts to poetry and Shakespeare. The bomber pilot who had been destined to die was instead permitted to live because he stood for a certain sort of English civilization.

The moral questions that haunted the Dresden raid were not in any way diminished by the sudden blinding flashes of light and the instantaneous atomization that made shadows stand permanently on walls when the US dropped atomic bombs on Hiroshima and Nagasaki in August 1945 to end the war. These were the weapons that transformed the world order and pointed to a future of warfare that Arthur Harris had been predicting, a future that he did not even see himself surviving. The atomic bomb and all its descendants (the technology passed to Stalin by spies enabling the Soviets to test their own first device in Kazakhstan in 1949) promised death on a scale never before imagined; David Niven's Peter Carter was already antiquated.

In the years that followed, Hiroshima and Nagasaki seemed to catalyse more debate in the West about the impact of Dresden, not least because there were many in Britain who believed that the numbers who were incinerated in the German firestorm – an echo of the inflated claims of both the Nazis and the Bombing Restriction Committee – outweighed the total of deaths from the Hiroshima atomic blast. Despite the 1961 publication of the four-volume official history *The Strategic Air Offensive Against Germany, 1939–1945*, by Sir Charles Webster and Noble Frankland, which came to a balanced judgement on the effectiveness and weaknesses of Harris's strategies, a view was hardening in some quarters that Bomber Command had done a uniquely terrible thing. In 1963 historian David Irving – later to become a figure of the most intense controversy – wrote *The Destruction of Dresden*, which suggested that the death toll may have been 135,000 and perhaps even as high as 200,000.[14] Reviewing this work for the *Observer*, former politician and diplomat Harold Nicolson agreed with its broad thesis and came very close to alleging that the bombing was a war crime.

'The British public like to persuade themselves that, whereas other nations indulge in atrocities, we ourselves never commit unholy acts,' wrote Nicolson. 'Yet there can be few operations of war as causeless, as purposeless, and as brutal as the attack on Dresden.' Nicolson was not interested in laying responsibility at the feet of Sir Arthur Harris; this, for him, went higher. He continued: 'It is difficult to dismiss the impression that we undertook this vast operation in order to impress the Russians with the power of the RAF.' Moreover, Nicolson – in the ecstasy of his anger – entered the territory that was later to give such succour to neo-Nazis: he wrote that, even compared to Hiroshima, the Dresden raid 'was the single greatest holocaust caused by war'.[15] Even if he had used the term lazily, it was a wildly tasteless and stupidly provocative thing to write.

In response to Nicolson's piece, a letter to the newspaper the following week was sent by E. Birkin of London SW6. Birkin was a Holocaust survivor:

I with many other inmates of concentration camps was trudging across Europe before the advancing Russians when we saw the flames of Dresden and the ruins of the city. It made us realize that the end was near. The morale of our guards, and of the German people whom we met, visibly deteriorated and their attitude to us, once at last they realized that Hitler's promises were false, improved remarkably. Also, it gave us renewed hope and strength to survive the last months of the war. In fact, that very night, we toasted our allies with soup.[16]

It was also in the 1960s that former bomb aimer Miles Tripp set about reuniting with his former crewmates. After the war, and demobilization, Tripp had married his girlfriend Audrey, with whom he had shared so many nights in Bury St Edmunds. He became a solicitor and wrote thrillers in his spare time which achieved their own success.[17] Tripp was alert to the way that the bombing of Dresden had become shorthand for unthinking destruction, but that was not quite how he and his former crewmates saw it; broadly, their view was that a war of that kind could never have been simply waged against hermetically sealed armies with no civilian casualties; that Nazism had been a tumour, and such a growth could not be cut out without damage to the surrounding flesh. In truth, the airmen did not remember a great deal about that one specific raid out of so very many, save its unusually long flight duration. Added to this, their chief thoughts on any mission concerned survival; so many thousands of feet up in the sky, it was difficult for them to imagine individuals on the ground as their bombs fell.

There was a curious paradox: all of them remembered the dread, the bad dreams, and many had developed conditions after the war – ulcers, stomach problems, fused vertebrae, trembling hands – which they attributed directly to the fierce stress of bombing missions. Yet at the same time, everyone in Tripp's crew unhesitatingly declared that it was an extraordinary period of their lives, and they would never have had it any other way. To a man they acknowledged how the world saw Dresden; all they could say in response was that the enemy had committed so many atrocities that the all-consuming aim of any mission was to wipe the Nazis out, for any of that Nazi tumour that remained might have regrown, leading to illimitable future atrocities. Tripp's comrades had scattered into a variety of lives, from local council employee to antique dealer. All were proud of the service that they had given.

None the less, throughout the late 1960s in Britain the view gained ground, especially in artistic circles, that the bombing of Dresden had been a sinisterly shameful episode; *Soldiers: An Obituary for Geneva*, a drama about Churchill, bombing and Dresden by the German playwright Rolf Hochhuth, opened in the West End in 1967.[18] Strikingly, one journalist writing a background feature described the Dresden subject matter as being about 'the biggest and quickest single massacre in history', adding that the atom bomb over Hiroshima 'killed only 71,000'.[19] The other element fuelling anti-bombing feeling at that time was perhaps the deepening moral mire of the American war in Vietnam; increasingly among the younger generation, this was an era in which bombing signified ruthless imperialism.

Sir Arthur Harris – who had finally been nudged by Churchill into accepting a baronetcy in 1953 – was interviewed in 1977 by Tony Mason for an internal RAF project. By then, Sir Arthur was eighty-four years old, but his memory was crisp. Again, he made it clear that he was not responsible for the selection of targets; that his entire time at the helm of Bomber Command had been spent 'under a shower of directives'. When it came to Dresden, and other cities, he insisted that the relentless pressure from his bomber raids depleted the strength of the German army because men were needed for anti-aircraft defence, and the manufacture of new weaponry and repairs. Sir Arthur, who had returned to Britain from South Africa with his family in the 1950s, was living in the willow-trailed town of Goring-on-Thames. There were no regrets, save for his gruff view expressed in 1977 that war ultimately 'never did anyone any good'.[20] He died in 1984, aged ninety-one.

In Dresden itself, in the post-war years, as citizens adjusted to the heavy pressures of a new world, new politics, new philosophy and new oppressions, there was a growing sense of the importance of memory; indeed, the struggles over remembrance would become bitter. At the same time, though, the city began regenerating, and restoring, and was eventually to find a new aesthetic that, unlike other areas of public life, was not entirely dominated by the crushing weight of Soviet ideology.

26. 'The Stalinist Style'

In the hard winters, the ruins were settled with snow; the landscape made monochrome, bombed-out interiors now incongruously white. Even those structures that were part-covered were vulnerable to the infiltration of blizzards. The Kreuzkirche would not be rebuilt and restored until 1955, ten years after its main roof was smashed through; but the Kreuzchor under the cantor Rudolf Mauersberger was very much a feature of the new life of the city under the communists, his choir performing in other public spaces outside of the Altstadt.

As well as Mauersberger's *Dresdner Requiem*, the choir gave renditions of a variety of new compositions, adapting leitmotifs from traditional folk music. One performance was watched and broadly enjoyed by Victor Klemperer, himself now restored to academic life – a professor once more, and reluctantly enmeshed in the stony procedures of the city's new authorities.[1] He was beguiled by the black-and-white uniforms of the Kreuzchor, and their stylized renditions, though he fleetingly thought of the boys as automatons.*

As for Victor and Eva Klemperer, the world that they moved through in those post-war years was alternately wondrous and crushing. Wondrous because of the daily experience of being treated with not just civility, but also respect; because of the new phase of Professor Klemperer's career that saw him travelling to academic conferences around Europe and even to China; because of the monographs

---

* This was far from the case: some of them – including Peter Schreier – would later go on to have the most brilliant musical careers. Schreier joined the choir full-time months after the bombing; he was ten years old. Even among many other young talents, his voice stood out and in the late 1940s his solos were recorded. After his voice broke, Schreier embarked upon a dazzling operatic career, taking him around Europe; but Dresden has always been his home. There is an interesting short biography of Schreier at www.bach-cantatas.com/Bio/Schreier-Peter.htm.

published, the talks given. Yet it was also crushing because Eva's health was continually very poor, and because they were conscious in this new Dresden of all the city's Jewish people who had been sent to their deaths. Their shadows were always there, together with the fear that the forces that killed them could yet be resurrected. In the early 1950s Eva died of a heart attack – she had gone for a nap and Klemperer found her, eyes open and face calm, when bringing her an evening drink. He was dazed with grief but, although he felt at the end of his own road, pushed on with his work, aching with loneliness. As the decade rolled by, he found a new wife, Hadwig. Klemperer lived until the beginning of 1960; he was seventy-eight when he died. His survival – and the survival of his extraordinary, detailed diaries of all those years of darkness – did much to help expose the full squalor of the Nazi cruelties.

Klemperer might have been unkind to describe uniformed Kreuzchor singers as automatons but certain people in those immediate post-war years certainly did resemble life-sized marionettes: the workers who were sent to clear the ruins. Some time after the bombing, special narrow-gauge railway lines were still being laid through the mountainous piles of rubble, in order to load up wagons with shattered debris and transport it away, preparing the ruined wilderness for fresh building. As well as the labourers assigned to clearing these fields of stone, unwitting passers-by were sometimes press-ganged by Soviet soldiers into putting in a shift as punishment if they were found not to be carrying all the correct documentation required of them. Yet the authorities wanted their renovation to be understood as the heroism of a new age. Posters were produced depicting broad-shouldered men and smiling women setting about reconstruction in a way that suggested that the wider society was also being rebuilt in a cleaner, healthier way.[2]

For one man, all this had been long dreamed of. Walter Ulbricht, a long-standing German communist with (to some ears) a distractingly high-pitched voice and (to some ears) an irritating 'Saxon accent',[3] who had been in exile throughout Europe in the 1930s and resident in Moscow for the course of the war, had been swift to return to Germany as the Nazis imploded. Under him, the German Communist Party was forcibly merged with its rival, the Social Democrats, to become the Socialist Unity Party. All rules and protocols came from Moscow; the seizure of power, which had started with nods to the need for democracy, was sharp and unchallenged. In Dresden, as in other East German cities, rationing was so severe that bread was made partly with acorns; there was scarcely the energy to form furious political opposition to this new regime. Ulbricht was a committed totalitarian, and it was his portrait that was swiftly to dominate every classroom, every lecture hall, every Rathaus. His image replaced that of Hitler on all postage stamps. (Before replacements became available, Hitler's image on each and every stamp had been simply drawn over by hand with a pen.)

In West Germany, there were 'de-Nazification' programmes that included civilians being shown photographs and films of the death camps. In the Soviet zone, encompassing the east of Berlin, Dresden, Weimar and Leipzig, among other cities, senior Soviet military officers and Soviet bureaucrats gravely set about re-educating the populace in different ways: former Nazi officials were quickly rounded up, interrogated and sent to prison camps in Russia. One level down, those citizens who had had particularly close ties with the Nazis, chiefly through work, were identified and in many cases denounced and driven from public life into a jobless purgatory.

For the rest of the civilian populace, the unsmiling efforts to change established thought started quickly. From theatre to factory shop floors, from the vulgar language used by working men in public bars to the rarefied discussions of academics, there were committees established to monitor and police attitudes, to inculcate respect among the middle classes for the working classes, to explain why expropriation of private industry was desirable, to convey and enforce the fundamental tenets of Marxism and dialectical materialism, and to censor books, newspaper articles, radio broadcasts and any works of art deemed insufficiently optimistic about the future under this new governance. (In terms of using vulgar language, middle-class professionals were gravely advised by Soviet officials not to follow the lead of the workers; instead of conveying unity, it might in fact smack of mockery, they thought.)[4] There were committees for every area of life, in every workplace, in every residential district; sitting at tables under dim lights, the men and women who set the agendas were flinty and unforgiving of deviation from the approved discourse; jobs could be terminated instantly and without explanation; entire civic departments could find themselves replaced overnight. The main authorities were deliberately capricious and unpredictable; they ensured compliance through the anxiety of insecurity. Alongside old-established shops there emerged new state-run outlets; and cinema-goers were now shown Russian films with subtitles.

For the city's children and students, this was when, educationally, they stopped facing west and instead turned to Moscow – and with some speed. The Russian language was added as a central pillar to the classroom curriculum as Dresden families understood that future employment opportunities – and chances of promotion – would be affected directly by this linguistic adaptability. The teaching of English, conversely, began to diminish; the vulgar tongue of the Americans, it might have been assumed, might itself only serve to introduce unwelcome ideas. Over the course of the coming generation, Russian became more common and familiar. There was also a subtle cultural shift in the 1950s and 1960s as families became accustomed to looking east for their holidays, taking long train journeys to the new resorts in Crimea and on the Black Sea coast.[5]

Free expression was essentially forbidden; it was not long before anyone in a bar wishing to tell a mildly anti-authoritarian joke would do so by first beckoning their friend outside, away from other ears. No one in the city had known real freedom since before 1933, although for those few still living who had been either persecuted or simply frozen out by the Nazi regime there were genuine, fresh opportunities here. From the hospitals to the art galleries there was quite simply a new and sharpened appetite for life; Dresdeners relished the restoration of the botanical gardens and the spring blossoming of the city's remaining and still abundant trees. On top of this, there was nowhere else throughout Europe that Dresdeners could look to as having an easier time of it, save perhaps the American zone of occupied Germany, which was rumoured to enjoy abundant supplies of food. The British zone, like Britain itself, was subject to severe rationing and the Dresdeners who had not been bombed out at least still had the security of their homes. In a continent that in the immediate post-war years was seething with millions of refugees, including the Sudeten Germans violently expelled from Czechoslovakia, the city on the Elbe was at least stable under its new controllers.

By 1949 Germany was officially two countries as the German Democratic Republic and the Federal Republic of Germany came into being. Over the course of the following decade, a great many in the GDR would emigrate to West Germany; equally, though, there were a great many more who chose not to take that opportunity. One such was the eminent electronics expert Professor Heinrich Barkhausen, who had returned to Dresden a year after the bombing. Initially, he and other scientific colleagues at the still bomb-damaged university faced a regime that was not keen for the city to regain its speciality in engineering, but over the years that attitude thawed. Indeed, Professor Barkhausen, in addition to being awarded a GDR National Prize (an accolade his university colleague Professor Klemperer briefly yearned for), also had the honour of a new university building being named after him. Designed in the austere but bright rectilinear style of the 1950s – students cycling up and down the wide avenue before it – the Barkhausen Building was home to the Low Wattage Technology Department; it also pursued work in the fast-evolving field of transistors.[6] Perhaps as a scientist, Barkhausen – who died in 1956 – had found it easier than most to absent himself from the endless ideological harassment; there were few debates about unsound attitudes in highly technical electronics diagrams and blueprints. The work could be seen straightforwardly as aiding the progress of the Eastern Bloc. More than this, Dresden managed to retain one of its more individual characteristics: as a centre of a wide range of precision manufacturing and technological innovation. As the years progressed, the city regained its reputation for such goods as finely made cameras; this in turn would come to attract visitors from less well-favoured regions of the bloc eager to buy some of this sophistication.

In terms of medicine, too, Dresden kept one of its most distinguished figures in those post-war years: Dr Albert Fromme, whose home had succumbed to the billowing flames that night, had simply without any fuss set up a new home within the Friedrichstadt hospital complex of which he was director. Rooms were found for himself and his family. Indeed, they were to stay there for several years, until he moved to a new property in a rather desirable leafy district overlooking the city close to the forests of Dresden Heath. He and his rebuilt hospital did some remarkable work, given the intense financial restrictions of the time, including a huge amount of research into cancer, on which he published a book in 1953.[7] Given the sparse technology, the Friedrichstadt hospital had some surprising successes treating breast cancer using radiotherapy, patients surviving what not that long before had been terminal conditions. And as Dr Fromme worked on, well into his seventies, the otherwise severe authorities garlanded him with grateful honours: he was made the rector of Dresden's first medical academy in 1954 and in the same year he was named Outstanding Scientist of the People.[8]

Dr Fromme also took an intense interest in the academies of science in other East German cities, from East Berlin to Leipzig. If he harboured doubts about the new regime, or opposition to the ideals of socialism, then he must have done so very discreetly; given, though, that he had refused to join the Nazi Party at a point when such a refusal could destroy a career, it is possible that Dr Fromme found a sympathetic resonance with the ideal of socialism, and indeed the universal provision of good health care for all. He retired only in the 1960s and in his frailty moved to join family in West Germany (the elderly were permitted to cross what had by then become a fiercely patrolled border).

Another survivor of both the bombing and the scourge of the Nazi regime had been welcomed back to the city following his evacuation. The artist and marionette maker Otto Griebel, with his wife and children, re-established themselves in 1946 and Griebel was appointed to teach at the Dresden College of Fine Arts.[9] Where others experienced discomfort and unease at the distant yet extraordinarily pervasive Soviet rule, Griebel instead saw a natural justice restored to the world, and for himself the prospect once again of painting allied with socialist ideals. His peers now included artists such as Curt Querner, a long-time communist, and as the GDR consolidated its new identity, so the new rulers sought to point the artists in the 'correct' directions. The innovative modernism of the 1920s now had to be subdued into works that were flavoured with socialist realism; and there were strictures on suitable subjects. But in this environment, Griebel none the less felt liberation: his earlier depictions of working men, for instance, although stylized, still captured an essence of proletarian heroism. Added to this, he was enthusiastic about the idea of art being used to further spread and cement socialism. Paintings in the 1950s and the 1960s produced in Dresden offered prospects of agriculture and industry in tones of sombre green, brown, grey and ochre, and of course the 1945 firebombing remained a theme of inspiration.[10] There were numerous debates about formalism; even the slightest brush stroke had political significance; and it was also important not to follow the new routes taken by American art, immersed as it was in capitalist imperialism. There was also an effort to ensure that art reached the workers. Like his scientific contemporaries, Griebel seemed remarkably successful at negotiating the rapids of an implacable regime: and he continued teaching into the 1960s. He passed away in 1972.

His son Matthias, aged eight at the time of the bombing, left school at fourteen in the 1950s specifically to learn about agriculture and to work on farms; later he became a farming adviser. Nothing could have been more impeccably socialist. And yet he had his own free-spirited artistic impulses that led him in the 1960s to become a cabaret performer.[11] He toured small clubs around the GDR and was scrutinized closely by the hard-eyed Stasi secret police, who had a large base on the hills to the north overlooking the ruins of the old city. Other young people throughout the fifties and sixties received even closer attention: the GDR penal code, which placed careful emphasis on antisocial behaviour and attitudes, could result in lifelong prison sentences. The slightest slip when it came to approaches to the class struggle could entail secret denunciation, interrogation and the destruction of families. Even after the death of Stalin in 1953, life in Dresden became no less suffocating and repressive. The local Stasi state security headquarters had numerous cells and interrogation rooms, preserving thematic continuity with the previous regime. When the GDR finally collapsed it was estimated that between

12,000 and 15,000 prisoners – mostly critics of the regime, or those who had sought to escape from the east – had passed through this detention block, prior to being sent to prisons and camps.

Despite the pervasive observation, the weight of that constant threat, most people in Dresden sought simply to live their lives. And the city was rising around them once more. Even for those, like the artist Eva Schulze-Knabe, who had found a perverse enchantment in sunset evenings gazing at the 'pink ruins'[12] with the blue skies above, there was the additional fascination of seeing the construction of the new housing projects. In Johannstadt and Neustadt and Friedrichstadt, great lines of six- and seven-storey blocks of apartments were built, some with balconies. The style was regimented and sternly geometrical; equality as architecture, planned with technocratic attention to detail of small square lawns and playgrounds before the tall blocks, and truncated parades of shops and amenities. In this new age, it was intended that all residents – from factory workers to craftsmen to bank managers – would be served by the same facilities with a uniform aesthetic. There were wide avenues too; wide enough certainly for tanks to drive down.

Even in an atmosphere of the most carefully observed equality there were still some new apartments that were favoured, such as the large flats built at the sides of the Altmarkt, on ground that had been dust and weeds. These apartments, for officials, had many rooms and wonderful views over the other reconstruction works taking place. The grand department stores were rebuilt, though now they were state owned and there were continuing controversies over shortages, especially of textiles and clothing. Men's suits were difficult to come by, and on one occasion the appearance in a state-run department store of five ladies' trench coats 'and a few coloured dust coats' – as advertised in a local newspaper – caused scenes so agitated that they were reported in the foreign press. 'Counters and show-stands were overturned'[13] as women fought over these rarities.

Nor was the impulse to create such a dramatic departure from the past especially unusual; indeed, in an age when both superpowers were looking out into the depths of space – sending satellites, launching men among the stars – it seemed natural. What was once Prager Strasse was reconfigured by the 1960s into a modernist state-owned shopping plaza; a concrete canyon lined with vast rectangular apartment blocks, and the plaza itself carefully planned with fountains and flower beds and benches. Yet if this hint of futurism seemed at all jarring to older residents, it was hardly unique; this new style of urban space had soulmates dotted around western Europe, and especially in Britain, from Croydon to Dundee. More than this, there were admiring visitors to Dresden from the West: in 1965, on the occasion of the twentieth anniversary of the bombing, young *Observer* journalist Neal Ascherson gazed around with some wonder. 'Walking through the old city, one is soon lost among the gutted walls of what could have been palaces or cathedrals,' he wrote. 'The city opens into a fawn coloured plain of stone dust, upon which new and graceful blocks of flats have been scattered.' The Altmarkt, meanwhile, had been reconstructed partly with 'heavy, ornate, but not unpleasant blocks in the Stalinist style'.[14]

The old flavour of the city had not dissipated entirely, though. One of the more prominent and much-loved landmarks received restoration after having been examined closely for political suitability. The Zwinger Palace, which had housed the city's art treasures, lay shattered throughout the 1940s and early 1950s; but there was a recognition even among the more hardline civic authorities that classical art was an important public need, the enjoyment of which must not be confined to middle-class intellectuals. Quite apart from the restoration of the galleries themselves was the initially stickier problem of the whereabouts of the Old Masters that Martin Mutschmann had had transported from the city long before the bombing.

Many of the collections had – rather like a great deal of technical and agricultural equipment – been taken to Russia after being unearthed from their shelters by the Soviet trophy hunters. Some were in the cellars of grand schlosser while others had with some velocity made their way to the west of Europe via silent dealers. There was some doubt as to whether the 1,200-odd paintings that were now in the hands of the Soviets would be retained in Moscow, but by the mid 1950s, amid careful publicity, the paintings were restored to their newly reconstructed galleries in the Zwinger Palace. In a city that was now notorious for the extent of its destruction – with one resident warning that citizens were becoming inured to the cult of ruins, like eighteenth-century poets – this was an important revitalizing moment: an acknowledgement that art in all its forms was the heart of the city. With the return of the Old Masters came the start of a wider artistic restoration: some 6,000 other pieces, from paintings to sculpture, were gradually returned to the city authorities.[15] Whenever the odd painting turned up in a London auction house, the GDR government successfully lobbied to have it sent back.

Music had also been at the heart of the city; but the fate of the bombed and hollowed out Semper Opera House, just next door to the Zwinger Palace, was very much less assured. In 1947 one city official had suggested that it be rebuilt and repurposed, not only as a people's opera house but as a people's cinema as well. There were others, though, who were very keen to destroy what remained with dynamite, contending that the old opera house, with its grand boxes above the stalls, embodied an irredeemably bourgeois spirit. If opera was to return, surely it would be better housed in a structure that did not exacerbate class divides? The only argument that prevented the wholesale destruction of the remnants was the feeling that Dresdeners as a whole regarded the opera as being central to the identity and the history of the city; that to eliminate it would be in some way to erase the past, of which so much had already been traumatically removed. And so the ruins stayed, close to the flowing Elbe. And it was not until the mid 1980s, after years of lobbying, that restoration work at last began.

There was music elsewhere by the late 1960s: strong performances, world-class renditions, to be heard in the newly built Palace of Culture on the Altmarkt, overlooking the site where so many thousands of bodies had burned on pyres. The chief conductor of the Dresden Philharmonic, Kurt Masur, inaugurated the building with a performance of Beethoven's Ninth Symphony. As a venue, the hall, with its sleek lines, glass frontage, copper roof and elaborately vast wall mosaic depicting proud socialist moments in Germany, was a deliberate aesthetic break from the style of the old city, but it attracted visitors from around the country (it also contained a theatre space and a banqueting hall with a tip-up floor that could be transformed into a dance floor). This was the socialist ideal: high arts for the masses. The Dresden Philharmonic was invited to delight Western audiences too, satisfying those old bourgeois appetites. It was at night that the building looked most striking: the light glowing forth from the entrance and the glass-fronted mezzanine onto the Altmarkt and the Kreuzkirche. Just before its construction was complete, Kurt Vonnegut – now a novelist and having been awarded a Guggenheim grant to develop his writing – returned to Dresden for the first time since February 1945, when he had been 'corpse mining'.

Vonnegut's extraordinary *Slaughterhouse-Five* was coalescing in his thoughts at that point; the novel in which fictional Billy Pilgrim in 1960s America finds himself jumping time-tracks back and forth across his own life. Those tracks led ineluctably back to 13 February 1945; Pilgrim was a fictional character but Vonnegut deliberately placed him at the centre of his own experiences of the bombing, and the apocalyptic aftermath. Those parts of the novel were intended to be read as the literal truth. It was this work that not only cemented Vonnegut as a darkly comic and compelling literary voice but also regalvanized the furious ethical debates about what had been done to the city. When Vonnegut was back in Dresden in 1967, the sheer enormity of what had happened – the full scale of which he had not been able to grasp as a prisoner – hit him like lightning. The fiction that emerged was that of ashy, laconic anger. In the novel, Vonnegut had characters repeating that the death toll had been 135,000 – the smaller but still exaggerated figure that had been in the air since earlier that decade when the historian David Irving gave that number – an estimate supplied by former Dresden civic official Hanns Voigt – in his account of the bombing. And the figure itself was one of the elements that helped light the fuse on a terrible revisionist movement that insisted on equating the destruction of Dresden with the Holocaust; that its citizens were victims of a deliberate criminal atrocity too.

This view – even now rejected with some anguish by the Dresden authorities – was to become a growing problem for the city as the remembrance of 13 February became ever more established as an annual event throughout the 1960s and 1970s. Vonnegut could hardly have anticipated such consequences; the broader theme of *Slaughterhouse-Five* concerned not so much numbers as simply the obscenity of the inferno and the horrors of attempting to reconstruct life afterwards, be it in Dresden or Hiroshima. In 1969 the novel was published and became an instant classic, but it also fixed the idea among its many readers that more than any of the many bombed German cities, Dresden was unique and extraordinary in all of its losses.

Grey sky-scraping offices in concrete, uncertain supplies of hot water, communal tables at restaurants – this was Dresden in the years of detente. Yet by the 1980s the city had recovered enough of its old aesthetic life to attract visitors not just from Russia and the Eastern Bloc but from the West too; left-leaning tourists, not allergic to the idea of the USSR and its satellite states, crossing the Iron Curtain to savour a cultural landmark that had not been overtaken by the trappings of shiny materialism. In addition to this, as work finally began on the reconstruction of the Semper Opera House in 1985, Dresden gained a new resident in the form of Vladimir Putin. In the days when he was a young KGB officer, Putin, his first wife Lyudmila, and their two young children, spent four years in the city. His intelligence activities – intercepts, bugged phones – were said to be low key, and perhaps by comparison with the Stasi – the East German domestic security service that was infused in every corner of public and private life, combining blanket surveillance and violence – they were. The young couple rather loved the city; Putin was already fluent in German and he and his wife found the streets and the surrounding leafy countryside deeply congenial.[16] They saved up for a car. Putin was said to have developed a fondness for the local Radeberger beer (the family lived in the east of Neustadt, near the north bank of the Elbe and not far from the Radeberger brewery).

In this sense, as a thirty-something KGB officer, Putin had a very much more pleasant life there than practically any of the citizens he passed on the streets. His one moment of serious alarm came in the autumn of 1989 with the breakdown of control across the German Democratic Republic that led to the fall of the Berlin Wall. In Dresden, angry citizens were already turning their attentions to the Stasi main headquarters. Putin correctly divined that they would also be marching on the KGB villa, and it was he who went out alone to face the crowd, imploring them calmly, in German, not to proceed any further because there were snipers in position who would not hesitate to shoot them down. Putin succeeded in containing the situation and spent the next three days creating a vast fire of incriminating KGB documentation.

Through all these curious years – the half-muffled artistic heart of the city beating with ever greater strength and confidence against the background of an ever more oppressive and decrepit regime – there was one melancholy landmark that reminded all Dresdeners of 13 February 1945: the broken stumps of the Frauenkirche, in the wide, desolate space of the Neumarkt. In all those slow decades of recon-struction, this joyous baroque temple was never considered any kind of priority by the authorities; rather, its amputated remains stood as a permanent reminder of the wickedness of the imperialist Americans and British, and their unprovoked targeting of such beauty. By the early 1980s the site had become a locus for Dresden's peace move-ment; just as in the West, where young people campaigned vociferously against nuclear arsenals, their peers in Dresden marched with equal zeal against all such weaponry. Sebastian Feydt – who is now pastor of the Frauenkirche – was there with his friends and banners. They also brought with them disabled German soldiers, without guns. Possibly the authorities permitted such demonstrations because the deployment of American medium-range nuclear missiles to West Germany was a source of constant Soviet insecurity, but that did not detract from the solemn sincerity of the young protestors, and their own fears for what seemed a hair-trigger future. With the annihila-tion of Dresden well within living memory, it did not require any great imagination to envisage the lightning flash and searing radio-active wind of nuclear detonation. There were already conspiracy theories that, during the war, the Allies had been planning to use Dresden as a testing ground for that very first atom bomb.

Meanwhile, though, Feydt's grandmother, who had loved the Frauenkirche, was an optimist: she foresaw that at some point in the future it would be perfectly restored. Might she also have envisaged the astounding recreation of so much else in Dresden? Not just the perfect baroque detailing on restored buildings from the Zwinger-garten to the Japanese Palace, but the restored villas, the replanted trees, even the careful renovations of what might have become lour-ing examples of cheap Soviet architecture. At the centre of all this stands the Frauenkirche; for what was also achieved – and still very much stands today – was the abiding principle of reconciliation, of cooperation and shared endeavour between Germany and Britain, even as the passionate debates about the criminality of the bombers continued. Dresden at last found a way of containing and preserving its darkest night, in such a way that the entire world might see, and understand, and not recoil.

27. Beauty and Remembrance

A great chain of people, arms linked, lining the square: overcoats, quilted jackets, hats, breath ghostly in the cold. It is the evening of 13 February. The sun has long set, and the deep note of the bell in the darkness produces stillness and reflection. The chime, repeated and repeated; everyone looking into the dark sky sees the same thing: the planes flying over. They are not there, but the relentlessly tolling bell somehow invokes a collective memory. Among all these people in the Altmarkt, standing near the Kreuzkirche, are visitors from overseas, from America to China. Everyone here, no matter where they have come from, knows what happened. This is the annual commemoration of the bombing.

The human chain is an idea partly in response to the ever-present attempts by others to hijack the anniversary: the far right-wingers who want Germans to be understood as martyrs to a war crime. There are extremists in every society, but Dresdeners appreciate that their city is an unusually sensitive shrine and that shrines can be desecrated if guards are dropped. It has taken many decades but Dresden can truly be said to be restored, both aesthetically and spiritually. And the dead are never forgotten.

Each year on this date there are other events, too: addresses by politicians outside the main council building; a rendition in the Kreuzkirche of Mauersberger's *Dresdner Requiem* (the piece is about an hour long, is performed to a completely packed audience and is almost overpoweringly moving); then, later, at 9.45 p.m., at the moment when the air-raid sirens found their full throat in 1945, all the bells in the city start to ring. The noise is deeply unsettling; in that echoing discordancy, the different notes and tones bouncing off so many restored walls and streets, there is a taste of gathering fear; of fast-approaching horror. Stand by the Frauenkirche as these bells ring out and you see crowds of people in the great square before it, rooted to the spot, and again staring at the sky. All the bells of the city, in their clangour, are urging escape; they speak of a world of order being violently overturned. They ring out until 10.03 p.m.; the minute the bombs started falling. In the sudden gaping silence, candles are lit and placed on the cobbles of the square; hundreds of them, in a specially marked area. For some, this is a moment of prayer – even of communion with forebears who died that night; for others an extraordinary glimpse of the depth of feeling that courses through the veins of the city still.

But all of this makes Dresden sound morbid, when in fact quite the opposite is true. The city today is extraordinarily light, alive and blithe. And the curious thing is this: the restoration ought to appear ersatz, yet there is not one moment when anything seems less than wholly authentic, from the rebuilt streets of the Altstadt, to the amazing repurposing of the castle by the river (now a literally dazzling museum, filled with porcelain treasures, golden ornaments and richly jewelled swords). The opera house is – as it was throughout the nineteenth and early twentieth centuries – world renowned for artistic range and innovation. And once more, this is a city that art lovers swarm to in great numbers. As well as the array of Old Masters in the Zwinger galleries, there is now in the Albertinum museum a brilliant display of nineteenth- and twentieth-century works: Caspar David Friedrich's most immersive and troubling landscapes a floor apart from the raw rigour of Otto Dix's First World War canvases. And those post-war communist artists are honoured too; portraits and studies that now have their own layers of political as well as aesthetic depth. The overall sense is that the city has been able to knit time together, drawing the past closer to the present, repairing the great rent caused by Nazism and the February 1945 catastrophe.

It has not been easy to reach this point of reconciliation, though, and in the patient and infinitely loving restoration of the Frauenkirche are to be found all the interlocking strands of grief, loss, guilt and responsibility. Ever since the dome's collapse there had been Dresdeners who yearned to see it rise again, but the GDR's priorities lay firmly elsewhere and there was simply not the money either from the Lutheran Church or from the local authorities even to consider it. Both the Catholic cathedral by the castle, and the Kreuzkirche, found financial champions for repair, and these works were relatively straightforward; but to re-erect the eccentric baroque structure on Neumarkt would take real engineering ingenuity as well as money. In an age when houses urgently had to be built, such frivolity could not be countenanced. It was proposed at one point that the fractured remnants of walls, and the heap of rubble, should simply be swept away.

But they were not, and for four decades, this haunted landmark symbolized a city in a twilight state. When the GDR and the Soviet Union collapsed, and the reunification of Germany followed, this attitude changed, partly because now a wider world was taking an interest. By 1992 it was agreed: the Frauenkirche would be rebuilt – in every particular – exactly as it was when the original architect George Bähr planned his vision in 1726. It would be easy to assume that modern technology would make easy work of this mighty eighteenth-century undertaking, but in fact the project soon became an intense exercise in applied mathematics and geometry as architects and engineers sought to recreate the extraordinarily delicate feat of counterbalance and support that made the magnificent stone dome, and the church's intricately galleried interior, possible. Here was a return to the principles of masonry; certainly computer modelling was useful but, in the end, this was a construction based on human ingenuity and care.

The work began: excavation of the rubble in order to use as many of the original eighteenth-century stones as possible; more sandstone quarried from the same source a few miles away; the rescue of one surviving bell and the recreation in workshops of others. And by this stage, as part of a determined effort in reconciliation, a British charity – the Dresden Trust – made its own wonderful contribution.

The idea had been sparked in part by a controversial event in London: the unveiling of a privately financed statue to Sir Arthur Harris in the Strand in 1992. The Queen Mother presided over the ceremony, but there were protestors who thought it was an outrage that such honour should be bestowed upon a man they regarded as a war criminal. The bitterness was sharp on both sides (and proved the start of a longer-running controversy concerning Bomber Command and the ways in which its aircrews should be remembered). Partly this was a conflict of culture, for it was the young left who voiced their opposition most stridently. Tangentially, the Harris statue subsequently being splashed with paint by activists was the catalyst for the Dresden Trust to start educating the younger generation about the bombing of the city and the wider conflict. One of the Trust's ideas was inspired: an offer to recreate the golden orb and cross that had been at the top of the Frauenkirche dome. Academics from Germany and Manchester met to discuss the elaborate patterning and dimensions of this massive ornament. The contract to construct it went to silversmiths Grant Macdonald of London; and serendipitously, one of the skilled craftsmen drafted to work on this intense project – Alan Smith – revealed himself to be the son of one of the bomber pilots who had taken part in the Dresden raid.

As with the structure of the main building, there were an array of challenges that required a form of mental time travel in order to summon back this golden eighteenth-century masterpiece, standing some twenty feet in height, comprising intricate elements originally known as The Clouds of Heaven, Jacob's Tears and The Rays of Glory, each descriptive of elaborate patterning in and around the base and the cross. When it was finished in 1999, the result was so beautiful that it was decided that it should tour Britain before being presented to Dresden. It also received patronage and acknowledgement of the proudest order when it was displayed to the royal family at Windsor Castle. The following year, amid grand ceremonies, the Duke of Kent accompanied it to Germany, where it was presented to the citizens of Dresden. Dr Alan Russell, one of the guiding lights of the Dresden Trust, which had secured so many charitable donations for this work, was certain that it would not only help with reconciliation but also serve as acknowledgement of British responsibility, a gesture that the British themselves might understand as a token of atonement.

The restoration of the church was complete by 2005, so perfect in every detail that it has in itself become a source of wonder for both tourists and pilgrims. Pastor Sebastian Feydt laughs that there are a few who find the interior a shade too colourful, the whites and the golds too bright, but that is how the church originally looked. Equally, the pale sandstone of the exterior is contrasted with 1930s photographs of the church that showed its outer walls blackened with soot. But time will attend to these differences. The stone will darken and, over the coming decades, the pale pinks and blues of the interior will naturally fade in intensity; and then the church will be exactly what it was.

Any work of restoration on such an amazingly intricate scale invites the unworthy thought that it can be no more than an elaborate simulacrum, that the new structure cannot philosophically be the same as the old, and so any attempt to make it so is simply an exercise in fine historical kitsch. But the visitor finds otherwise, for in absorbing the richness of the circular interior and climbing the narrow spiral stairs right up past the stone dome to the top of the church there is a sense of both solidity and deep pride that wholly removes any suggestion of inauthenticity. Then there is the view from that high exterior. Not every building in the reconstructed Altstadt streets conforms exactly to its forebear, but the shape of the roofs and the patterns of the streetscape themselves are faithful to those of the 1930s. The gaze is then drawn to the tranquil winding Elbe and the wooded hills beyond.

Before the Frauenkirche reconstruction there had been another move to rebuild a relationship with England. In 1959 Dresden was twinned with the city of Coventry, itself extensively rebuilt after the 1940 bombing attack that had burned out its medieval heart, destroyed its cathedral and melted iron to the point where molten rivulets of dissolved plumbing hissed down glowing walls. In Dresden, people – specifically older people – are solicitous about mentioning Coventry whenever the subject of air raids is raised; indeed, there are Dresdeners who think a very great deal more about Coventry than most people in England.

The debate in recent years has become more specifically about whether the bombing of Dresden was a war crime. From the work of the late W. G. Sebald, who wrote *On the Natural History of Destruction*, to the fissile thesis of Jörg Friedrich's *The Fire* (that German civilians were indeed very much victims) to a philosophical work by A. C. Grayling, *Among the Dead Cities*, the ethics have been explored with some vigour, not to mention melancholy and anger. The phrase 'war crime' has a legal precision which has been examined by academic Donald Bloxham[1] in this context: weighing up the condemnations of – and possible justifications for – area bombings and placing Dresden in the context of other atrocities committed by both Germans and British.

We might also, after seventy-five years, say this: 'war crime' above all implies intentionality and rational decision-making, and this raises another possibility. War creates its own nauseous gravity, and towards the end of a six-year conflict, with millions dead, all sides exhausted, could it be that these city bombings were not vengeful or consciously merciless, but ever more desperate reflexive attacks launched to make the other side simply *stop*? Just as it cannot be assumed that individuals always act with perfect rationality, so the same must be said for entire organizations acting with one will. Much as the Frauenkirche and its dome and its mighty stones were (and are) held in place by unseen counterbalancing geometric forces, so war might be viewed as analogous to the dislocation of society's fine balance; that any conflict of such duration and scale will in the end create repercussions that start to chip away at the foundations of sanity itself, and in so doing reveal the inherent delicacy of civilization. The question after all this time is this: given the unalterable horror of 25,000 people being killed in one night, and given that the bombing was unquestionably an atrocity, intended or not, is there anything at all to be gained now in terms of solace or restitution by pursuing legally precise accusations?

For some Germans, there has possibly always been a greater sense of balance in the arguments. In his 1947 novel *Doctor Faustus*, concerning the life of a genius composer prior to and during the rise of Hitler, German author Thomas Mann's narrator observes: 'we have experienced the destruction of our noble cities from the air, a destruction that would cry to heaven if we who suffer were not ourselves laden with guilt. As it is, the cry is smothered in our throats: like King Claudius's prayer, it can "never to heaven go".'

There are many in Dresden now who are also careful to acknowledge the origins of the war, before making broader judgements on the bombing. But in any case, and in so many other ways, the city itself has made it plain that the key is remembrance, and that the bombing must be taken not as a singular event but rather as a universal symbol of the horror of all wars. Dresden has a beautifully designed military history museum, sitting north of the city on the gentle hill overlooking the distant spires. The structure – a former nineteenth-century military barracks – has a distinctive addition, or extension, shaped like vast geometric shrapnel, several storeys high, sticking into the front of the building. It was designed by Daniel Libeskind, and in the top floor of this 'shrapnel' extension, almost open to the sky, is a permanent exhibit dedicated to the bombing: nothing more than a series of stones and cobbles laid out upon the floor.

If you leave the museum and go back down the hill to the river and the Altstadt, you pass through cheerful nineteenth-century streets filled with students and trendy cafes and little craft shops, a diorama of diversity and youth and relaxation. Since reunification, Dresden has received a great deal of federal funding: the tram system is swish and fast, the museums and galleries are rich and illuminating, a new modernist synagogue complex stands by Brühl's Terrace and the theatre and the opera attract artists from around the world. There are visitors in abundance; and in many other ways the city has wholly rediscovered and embraced its old cosmopolitan soul. Near the Palace of Culture and the Frauenkirche, the streets in the summer echo and resonate with music; the buskers here are of quite a different quality from those to be found in any other European city. Violinists play nineteenth-century classics; a cappella tenors give ad-lib excerpts from operas. There can be a giddy exultation in the amber glow of a warm sunset, and as exquisite notes are briefly conjoined with the jangling bells of the Hofkirche the sheer depth of noise conveys the sense of life more fully than anything else.

Even in the icy air of December, Dresden is full, glowing in the sort of Christmas kitsch that reflects childhood dreams. In the short afternoons, as the sky turns sapphire, then darker still, the wide space of the Altmarkt becomes a delightful wooden maze of log-cabin market stalls, selling mulled wine and assorted gifts, and the whole square is illuminated in rich reds and greens. At each turn of the hour, in the crisp, cold dark, the heavy bell of the Kreuzkirche rings out deeply. And you momentarily remember that you are never more than a few steps away from the past.

Acknowledgements

First, my enormous gratitude and thanks to the Dresden Stadtarchiv and all those who work there; its vast collection extends far beyond all those haunting diaries and accounts of the night of 13 February 1945. Here, just a short leafy journey from the city centre on the number 7 tram, are books, maps, documents, even ledgers, stretching back through 800 years of colourful Dresden history. My particular thanks to the director, Thomas Kubler, whose terrific energy and insight set me on the right paths; and to Claudia Richert, who is hugely knowledgeable and equally sharp.

Elsewhere in Dresden, I owe huge thanks to Peter Schaffrath, both for warm hospitality and for the most invaluable tour of the city that opened my eyes to other corners of its history; to Maximilian Limbourg, for introducing me to Herr Kubler and Herr Schaffrath, and also guiding me through crucial aspects of Dresden culture, architecture and industry. My gratitude as well to Pastor Sebastian Feydt, who oversees the Frauenkirche, for taking so much time to see me, and for so many fascinating stories.

I was introduced to him by Eveline Eaton, chair of the Dresden Trust; also measurelessly helpful has been artist Monica Petzal, also of the Dresden Trust. The Trust is a British charity devoted, as it states, to 'healing the wounds of war'; it has been involved in some terrific work with the city, from the crafting of the exquisite orb and cross mentioned in the final chapter, to the recent planting of trees in Neumarkt. For full details of their rich and varied projects with the city, visit www.dresdentrust.org.

Thank you to Paul Addison, Sebastian Cox and Nadine Zimmerli for reading and commenting on the manuscript. Any mistakes that remain are my own.

My thanks also to Christ Church College, Oxford, at which can be found the papers of Viscount Portal, and to Steven Archer, who made me most welcome in the library. My gratitude to the archivists at the RAF Museum in Hendon, where can be found the private papers of Sir Arthur Harris. Equally fascinating are the collections of the memories and experiences of aircrews to be found at the Imperial War Museum, London. Additional thanks to the London Library, which holds some unexpected and hugely useful treasures deep in its stacks, to the British Library, which has made period newspaper research so addictive that it is difficult to leave at closing time, and also to the National Archives, Kew, where the range and abundance of primary sources are equally mesmerizing.

At Viking, my debt to publisher Daniel Crewe is enormous, first and not least because the idea for the book was his. And I am also hugely grateful for his raptor eye and keen judgement in terms of the initial drafts. Thanks also to assistant editor Connor Brown, sharp with ideas and suggestions. Countless thanks to copy-editor Trevor Horwood for laser-beam scrutiny and aliveness to history and the power of language; to Emma Brown for formidable editorial management; to Sarah Scarlett for her work on the English language rights; to Sam Fanaken for ensuring the book's sales profile; and to Rose Poole in marketing and Olivia Mead in publicity for helping to make certain that the anniversary of Dresden will be remembered and marked.

Huge thanks as always to my brilliant agent Anna Power, who started all this, and also to Helene Butler, who has worked tirelessly across a range of territories.

A quick apology to my father for the tardiness of his own promised trip to Dresden – we will get there very soon; and a thank you to my mother, who *did* get her promised trip there, and who was mesmerized by – among other things – the vast GDR mosaic upon the Palace of Culture. The city itself is so hospitable, and so beautiful, so rich in art and music and also in fascinating walks through friendly streets, that I wish we were all there right now.

Selected Bibliography

Paul Addison and Jeremy A. Crang (eds.), *Firestorm: The Bombing of Dresden 1945* (Pimlico, 2006)

Jörg Arnold, *The Allied Air War and Urban Memory: The Legacy of Strategic Bombing in Germany* (Cambridge University Press, 2011)

Paul Betts, *Within Walls: Private Life in the German Democratic Republic* (Oxford University Press, 2010)

Martin Bowman, *Castles in the Air: The Story of the B17 Flying Fortress Crews of the US 8th Air Force* (Patrick Stephens, 1984)

Giulio Douhet, *The Command of the Air* (Faber and Faber, 1943)

Freeman Dyson, *Disturbing the Universe* (Harper & Row, 1979)

Sheila Fitzpatrick, *Mischka's War: A Story of Survival from War-Torn Europe to New York* (I. B. Tauris, 2017)

Roger Freeman, *Bases of Bomber Command: Then and Now* (Battle of Britain International, 2001)

Jörg Friedrich, *The Fire: The Bombing of Germany, 1940–1945* (Columbia University Press, 2006)

Mary Fulbrook and Andrew Port (eds.), *Becoming East German: Socialist Structures and Sensibilities After Hitler* (Berghahn Books, 2013)

Stephen A. Garrett, *Ethics and Airpower in World War II: The British Bombing of German Cities* (St. Martin's Press, 1993)

Robert Gerwarth, *The Vanquished: Why the First World War Failed to End, 1917–1923* (Allen Lane, 2016)

A. C. Grayling, *Among the Dead Cities: Is the Targeting of Civilians in War Ever Justified?* (Bloomsbury, 2006)

Sir Arthur Harris, *Bomber Offensive* (Collins, 1947)

Max Hastings, *Bomber Command* (Michael Joseph, 1979)

E. T. A. Hoffmann, *Selected Writings of E. T. A. Hoffmann*, trans. Leonard Kent and Elizabeth Knight (University of Chicago Press, 1969)

Tony Judt, *Postwar: A History of Europe Since 1945* (Heinemann, 2005)

Erich Kästner, *When I Was a Little Boy*, trans. Isabel and Florence McHugh (Jonathan Cape, 1959)

Ian Kershaw, *The End: Hitler's Germany, 1944–45* (Allen Lane, 2011)

Victor Klemperer, *I Shall Bear Witness: The Diaries of Victor Klemperer 1933–41*, trans. Martin Chalmers (Weidenfeld and Nicolson, 1998)

————, *To the Bitter End: The Diaries of Victor Klemperer 1942–45*, trans. Martin Chalmers (Weidenfeld and Nicolson 1999)

————, *The Lesser Evil: The Diaries of Victor Klemperer 1945–59*, trans. Martin Chalmers (Weidenfeld and Nicolson, 2003)

Fritz Löffler, *Otto Dix: Life and Work* (Holmes and Meier, 1982)

Heinrich Magirius, *Die Dresdner Frauenkirche von Georg Bähr. Entstehung und Bedeutung* (Deutscher Verlag für Kunstwissenschaft, 2005)

Thomas Mann, *Doctor Faustus* (Secker and Warburg, 1949)

Masterpieces from Dresden, guide accompanying the Royal Academy exhibition of art from the Gemäldegalerie Alte Meister (Thames and Hudson, 2003)

Anne McElvoy, *The Saddled Cow: East Germany's Life and Legacy* (Faber and Faber, 1992)

Leo McKinstry, *Lancaster: The Second World War's Greatest Bomber* (John Murray, 2009)

Ingelore Menzhausen, *Early Meissen Porcelain in Dresden* (Thames and Hudson, 1990)

Donald Miller, *Eighth Air Force: The American Bomber Crews in Britain* (Aurum, 2007)

Michael Miller and Andreas Schulz, *Gauleiter: The Regional Leaders of the Nazi Party and Their Deputies* (R. James Bender Publishing, 2012)

Roger Moorhouse, *Berlin at War: Life and Death in Hitler's Capital, 1939–45* (Bodley Head, 2010)

Richard Overy, *The Bombing War: Europe 1939–1945* (Allen Lane, 2013)

Henry Probert, *Bomber Harris: His Life and Times – The Biography of Marshal of the Royal Air Force Sir Arthur Harris* (Greenhill Books, 2001)

Walter Reichart, *Washington Irving and Germany* (University of Michigan Press, 1957)

Alan Russell, *An Englishman Speaks Out – On Dresden, On Destruction, On Reconciliation and Rebuilding* (Dresden Trust, 2015)

————, *A Trust for Our Times: The Story of the Dresden Trust* (Dresden Trust, 2015)

W. G. Sebald, *On the Natural History of Destruction* (Hamish Hamilton, 2003)

Richard Strauss and Stefan Zweig, *A Confidential Matter: The Letters of Richard Strauss and Stefan Zweig, 1931–1935*, trans. Max Knight (University of California Press, 1977)

Daniel Swift, *Bomber County* (Hamish Hamilton, 2010)

Dirk Syndram, *The Green Vault in Dresden: Renaissance and Baroque Treasury Art*, trans. Daniel Kletke (Staatliche Kunstsammlungen Dresden, 2004)

Frederick Taylor, *Dresden: Tuesday 13 February 1945* (Bloomsbury, 2004)

Adam Tooze, *The Deluge: The Great War and the Remaking of Global Order, 1916–1931* (Allen Lane, 2014)

Miles Tripp, *The Eighth Passenger: A Flight of Recollection and Discovery* (Heinemann, 1969; repr. Leo Cooper, 1993)

Kurt Vonnegut, *Slaughterhouse-Five; or The Children's Crusade – A Duty-Dance with Death* (Cape, 1970)

——, *Kurt Vonnegut: Letters*, ed. and intro. Dan Wakefield (Vintage, 2013)

Richard Wagner, *My Life* (Constable, 1911)

H. G. Wells, *The War in the Air* (George Bell, 1908)

Stefan Zweig, *The World of Yesterday: Memoirs of a European* (Cassell, 1943; repr. Pushkin Press, 2009)

Notes

1. The Days Before

1 Gerhard Ackermann, interviewed in the popular German newspaper *Bild*, 1 January 2018, a piece focusing slightly more upon his lifelong addiction to cinema-going rather than upon Dresden.

2 Corey Ross, 'Mass Culture and Divided Audiences: Cinema and Social Change in Inter-War Germany', *Past & Present*, no. 193 (November 2006).

3 Ibid.

4 Interview with Churchill's interpreter Hugh Lunghi for National Security Archive, 1 July 1996.

5 Ibid.

6 Jörg Arnold, *The Allied Air War and Urban Memory* (Cambridge University Press, 2011).

7 Dresden City Archives, series 6.4.53.1 (hereafter DCA), file 500.

8 DCA, file 477.

9 Tami Davis Biddle, 'Dresden 1945: Reality, History and Memory', *Journal of Military History*, vol. 72, no. 2 (2008).

10 DCA, file 107.

11 Victor Klemperer, *To the Bitter End: The Diaries of Victor Klemperer 1942–45*, trans. Martin Chalmers (Weidenfeld and Nicolson, 1999).

12 DCA, file 500.

13 Ibid.

14 Klemperer, *To the Bitter End*.

15 DCA, file 107.

16 An article in the arts journal *The Burlington Magazine* in April 2007 described the station as being one of Europe's most 'ethereal'.

17 See www.das-neue-dresden.de/kaufhaus-alsberg for an article on the architectural history, as well as the expropriation by the Nazis.

18 There is a haunting portrait of Elsa Frölich, and her daughter Sunni, drawn by fellow communist Lea Grundig in the mid 1930s; both Frölich and Grundig would flourish under the post-war regime.

19 DCA, file 475. Pleasingly, the brewery's tunnels have recently been repurposed by Dresden University physicists for atom-colliding experiments.

20 The dairy today has a dedicated website (www.pfunds.de) and is still one of Dresden's most pleasing and unexpected aesthetic spectacles.

21 Today the site is a stately and rather old-fashioned hotel; see www. schloss-eckberg.de.

2. In the Forests of the Gauleiter

1 A memo sent from Lord Cherwell to Churchill on 30 March 1942 in which he speculated about 'de-housing' one third of the German population; as cited in Richard Overy, *The Bombing War: Europe 1939–1945* (Allen Lane, 2013).

2 Harris Papers, RAF Museum Archive, Hendon, file 40.

3 Harris Papers – 'Correspondence with Supreme Headquarters Allied Expeditionary Force'.

4 Sir Arthur Harris, *Bomber Offensive* (Collins, 1947).

5 Ibid. Harris, although styling himself as a curt colonial, had a feel for passionate and emotional rhetoric, of which there were echoes to be heard in his message to Bomber Command – 'Special Order of the Day' – issued on 10 May 1945, Harris Papers, folder 40.

6 Harris, *Bomber Offensive*.

7 Ibid.

8 Ibid. He deployed the term in correspondence with his superiors.

9 DCA, file 101.

10 DCA, file 802.

11 Victor Klemperer, *I Shall Bear Witness: The Diaries of Victor Klemperer 1933–41*, trans. Martin Chalmers (Weidenfeld and Nicolson, 1998).

12 The artist Monica Petzal – a key figure in the Dresden Trust – has written fascinatingly of her mother, Hannelore Isakowitz, who was brought up in

the city; as a girl, Hannelore saw Dresden at its height of sophistication and artistic richness. Monica Petzal's work, which exhibits in a range of galleries, explores the ghostly echoes of that city. For more information on her work see www.monicapetzal.com.

13 Dr Margarete Blank is often written about in German journals; and not just because of her execution at the hands of the Nazis. There are also portraits of the life of a female doctor in the early years of the twentieth century, and also articles to do with the way her memory was used by the post-war communists. For a concise and illuminating short biography see www.leipzig.de.

14 For a concise biography of Mutschmann see www.spitzenstadt.de.

15 Bizarrely, this item turned up on the online auction site www.liveauc tioneers.com in February 2017, complete with a snap of Mutschmann's inscription.

16 *Daily Telegraph*, 27 January 1933.

17 E. T. A. Hoffmann's 'The Automata' was published in 1814. Two years later, in 'The Sandman', there is an even creepier fragment involving a young woman called Olimpia who beguiles the young hero; that young man is then driven mad when he discovers that she is clockwork, and he sees her eyes upon the floor.

18 The Nazi war on jazz music is fascinatingly explored in Michael H. Kater, 'Forbidden Fruit? Jazz in the Third Reich', *American Historical Review*, vol. 94, no. 1 (February 1989).

19 Patrick Merziger, 'Humour in Nazi Germany: Resistance and Propaganda?', *International Review of Social History*, vol. 52 (December 2007).

20 *Daily Telegraph*, 25 May 1935.

21 *Daily Telegraph*, 25 April 1935.

22 *Daily Telegraph*, 20 October 1937.

23 An interesting short biography can be found at db.yadvashem.org/ deportation/supervisors.

24 A terrifying portrait of Hans Clemens can be found in Klemperer, *To the Bitter End*, and a fascinating piece in *Der Spiegel* (www.spiegel.de) from 16 February 2011 details his murky post-war career in Soviet espionage.

25 For an interesting and concise biography of Dr Kluge see Sächsische Biografie, http://saebi.isgv.de/biografie/Rudolf_Kluge_(1889-1945).

26 See Sächsische Biografie, saebi.isgv.de/biografie/Hans_Nieland_(1900–1976).

27 http://saebi.isgv.de/biografie/Rudolf_Kluge_(1889-1945).

3. The Dethroning of Reason

1 For an extraordinary essay concerning Wagner, his friendship with the synagogue's architect Semper, and his desire to have a copy of the lamp that hung before the tabernacle doors see Colin Eisler, 'Wagner's Three Synagogues', *Artibus et Historiae*, vol. 25, no. 50 (January 2004).

2 Helen Rosenau, 'Gottfried Semper and German Synagogue Architecture', *Leo Baeck Institute Year Book*, vol. 22 (January 1977).

3 Ibid.

4 Ibid.

5 Ibid.

6 For the restoration of the synagogue and its star, see 'Dresden Synagogue Rises Again', news.bbc.co.uk/1/hi/world/europe/1647310.stm.

7 The demolition was filmed by the Technisches Hilfswerk, a civil protection organization controlled by the German federal government; fragments of the film are to be found on YouTube, though it is the sort of footage that attracts unsavoury viewers.

8 The story of Erich Isakowitz is related by his granddaughter, the artist Monica Petzal. As well as creating powerful and haunting works inspired by her family and the city, Petzal has written of her family in brochures to accompany 'Indelible Marks: The Dresden Project'. For further information, see www.monicapetzal.com.

9 Ibid.

10 Ibid.

11 Klemperer, *I Shall Bear Witness*.

12 Ibid.

13 Stefan Zweig, *The World of Yesterday: Memoirs of a European* (Cassell, 1943; repr. Pushkin Press, 2009).

14 Timothy W. Ryback, *Hitler's First Victims: And One Man's Race for Justice* (Bodley Head, 2015).

15 See www.monicapetzal.com.

16 Klemperer, *I Shall Bear Witness*.

17 Zweig, *The World of Yesterday*.

18 Klemperer, *I Shall Bear Witness*.

19 Ibid.

20 These insights among others are discussed by John Wesley Young, in 'From LTI to LQI: Victor Klemperer on Totalitarian Language', *German Studies Review*, vol. 28 (February 2005).

21 Henry Ashby Turner, Jr, 'Victor Klemperer's Holocaust', *German Studies Review*, vol. 22 (October 1999).

22 Young, 'From LTI to LQI'.

23 Stills from surviving film clips can be seen at en.stsg.de/cms/node/815 – the Saxon Memorial Foundation.

4. Art and Degeneracy

1 The subject of *Hamlet* in Dresden – and other Shakespeare adaptations around the country in the seventeenth century – is discussed by Simon Williams in *Shakespeare on the German Stage* (Cambridge University Press, 2004).

2 DCA, file 802.

3 Ibid.

4 The exhibits of such richly jewelled swords – and other wonders in gold, porcelain and tapestry – are now permanently on show in the Dresden Royal Palace. The site www.schloesserland-sachsen.de/en/palaces-castles-and-gardens/dresden-royal-palace/ gives a taste of the other aesthetic wonders.

5 As with the Royal Palace and its Green Vault, the Zwinger Galleries – literally across the road – are so fully restored that it is possible to spend days in them. For an overview of their exhibitions and works, it is worth looking at www.der-dresdner-zwinger.de/en/home/.

6 Ibid.

7 Ibid.

8 Dresden's modern art museum, the Albertinum, contains many of Friedrich's works among its dazzling array of exhibits. See albertinum.skd.museum/en.

9 For a discussion of Nolde see Michael Hoffmann, 'At One with the Universe', *London Review of Books*, 27 September 2018.

10 See Ian Buruma, 'Art of a Degenerate World', *New York Review of Books*, 27 September 2018.

11 Dix's nightmares and the psychological impact of war upon his work are explored in fascinating detail by Paul Fox in 'Confronting Postwar Shame in Weimar Germany: Trauma, Heroism and the War Art of Otto Dix', *Oxford Art Journal*, vol. 29, no. 2 (June 2006).

12 Felixmüller was a friend of the Isakowitz family; examples of his work are at www.monicapetzal.com.

13 A short illustrated overview of Griebel's work can be found at weimar art.blogspot.com/2010/06/otto-griebel.html.

14 A further analysis of the exhibition and its internal aesthetic conflicts is Neil Levi, "Judge for Yourselves!" – The *'Degenerate Art* Exhibition as Political Spectacle', *October*, vol. 85 (Summer 1998).

15 There is an interesting blogspot on the original Dresden 'Degenerate Art' exhibition and the works featured, plus the evolution of this artistic persecution, at hausderkunst.de/en/notes/beschlagnahme-der-entarteten-kunst-1937-1938.

16 As well as an illuminating range of his work in the Dresden Albertinum (see note 8 above), there is a good essay on earlier subjects before his dismissal and reluctant move into landscape studies by Sabine Rewald in 'Dix at the Met', *Metropolitan Museum Journal*, vol. 31 (1996).

17 For a short biography of Mauersberger and a range of photographs through the decades see www.bach-cantatas.com/Bio/Mauersberger-Rudolf.htm.

18 An interesting blog on Mauersberger and the Kreuzchor together with excerpts from his *Dresdner Requiem* can be found at www.overgrown path.com/2006/02/dresden-requiem-for-eleven-young.html.

19 Siegfried Gerlach, *George Bähr. Der Erbauer der Dresdner Frauenkirche. Ein Zeitbild* (Böhlau, 2005).

20 Perhaps rather startlingly, a recording was made of this 1944 performance and was available into the 1990s.

21 Robert Giddings, 'Wagner and the Revolutionaries', *Music & Letters*, vol. 45, no. 4 (October 1964).

22 Hans Rudolf Vaget, 'Wagnerian Self-Fashioning: The Case of Adolf Hitler', *New German Critique*, no. 101 (Summer 2007).

23 Elena Gerhardt, 'Strauss and His Lieder', *Tempo*, no. 12 (Summer 1949), is a charming personal reminiscence that also mentions the occasion he took the Dresden Opera Company to London in 1936.

24 Zweig, *The World of Yesterday*, for this and what follows.

25 Zweig's time as an exile in Brazil was dramatized in a film reviewed – with some background – in *The Economist* in 2016: www.economist.com/prospero/2016/06/22/stefan-zweig-in-exile-a-european-in-brazil.

26 Thomas Eisner, 'Fritz Busch: A Friend Remembered', *Musical Quarterly*, vol. 85 (Autumn 2001).

27 Raffaele De Ritis, 'Circus Sarrasani', www.circopedia.org/Circus_Sarrasani.

28 Ibid.

29 Hay's memoir – 'An Old Airman's Tale', as told to Malcolm Brooke – is available at www.bomberhistory.co.uk.

5. The Glass Man and the Physicists

1 For a short biography see https://ethw.org/Heinrich_Barkhausen.

2 There is more at the Dresden university website: https://tu-dresden.de/ing/elektrotechnik/dic-fakultaet/profil/100-jahre-schwachstromtechnik.

3 Sheila Fitzpatrick, *Mischka's War: A Story of Survival from War-Torn Europe to New York* (I. B. Tauris, 2017).

4 Ibid.

5 Ibid.

6 Clare Le Corbeiller, 'German Porcelain of the Eighteenth Century', *Metropolitan Museum of Art Bulletin*, vol. 47 (Spring 1990).

7 Ibid.

8 Ibid.

9 Edmund de Waal wrote movingly about this theme in the *Guardian*, 18 September 2015.

10 Ibid.

11 Ibid.

12 Eike Reichardt, *Health, 'Race' and Empire: Popular-Scientific Spectacles and National Identity in Imperial Germany, 1871–1914* (Lulu.com, 2008).

13 Ibid.

14 Ibid.

15 Paul Weindling, *Health, Race and German Politics Between National Unifi-cation and Nazism, 1870–1945* (Cambridge University Press, 1993). The Hygiene Eye painting was by Franz von Stuck.

16 Vintage examples of these cameras can be found pictured lovingly on a great number of websites. More on the history of the firm can be found in Michael Buckland, 'Histories, Heritages and the Past: The Case of Emanuel Goldberg', in W. Boyd Rayward and Mary Ellen Bowden (eds.), *The History and Heritage of Scientific and Technological Information Systems* (Information Today, 2002).

17 Ibid.; Buckland's essay focuses on how Professor Goldberg's name was both systematically and accidentally erased from histories of scientific innovation.

18 Klemperer, *I Shall Bear Witness*.

6. 'A Sort of Little London'

1 DCA, file 855, for this and what follows.

2 DCA, file 107.

3 Tami Davis Biddle, 'Sifting Dresden's Ashes', *Wilson Quarterly*, vol. 29 (Spring 2005).

4 Jeremy Black, *The British and the Grand Tour* (Routledge Revivals, 2011).

5 Walter A. Reichart, 'Washington Irving's Influence in German Litera-ture', *Modern Language Review*, vol. 52, no. 4 (October 1957).

6 Nadine Zimmerli, 'Elite Migration to Germany: The Anglo-American Colony in Dresden Before World War 1', in Jason Coy et al. (eds.), *Migrations in the German Lands, 1500–2000* (Berghahn Books, 2016).

7 Ibid.

8 Digital versions of these advertisements, as featured in the *Daily Tele-graph* and *Daily Mail*, can be seen at the British Library Newspaper Archive.

9 Charles Shields, *And So It Goes: Kurt Vonnegut, a Life* (Henry Holt, 2011).

10 Kurt Vonnegut, *Kurt Vonnegut: Letters*, ed. and intro. Dan Wakefield (Vintage, 2013).

11 Ibid.

12 Victor Gregg with Rick Stroud, *Dresden: A Survivor's Story, February 1945* (Bloomsbury, 2019), for this and what follows.

13 Miles Tripp, *The Eighth Passenger: A Flight of Recollection and Discovery* (Heinemann, 1969; repr. Leo Cooper, 1993), for this and what follows.

7. The Science of Doomsday

1 Harris, *Bomber Offensive*, for this and what follows.

2 Ibid.

3 Cited in Abigail Chantler, *E. T. A. Hoffmann's Musical Aesthetics* (Routledge, 2006).

4 An interesting essay by Patrick Wright – 'Dropping Their Eggs' in the *London Review of Books*, 23 August 2001 – explores how the RAF's Hugh Trenchard deployed that startling phrase to describe how bombs would fall on city centres before the end of the First World War.

5 Malcolm Smith, ' "A Matter of Faith": British Strategic Air Doctrine Before 1939', *Journal of Contemporary History*, vol. 15 (July 1980).

6 The anxieties surrounding the possibilities of city bombing are explored in Overy, *The Bombing War*.

7 As discussed in Philip K. Lawrence, *Modernity and War: The Creed of Absolute Violence* (Macmillan, 1997).

8 As cited in Hew Strachan, 'Strategic Bombing and the Question of Civilian Casualties up to 1945', in Paul Addison and Jeremy A. Crang (eds.), *Firestorm: The Bombing of Dresden 1945* (Pimlico, 2006).

9 Ibid.

10 Ibid.

11 Ibid.

12 Stewart Holbrook, 'The Peshtigo Fire', *American Scholar*, vol. 13, no. 2 (Spring 1944), is an extremely atmospheric retelling of the catastrophe. See also 'Nature's Nuclear Explosion', in Denise Gess and William Lutz, *Firestorm at Peshtigo: A Town, Its People, and the Deadliest Fire in American History* (Holt, 2003).

13 Philip G. Terrie, ' "The Necessities of the Case": The Response to the Great Thumb Fire of 1881', *Michigan Historical Review*, vol. 31, no. 2 (Fall 2005).

14 Ibid.

15 A fascinating piece on the earthquake can be found in *The Smithsonian* magazine at https://www.smithsonianmag.com/history/the-great-japan-earthquake-of-1923.

16 J. Charles Schencking, 'The Great Kanto Earthquake and the Culture of Catastrophe and Reconstruction in 1920s Japan', *Journal of Japanese Studies*, Summer 2008.

17 *The Smithsonian*, as note 15.

18 Ibid.

19 Churchill wrote this in a speculative piece about future weaponry in the *Pall Mall Gazette*, 1924.

20 Strachan, 'Strategic Bombing'.

21 Ibid.

22 Harris, *Bomber Offensive*.

23 Remarkably, a recording of Mann's broadcast can be found at www.dialoginternational.com/dialog_international/2012/12/listen-germany-thomas-mann-on-the-firebombing-of-lubeck.html.

8. The Correct Atmospheric Conditions

1 According to Pia de Jong in a charming piece for the Institute of Advanced Study, it was young Dyson himself who came up with the phrase: his father overheard him using it, was tickled, and sent it to *Punch* magazine. The article is at www.ias.edu/ideas/2013/de-jong-dyson.

2 National Archives AIR 40/1680.

3 As recounted in Freeman Dyson, 'A Failure of Intelligence', *MIT Technology Review*, 1 November 2006, a mesmerizing piece that can be read at www.technologyreview.com/s/406789/a-failure-of-intelligence.

4 Aldous Huxley, *Ends and Means: An Enquiry into the Nature of Ideals and into the Methods Employed for Their Realization* (Chatto and Windus, 1937).

5 Dyson, 'A Failure of Intelligence'.

6 Ibid.

7 Ibid.

8 Freeman Dyson, *Disturbing the Universe* (Harper & Row, 1979).

9 David Lodge, 'Dam and Blast' (1982), in his collection *Write On* (Secker & Warburg, 2012). Lodge also pointed out that, although

his father was in the air force, he somehow avoided going up in a plane.

10 Tami Davis Biddle, 'Bombing by the Square Yard: Sir Arthur Harris at War, 1942–1945', *International History Review*, vol. 21, no. 3 (September 1999).

11 Jörg Friedrich, *The Fire: The Bombing of Germany, 1940–1945* (Columbia University Press, 2006).

12 Ibid.

13 National Archives AIR 20/4831.

14 Ibid.

15 Ibid.

16 Lord Portal Papers, Christ Church, Oxford, folder 10, file 3A.

17 Ibid., file 3B.

18 Ibid.

19 Ibid.

20 Ibid., file 3C.

21 Ibid.

22 Ibid.

23 Ibid., file 3D.

9. Hosing Out

1 Daniel Swift, *Bomber County* (Hamish Hamilton, 2010).

2 A. C. Grayling, *Among the Dead Cities: Is the Targeting of Civilians in War Ever Justified?* (Bloomsbury, 2006).

3 Vera Brittain, *Seed of Chaos: What Mass Bombing Really Means* (New Vision, 1944).

4 Lord Dowding, a spiritualist, wrote on the subject in, among other books, *Twelve Legions of Angels* (Jarrolds, 1946).

5 Letter from Michael Scott, RAF Wattisham, published in Andrew Roberts (ed.), *Love, Tommy: Letters Home, from the Great War to the Present Day* (Osprey Publishing, 2012).

6 Frank Blackman, quoted in Swift, *Bomber County*.

7 Tripp, *The Eighth Passenger*.

8 Ibid.

9 Russell Margerison, *Boys at War* (Northway Publications, 2009).

10 Swift, *Bomber County*.

11 Hay, 'An Old Airman's Tale'.

12 Ibid.

13 Ibid.

14 Swift, *Bomber County*.

15 Ibid.

16 Bill Burke, 'The Sheer Thrill of Being a Member of an Operational Marking Team', www.627squadron.co.uk/afs-bookpartIII-SheerThrill.html.

17 Tripp, *The Eighth Passenger*.

18 Burke, 'The Sheer Thrill'.

10. *The Devil Will Get No Rest*

1 www.iwm.org.uk/history/tips-for-american-servicemen-in-britain-during-the-second-world-war.

2 See www.americanairmuseum.com, part of the Imperial War Museum's website.

3 For Fielder's obituary, published by several Pittsburgh newspapers, see www.legacy.com/obituaries/postgazette/obituary.aspx?n=morton-irwin-fiedler.

4 Gordon Fenwick interviewed in the 384th Group magazine. As well as having an entry on the American Air Museum site, Fenwick has been interviewed frequently in the US press and television.

5 Ibid.

6 Pleasingly, the idea of the 'friendly invasion' is now a tourist attraction in Norfolk – see www.visitnorfolk.co.uk/things-to-do/Friendly-Invasion-in-Norfolk.aspx.

7 The term 'spillage' appears in Charles W. McArthur, *Operations Analysis in the U.S. Army Eighth Air Force in World War II* (American Mathematical Society, 1990).

8 Mentioned in an introduction to the subject at the Imperial War Museum by Carl Warner at www.iwm.org.uk/history/american-airmen-in-britain-during-the-second-world-war.

9 More information (plus pictures) at the American Air Museum website, http://www.americanairmuseum.com/place/136207.

10 In my *The Secret Life of Bletchley Park* (Aurum, 2010), Wrens recalled the urgency to attend a concert by Glenn Miller and his band at Bedford, which was close to the codebreaking centre.

11 Fenwick, in 384th Group magazine.

12 Eugene Spearman, ww2awartobewon.com/wwii-articles/bremen-mission-384th-bomb-group/.

13 There is a very interesting essay about James Stewart's acting career before and after the war by Geoffrey O'Brien in the *New York Review of Books*, 2 November 2006, which, although it only touches on his bombing experiences, none the less suggests that there was a duality to Stewart's screen persona after the war.

14 Thomas Childers, ' "*Facilis descensus averni est*": The Allied Bombing of Germany and the Issue of German Suffering', *Central European History*, vol. 38, no. 1 (March 2005).

15 Ibid.

16 Ibid.

17 For background see Smithsonian Institute, airandspace.si.edu/collection-objects/messerschmitt-me-262-1a-schwalbe-swallow.

18 Fenwick, in 384th Group magazine.

11. The Day of Darkness

1 DCA, file 803.

2 Ibid.

3 DCA, file 107.

4 DCA, file 802.

5 DCA, file 133.

6 DCA, file 855.

7 DCA, file 523.

8 DCA, file 477.

9 DCA, file 475.

10 Ibid.

11 DCA, file 855.

12 DCA, file 500.

13 Klemperer, *To the Bitter End*.

14 Ibid.
15 Ibid.
16 DCA, file 802.
17 Ibid.
18 Ibid.
19 Ibid.
20 Ibid.
21 Fitzpatrick, *Mischka's War*.
22 Tripp, *The Eighth Passenger*.
23 Ibid.
24 Ibid.
25 DCA, file 107.
26 Ibid.
27 DCA, file 133.
28 DCA, file 472.
29 DCA, file 104.
30 Tripp, *The Eighth Passenger*.
31 Ibid.
32 Ibid.
33 Klemperer, *To the Bitter End*.
34 Vonnegut, *Letters*.
35 Ibid.
36 Gregg, *Dresden*.
37 *Bild*, 13 February 2017.
38 Hay, 'An Old Airman's Tale'.

13. *Five Minutes Before the Sirens*

1 DCA, file 107.
2 More on the 'Bob Gerry Troupe' and their interesting post-war career at http://www.circopedia.org/Bob_Gerry_Troupe.
3 Griebel's memoir, *Ich war ein Mann der Strasse. Lebenserinnerungen eines Dresdner Malers* (I Was a Man on the Street: The Memoirs of a Dresden Painter) (Röderberg, 1986), now out of print, has been widely cited for his intense and at times grotesque account of that night.

4　Fitzpatrick, *Mischka's War*.
5　DCA, file 802.
6　DCA, file 133.
7　DCA, file 477.
8　DCA, file 116.

13. Into the Abyss

1　DCA, file 109.
2　Ibid.
3　DCA, file 803.
4　Ibid.
5　DCA, file 477.
6　Vonnegut, *Letters*.
7　DCA, file 802.
8　Ibid.
9　DCA, file 533.
10　Ibid.
11　DCA, file 472.
12　Ibid.
13　Klemperer, *To the Bitter End*.
14　Pleasingly, a number of Mauersberger's folk songs have been issued on CD.
15　DCA, file 847.
16　Ibid.
17　Ibid.
18　DCA, file 107.
19　Ibid.
20　Ibid.

14. Shadows and Light

1　The Imperial War Museum has an extended and wholly fascinating interview with William Topper which can be heard at www.iwm.org.uk/collections/item/object/80015851 and which informs much of what follows.

2 DCA, file 104.

3 DCA, file 802.

4 DCA, file 107.

15. 10.03 p.m.

1   DCA, file 109.

2   DCA, file 803.

3   Fitzpatrick, *Mischka's War.*

4   DCA, file 475.

5   Ibid.

6   DCA, file 477.

7   Ibid.

8   Ibid.

9   DCA, file 107.

10 Ibid.

11 DCA, file 802.

12 Ibid.

13 Ibid.

14 DCA, file 472.

15 Klemperer, *To the Bitter End.*

16 Ibid.

17 DCA, file 477.

16. The Burning Eyes

1   DCA, file 477.

2   Ibid.

3   DCA, file 475.

4   Ibid.

5   Ibid.

6   DCA, file 472.

7   Ibid.

8   DCA, file 104.

9 Ibid.

10 Although not currently in print, Griebel's *Ich war ein Mann der Strasse* has a number of in print episodes that have been cited by admirers.

11 Fitzpatrick, *Mischka's War*.

12 Michal Salomonivic, interviewed on Czech Radio (www.radio.cz).

13 DCA, file 506.

14 Ibid.

15 Ibid.

16 Ibid.

17 Ibid.

18 DCA, file 533.

19 DCA, file 109.

20 DCA, file 802.

21 Ibid.

22 Ibid.

23 Ibid.

24 Ibid.

25 Ibid.

26 DCA, file 107.

27 Ibid.

28 Ibid.

29 Ibid.

30 Ibid.

31 Ibid.

32 Klemperer, *To the Bitter End*.

33 Ibid.

17. Midnight

1 As cited in Tripp, *The Eighth Passenger*.

2 Fitzpatrick, *Mischka's War*.

3 Friedrich, *The Fire*.

4 Ursula Elsner, interviewed in the *Daily Telegraph*, 8 February 2015.

5 Biddle, 'Sifting Dresden's Ashes'.

6 DCA, file 506.

7 DCA, file 109.

8 DCA, file 472.

9 Friedrich, *The Fire*.

10 DCA, file 104.

11 An account from Dresden zoo inspector Otto Sailer-Jackson, cited in Alexander McKee, *The Devil's Tinderbox: Dresden 1945* (Souvenir Press, 2000).

12 Fitzpatrick, *Mischka's War*.

18. The Second Wave

1 Tripp, *The Eighth Passenger*, for this and what follows.

2 Hay, 'An Old Airman's Tale'.

3 Tripp, *The Eighth Passenger*.

4 A BBC tribute to Harry Irons can be found at www.bbc.co.uk/news/uk-england-london-46201076.

5 Fitzpatrick, *Mischka's War*.

6 Klemperer, *To the Bitter End*, for this and what follows.

7 DCA, file 472.

8 DCA, file 104.

9 DCA, file 477.

10 Ibid.

11 DCA, file 107.

12 Ibid.

13 DCA, file 802, for this and what follows.

14 DCA, file 533, for this and what follows.

15 Fitzpatrick, *Mischka's War*.

16 A chilling account, given by Otto Sailer-Jackson, is cited in several sources, including McKee, *The Devil's Tinderbox*.

17 Friedrich, *The Fire*.

18 DCA, file 109.

19 Ibid.

20 A fascinating account both of Dorothea Speth's experiences, and also about the lives of Mormons in Dresden, can be found at rsc.byu. edu/archived/harm-s-way-east-german-latter-day-saints-world-war-ii/ dresden-district/dresden-altstadt.
21 DCA, file 475.
22 Klemperer, *To the Bitter End*.

19. From Among the Dead

1 DCA, file 802.
2 Ibid.
3 DCA, file 472.
4 Fitzpatrick, *Mischka's War*.
5 DCA, file 477.
6 Ibid.
7 DCA, file 109.
8 DCA, file 475.
9 Fitzpatrick, *Mischka's War*.
10 Klemperer, *To the Bitter End*, for this and what follows.

20. The Third Wave

1 Interviewed in various American newspapers. His war records can be seen at 384thbombgroup.com.
2 Ibid.
3 Ibid.
4 Overy, *The Bombing War*.
5 Cited in Childers, ' "*Facilis descensus averni est*" '. In 1982 Fussell wrote a searingly powerful essay about his war experiences – and the horror of that winter of 1944/45 – for *Harper's* magazine which can be read at harpers.org/sponsor/thewar/wwiiharpers/my-war-how-i-got-irony-in-the-infantry/.
6 Overy, *The Bombing War*.
7 DCA, file 107, for this and what follows.

8 DCA, file 533.

9 DCA, file 802, for this and what follows.

10 As noted on the IWM site americanairmuseum.com.

11 DCA, file 475.

12 DCA, file 477.

21. Dead Men and Dreamers

1 DCA, file 107.

2 Ibid.

3 DCA, file 475.

4 DCA, file 802.

5 Klemperer, *To the Bitter End*.

6 DCA, file 116.

22. The Radiant Tombs

1 Ralph Blank et al., *Germany and the Second World War, vol. IX* (Clarendon Press, 2008).

2 Klemperer, *To the Bitter End*.

3 Friedrich, *The Fire*.

4 Vonnegut, *Letters*.

5 Kurt Vonnegut, *Slaughterhouse-Five; or The Children's Crusade – A Duty-Dance with Death* (Cape, 1970).

6 Ibid.

7 DCA, file 107.

8 Gregg, *Dresden*.

9 DCA, file 477.

10 Matthias Griebel, interviewed in *The New York Times*, 11 February 1995.

11 Ibid.

12 Klemperer, *To the Bitter End*.

13 DCA, file 802.

14 Ibid.

15 DCA, file 109.

23. The Meanings of Terror

1 *Daily Mirror*, 15 February 1945.
2 *Daily Telegraph*, 15 February 1945.
3 Ibid.
4 Ibid.
5 Tripp, *The Eighth Passenger*.
6 Ibid.
7 Biddle, 'Sifting Dresden's Ashes'.
8 Ibid.
9 *Daily Telegraph*, 17 February 1945.
10 *Daily Telegraph*, 5 March 1945.
11 *Daily Mail*, 5 March 1945.
12 Ronald Schaffer, 'American Military Ethics in World War II: The Bombing of German Civilians', *Journal of American History*, vol. 67, no. 2 (September 1980).
13 *Manchester Guardian*, 7 March 1945.
14 Ibid.
15 Ibid.
16 Harris Papers, folder H55, document 71A.
17 Ibid., document 73A.
18 Ibid., document 72A.
19 Ibid., folder 4B, document dated 28 March 1945.
20 Ibid.
21 Ibid., document dated 29 March 1945.
22 Ibid.
23 Ibid., document dated 1 April 1945, stamped 'personal'.

24. The Music of the Dead

1 DCA, file 802.
2 Ibid.
3 DCA, file 115.

4 *Der Freiheitskampf*, Dresden edition, 16 April 1945, for this and what follows.

5 Fitzpatrick, *Mischka's War*.

6 Griebel, *Ich war ein Mann der Strasse*, quoted in a fascinating essay by Francesco Mazzaferro which can be seen at letteraturaartistica.blogspot. com/2018/10/otto-griebel29.html.

7 As cited in an absorbing essay by Johannes Schmidt: 'Dresden 1945: Wilhelm Rudolph's Compulsive Inventory', *Art in Print*, vol. 5, no. 3 (2015), artinprint.org/article/wilhelmrudolph/.

8 The Carus Classics 2013 CD issue of *Dresdner Requiem* has interesting sleeve notes by Matthias Herrmann, a detailed look at Mauersberger's musical inspirations and English translations of the requiem's lyrics.

9 Schmidt, 'Dresden 1945'.

10 DCA, file 475.

11 Ibid.

12 There is some interesting background on Elsa Frölich and her husband as well as Dresden's other underground communists at www.stadtwikidd. de/wiki/Elsa_Frölich (in German).

13 Victor Klemperer, *The Lesser Evil: The Diaries of Victor Klemperer 1945–59*, trans. Martin Chalmers (Weidenfeld and Nicolson, 2003).

14 There is some information on Nieland's surprising post-war life and rehabilitation to be seen at Sächsische Biografie, saebi.isgv.de/biografie/ Hans_Nieland_(1900-1976).

25. Recoil

1 A very interesting – and frightening – piece about Kästner and his relationship with the Nazis (and the burning of his books) can be seen at Spiegel Online: www.spiegel.de/international/zeitgeist/nazi-book-burning-anniversary-erich-kaestner-and-the-nazis-a-894845.html.

2 Erich Kästner, *When I Was a Little Boy*, trans. Isabel and Florence McHugh (Jonathan Cape, 1959).

3 DCA, file 802.

4 DCA, file 477.

5   Harris Papers, folder 40, document dated 10 May 1945.

6   Harris, *Bomber Offensive*.

7   Ibid.

8   Harris Papers, folder 3A, letter dated 18 June 1945.

9   Letter from Taylor to *The New York Times*, published 18 January 1992.

10 This is part of an epic oral interview conducted by Hugh A. Ahmann for the United States Air Force Oral History Program, the transcript of which can be read at www.trumanlibrary.gov/library/oral-histories/landryrb#146.

11 Dyson, 'A Failure of Intelligence'.

12 Max Seydewitz, speaking in February 1950; the speech was widely reported in British newspapers.

13 Harris Papers, folder 40, 'Lectures, Speeches, Talks etc.'.

14 David Irving, *The Destruction of Dresden* (Kimber, 1963).

15 *Observer*, 5 May 1963.

16 *Observer*, 12 May 1963; Birkin was one of several readers taking issue with Nicolson.

17 Tripp, *The Eighth Passenger*.

18 As discussed by Mark Arnold-Foster in the *Guardian*, 14 February 1967.

19 Ibid.

20 This fascinating interview was screened by the BBC on 11 February 2013.

26. 'The Stalinist Style'

1   Klemperer, *The Lesser Evil*.

2   Some of the propaganda posters from this period – stylized and striking – are on display to very fine effect at the Dresden Museum of Military History.

3   The accent was even mentioned in his obituary in *The New York Times* on 2 August 1973.

4   Klemperer, *The Lesser Evil*.

5   Ibid.

6   Like so much of Dresden's Soviet post-war architecture, there is something now quite strangely evocative about the Barkhausen building; pictures to be found at navigator.tu-dresden.de/gebaeude/bar?language=en.

7 For a concise biography of Dr Fromme see Sächsische Biografie, saebi. isgv.de/biografie/Albert_Fromme_(1881-1966).

8 Ibid.

9 According to some accounts, Griebel was based in the Workers' and Peasants' Department of the college, the purity of which must have appealed.

10 The rooms of post-war painting now in the Albertinum Gallery (where in 1945 the civic authorities were based) are fascinating, and they raise the further question of whether art and ideology in the wider world are more frequently fused than we imagine.

11 In later life, Matthias Griebel became director of the Dresden City Museum; he has been frequently interviewed, and profiled admiringly, such as in this piece for *Disy* magazine at www.disy-magazin.de/ Matthias-Griebel.337.0.html.

12 Klemperer, *The Lesser Evil*.

13 This shop fracas was reported in the *Daily Telegraph* on 27 March 1953.

14 Neal Ascherson, in the *Observer*, 13 February 1965.

15 This gradual restoration features as a sort of mini-exhibit in its own right in the Zwinger galleries today.

16 Some of the details were recalled by Lyudmila in Vladimir Putin, *First Person* (PublicAffairs, 2000), a 'Self-Portrait' featuring interviews with the then new president. There was also interesting BBC news coverage in September 2015 tying in with Chris Bowlby's Radio 4 documentary *The Moment that Made Putin*.

27. Beauty and Remembrance

1 Donald Bloxham, 'Dresden as a War Crime', in Addison and Crang (eds.), *Firestorm*.

Index